NATURAL HISTORY OF THE ISLANDS OF CALIFORNIA

CALIFORNIA NATURAL HISTORY GUIDES, 61

NATURAL HISTORY OF THE ISLANDS OF CALIFORNIA

ALLAN A. SCHOENHERR

C. ROBERT FELDMETH

MICHAEL J. EMERSON

ILLUSTRATIONS BY
DAVID MOONEY AND MICHAEL J. EMERSON

UNIVERSITY OF CALIFORNIA PRESS

Berkeley   Los Angeles   London

The publisher gratefully acknowledges the contribution provided by the General Endowment Fund, which is supported by generous gifts from the members of the Associates of the University of California Press.

University of California Press
Berkeley and Los Angeles, California
University of California Press, Ltd.
London, England

Cover illustration:
View westward from East Anacapa Island.

Library of Congress Cataloging-in-Publication Data

Schoenherr, Allan A.
  Natural history of the islands of California / Allan A. Schoenherr,
C. Robert Feldmeth, and Michael J. Emerson; illustrations by David
Mooney and Michael J. Emerson.
      p.   cm.   (California natural history guides; 61)
    ISBN 0-520-21197-9 (cloth: alk. paper)
    1. Natural history—California. 2. Islands—California. I. Feldmeth,
C. Robert. II. Emerson, Michael J. III. Title. IV. Series.
  QH105.C2S367   1999
  508.794'0914'2—dc21   97-43756
                                                              CIP

Printed in the United States of America

9   8   7   6   5   4   3   2   1

The paper used in this publication meets the minimum
requirements of American National Standard for Information
Sciences—Permanence of Paper for Printed Library Materials,
ANSI Z39.48-1984.

CONTENTS

This book is dedicated to C. Robert Feldmeth, who conceived the idea of a book on the islands of California and whose untimely death prevented him from seeing it brought to fruition. He intended to dedicate the book to his wife Judy and his children Damon, Joshua, Paige, and Brad.

PREFACE

In the early 1970s C. Robert Feldmeth conceived the idea for this book. Because his experience was primarily on the Southern Channel Islands, he enlisted the aid of Michael J. Emerson to write about and contribute a series of line drawings of the biota of the Northern Channel Islands. In addition, David Mooney was asked to do a series of line drawings to fill in gaps in the existing set of figures. Prior to publication, the untimely deaths of Feldmeth and Emerson seemed to put final publication of the book into limbo, until Allan A. Schoenherr, author of *A Natural History of California,* was enlisted to complete the manuscript and prepare it for publication.

Robert Feldmeth explained what inspired him to write this book as follows:

> Islands have fascinated explorers since the time of the first sailing ships, and even before that time early peoples constructed rafts or simple canoes to reach distant shores. Biologists from Charles Darwin on have found islands to be laboratories of evolution: isolated land masses separated from the continents by impassable barriers of water. Just off the California coast there is an island archipelago, not as dramatic in isolation as the Galápagos nor as scenic as Hawaii but populated with an interesting flora and fauna. These California islands are easily accessible to millions of people interested in nature. One purpose of this book is to stimulate their interest in the natural history of the California islands.
>
> My interest in the California islands began as a young boy as I boarded the big white steamer, the SS *Catalina,* in San Pedro and first crossed the channel to Santa Catalina Island. Although I have since had the opportunity to make many trips to the islands of California and many other parts of the world, the same sense of excitement and adventure still comes to me

as a deep, blue-water channel is crossed and a shimmering island mass appears through the haze. To go ashore in a small boat, and then climb a rugged canyon and view unique plants and animals as one ascends to the summit, is to me one of the most thrilling experiences a naturalist can have. This book was written to allow visitors to California's islands to share that excitement and to learn something about their geology, flora, fauna, and prehistory. The information presented here has been accumulated since 1972, when I first taught a university extension field course on the natural history of the California islands for the University of California at Los Angeles. Since that time it has been my privilege to take hundreds of people to the islands off the California coast, where it is possible not only to see a part of California that has not changed much in the last 150 years but also to view fine examples of island ecology and biogeography.

In attempting to cover the natural history of the California islands we have been able to include only a brief glimpse of each. Many readers may find that their own area of interest has been only briefly surveyed. Our hope is that those with great interest and little knowledge of the islands will be able to use this book as a key with which to unlock the vast field of island natural history and that those with specific interests will follow this work with an examination of the detailed accounts that each island deserves.

ACKNOWLEDGMENTS

C. Robert Feldmeth, in his version of the book, wished to acknowledge the following persons: Dr. Robert Barrett, former director of the Department of the Sciences (University of California at Los Angeles Extension), offered encouragement and help in initiating and programming many of the earliest natural history trips to the islands. Dr. Robert Thorne, of Rancho Santa Ana Botanic Garden, accompanied him on numerous trips as co-instructor and patiently conveyed a portion of his knowledge of island flora. His close colleague, Dr. Daniel Guthrie, having visited most of the islands, had provided him with a large amount of information on terrestrial vertebrates and the archaeology of San Miguel Island. He also assisted him in many aspects of the preparation of this book. Dr. Robert Given, past director of the University of Southern California's Marine Science Center, was also a willing resource person for information on subtidal organisms and their ecology. Finally, Mr. Mark Hoeffs, the curator of the Wrigley Memorial Botanical Garden, gave of his time and knowledge on numerous occasions. The library staffs of the California Academy of Sciences, the Point Reyes Bird Observatory, and the Santa Barbara Museum of Natural History (Channel Island Archives) were also most kind in providing their aid.

Bob Feldmeth was particularly gratified for the contribution of Michael Emerson, who wrote the first draft of the chapter on the Northern Channel Islands, contributed many line drawings, and, sadly, passed away before seeing his work in print. His work was part of a masters thesis completed at the University of California, Santa Barbara, and his contribution to and cooperation in the preparation of the book were invaluable.

I wish to acknowledge the conversations, friendship, and help provided by Bob Feldmeth, which inspired me to take up where he left off and complete this book. I especially wish to acknowledge the cooperation and understanding of Bob's wife Judy and Michael Emerson's sister Sharon, who watched patiently while I finished up the work that their loved ones had begun.

Much of the artwork in this book was provided by David Mooney, who also waited patiently as this book slowly evolved. Unless otherwise noted, the photographs are mine. Further thanks go to the many persons cited in the text who gave me permission to use work from previously published materials.

My contribution to this book would not have been possible without access to the islands themselves. I am indebted to Dr. William Mautz for inviting me to accompany him on trips to San Clemente Island and to Dr. Lon McClanahan and Donald Newman of the Marine Studies Consortium at California State University, Long Beach, for shuttling me back and forth to Santa Catalina and Santa Barbara Islands.

I am particularly grateful to innumerable people who cooperated with me in my quest to gather unpublished information. Among them are Drs. William Lidicker, Robert Ornduff, and David Wake of the University of California at Berkeley. Dr. Daniel Guthrie of the W. M. Keck Science Center of the Claremont Colleges kindly shared an unpublished manuscript on the archaeology of San Miguel Island. Similarly, Dr. Peter Bowler of the University of California at Irvine shared information on the little-known lichen flora of the Channel Islands. Roy Van de Hoek of the Los Angeles County Catalina Island Interpretive Center shared his unpublished data on introduced birds and mammals, and also provided me with insight into the present status of the biota on Santa Catalina Island. Bill Faulkner, interpreter for Channel Islands National Park, also provided innumerable bits and pieces of unpublished information about the Northern Channel Islands. Thomas Oberbauer of the San Diego County Department of Planning and Land Use, who is a recognized expert on the flora of San Clemente and Santa Catalina Islands, kindly provided many helpful comments that helped me to understand botanical aspects of those islands.

Attempts to gather information about the islands in San Francisco Bay were particularly frustrating, and many people gave generously of their time and insight in that endeavor. I particularly thank Fred McCollum, the caretaker of Brooks Island, for returning my phone calls, answering questions, and arranging for my visit to that island. Harry and Jean Levine also provided valuable information about Brooks Island as well as suggesting important contact persons. Richard Spight, who is gathering historical information about the Marin Islands, shared ideas with me over the phone. I am indebted to Michael Vasey and Philip Greene, who shared unselfishly of their insights into birds and their distribution in San Francisco Bay. For information on Alcatraz Island I am grateful to Elizabeth McClintock, who sent me her handwritten notes; to National Park Service Ranger Will Reyes, who sent me selected photocopied material; and to Michael Boland, who sent me a copy of his book, *Gardens of Alcatraz.* James Houston, author of *Californians: Searching for the Golden State,* also sent me copies of materials he had collected about the islands in San Francisco Bay. Finally, the following people mailed me useful information: Lieutenant Commander Yost sent me information about Treasure Island; Steve Edwards of the East Bay Regional Park District sent me information on Browns Island; and the docents of Angel Island sent me a copy of their training manual.

To anyone I may have forgotten, I offer my sincere thanks for helping to wrap up this project.

Allan Schoenherr
Laguna Beach

INTRODUCTION

The purpose of this book is twofold: to provide general information for anyone interested in the California islands and to serve as a field guide for visitors to the islands. The book covers both general history and natural history, from the geological origins of the islands through their aboriginal inhabitants and their marine and terrestrial biotas. Detailed coverage of the flora and fauna of one island alone would completely fill a book of this size; hence only the most common, most readily observed, and most interesting species are included.

The names used for the plants and animals discussed in this book are the most up-to-date ones available, based on the scientific literature and the most recently published guidebooks. Common names are always subject to local variations, and they change constantly. Where two names are in common use, they are both mentioned the first time the organism is discussed. Ironically, in recent years scientific names have changed more recently than common names, and the reader concerned about a possible discrepancy in nomenclature should consult the scientific literature. If a significant nomenclatural change has escaped our notice, we apologize. For plants, our primary reference has been *The Jepson Manual: Higher Plants of California,* edited by James C. Hickman, including the latest lists of errata. Variation from the nomenclature in that volume is due to more recent interpretations, as explained in the text.

Certain abbreviations used throughout the text may not be immediately familiar to the general reader; they are as follows: sp., species (singular); spp., species (plural); n. sp., newly described species; and var., variety.

Because this book covers only California islands, some definitions are in order. Although the islands off northern Baja California, Mexico, are in the California floristic province, we do not discuss them except as they relate to biogeographic distributions. Numerous small islets and rocks occurring along the coast are not considered, and the many large islands in the Sacramento and San Joaquin River deltas are also not covered. The main emphasis of the book is the Channel Islands that range along the coast from Point Conception in central California to San Clemente in southern California. We have also included the Farallon Islands or Farallones, Año Nuevo Island, and several islands in San Francisco Bay, including Alcatraz, Angel Island, Brooks Island, Browns Island, the Marin Islands, and Yerba Buena Island.

The islands have been grouped geographically so that the Northern Channel Islands (Anacapa, San Miguel, Santa Cruz, and Santa Rosa), the outer Southern Channel Islands (San Clemente, San Nicolas, and Santa Barbara), and the islands in San Francisco Bay are discussed together. The most frequently visited of the Southern Channel Islands, Santa Catalina, is discussed in its own chapter. Significant introductory material relevant to other islands is also found in the chapter on Santa Catalina Island. Each chapter focuses on an island's history and natural history, with a special emphasis on features that are interesting or unique. Although plant communities are covered for every island, a community is discussed in detail only in the chapter dealing with the island on which it is dominant. Thus the most thorough discussions of Coastal Sage Scrub and Island Chaparral occur in the chapter on Santa Catalina Island, and Mixed Evergreen Forest is discussed only in the chapter on islands in San Francisco Bay.

Several chapters discuss features that relate in general to all of the islands. Chapter 1 deals with biogeography and ecology, Chapter 2 with geology, Chapter 3 with early human history, and Chapter 4 with marine life.

Santa Catalina Island, the most visited of all the California islands, receives up to 10,000 people per day during the summer months, and more than 1.3 million people visit Santa Catalina by boat each year. At Channel Islands National Park, about 220,000 people go to the visitor center each year and about 40,000 people actually set foot on one or more of the Northern Channel Islands. In the San Francisco Bay area, visitorship is rapidly increasing. In 1997 Alcatraz was the most-visited island, with about 1.2 million visitors, and visitorship on Angel Island was nearly 300,000.

Santa Barbara Island and the Northern Channel Islands (Anacapa, San Miguel, Santa Cruz, and Santa Rosa) make up Channel Islands National Park. Anacapa, Santa Barbara, and Santa Cruz Islands are regularly visited by groups interested in birds, seals, sea lions, or various other aspects of the islands' natural history. Because good field guides to the birds and marine mammals of these islands already exist, only the more common species are included here. However, because information on terrestrial plants is primarily located in scientific publications and not yet in field guides, plants are covered in more detail, with emphasis on unique or endemic species.

The reader interested in more specific information on a given subject or island can consult the scientific literature, and a list of selected references on California islands has been included. Companions to this volume include *Introduction to Seashore Life of the San Francisco Bay Region and the Coast of Northern California* by Joel W. Hedgpeth, *Seashore Plants of California* by E. Yale Dawson and Michael S. Foster, *Underwater California* by Wheeler J. North, *Marine Mammals of California* by Robert T. Orr and Roger C. Helm, *Marine Food and Game Fishes of California* by John E. Fitch and Robert J. Lavenberg, *Seashore Life of Southern California* by Sam Hinton, *Water Birds of California* by Howard L. Cogswell, and *A Natural History of California* by Allan A. Schoenherr.

There are numerous ways to reach Santa Catalina; ferries depart several times daily on a year-round schedule from Long Beach, Newport Beach, and San Pedro. A ferry has also been proposed for Dana Point Harbor. Contact Catalina Express in Long Beach or San Pedro, Catalina Cruises in Long Beach, or Catalina Passenger Service in Newport Beach. Air transportation is provided by Island Express in Long Beach and San Pedro, and Island Hopper/Catalina Airlines in San Diego. Tours and lodging are available for visitors to Avalon or Twin Harbors, and campsites are available at Blackjack Mountain, Hermit Gulch, Little Fishermans Cove, Little Harbor, and Parsons Landing.

Channel Islands National Park can be reached by boat or air. The boat concessionaire is Island Packers in Ventura, and air travel can be arranged by calling Channel Islands Aviation in Camarillo. All of the islands offer campsites. Bed-and-breakfast options at Smugglers' Cove and Scorpion Ranch on Santa Cruz Island are no longer available. For more information, contact Channel Islands National Park in Ventura.

San Clemente and San Nicolas Islands are the property of the U.S. Navy. Visitors are not allowed on these islands without special permission, although the coastline, with its many coves and abundant marine life, is accessible to fishermen and sailors.

Of the islands in San Francisco Bay, Alcatraz and Angel Islands are the easiest to visit. Ferries transport visitors to Angel Island from Berkeley, San Francisco, and Tiburon daily during the summer. Moorings and slips are available for boats in Ayala Cove on Angel Island. Most of the island features good hiking and bicycling roads. Many visitors bring picnic lunches and spend the day playing baseball, hiking, or sunning on such beaches as Swimmer's Beach. Ferries to Alcatraz Island are also frequent during the summer months, departing from Fisherman's Wharf in San Francisco. Access to the remainder of the islands in San Francisco Bay is limited without a special permit, but Dolphin Charters in El Cerrito offers tours of the northern California islands, including the Farallons.

CHAPTER ONE

ISLAND ECOLOGY AND BIOGEOGRAPHY

WHAT MAKES ISLANDS SO INTERESTING?

It seems that islands have always been fascinating to humans. When the first Western European explorers sailed in search of trade routes around the world, they found many islands populated with aboriginal cultures. Today people still travel with great anticipation to islands. In particular, on any given weekend large numbers of passengers excitedly board ferries or small airplanes to journey to one of California's islands. Half the excitement is getting there, but once on an island, visitors discover a California "time warp," a place seemingly frozen in time. Except for Avalon (Plate 11A) on Santa Catalina, a few military bases, and park personnel on other islands, human habitation is minimal. Wild California as it appeared in "the old days" is visible everywhere, with the added attraction of unique plants and animals. It is the singular character of these and other islands that makes them so interesting.

Although the climate of an island may not differ significantly from that of the coastal zone of the adjacent mainland, an island's size and distance from the mainland have a profound influence on the organisms that inhabit it. Islands are therefore unique evolutionary laboratories. Biologists find islands so fascinating that many have spent entire careers studying their *ecology* (the interaction of environment and organisms) and *biogeography* (plant and animal distribution). Charles Darwin's voyage on the HMS *Beagle* and his vivid description of the unusual flora and fauna of the Galápagos Islands gave birth to the study of the natural history of islands. Darwin's observations of different yet related animals and plants from the various islands provided powerful evidence for his hypothesis on the role of natural selection in the formation of species. Today island

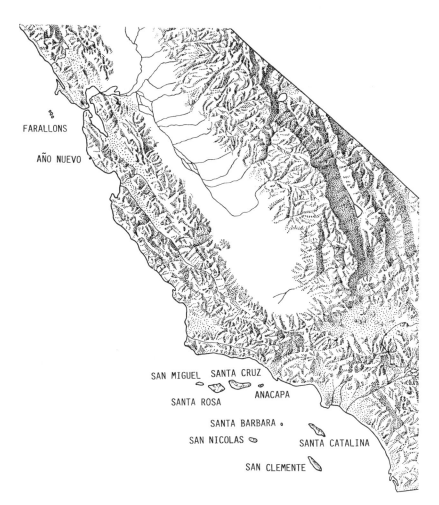

Figure 1. The islands of California, excluding the islands of San Francisco Bay.

ecology and biogeography are two of the most active and exciting areas of modern biology.

The islands of California (Fig. 1), and more specifically the Channel Islands off the coast of southern California, offer a remarkable opportunity to observe at close range the effect that isolation by water has upon the development of the flora and fauna of a particular land mass. These islands are all relatively accessible but vary greatly in size, distance from the mainland, and habitat type (Table 1). Furthermore, because sea level has not remained constant, the islands have not always been the same size or situated the same distance from the mainland. There is considerable geo-

TABLE 1 A COMPARISON OF CALIFORNIA'S ISLANDS

	AREA, MI² (KM²)	ELEVATION, FT (M)	DISTANCE TO MAINLAND, MI (KM)	NATIVE TAXA OF PLANTS[a]	AMPHIBIANS	REPTILES	RESIDENT BIRDS[a]	MAMMALS[a]
Southern California Islands								
Northern Channel Islands								
Anacapa	1.1 (2.9)	930 (283)	13 (20)	190 (1)	1	2	21	2 (1)
San Miguel	14 (37)	830 (253)	26 (42)	198	1	2	15 (1)	3 (2)
Santa Cruz	96 (249)	2470 (753)	19 (30)	480 (8)	3	6	42 (1)	12 (4)
Santa Rosa	84 (217)	1589 (484)	27 (44)	387 (4)	2	2	25	4 (3)
Southern Channel Islands								
San Clemente	56 (145)	1965 (599)	49 (79)	272 (17)	—	2	24 (2)	6 (2)
San Nicolas	22 (58)	910 (277)	61 (98)	139 (2)	—	3	13	2 (2)
Santa Barbara	1.0 (2.6)	635 (149)	38 (61)	88 (2)	—	3	13	2 (1)
Santa Catalina	76 (194)	2125 (648)	20 (32)	421 (7)	3	8	33	9 (4)

	AREA, MI² (KM²)	ELEVATION, FT (M)	DISTANCE TO MAINLAND, MI (KM)	NATIVE TAXA OF PLANTS[a]	AMPHIBIANS	REPTILES	MAMMALS[a]
Northern California Islands							
Northern Coast Islands							
Año Nuevo	95 (9.8)	60 (18)	0.5 (0.8)	—	—	—	1
Farallon Islands	92 (36)	385 (109)	20 (33)	13 (1)	1	—	—
San Francisco Bay Islands							
Alcatraz	22 (9)	138 (44)	1.5 (2.4)	12	1	—	1
Angel	760 (300)	781 (300)	0.5 (0.8)	282	2	7	4 (1)
Brooks	45 (18)	160 (52)	0.5 (0.8)	—	3	3	1
Browns	750 (275)	4 (1.3)	0.2 (0.3)	95	—	—	2
East Marin	11 (4.2)	70 (23)	0.5 (0.8)	53	1	1	—
Red Rock	9 (3.5)	169 (54)	1.5 (2.4)	5	2	—	—
Treasure	403 (159)	4 (1.3)	1.5 (2.4)	—	—	—	—
West Marin	3 (1.1)	70 (23)	0.5 (0.8)	28	1	—	—
Yerba Buena	152 (60)	400 (130)	1.5 (2.4)	12	1	1	—

[a]The number of endemic species is indicated in parentheses.

logical and biological evidence to suggest, for example, that the islands off Ventura and Santa Barbara were once separated by a narrow channel of only a few miles, making it relatively easy for many types of plants and animals to colonize these islands. Islands such as these—easily colonized because they are near to, or were once a part of, the mainland—are called *continental islands.* Other islands to the south, probably always far from the mainland, could be colonized only by crossing distances of up to 157 miles (252 km) of open ocean. Islands that are distant from the mainland and that have never been attached to it are called *oceanic islands.* Major faults separate California's islands from each other and from the mainland; thus the islands have not always been located where they presently lie. These differences enhance interest in comparative biogeographical studies of plant and animal inhabitants.

Life forms that inhabit islands grow and interact in isolation. This isolation tends to favor the establishment of unique organisms because these immigrants continue to evolve after their arrival on islands. Species isolated on islands can also remain as relicts or remnants of populations that formerly enjoyed widespread distribution on the mainland. Thus insular plants and animals can provide insight into the mechanisms of evolution and also give us a glimpse of organisms that are now extinct elsewhere. These unique organisms, which enjoy limited or localized distribution, are said to be *endemic.*

ISLAND ENDEMISM

Because of their lack of human habitation and long isolation, California islands offer excellent resources for studies of evolution and natural history. Numerous species of plants (Table 2) and some animals are limited in distribution to one or more of the islands. For example, Island Ironwood trees, *Lyonothamnus floribundus* (Fig. 2; Plate 5A,B), are found on several islands, but they are absent from the mainland today. On the other hand, they have been found as fossils in places as distant and unlikely as Death Valley. Near the end of the Pleistocene ice ages, about 12,000 years ago, Ironwoods were probably widespread on the mainland. These distinctive members of the rose family (Rosaceae) presumably were unable to adapt to the warmer, drier climate that arose after the last ice age. Yet these nearly extinct trees persist on a few steep hillsides in the Channel Islands, where, presumably in the absence of competition, they survive in a cool, foggy climate that may somewhat resemble that of the past.

Many island endemics are considered varieties or subspecies of mainland plants, but only Island Ironwood is differentiated to the genus level (*Lyonothamnus*). Furthermore, Island Ironwood has differentiated into

TABLE 2   ENDEMIC VASCULAR PLANTS OF THE CALIFORNIA ISLANDS

FAMILY AND SPECIES	ISLANDS
Dicots	
Apiaceae (celery family)	
San Nicolas Island Lomatium (*Lomatium insulare*)—Rare	ni
Asteraceae (sunflower family)	
Island Sagebrush (*Artemisia nesiotica*)	ba,cl,ni
Nevin's Eriophyllum (*Eriophyllum nevinii*)—Rare	ba,ca,cl
San Clemente Island Hazardia (*Hazardia cana*)—Rare	cl
Island Hazardia (*Hazardia detonsa*)	an,cr,ro
Island Tarweed (*Hemizonia clementina*)	an,ba,ca,cl,ni
Leafy Malacothrix (*Malacothrix foliosa*)	an,ba,cl,ni
Santa Cruz Island Malacothrix (*Malacothrix indecora*) —Endangered	cr,mi
Junak's Malacothrix (*Malacothrix junakii*)	an
Cliff Malacothrix (*Malacothrix saxatilis* var. *implicata*)	an,cr,mi,ni,ro
Island Malacothrix (*Malacothrix squalida*)—Endangered	an,cr
Blair's Munzothamnus (*Stephanomeria blairii*)—Rare	cl
Berberidaceae (barberry family)	
Island Barberry (*Berberis pinnata* ssp. *insularis*) —Endangered	an,cr,ro
Boraginaceae (borage family)	
Trask's Cryptantha (*Cryptantha traskiae*)	cl,ni
Brassicaceae (mustard family)	
Hoffman's Rock Cress (*Arabis hoffmannii*)—Endangered	cr,ro
Santa Cruz Island Rock Cress (*Sibara filifolia*)—Endangered	ca,cl,cr
Santa Cruz Island Fringepod (*Thysanocarpus conchuliferus*)—Endangered	cr
Cistaceae (rockrose family)	
Island Rush-rose (*Helianthemum greenei*)—Threatened	ca,cr,mi,ro
Convolvulaceae (morning-glory family)	
Island Morning-glory (*Calystegia macrostegia*)	all
Crassulaceae (stonecrop family)	
Santa Rosa Island Live-forever (*Dudleya blochmaniae* ssp. *insularis*)—Rare	ro
Candleholder Dudleya (*Dudleya candelabrum*)—Rare	cr,ro
Greene's Dudleya (*Dudleya greenei*)	an,cr,mi,ro
Santa Catalina Island Live-forever (*Dudleya hassei*)	ca
Santa Cruz Island Live-forever (*Dudleya nesiotica*) —Threatened	cr
Santa Barbara Island Live-forever (*Dudleya traskiae*) —Endangered	ba
Bright Green Dudleya (*Dudleya virens*)	ca,cl,ni
Crossosomataceae (crossosoma family)	
Catalina Crossosoma (*Crossosoma californicum*)	ca,cl
Ericaceae (heath family)	
Santa Catalina Island Manzanita (*Arctostaphylos catalinae*)—Rare	ca
Santa Rosa Island Manzanita (*Arctostaphylos confertiflora*)—Endangered	ro

(*Continued*)

TABLE 2   (*Continued*)

FAMILY AND SPECIES	ISLANDS
Ericaceae (*Continued*)	
Santa Cruz Island Manzanita (*Arctostaphylos insularis*)	cr
Island Manzanita (*Arctostaphylos tomentosa* ssp. *insulicola*)	cr,ro
Subcordate Manzanita (*Arctostaphylos tomentosa* ssp. *subcordata*)	cr,ro
McMinn's Manzanita (*Arctostaphylos viridissima*)	cr
Fabaceae (pea family)	
San Miguel Milkvetch (*Astragalus miguelensis*)	an,cl,cr,mi,ro
San Clemente Island Milkvetch (*Astragalus nevinii*)—Rare	cl
Trask's Milkvetch (*Astragalus traskiae*)—Rare	ba,ni
San Clemente Island Bird's-foot Trefoil (*Lotus argophyllus* var. *adsurgens*)—Endangered	cl
Island Bird's-foot Trefoil (*Lotus argophyllus* var. *argenteus*)	ba,ca,cl,ni
Santa Cruz Island Bird's-foot Trefoil (*Lotus argophyllus* var. *niveus*)—Endangered	cr
Island Deerweed (*Lotus dendroideus* var. *dendroideus*)	an,ca,cr,ro
Trask's Island Lotus (*Lotus dendroideus* var. *traskiae*) —Endangered	cl
Island Pinpoint Clover (*Trifolium gracilentum* var. *palmeri*)	ba,ca,cl,ni
Fagaceae (oak family)	
MacDonald Oak (*Quercus ×macdonaldii*)	ca,cr,ro
Island Scrub Oak (*Quercus pacifica*)	ca,cr,ro
Island Oak (*Quercus tomentella*)	an,ca,cl,cr,ro
Grossulariaceae (gooseberry family)	
Santa Cruz Island Gooseberry (*Ribes thacherianum*)—Rare	cr
Hydrophyllaceae (waterleaf family)	
San Clemente Island Phacelia (*Phacelia floribunda*)—Rare	cl
Northern Channel Islands Phacelia (*Phacelia insularis* ssp. *insularis*)—Endangered	mi,ro
Lyon's Phacelia (*Phacelia lyoni*)	ca,cl
Malvaceae (mallow family)	
Northern Channel Island Malva Rosa (*Lavatera assurgentiflora* ssp. *assurgentiflora*)	an,mi
Southern Channel Island Malva Rosa (*Lavatera assurgentiflora* ssp. *glabra*)	ca,cl
San Clemente Island Bush Mallow (*Malacothamnus clementinus*)—Endangered	cl
Santa Cruz Island Bush Mallow (*Malacothamnus fasciculatus* ssp. *nesioticus*)—Endangered	cr
Onagraceae (evening primrose family)	
San Clemente Island Evening Primrose (*Camissonia guadalupensis* ssp. *clementina*)—Rare	cl
Papaveraceae (poppy family)	
Channel Island Tree Poppy (*Dendromecon harfordii*)	ca,cl,cr,ro
Island Poppy (*Eschscholzia ramosa*)	ba,ca,cl,cr,ni,ro
Santa Barbara Island Cream Cups (*Platystemon californicus* var. *ciliatus*)	ba
Polemoniaceae (phlox family)	
Island Gilia (*Gilia nevinii*)	an,ba,ca,cl,cr,ni,ro

TABLE 2   (*Continued*)

FAMILY AND SPECIES	ISLANDS
Polemoniaceae (*Continued*)	
Hoffmann's Slender-flowered Gilia (*Gilia tenuiflora* ssp. *hoffmannii*)—Endangered	ro
Pygmy Linanthus (*Linanthus pygmaeus* ssp. *pygmaeus*)	cl
Polygonaceae (buckwheat family)	
Santa Cruz Island Buckwheat (*Eriogonum arborescens*)	an,cr,ro
Santa Barbara Island Buckwheat (*Eriogonum giganteum* var. *compactum*)	ba
San Clemente Island Buckwheat (*Eriogonum giganteum* var. *formosum*)	cl
Santa Catalina Island Buckwheat (*Eriogonum giganteum* var. *giganteum*)	ca
Island Buckwheat (*Eriogonum grande* var. *grande*)	an,ca,cl,cr
Red Buckwheat (*Eriogonum grande* var. *rubescens*)	an,cr,mi,ro
San Nicolas Island Buckwheat (*Eriogonum grande* var. *timorum*)—Endangered	ni
Ranunculaceae (buttercup family)	
San Clemente Island Larkspur (*Delphinium variegatum* ssp. *kinkiense*)—Rare	cl
Thorne's Royal Larkspur (*Delphinium variegatum* ssp. *thornei*)—Rare	cl
Rhamnaceae (buckthorn family)	
Feltleaf Ceanothus (*Ceanothus arboreus*)	ca,cr,ro
Island Ceanothus (*Ceanothus megacarpus* var. *insularis*)	an,ca,cl,cr,ro
Big-pod Ceanothus (*Ceanothus megacarpus* var. *megacarpus*)	ca,cl,cr
Island Redberry (*Rhamnus pirifolia*)	ca,cl,cr,ro
Rosaceae (rose family)	
Catalina Island Mountain Mahogany (*Cercocarpus traskiae*)—Endangered	ca
Island Ironwood (*Lyonothamnus floribundus* ssp. *aspleniifolius*)—Rare	cl,cr,ro
Santa Catalina Island Ironwood (*Lyonothamnus floribundus* ssp. *floribundus*)—Rare	ca
Rubiaceae (madder family)	
Narrow-leaved Bedstraw (*Galium angustifolium* ssp. *foliosum*)	an,cr,ro
Sea-cliff Bedstraw (*Galium buxifolium*)—Endangered	cr,mi,ro
San Miguel Island Bedstraw (*Galium californicum* ssp. *miguelensis*)	mi,ro
San Clemente Island Bedstraw (*Galium catalinense* ssp. *acrispum*)—Endangered	cl
Santa Catalina Island Bedstraw (*Galium catalinense* ssp. *catalinense*)	ca
Nuttall's Island Bedstraw (*Galium nuttallii* ssp. *insulare*)	ca,cr,ro
Saxifragaceae (saxifrage family)	
Island Alumroot (*Heuchera maxima*)—Rare	an,cr,ro
Island Jepsonia (*Jepsonia malvifolia*)	ca,cl,cr,ni,ro
San Clemente Island Woodland Star (*Lithophragma maximum*)—Endangered	cl

(*Continued*)

TABLE 2   *(Continued)*

FAMILY AND SPECIES	ISLANDS
Scrophulariaceae (figwort family)	
San Clemente Island Indian Paintbrush (*Castilleja grisea*)—Rare	cl
Island Paintbrush (*Castilleja lanata* ssp. *hololeuca*)—Rare	an,cr,mi,ro
Soft-leaved Indian Paintbrush (*Castilleja mollis*)—Endangered	ro
Santa Cruz Island Monkeyflower (*Mimulus brandegei*)—Rare	cr
Island Monkeyflower (*Mimulus flemingii*)	an,cl,cr,ro
Santa Catalina Figwort (*Scrophularia villosa*)—Rare	ca,cl
Solanaceae (nightshade family)	
Santa Catalina Island Desert-thorn (*Lycium brevipes* var. *hassei*)—Extinct(?)	ca,cl
San Nicolas Island Desert-thorn (*Lycium verrucosum*)—Extinct(?)	ni
Island Nightshade (*Solanum clokeyi*)	cr,ro
Wallace's Nightshade (*Solanum wallacei*)	ca
Monocots	
Liliaceae (lily family)	
San Clemente Island Brodiaea (*Brodiaea kinkiensis*)—Rare	cl
San Clemente Island Triteleia (*Triteleia clementina*)—Rare	cl
Poaceae (grass family)	
California Dissanthelium (*Dissanthelium californicum*)—Extinct(?)	ca,cl

Note: Key to abbreviations: an, Anacapa; ba, Santa Barbara; ca, Santa Catalina; cl, San Clemente; cr, Santa Cruz; mi, San Miguel; ni, San Nicolas; ro, Santa Rosa.

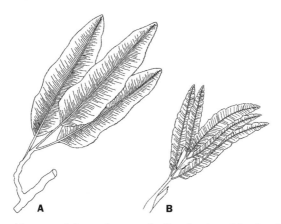

Figure 2. Island Ironwood, *Lyonothamnus floribundus,* is an island endemic that has become differentiated into two subspecies. (A) Santa Catalina Island Ironwood, *Lyonothamnus floribundus* ssp. *floribundus,* is endemic to Santa Catalina Island. It is characterized by linear to oblong leaves about 6 in. (15 cm) long. (B) Island Ironwood or Fern-leaved Ironwood, *Lyonothamnus floribundus* ssp. *aspleniifolius,* is an island endemic found on San Clemente, Santa Cruz, and Santa Rosa Islands. It is characterized by compound leaves with linear leaflets about 2 in. (3 cm) long.

two dissimilar subspecies. The Santa Catalina Ironwood, *Lyonothamnus floribundus* ssp. *floribundus* (Fig. 2A; Plate 5A), is found only on Santa Catalina Island, and as such it is referred to as a Santa Catalina endemic. In contrast, the Island Ironwood or Fern-leaved Ironwood, *Lyonothamnus floribundus* ssp. *aspleniifolius,* is found on San Clemente, Santa Cruz, and Santa Rosa Islands. The Island Ironwood is therefore referred to as an *island endemic* because its natural range is entirely on islands, although it is not restricted to a single one. The two subspecies also qualify as relicts because the island populations represent remnants of formerly widespread distributions. This type of endemism is sometimes called *relictual endemism.*

Another aspect of the ironwood's biogeography is less easily explained. Of the two relict subspecies, the more ancient form, Island Ironwood, was widespread throughout the continental interior. Santa Catalina Ironwood occurs in later deposits limited to the mainland coast. Movement of land along the San Andreas fault may explain the present distribution (as will be discussed later), but how the older, interior form colonized the majority of coastal islands—particularly San Clemente Island, south of Santa Catalina—and then survived extensive flooding during the ice ages remains an enigma. The answer to this question may eventually reveal a great deal about the ancient history of the islands. The long tenure of this tree on the islands is further emphasized by the presence of two apparently relict species of moths (*Ypsolopha lyonothamnae* and *Caleotechnites* n. sp.) whose larvae are known to feed only on the leaves of Island Ironwood.

Among shrubs, an example of relictual endemism is the unique family the Crossosomataceae. There are only two species of these roselike shrubs. One species, Catalina Crossosoma or California Thorn Apple, *Crossosoma californicum* (Plate 6D), occurs only on the dry, rocky slopes and canyons of San Clemente and Santa Catalina Islands. It also occurs on Guadalupe Island far to the south, off Baja California, and on the Palos Verdes Peninsula, which was formerly an island when sea level was higher. The other species, known simply as Crossosoma or Ragged Rock-flower, *Crossosoma bigelovii,* has become adapted to dry, rocky canyons in the Colorado Desert, where there is significant summer precipitation.

In contrast to the process by which relictual endemism occurs, endemics also result from a founder population that diverges genetically from its ancestral species. The habitats afforded by islands allow new colonists to expand or shift ecologic niches. Such changes may alter the results of natural selection to allow new characteristics to be selected and hence new species, subspecies, or varieties to emerge. These new populations, now different from their mainland ancestors, are termed *autochthonous endemics.* The term *autochthonous,* derived from Greek roots, means "self-earth"; the

Figure 3. The Deer Mouse, *Peromyscus maniculatus*. This mouse is represented by a different endemic subspecies on each of the eight Channel Islands. It is also found on Alcatraz Island in San Francisco Bay.

implication is that the species arose by itself from the land on which it lives. An example of such an endemic is the Deer Mouse, *Peromyscus maniculatus* (Fig. 3), which occurs on all eight of the Channel Islands; each island has its own described subspecies, although recent analyses seem to distinguish unique subspecies for only Anacapa and San Clemente Islands. The Deer Mouse is also found on Alcatraz Island in San Francisco Bay, although its presence there may be due to an accidental human introduction.

Birds on the California islands are mostly similar to their mainland relatives. Some differentiation has occurred at the subspecies level, but not to the degree that is typical of other vertebrates. Study of avian differentiation is of course complicated by the fact that birds are highly mobile. Of the birds that have become differentiated, the Island Scrub Jay, *Aphelocoma insularis* (Plate 1B), of Santa Cruz Island, is the only endemic species of bird on the California islands. This jay differs from the Western Scrub Jay, its mainland counterpart, by being bluer and larger, and having different mating behavior. It also has a different call: the island species sounds like a Western Scrub Jay with laryngitis.

Among shrubs of the buckwheat family (Polygonaceae), there is an unusually high degree of autochthonous endemism on the California islands. At least twenty endemic species or subspecies have been identified. Among the unique giant buckwheats distributed over seven different islands, three varieties of *Eriogonum giganteum* (Fig. 50) and three varieties of *Eriogonum grande* (Fig. 72) have been described.

The largest number of island endemics is contained within the group of leaf succulents known as live-forevers (*Dudleya* spp.) (Figs. 55 and 79).

Including undescribed and controversial taxa, nine species of these cliff-dwelling, drought-tolerant plants have distributions restricted to the islands. Other groups that include a significant number of endemics include the following: Manzanitas (*Arctostaphylos* spp.) (Figs. 56, 82, 123, and 184), Bedstraws (*Galium* spp.), "Dandelions" (*Malacothrix* spp.) (Figs. 74, 75, and 137; Plate 6E), Phacelias (*Phacelia* spp.) (Fig. 100), and two members of the pea family (Fabaceae): Deer weeds (*Lotus* spp.) (Figs. 73 and 133) and Milkvetches or Locoweeds (*Astragalus* spp.) (Fig. 98). Because of their limited distribution and because of widespread environmental degradation, many of these plants have been classified by the state and federal governments as endangered or threatened.

In the United States, California is the center of diversity for pines and oaks. It is only fitting, therefore, that its islands should be characterized by distinctive representatives of these large, attractive plants.

Among the oaks, some species are shrubs and some are trees. Of the tree species also found on the mainland, Coast Live Oak, *Quercus agrifolia* (Fig. 183A), is found on Santa Cruz and Santa Rosa Islands within the Northern Channel Island group and on Angel Island in San Francisco Bay. The most widely distributed oak in California, Canyon Live Oak or Golden-cup Oak, *Quercus chrysolepis,* is also found on Santa Catalina and Santa Cruz. There is some controversy over its presence on San Clemente Island. Of the deciduous oaks, Blue Oak, *Quercus douglasii* (Fig. 93A), and Valley Oak, *Quercus lobata* (Fig. 93B), occur in a few groves on Santa Catalina and Santa Cruz Islands. Two oak species are associated specifically with the islands. The most widely distributed island endemic is Island Oak, *Quercus tomentella* (Fig. 92), a tree mostly of north-facing slopes and canyons. It grows on Anacapa, San Clemente, Santa Catalina, Santa Cruz, and Santa Rosa Islands, as well as Guadalupe Island, far to the south. Young twigs on this species are conspicuously hairy. The dark green leaves are oblong and 2–3 in. (50–75 mm) long, with smooth to serrated margins. The undersides of the leaves are hairy.

Another insular oak is a tree form known as MacDonald Oak, formerly *Quercus macdonaldii.* This tree grows in locations similar to those of the Island Oak, but it is found only on Santa Catalina, Santa Cruz, and Santa Rosa Islands. It also has hairy twigs, and the undersides of the leaves are faintly hairy. It differs from Island Oak by having several shallow lobes on each leaf. As unlikely as it may seem, this species is believed to have arisen by hybridization between Valley Oak and Island Scrub Oak, *Quercus pacifica* (Fig. 87). Although its taxonomic status is not clear, it is often referred to by its hybrid name, *Quercus ×macdonaldii.* Scrub Oaks are widely distributed on these islands today, but the number of Valley Oaks is limited. Valley Oak must have been far more common in the past.

MacDonald Oak appears to enjoy limited distribution on the mainland as well, growing in isolated localities as far south as Morro Canyon in Crystal Cove State Park, Orange County.

There are three species of scrub oaks on the islands. The shrub form of Interior Live Oak, *Quercus wislizenii* var. *frutescens* (Fig. 183B), is found on Angel Island. On Santa Cruz Island, what was formerly considered to be a shrub form of Interior Live Oak is now known as Santa Cruz Island Oak, *Quercus parvula* var. *parvula*. It also occurs in adjacent Santa Barbara County on the mainland. A newly described species is now known as Island Scrub Oak, *Quercus pacifica* (Fig. 87). It is endemic to Santa Catalina, Santa Cruz, and Santa Rosa Islands, where it is locally common. It was formerly considered synonymous with the California Scrub Oak, *Quercus berberidifolia*. Island Scrub Oak differs from the Santa Cruz Island Oak by having rounded leaf tips and small hairs on the undersurface of the leaves. Interior Live Oak and Santa Cruz Island Oak have a shiny green color to both sides of their leaves.

Pine species on the California islands are neither numerous nor widespread, but their distributions are worth studying. (For additional information on the island pines see Chapter 6.) The presence of Torrey Pine, *Pinus torreyana* (Fig. 94A; Plate 13B), on Santa Rosa Island is particularly worthy of note. This large-coned, long-needled species occurs only on the mainland near Del Mar and on Santa Rosa Island. Its distribution may be the smallest of any pine species in the world. The island population is characterized by larger cones, and the trees are smaller. Some authorities consider Torrey Pines on the island to belong to a separate subspecies known as the Santa Rosa Island Pine, *Pinus torreyana* ssp. *insularis*.

Among the closed-cone pines, two or three species have island populations. Bishop Pine, *Pinus muricata* (Fig. 94B; Plate 12B), has the widest distribution. It occurs on upper coastal terraces from Humboldt County to Santa Barbara County, and on Santa Cruz Island. It is also found on the mainland of Baja California near La Erendira. A close relative of the Bishop Pine, the Santa Cruz Island Pine, which formerly was considered a separate species (*Pinus remorata*), occurs on Santa Cruz and Santa Rosa Islands as well as the mainland near Lompoc. Many authorities do not recognize this as a distinct species, but instead group it with Bishop Pine.

The Monterey Pine, *Pinus radiata*, occurs naturally today at three locations on the California coast (near Año Nuevo Point, Monterey, and Cambria) and also on Cedros and Guadalupe Islands off the Baja California coast. Guadalupe Island, a volcanic outcrop 157 miles (252 km) from the mainland, is a true oceanic island. All of the species must have reached there by dispersal, so how these trees got there is the subject of some debate. Also subject to debate is the question of which of the closed-cone pines actually inhabit Cedros and Guadalupe Islands. Some authorities contend that both species occur on both islands. Others describe them both as varieties of Bishop Pine. The latest interpretation is that Monterey Pine is highly variable with respect to cone size, cone shape, and numbers of needles per cluster (fascicle), and that nearly endless variation in these characteristics is present in the trees on both islands. Nevertheless, at this time the species is represented by endemic varieties on Cedros and Guadalupe Islands. Hence the trees on Guadalupe Island, which tend to have large cones and needles in clusters of three, have been assigned to the taxon *Pinus radiata* var. *binata*. The trees on Cedros Island, which tend to resemble Bishop Pines in having smaller cones and needles in clusters of two, are called *Pinus radiata* var. *cedroensis*.

Monterey Pine now has the widest distribution of any pine species in the world. It has been planted on every continent that has a suitable climate, and it may be the most common tree species in New Zealand. The pine trees associated with habitation on nearly all of the California islands are usually Monterey Pines that were planted during the recent past. In San Francisco Bay the larger islands, such as Angel and Yerba Buena, have a large number of Monterey Pines.

The natural distribution of closed-cone pines on the west coast is associated with rather precise ecological conditions. They are frequently associated with specific types of depauperate, fine-grained soils such as acidified sandstones, serpentinites, or diatomites. In this respect they occur on "ecological islands," and their distribution on California's islands thus places them on islands within islands!

Closed-cone pines are also associated with fire as the mechanism that forces their cones to open, and they are dependent on fog drip to provide adequate moisture. On Santa Cruz Island in the 1980s, many Bishop Pines appeared to be dying of old age. Some authorities contended that this die-off was due to long periods of fire suppression, whereas others blamed the introduced sheep. A contrasting view was that fires had been common enough to stimulate regeneration, and that we were instead seeing a natural response to changing climate—the same process that isolated the species in the first place. Today, regeneration is once again apparent.

COLONIZATION OF ISLANDS: HOW DO THEY GET THERE?

Land Bridges

One way in which organisms can move to islands is by crossing land bridges (although these may no longer exist). Typically these represent a portion of land that was formerly attached to the mainland and became lost by erosion. Alternatively the connection, now under water, became exposed by a lowering of sea level. During the great ice ages—an epoch known as the Pleistocene (circa 2 million to 12,000 years ago)—great sheets of glacial ice periodically covered much of northern North America. A large amount of water was trapped as ice in these vast glaciers and hence sea level was considerably lower than it is at present. It is estimated that during the maximum glaciation of these relatively recent glacial periods, shorelines were as much as 400 ft (120 m) below their present position. Many islands located on continental shelves around the world were thus connected to the mainland by dry land. These land corridors allowed easy distributional access to the islands for both plants and animals. Although it appears that none of the Channel Islands was connected to the mainland during the Pleistocene, the Farallon Islands probably were. Año Nuevo and the islands in San Francisco Bay, such as Alcatraz and Angel Island, almost certainly were.

Lowering of sea level not only changes the distance of an island from the mainland, it also changes its shape and size. During the period of maximum lowering, the four Northern Channel Islands became one large island, sometimes referred to as "Santa Rosae," but even during that time there remained a channel of at least 4.5 miles (7 km) separating it from the mainland. Hence all of the plants and animals we see on the Channel Islands most likely descended from colonists that reached these islands by moving across an expanse of water. But how did they cross those channels?

Swimming and Flying

Flying animals—such as insects, birds, and bats—reached even the most distant California islands without difficulty. It is not uncommon for exhausted birds to land on boats far out to sea. For example, in October 1996, a Barn Owl, *Tyto alba,* landed on a fishing boat 15 miles beyond San Clemente Island. That species does occur on the island, but it would not be impossible for the bird to have flown or been blown all the way from the mainland.

Many insects are good fliers, but the insects of the islands have not been thoroughly studied. Although most of the butterflies on the islands are members of the same species as those found on the mainland, the Avalon Hairstreak, *Strymon avalona,* may have one of the smallest distributions of any insect species in the world. It is found only on Santa Catalina Island. Its nearest relative, the Gray Hairstreak, *Strymon melinus,* is found throughout North America and is known from all eight Channel Islands.

About 750 species of moths and butterflies (Lepidoptera) are found on the Channel Islands. There are about 370 species on Santa Catalina Island and 550 on Santa Cruz Island. A total of twenty-six species are considered endemics (Table 3), and 60 percent of them are restricted to a single island. All but the outermost islands, San Miguel and San Nicolas, have at least one endemic.

In comparing common moths and butterflies on Santa Cruz Island with those on the adjacent mainland, among five groups of conspicuous, larger forms, 30–62 percent of the species were represented on the island. In contrast, when comparing small leaf-mining species, it was discovered that 71 percent of the species were represented on the island. More specifically, when examining those species that use common host plants such as oaks, willows, and California Lilacs (*Ceanothus* spp.), it was discovered that fully 87 percent of the leaf-miners were on the island whereas only 35 percent of the butterflies (Swallowtails and Skippers) were represented. This seeming contradiction in species richness is possibly explained by the increased probability of the minute leaf-miners surviving in small patches of host plants.

But how do lizards, snakes, and mammals get to islands? Swimming, except perhaps for snakes, seems to be an unlikely means of crossing and probably cannot be considered a viable dispersal mechanism except over very short distances. Part of the evidence cited by biogeographers in the past in support of a land bridge to the Northern Channel Islands is that fossils of a pygmy elephant—the Exiled Mammoth, *Mammuthus exilis*—have been found on San Miguel, Santa Cruz, and Santa Rosa Islands. Although supporters of the land bridge hypothesis contend that it is not possible for an elephant, no matter how small, to reach an island by any means other than walking, critics point out that Indian Elephants (*Elephas maximus*) are good swimmers, and that a 4.5-mile (7-km) swim would not be out of the question. Furthermore, fossil remains of elephants, most of which were dwarf varieties, have been found on at least ten islands in the Mediterranean Sea.

So if swimming or flying is out of the question for most animals and all plants, how then did these organisms cross to the islands?

Rafting

It appears that the likeliest explanation for the presence of most animals on the islands is that they could have crossed the channel on rafted masses of vegetation. These rafts, which consist of branches or even whole trees, are washed downstream by significant winter floods that occur in California every 30–50 years. Rivers such as the Los Angeles, San

TABLE 3 ENDEMIC MOTHS AND BUTTERFLIES OF CALIFORNIA CHANNEL ISLANDS

SUPERFAMILY AND SPECIES	ISLAND
Nepticuloidea	
Stigmella n. sp.	cl,cr
Tineoidea	
Acrocercops insulariella	cr
Gelechioidea	
Agonopterix toega	cl
Holcocera phenacocci	an,ba,ca,cr
Caleotechnites n. sp.	cl,cr
Chionodes n. sp.	an,ba,ca,cr
Ephysteris n. sp.	cr
Scrobipalpula n. sp.	cl
Vladimiria? n. sp.	cl,cr
Yponomeutoidea	
Ypsolopha lyonothamnae	cl,cr
Tortricoidea	
Argyrotaenia franciscana insulana (Island Tortix)	an,cr,mi,ni,ro
Argyrotaenia isolatissima (Solitary Tortix)	ba
Pyraloidea	
Evergestis angustalis calalinae	ca
Sosipatra proximanthophila	ca,cr
Vitula insula	ca,cr
Geometroidea	
Pero catalina (Catalina Leafwing)	ca
Pero n. sp. nr. *gigantea*	cl
Pterotaea cringera	cl
Noctoidea	
Arachnis picta insularis (Anacapa Painted Tiger Moth)	an
Arachnis picta meadowsi (Catalina Painted Tiger Moth)	ca
Lophocampa indistincta	an,ca,cr,ro(?)
Feralia meadowsi (Catalina Miller)	ca,cr(?)
Zosteropoda clementei	cl,cr,ro
Hesperioidea	
Ochlodes sylvanoides santacruza (Santa Cruz Woodland Skipper)	cr
Papilionoidea	
Anthocharis cethura catalina (Catalina Orange-tip)	ca
Strymon avalona (Avalon Hairstreak)	ca
Euphydryas editha insularis (Island Checkerspot)	ro

Source: After Powell (1994).

Note: Key to abbreviations: an, Anacapa; ba, Santa Barbara; ca, Santa Catalina; cl, San Clemente; cr, Santa Cruz; mi, San Miguel; ni, San Nicolas; ro, Santa Rosa.

Gabriel, Santa Ana, and Santa Clara drain large areas and, during flood time, carry considerable amounts of debris downstream and far out to sea. Assuming that a snake, lizard, or rodent were to cling to a tree or branch as it was washed along in a flood, it might be possible for the animal to ride such a raft long enough for currents or wind to push it across a channel to an island. Such rafts, containing animals, have been observed far out at sea all over the world, and they probably have been the means of migration of many animal species to the California islands. In 1955 a live Black-tailed Jack Rabbit, *Lepus californica,* was found floating on a kelp raft near San Clemente Island, 39 miles (62 km) from the California mainland.

Nevertheless, it remains apparent that chance, not logic, dictates which animals reach islands. Some biogeographers refer to this concept as "sweepstakes dispersal." It explains why so many animals common on the mainland—such as rabbits (*Lepus* spp., *Sylvilagus* spp.), Mule Deer (*Odocoileus hemionus*), Coyotes (*Canis latrans*), and Striped Skunks (*Mephitis mephitis*)—have not made it to the islands. Most animals riding these rafts probably do not safely make it to an island, but over many thousands of years all that is needed is an occasional successful crossing by a pregnant female or a male and female of the same species. The probability of such a crossing is of course quite low, but over time it has happened, even on some of the most remote islands.

There is a population of Arboreal Salamanders, *Aneides lugubris* (Fig. 62), on the Farallon Islands. This salamander is frequently associated with oak trees, although there are no native oaks on the Farallons. Throughout most of its range the salamander is characterized by small, yellow spots; yet on the islands the salamanders show a pattern of large spots that is also typical of the forms in the Gabilan Range east of Monterey. The Farallon Islands and the Gabilan Range are both west of the San Andreas fault; the Farallons are pure, weathered granite and the Gabilans also contain much granite. It has been postulated that the Gabilans and Farallons were once part of a long peninsula. It is apparent that the Gabilan Range was once also an island. Whether or not the Farallons were ever large enough to have remained continuously above sea level is subject to some conjecture. It is possible that the salamanders were carried to the island on a log raft, or it may be that these wave-lashed outcrops are all that remains of a former large land mass. Small-spotted members of this species are also found on Santa Catalina Island and several of the islands in San Francisco Bay, but they have not been studied thoroughly enough to determine how different they may be from mainland forms.

The most sedentary of all California salamanders, the slender salamanders (*Batrachoseps* spp.), are the most common amphibians on the California islands. On Santa Catalina and Los Coronados is found the Garden Slender Salamander, *Batrachoseps pacificus major*. It is also found on Todos Santos Island near Ensenada. At present it is assigned to the same subspecies that occurs on the adjacent mainland. To date, however, electrophoretic studies that could establish differentiation have not been published. A different subspecies, the Channel Islands Slender Salamander, *Batrachoseps pacificus pacificus* (Fig. 104), occurs on the four Northern Channel Islands. This subspecies has also been assigned to the same subspecies as occurs on the adjacent mainland. However, electrophoretic analysis of these island forms indicates that they are different enough to have been separated from the mainland forms for at least 4 million years. Santa Cruz Island, which is composed of two geological terranes, has two kinds of slender salamanders! (See the following discussion under "Vicariant Transport" for the significance of the two terranes.) The Black-bellied Slender Salamander, *Batrachoseps nigriventris*, also occurs on Santa Cruz Island. It too is believed to have diverged from its mainland counterpart at least 4 million years ago. Seven of the islands in San Francisco Bay have populations of the California Slender Salamander, *Batrachoseps attenuatus* (Fig. 190). Because these islands had mainland connections during periods of lower sea level, it is likely that the salamanders on the islands in San Francisco Bay are relicts.

Among the Channel Islands, snakes are found only on Santa Catalina, Santa Cruz, and Santa Rosa—relatively large, close islands. On Santa Catalina, surprisingly, snake species (five) outnumber lizards (three). The Western Rattlesnake, *Crotalus viridis* (Fig. 61), is found on Santa Catalina Island. Rafting seems the most logical mode of transport for snakes, although most species swim quite well. Some authorities contend that the rattlesnakes were introduced in a shipment of hay bales, despite the fact that snakes, particularly rattlesnakes, often wash up on beaches after major storms. After one such storm in 1995 a total of twenty-six snakes, mostly rattlesnakes, were collected from Del Mar and Solana Beaches in San Diego County.

Insects, spiders, and such other arthropods as millipedes and centipedes on California islands have not been thoroughly studied. Butterflies and moths (Lepidoptera) have been collected from every island, but other than the attractive or conspicuous forms, grasshoppers and their relatives (Orthoptera) seem to be the only group that has been studied with any intensity. Entomologists have identified fifty-two species of Orthoptera, and twelve of these are considered to be endemic. Among the endemic species, the Silk-spinning Crickets (*Cnemotettix*) (Fig. 103B) seem to have been particularly successful colonizers. They have diversified into at least four endemic species on the Channel Islands. These burrowing insects, related to Jerusalem Crickets (*Stenopelmatus*), are flightless, so they most likely arrived by rafting. An endemic shield-backed katydid, *Neduba propsti*, has been described for Santa Catalina Island.

Air Flotation

Even if they could not fly, small insects and many seeds were undoubtedly blown across to islands, especially during times when strong winds blew offshore with considerable force. Surprisingly, spiders are well suited as colonizers on islands, presumably because they are able to spin long strands of silk that act like balloons or parachutes. Even the Hawaiian islands have native species of spiders. Among plants, those with plumed seeds are well suited for wind dispersal. Many members of the sunflower family (Asteraceae) and many riparian species such as cottonwoods and cattails have plumed seeds capable of long-distance wind dispersal.

Passive Transport

Birds can transport insect or snail eggs as well as seeds on their feet or feathers. Many plants may also have arrived as seeds after fruits were eaten by mainland birds and their seeds were deposited after the birds' arrival on the island. Apparently domestic "Cherry Tomatoes" were introduced to the Los Coronados Islands by Western Gulls in this manner. Furthermore, migratory fruit-eating birds regularly pass along the coast and visit the islands.

Indeed the means of dispersal has probably been selected for in many plant species. Seeds equipped for air flotation, barbed seeds suited for attachment to birds' feet or feathers, and fruits that allow ingestion and the later deposition of seeds in feces are all mechanisms that ensure the movement of seeds to new locations. These means of dispersal are believed responsible for plant colonization of islands as remote as those in the Hawaiian group, and they most certainly also apply to the California islands.

Vicariant Transport

Vicariance is a form of transport associated with plate tectonics. Life forms are transferred from one point to another along with geological terranes, as if they were passengers on a huge ferry. Plate tectonics is explained in Chapter 2, but for now imagine that a piece of land that was formerly attached to the mainland becomes an island as it is torn loose along a fault system, and that it carries its cargo of life forms along with it.

The movement northward of land west of the San Andreas fault provides a possible example of vicariant transport. Miocene fossils of the two subspecies of Island Ironwood are located on opposite sides of the San Andreas fault. Fossils of Santa Catalina Island Ironwood have been found only along the coast on the western side of the fault. Island Ironwood from San Clemente, Santa Cruz, and Santa Rosa Islands, which is significantly different in appearance from the Santa Catalina Island subspecies, has left a fossil record to the north and east of the fault. The implication is that during the Miocene, prior to the northward movement west of the fault, ancestors of the two subspecies were divided along a simple north-south axis, and they have been carried to their present location by movement of the land. (It is, however, difficult to explain the presence of Island Ironwood on San Clemente Island, to the south of Santa Catalina.)

Vicariant biogeography is a plausible explanation for the appearance on islands of freshwater fishes or highly sedentary animals such as salamanders. In fact, the appearance of two species of Slender Salamanders (*Batrachoseps nigriventris* and *Batrachoseps pacificus*) on Santa Cruz Island may well be explained by vicariant biogeography.

It is tempting to search for alternative explanations for the presence of these salamanders on islands. Amphibians are unable to swim in salt water, so any hypothesis that involves dispersal from the mainland must involve some sort of rafting. It is entirely possible that sedentary salamanders might float across on a piece of wood or debris washed out by heavy rains. This explanation might particularly apply to the presence of the Arboreal Salamanders, *Aneides lugubris,* on the islands. On the other hand it is difficult to believe that salamanders, which usually occur under rocks and logs, could reach so many islands in this manner. Perhaps the two species rode to their present locations as passengers on land masses. Geological evidence indicates that the portions of Santa Cruz Island on each side of the fault were formerly separate islands and that the salamanders have mostly remained on their original terranes since the two halves became joined. One researcher studying *Batrachoseps* in the Coast Ranges found that the greatest distance a salamander moved during its lifetime was about 4 ft (1.2 m).

Of special interest in the biogeography of California's islands is the presence of the Island Night Lizard, *Xantusia riversiana* (Fig. 151; Plate 1C), on three islands. Dense populations of these lizards are found on San Clemente, San Nicolas, and Santa Barbara Islands. Electrophoretic studies show that these lizards are clearly the most divergent of all the vertebrates on the islands. They are different enough from their mainland relatives that some authorities have placed them in a different genus altogether (*Klauberina*).

Similar to salamanders, Island Night Lizards are without question sedentary, spending most of their time under rocks or in cracks. Mark-and-recapture studies on San Clemente Island have shown that over a period of years lizards are frequently recaptured under the same rock. Average home ranges are about 10 ft (3 m) across. The greatest distance a marked lizard is known to have moved is 30 ft (10 m). The population density of these lizards on San Clemente Island is remarkable. Studies indicate that, thanks to a lack of competitors and predators, there are over 3500 lizards per acre (1450/ha), amounting to a biomass of 55 to 85 lb/acre (10–16 kg/ha).

Relatives on the mainland include the Desert Night Lizard, *Xantusia vigilis,* and the Granite Night Lizard, *Xantusia henshawi.* Desert Night Lizards are commonly found in association with yucca plants, and Granite Night Lizards are found in cracks in rocks in the Peninsular Ranges. A fossil night lizard, similar but not identical to the island form, is represented in the San Diego area in sediments that have been determined to be at least 40 million years of age.

Electrophoretic studies imply that the island form has been separated from its mainland relatives for at least 10–15 million years. The two mainland forms appear to have diverged from each other about 7 million years ago. By correlating the electrophoretic data with the age of the fossils, we may speculate that the Island Night Lizard became separated from the mainland forms between 10 and 40 million years ago, and it may have been an island dweller since then.

Distribution of the night lizard family (Xantusiidae) is similar to that of other animals that seem to have been translocated on extant terranes. Members of the family occur in Cuba, tropical Middle America, and the arid Southwest. The Island Night Lizard may have evolved on San Clemente Island and ridden to its present locality from a former position, attached to mainland Mexico. There is no evidence that San Clemente Island was ever completely submerged, and the time span of tens of millions of years is appropriate for this type of transport.

The other two islands on which the Island Night Lizard occurs are not high enough to have remained above sea level. It is therefore believed that the lizards were somehow transported to the other islands sometime in the last million years. Electrophoretic studies also substantiate this idea: there is very little difference among the lizards of the different islands. This type of transport would require rafting, and a problem with this hypothesis is that the currents move the wrong way for rafts to disperse passively northward. Another hypothesis is that the lizards were carried as pets by Native Americans who inhabited the islands, but this suggestion does not explain why the lizards are not found on all the islands.

ESTABLISHING RESIDENCE:
ISLAND BIOGEOGRAPHY THEORY

Upon reaching an island, an organism must also find suitable habitat, after which competition becomes an equally important factor. Locating a small island surrounded by miles of uninhabitable sea is enough of a challenge for any terrestrial species, but finding a suitable place to live on that island is even more difficult. One advantage for the colonist is the fact that isolation generally keeps the species count low. In its original mainland habitat the colonist had to compete with many species, whereas on the relatively isolated island it may encounter only a few competitors.

Assume the colonist arrives, finds appropriate food resources, and reproduces. It has now established a founder population in a new place. Because so few individuals were involved in the founding, the genetic makeup of the population may not be representative of the gene pool for the same species on the mainland. Hence the new island population may start off with a distinctive set of characteristics and thus gets a head start on being endemic or unique. An example of this phenomenon could be the Two-striped Garter Snake, *Thamnophis hammondii,* which was formerly known as the Santa Catalina Island Garter Snake, *Thamnophis couchi hammondi.* Although still considered members of the same subspecies as those on the mainland, members of this isolated population have a unique color pattern. It lacks distinctive stripes and is a deep olive brown with a pale, buff-colored chin and lips. On the mainland this pattern is not representative of the species as a whole except for a population that occurs near Lompoc in Santa Barbara County. It has been calculated that it would be possible for one of these snakes, perhaps a gravid female, to be washed into the sea by the Santa Ynez River and be carried by known currents to Santa Catalina Island in a little over three weeks. Although the probability of such an event occurring is admittedly low, it is within the realm of possibility. Snakes are good swimmers and floaters, and they also can ride logs. It is also interesting that this color pattern closely matches that of the Lower California Garter Snake, *Thamnophis digueti,* found in a few bodies of fresh water in south-central Baja California.

In the late 1960s R. H. MacArthur and E. O. Wilson, in their now-classic book *The Theory of Island Biogeography,* established a set of principles for island populations that have been supported by research on islands all over the world, including the California islands. First, they proposed that two basic factors influence the number of species on an island: rates of immigration balanced by rates of extinction. An island, therefore, has an equilibrium point at which ecological saturation occurs and the total number of species, or the carrying capacity, is maximized. If the number of species on an island is at or near saturation, rates of immigration and extinction must be in equilibrium.

A very important concept in island biology is that once an island becomes saturated, the total number of species tends to remain the same. Even though species composition may change over time, the number of extinctions should equal the number of colonizations. Although there is not always agreement on these numbers when comparing animals, such as mammals, that have limited ability to cross water barriers, animals that are good dispersers seem to fit the pattern well. Data collected from 1917 to 1968 on the number and types of breeding land birds on the California islands indicate that in nearly every case the total number of species remained stable, with the number of extinctions equal to the number of colonizations. Butterflies, on the other hand, seem to be undersaturated on the islands, probably because of the extreme disturbance to the native plant communities. The numbers of butterflies are closely related to the numbers of host plants upon which they live, as either larvae or adults.

Comparison of the total number of species on an island with that on an equivalent area on the mainland usually reveals that saturation on the island occurs with fewer species. There are probably several reasons for this phenomenon. First, species that require large ranges are automatically selected against. Second, an area on the mainland includes many species that are only on the fringe of their preferred habitats and that are more common in adjacent areas. These two types of species are seldom found on islands. Perhaps of greatest importance is the fact that the total diversity of habitats on an island tends to be reduced and niches tend to be more generalized; this seems particularly true where human disturbance has monotonized the landscape.

Another factor that could affect the number of species on an island is time. For example, comparison of the numbers of reptile species on the various islands in the Gulf of California (Sea of Cortes) shows that the numbers on the California islands, including those on the Pacific side of Baja California, are smaller than would be expected. It has been hypothesized that unstable climate associated with the ice ages reduced the time available for colonization. Most authorities allow about 10,000 years of appropriate climate since the end of the last period of glaciation. Land birds, which can colonize more rapidly, have had sufficient time to reach saturation, but reptiles have not had enough time. This hypothesis may also be invoked to explain why the numbers of mammals and amphibians on the California islands are unexpectedly low.

Several interacting factors affect the number of organisms that reach an island. Small islands are more difficult to colonize than large islands because they present smaller targets. Distant islands are more difficult to reach than islands close to the mainland. It is evident, therefore, that small islands located far from the mainland will have fewer total species, whereas large islands near the mainland will have the greatest number of species. Species on small, close islands and large, distant islands should be intermediate in number.

MacArthur and Wilson's model is well supported by the numbers of native plants and animals on California's Channel Islands. For example, Santa Barbara Island (small and distant) and Santa Catalina Island (close and large) well illustrate the size-distance relationships. Santa Barbara is 1 square mile (2.56 km^2) in size and is 38 miles (61 km) from the mainland. It has 88 taxa of plants and 16 species of vertebrate animals. Santa Catalina has a total area of 76 square miles (194 km^2), is 20 miles (32 km) from the mainland, and is occupied by 421 taxa of plants and 53 species of vertebrate animals. Reference to Table 1, which compares the numbers of plant and animal species on the different islands, verifies that these concepts hold.

EVOLUTION ON ISLANDS

New habitats, different climates, and the absence of competitors have allowed many unusual specializations to develop on the world's islands, including those off California. Four of the most common phenomena are gigantism, dwarfism, loss of mobility, and niche shifts.

Gigantism

Imagine the establishment of a small herbaceous (nonwoody) plant on a California island. With milder temperatures, moisture available from marine air, no grazing animals, and fewer competitors than in mainland communities, it might be able to evolve into a larger, upright, branched shrub. Just such an evolutionary sequence has probably occurred for a member of the sunflower family (Asteraceae): the Giant Coreopsis, *Coreopsis gigantea* (Fig. 161; Plate 9), which is found on all the Channel Islands except San Clemente. On the adjacent mainland, the genus is represented by annual desert wildflowers and a low-growing sea-bluff perennial known as Sea Dahlia or Maritime Coreopsis, *Coreopsis maritima*. On the islands and in several restricted coastal areas of the adjacent mainland, however, Giant Coreopsis is a thick-stemmed, large, woody plant reaching a height of 4–6 ft (1–2 m) or more. During the spring months, candelabra-like branches support a luxuriant foliage and large yellow flower heads. Although most authorities cite Giant Coreopsis as an example of island gigantism, it is also possible that is a relict that has left no fossil record on the mainland.

Another sunflower relative that becomes much larger on the islands is one of the Woolly Sunflowers (*Eriophyllum*). Nevin's Eriophyllum, *Eriophyllum nevinii,* is another sea bluff–dwelling species. It is found on San Clemente, Santa Barbara, and Santa Catalina Islands. Among the buckwheats, Saint Catherine's Lace (*Eriogonum giganteum*) (Fig. 50), Santa Cruz Island Buckwheat (*Eriogonum arborescens*) (Fig. 71), and Island Buckwheat (*Eriogonum grande*) (Fig. 72) are also considerably larger than their mainland relatives. One of the most unusual plants on the islands is Blair's Munzothamnus, *Stephanomeria blairii.* Found only on San Clemente Island, this shrub reaches a height of up to 4 ft and is conspicuously different from other members of its family.

The first impression one forms upon viewing the canyons and north-facing slopes of Santa Catalina Island is that there are many trees. Closer inspection reveals that they are actually large shrubs that are the same as, or closely related to, the species found on the mainland. This form of gigantism becomes more apparent as one becomes more familiar with the plants of the Channel Islands.

A tree that many associate with Santa Catalina Island is the Catalina Cherry, *Prunus ilicifolia* ssp. *lyonii* (Plate 5C,D). Catalina Cherry is the tree version of a common chaparral shrub known as Holly-leaved Cherry, *Prunus ilicifolia* ssp. *ilicifolia.* Cherry Cove, a popular mooring on the east side of the island, is named in its honor. Groves of Catalina Cherry also occur in canyons on San Clemente, Santa Cruz, and Santa Rosa Islands. Individual trees may reach 50 ft (15 m) in height.

Gigantism is also found among the vertebrates on California's islands. The Island Night Lizard, *Xantusia riversiana,* mentioned earlier, is considerably larger than mainland night lizards. Most rodents are also larger than their mainland relatives. Examples include the Santa Catalina Island Harvest Mouse (*Reithrodontomys megalotis catalinae*) (Fig. 67), the Deer Mouse (*Peromyscus maniculatus*) (Fig. 3), the Santa Catalina Island Ground Squirrel (*Spermophilus beecheyi nesioticus*) (Fig. 66), and the Spotted Skunk (*Spilogale gracilis amphialus*) (Fig. 114). Extinct mice—the Anacapa Mouse, *Peromyscus anyapahensis,* and the Giant Island Mouse, *Peromyscus nesodytes,* of Santa Rosa and San Miguel Islands—were several times the size of their mainland relatives, which in turn are similar in size to the House Mouse (*Mus musculus*). Both extinct mice are known from Pleistocene fossils, but remains of the Giant Island Mouse are also found in the middens (refuse piles) of Native Americans, indicating that this rodent coexisted with early humans until some 2000 years ago.

10 cm

ME

Figure 4. Island Fox, *Urocyon littoralis*. This island endemic is represented by a different subspecies on six of the eight Channel Islands. It is absent from the two smallest Channel Islands, Anacapa and Santa Barbara.

Dwarfism

Whereas small animals, such as lizards and rodents, seem to grow larger on islands, animals that start out large seem to get smaller. The explanation for dwarfism is that islands have a limited food supply. A population of small animals, requiring less food, should do better where food is scarce.

For example, the Island Fox, *Urocyon littoralis* (Fig. 4; Plate 1A), is smaller than the closely related mainland Gray Fox, *Urocyon cinereoargenteus*.

But by far the most spectacular example of dwarfism among mammals is the pygmy Exiled Mammoth, *Mammuthus exilis*. The Pleistocene fauna of southern California has been reconstructed from the fossils deposited in the tar pits at Rancho La Brea. Along with sabretooth cats and dire wolves, two species of elephants were present. The ancestral species for the Exiled Mammoth appears to have been a full-sized species, *Mammuthus columbi,* that occurred on the mainland. As mentioned previously, fossil elephants on at least ten islands in the Mediterranean Sea were also dwarfs.

Loss of Mobility

Island animals and plants also seem to lose their mobility, a trend that is coincident with the change in life history strategy that causes them to grow larger. The dispersal mechanisms that brought them to the island might become a disadvantage once a population becomes established: island plants and animals do not benefit if they are carried away from the island. Thus birds (such as the Channel Island fossil goose *Chendytes*) become flightless and certain terrestrial animals become sedentary. Plants lose their mechanisms for wind dispersal: plumes on seeds disappear, and seeds become larger.

Niche Shifts

In association with fewer species and in the absence of competition, a species may be able to occur in great abundance on an island, a phenomenon known as *competitive release.* In such a case there is a tendency for genetic variability to express itself; the larger the population, the greater the variation. This diversity allows a species to occupy a broad range of habitats, and over time it may come to occupy an ecological niche that is different from that of its mainland relatives. Such niche shifts are illustrated by a number of species of land birds on the Channel Islands.

On Santa Cruz Island, the number of breeding-bird pairs per acre of chaparral is similar to that on the mainland, yet Santa Cruz Island has only two-thirds the number of species. Common species such as the California Thrasher, *Toxostoma redivivum,* and the California Towhee, *Pipilo crissalis,* are missing on the islands. Bewick's Wren, *Thryomanes bewickii* (Fig. 64J), is twice as common, and Hutton's Vireo, *Vireo huttoni,* is four times as common as it is on the mainland. On Santa Cruz Island, common insectivorous birds such as the Wrentit (*Chamaea fasciata),* Bushtit (*Psaltriparus minimus*), and Plain Titmouse (*Parus inornatus*) are missing. In island chaparral they are replaced by Bewick's Wren, Hutton's Vireo, and the Orange-crowned Warbler, *Vermivora celata* (Fig. 109), which is uncommon in mainland chaparral but common on the islands. Furthermore, in the absence of the California Thrasher, the Northern Mockingbird, *Mimus polyglottos* (Fig. 64G), has taken over its niche as the mimic thrush, whereas the endemic Island Scrub Jay, *Aphelocoma insularis,* has become a common ground feeder. In addition, in the absence of competition from Steller's Jay, *Cyanocitta stelleri,* the Island Scrub Jay has moved into the Closed-cone Pine Forest and added pine seeds to its diet.

HUMAN IMPACTS ON ISLAND ECOLOGY

Native Americans may first have visited the Channel Islands about 12,000 years ago, and they probably occupied the larger islands continuously beginning about 7000 years ago. They exerted an impact on island vegetation through food-gathering activities (see Chapter 3), including setting fires, and perhaps by cutting down certain trees or shrubs for shelter, for fuel, or to make baskets. Because they moved from mainland to island and from island to island by canoe, these earliest inhabitants may have been responsible for the introductions of new plants and animals.

Native Americans exploited shellfish, such as abalone and mussels. They also fished and killed birds and mammals, and thus certainly exerted some adverse impact on the flora and fauna of the islands. Their hunting activities may have brought about the extinction of the fossil flightless goose. They also were known to set periodic fires, probably to encourage production of certain plants, such as Chia, *Salvia columbariae,* that produced edible seeds.

The presence of the Island Fox, *Urocyon littoralis* (Fig. 4; Plate 1A), on several islands is sometimes explained as an example of transport by Native Americans. Island Foxes occur on the six largest islands, including San Clemente, San Miguel, San Nicolas, Santa Catalina, Santa Cruz, and Santa Rosa. Although there is some difference of opinion regarding classification, each island is considered to have its own subspecies, implying that the foxes have been isolated on the islands for quite some time. The Island Fox's nearest relative appears to be the Gray Fox, *Urocyon cinereoargenteus,* of the adjacent mainland. It was once proposed that the Island Fox is more closely allied to three small species of foxes that occur in Yucatán, Mexico, and Guatemala, in which case the Island Fox could represent another example of the vicariant distribution mechanism noted previously for the Island Night Lizard. The fact that Island Foxes have differentiated to a greater degree than any other island mammal adds support to the idea that they may have been isolated for longer than we think.

With the aid of such techniques as analysis of mitochondrial DNA, electrophoresis, and anatomical and archaeological studies, scientists have concluded that the foxes arrived first on the Northern Channel Islands at least 16,000 years ago. This colonization presumably took place during a period of lowered sea level, when the islands were closer to the mainland and connected to each other as the single island Santa Rosae. By 9500 years ago, sea level had risen to approximately its present level, isolating the foxes into the three northern populations, which subsequently differentiated. Based on similarities and differences among the different island populations, as well as the archaeological record, it appears that foxes from San Miguel Island were taken to San Clemente Island first, and then to San Nicolas. The record of foxes appears on San Clemente Island in remains that have been dated to 3400 years ago, as opposed to those on San Nicolas Island, which are only 2200 years old. Interestingly there is practically no genetic variability in the San Nicolas foxes, implying that they arose from a very small population, perhaps numbering only two ancestors.

In contrast, the foxes on Santa Catalina Island appear to have been derived from northern and southern sources, the implication being that Native Americans carried foxes to Santa Catalina several times.

If Native Americans in fact carried foxes around as pets, it would have been a long time ago. On the other hand, differences in the subspecies might be less significant than we think. Size and color differences are known to evolve rapidly, but the genetic data are more conclusive. These types of changes are typical of animals and plants on all sorts of ecological islands. It is possible that Island Foxes do not deserve subspecific status. It is also possible that the different island populations simply represent the descendants of foxes of different sizes or colors that the Native Americans left on the islands, a phenomenon known as the *founder effect*.

The arrival of European explorers in 1542 (Cabrillo) and 1601 (Vizcaíno) exposed the islands and their inhabitants to potentially significant alterations. Domestic animals such as pigs and goats may have been released. Infectious diseases could have been introduced to Native Americans, and extensive woodcutting may have occurred. However, these explorers had only brief contacts with the islands, and it appears that for the next two hundred years the island's flora and fauna were spared the impacts of western civilization.

Beginning in 1769, however, California was colonized by Spanish missionaries. A series of missions was built along the coast, and domestic plants and animals were brought to California. During the next fifty years, an influx of Europeans and Americans seriously altered the ecosystems of the islands. Russian, English, and American fur traders visited all of the California islands, bringing about the local elimination of the Sea Otter (*Enhydra lutris*) (Fig. 36), the Northern Fur Seal (*Callorhinus ursinus*), and the Northern Elephant Seal (*Mirounga angustirostris*) (Figs. 38 and 167) as well as the decimation of the Native American inhabitants through introduced diseases.

During this period, goats, pigs, and sheep (Fig. 5) were variously introduced to most of the islands. These animals soon reverted back to a wild (feral) state and reproduced rapidly, probably extirpating many plant species and certainly altering almost all plant communities. Abundant vegetation and the lack of predators enabled their large populations to damage seriously the fragile plant communities that had existed for thousands of years, isolated from such grazing pressure.

In the 1830s many settlers moved to the islands to raise livestock and to farm. Portions of even tiny Santa Barbara Island were plowed and planted, rabbits were released, and later sheep were introduced. The tremendous influx of immigrants to California in the 1850s brought even greater pressure to the islands. Egg collectors supplied the booming

Figure 5. Introduced animals of the California islands. (A) Goats, *Capra hircus*, on San Clemente Island (1986). (B) Sheep, *Ovis aries*, on Santa Cruz Island (1997). (C) Bison, *Bison bison*, on Santa Catalina Island (1990). (D) Feral Hog, *Sus scrofa*, on San Clemente Island (1986).

population of San Francisco through weekly visits to the murre rookeries on the Farallon Islands, while more and more squatters occupied the Channel Islands off southern California. Some mining occurred on Santa Catalina Island in the early 1860s, while sheep and cattle ranching continued on the larger islands.

Figure 5. (*Continued*)

By the middle of the nineteenth century the Mexican government had sold or given the two largest Northern Channel Islands to prominent local families. After California joined the United States in 1850, the islands changed hands several times and were developed into farms and ranches. The new settlers brought with them a diverse collection of plants and animals that were totally alien to the insular ecosystem.

In the late nineteenth century, land developers bought Santa Catalina

Island and built the resort community of Avalon. Subsequent development of Santa Catalina included the settlement of Two Harbors and the establishment of several rock quarries and numerous yachting facilities in the many protected coves.

The isolated nature of the islands along with private ownership during the twentieth century helped protect them to some degree from human influence. In 1938, formal protection was bestowed on Santa Barbara and Anacapa Islands when they became the Channel Islands National Monument. Most of Santa Catalina Island and a substantial portion of Santa Cruz Island have been set aside as natural areas, administered by nonprofit conservancies. In 1975 the Catalina Conservancy took over management of 86 percent of Santa Catalina, and the western 90 percent of Santa Cruz Island came under the protection of The Nature Conservancy in 1978. The Channel Islands National Park was established in 1980, encompassing the National Monument and the rest of the Northern Channel Islands. In 1986 Santa Rosa Island was acquired from the Vail and Vickers Cattle Company by the National Park Service for $29 million, and funds raised for the purchase of the eastern end of Santa Cruz Island permitted a 75 percent interest to be removed from private control. In 1997, through the application of a "legislative taking" law passed by Congress, the final 25 percent of the eastern end was acquired by the National Park Service. These acquisitions have eliminated private ownership of the Northern Channel Islands and placed them in the hands of agencies dedicated to preservation. San Miguel Island is jointly administered by the National Park Service and the U.S. Navy, which retains the option of resuming use of the island. San Clemente and San Nicolas Islands are still the property of the U.S. Navy, and access is limited to persons having official business there. The Farallon Islands are now a National Wildlife Refuge, administered by the U.S. Fish and Wildlife Service.

The islands in San Francisco Bay have passed through the same phases of ownership, including a significant military presence and the use of Alcatraz as a federal prison. Today the islands are all under public ownership.

Channel Islands National Park has been declared an international biosphere reserve under the U.S. Man and the Biosphere Program, which was created to establish and support a network of reserves intended to represent the various biogeographical areas of the United States. The islands still retain some of the pristine quality that Native Americans knew, and it is hoped that diligent conservation will offset the abuse they have suffered during the past century.

New threats to the ecosystem of the islands are posed by increased oil production in the Santa Barbara Channel, pollution from mainland agricultural and urban development, sonic booms from Vandenberg Air Force Base just to the north (which may disrupt the breeding of sea birds and pinnipeds), uncontrolled public visitation, and the introduction of additional nonnative plants and animals.

Introduced Animals

The devastation wreaked by nonnative animals is nowhere more apparent than on islands. The most serious problem results from the introduction of large herbivores. Island plants evolved in the absence of large herbivores, and therefore many of them have no defenses. In the absence of large carnivores, the herbivores overpopulate the islands within a short time, and herbivores that are left unattended on an island soon strip it of most of its vegetation.

Goats, *Capra hircus* (Fig. 5A), seem to do the most damage, for they will eat practically anything. Goats were present on Santa Barbara, San Clemente, and Santa Catalina, and on Brooks and Yerba Buena Islands in San Francisco Bay. Indeed Yerba Buena Island was once known as Goat Island. Goats were introduced to Santa Catalina in 1827, and they are still there. In 1989, a systematic program to remove goats and pigs from Santa Catalina was begun. About twice a year, helicopter-assisted hunts are conducted, in which sharpshooters with 12-gauge shotguns fire from the air. By 1998 most of the animals were gone from the west side of the island, but as many as 1000 goats and 3000 pigs may remain in the canyons on the east side of the island near Avalon. The only thing that has prevented them from denuding the entire island is a series of fences that have confined them to localized areas. Nevertheless, forty-eight native plant species have been lost on Santa Catalina since the introduction of goats.

Fencing could have helped San Clemente Island, too, but attempts to control the goats there came too late. As noted previously, the U.S. Navy owns and operates San Clemente Island, using it for target practice and as a missile-tracking station. By the 1980s goats had turned the island into a wasteland. The only native vegetation that survived in reasonable health included cacti and those shrubs that grew in canyons with walls too steep to climb. Native oaks were pruned flat on their undersides, and no seedlings were allowed to grow more than an inch (25 mm) or so before being nibbled off.

Because of the presence on San Clemente Island of plants and animals protected by the Endangered Species Act, the Navy took action to reduce or eliminate the goat population. A plan to shoot the goats systematically was announced, but the Fund for Animals, an animal-rights group, succeeded repeatedly in stopping its implementation. At one time there were close to 15,000 goats on the island. Over a period of several years, various efforts to round them up alive reduced the number to perhaps 1500. Herds of goats were transplanted to a variety of localities in the continental United States. In 1986, the Fund, at the Navy's expense, was allowed to trap remaining goats by dropping nets on them from helicopters. The goats were again transferred to the mainland, where they were put up for adoption. Yet the goat adoption program faced the same problem that had hampered the burro adoption program in the Southwestern desert: not enough people wanted goats. Nevertheless nearly 900 goats were removed from the island.

But the problem was still not solved, because all of the goats had not been removed. In 1991, the Navy finally removed the last of the goats, using "Judas goats" (tame female goats in heat) to lure the remainder of the feral animals into captivity. To this day the Navy remains alert to the presence of stray goats. The vegetation is beginning to show promising signs of recovery, but certain plant species will never recover from the impact of goat feeding.

Sheep, *Ovis aries* (Fig. 5B), are nearly as bad as goats. San Miguel, San Nicolas, and Santa Cruz Islands have been home to sheep since the 1800s, and Brooks Island, in San Francisco Bay, was once known as Sheep Island. Of all the Channel Islands, San Nicolas may have been hit the hardest. By 1890 there were more than 30,000 sheep on San Nicolas; they consumed much of the native vegetation, and by 1930 the island was in very poor condition. In 1933 the Navy acquired the island and built a weather station. The last sheep rancher left the island in 1941, when his lease was revoked, and by then there was very little vegetation left. In an effort to reduce erosion, the Navy applied fertilizer and grass seed from an airplane. Today, all sheep have been removed and nonnative grasses constitute most of the surviving vegetation. Lower mesas, eroded sandstone slopes, and dune areas still contain areas of native vegetation, including certain rare species. At this point, San Nicolas is a good candidate for study of the processes of natural island colonization.

San Miguel was nearly as bleak a place as San Nicolas. It was denuded by sheep grazing, and most of its topsoil has blown away. A fossil forest—with interesting limestone concretions on old tree roots exposed by erosion—is one of the bizarre attractions on the island (Fig. 118). With the removal of the sheep, San Miguel is showing remarkable signs of recovery.

Santa Cruz Island has had sheep since the 1850s. By the late 1970s, all regions above the fence line showed damage from grazing, and very little native vegetation within reach of the sheep was left. All shrubs had been pruned on the underside as high as a sheep could reach. Seedlings were unable to become established. If the sheep were not brought under control, the native plants would eventually die of old age. Fortunately, Santa Cruz Island is today managed by a combination of The Nature Conservancy and the National Park Service. The Conservancy has added fences, and between 1983 and 1986 they removed over 30,000 sheep. In 1997, after the National Park Service took over the eastern end of the island, they began to remove the remaining 2000 sheep. The sheep are being captured alive and returned to the mainland. The island's recovery seems promising: including introduced species, there are now some 650 kinds of plants on Santa Cruz. Ironwood and Bishop Pine seedlings are reappearing, and Silver Deerweed, *Lotus argophyllus* var. *niveus* (Fig. 133)—once on the brink of extinction—is flourishing. Live-forevers, *Dudleya greenei* (Fig. 79B) and *Dudleya nesiotica* (Fig. 79A), once confined to steep cliff faces, are expanding their ranges. Sheep still remain on the eastern 10 percent of the island, which is still denuded. Constant attention to the fences is required to prevent escapees from invading the western part of the island.

Cattle, *Bos taurus,* have over the years been herded on Santa Catalina, Santa Cruz, and Santa Rosa, as well as Alcatraz, Brooks, and Yerba Buena Islands in San Francisco Bay. Now there is only one herd left, on Santa Rosa Island. The Nature Conservancy removed the cattle, about 1800 head, from Santa Cruz Island. The herd on Santa Rosa Island shares resources with introduced Mule Deer, *Odocoileus hemionus,* and Wapiti (Roosevelt Elk), *Cervis elaphus.* Although the elk and deer are not native, their population level is controlled by hunting, with the goal of limiting the two herds to about 700 animals each. The acquisition in 1986 of Santa Rosa Island by the National Park Service included all land except for the residence and 7.6 acres (3 ha) of the surrounding land. The owner, the Vail and Vickers Cattle Company, retained the right to continue cattle ranching over the entire island and commercial deer and elk hunting until the year 2011, 25 years from the date of purchase. Under a range management plan, stocking rates are adjusted based on monitoring of residual dry matter (remaining edible forage) in upland sites. In 1995, with about 6500 head of cattle remaining, the National Park Service proposed that about 20 percent of the pastureland be allowed to "rest" and that the cattle be removed from it. After it recovers, the plan is to allow cattle on that parcel only during the winter months. In addition, an electric fence was placed around the habitat of three rare plant species. In 1996, however, the National Parks and Conservation Association, stating that cattle still were allowed to roam the entire island, sued the National Park Service for mismanagement. The subsequent settlement required elimination of cattle in 1998.

The elk on Santa Rosa Island grow to uncommonly large size. Is this another example of island gigantism? Half of the sixteen trophy Roosevelt Elk listed in Safari Club International's record book were shot on Santa Rosa. Hunters pay $6000 for a five-day permit to shoot a six-by-six elk (one that has six points on each antler).

A most unlikely introduced herbivore is the Bison (American Buffalo), *Bison bison* (Fig. 5C). Today there are about 500 of them on Santa Catalina Island, in a population that is also controlled. The Bison were introduced to the island in 1924 during the filming of a silent movie, *The Vanishing American.* From the original fourteen animals released, the herd has grown significantly, to the detriment of native vegetation. However, Bison now graze primarily on introduced grasses. The dramatic difference between the damage produced by goats and Bison can be seen where the two herds graze on opposites sides of a fence. The vegetation on the side where the goats live is invariably chewed off to the ground (Fig. 68).

A secondary influence of Bison on Santa Catalina has been the appearance of Brown-headed Cowbirds, *Molothrus ater,* flocks of which follow Bison herds and feed on their droppings. Unfortunately, the cowbirds are nest parasites that also lay their eggs in the nests of various native songbirds that reside on the island. Their ultimate effect on the abundance of the island's native birds has yet to be assessed.

Santa Barbara Island, the smallest of the Channel Islands, has been affected by farming, sheep ranching, and the introduction of feral rabbits. The European Rabbit (Belgian Hare), *Oryctolagus cuniculus* (Fig. 159), was introduced about 1915 by a farmer, and apparently reintroduced by the Navy in 1942. The rabbits flourished, and native vegetation was seriously damaged. From 1979 through 1981, the National Park Service removed the rabbits and native vegetation is now recovering. The endemic Santa Barbara Live-forever, *Dudleya traskiae,* once thought to be extinct, is once more expanding its range. The European Rabbit was also an inhabitant of the Farallon Islands.

Perhaps the most serious threat to the native island biota is the presence of introduced Wild Pigs or Feral Hogs, *Sus scrofa* (Fig. 5D). The pigs are members of the same species as the domestic hog or pig, and they are abundant on Santa Catalina and Santa Cruz Islands. They formerly were abundant on San Clemente and Santa Rosa as well, but extermination programs have succeeded in removing them from those islands, and their removal from Santa Catalina Island is under way. Pigs are omnivorous. They do not see well, but they use their excellent sense of smell to locate various underground roots, tubers, or bulbs. In order to find these carbohydrate-rich underground storage organs, boars turn over the soil, uprooting whatever is on the surface. Among their favorite foods are the bulbs of Blue Dicks, *Dichelostemma capitatum* (Fig. 198), and Mariposa Lilies (*Calochortus* spp.) (Plate 10C). After a group of Wild Pigs has moved through an area, it looks as if it has been rototilled, with large areas of bare earth the typical result. When it rains, the disturbed topsoil is carried away, and patches remain bare for years.

Human visitors to the islands must realize that a Wild Boar is one of the most dangerous animals that may be encountered. If cornered, boars are ferocious. Their large canine teeth project upward as tusks, and although wild males may have shorter tusks than their domestic counterparts, the arrangement remains useful for digging—and waylaying opponents.

Not too many carnivores have been introduced to islands, because in general they are not good to eat. Herbivores have been introduced to provide a source of food or sport hunting for humans. The early introductions of goats were intended to provide fresh meat for sailors. Introductions of cattle and sheep were intended to capitalize on the presence of unfenced range, free of predators. Boars were introduced to provide food, and also for sport hunting.

The introductions of these animals have not been limited to islands, but, put simply, islands are more susceptible to overcrowding. Where populations of pigs, goats, sheep, and other herbivores roam free on various parts of the mainland, particularly in the Coast Ranges, natural predators such as mountain lions help to control them.

The carnivores that have been introduced to islands are principally escaped pets. Domestic dogs and cats, at one time or another, seem to have been present on all of the islands. Feral dogs seemed to be more of a problem in the past. At first one of the limiting factors controlling sheep populations on San Nicolas Island was the pack of dogs descended from animals kept by the original Native American inhabitants. However, it did not take long for the sheepherders to remove all the dogs.

Cedros Island, a large, steep island off Baja California, is one of the least disturbed of all the islands along the Pacific coast. A population of native deer coexisted there with introduced goats. Apparently the deer are able to thrive on the island without overpopulation, and a pack of wild dogs kept the goats under control.

Feral cats abound on many islands. The presence of these cats is a major problem for sea birds because of the exposed nature of their nests. It is also a problem for native rodents and land birds. The San Clemente Island Loggerhead Shrike, *Lanius ludovicianus mearnsi,* an endangered species, is particularly threatened by feral cats. However, some birds seem to survive, possibly by taking refuge in cactus patches or trees. On the other hand, cats tend to keep introduced rats and mice under control.

Introduced Plants

On some islands, nonnative plants greatly outnumber native ones in terms of area covered. This is particularly true on islands such as San Clemente, San Miguel, San Nicolas, Santa Barbara, and Santa Rosa, where grassland covers most of the landscape. Nonnative plants account for a high of 48 percent of species on San Nicolas Island and a low of 20 percent on Santa Rosa Island. Thus a smaller number of alien plants covers a large amount of area.

In the case of the grass family (Poaceae), nonnative species greatly outnumber native ones and also cover more acreage. For example, on Santa Cruz Island, there are twenty-eight species of native grasses and forty-two nonnative species. The total area covered by grassland on Santa Cruz represents 57 percent of the island's surface. On Santa Rosa Island grassland covers 67 percent of the total area. These grassland communities are today composed largely of nonnative ephemeral grasses (Fig. 59), such as oats (*Avena* spp.), bromes (*Bromus* spp.), barleys (*Hordeum* spp.), and ryegrasses (*Lolium* spp.).

Where did these grasses come from and why do they replace the native ones? Introduced grasses come primarily from the eastern Mediterranean, where they evolved over thousands of years under pressure from domestic grazing animals. They were introduced to California in the food, fur, and digestive tracts of domestic animals brought from Europe, particularly after the Gold Rush. They thrive in California because its climate is very similar to that of the Mediterranean.

How do nonnative grasses replace the native species? Native grasses, which are primarily perennial bunch grasses, die back each year during the summer drought. These plants invest much of their energy in root growth rather than seed production. The root systems remain dormant until the winter rains stimulate regrowth of the aboveground foliage. In contrast, ephemeral grasses endure periods of drought as seeds; the entire plants, including the roots, die during the dry season. When it rains, the seeds germinate and the plants grow, reproduce, and set seed once again, all during one season (which is why they are said to be ephemeral or annual). In addition, nonnative grazing animals trample the roots of the perennial native grasses. Thus the ephemeral species, which invest most of their energy in seed production, have an advantage. The hooves of domestic grazers not only kill the roots of the native grasses, they also compact the soil, increasing runoff and erosion. Water that should percolate into the ground runs off and becomes unavailable to the root systems that remain. Yet the shallow penetration of the water is sufficient to stimulate the growth of the shallow-rooted, nonnative ephemeral species, and replacement is under way.

Within the grasslands, other nonnative ephemeral plants also take over. Most of these herbaceous ephemerals are what we call weeds; they include primarily mustards (*Brassica* spp.), filarees (*Erodium* spp.), Bur-clover and/or Alfalfa (*Medicago* spp.), and Sweet Clover (*Melilotus* spp.). Most of these plants were introduced for similar reasons as the nonnative grasses, in association with livestock, although deliberate introductions of food or medicinal plants also occurred. For example, Horehound, *Marrubium vulgare*, a member of the mint family (Lamiaceae), was introduced from Europe to make medicinal tea or candy that can be used to soothe a sore throat.

Sweet Fennel, *Foeniculum vulgare*, is a European native that was introduced for its essential oils. Many people are familiar with this plant because of its licorice odor. The leaves, roots, and seeds are edible. The seeds are used for seasoning in Italian dishes, and the spice is sometimes called anise. It is a common weed on all of the Channel Islands and the mainland. Ironically nonnative grazers seemed to control the spread of this noxious weed. Yet now that the sheep have been removed from most of Santa Cruz Island, a program has been initiated to remove the Fennel manually, lest it take over vast acreage. Fennel is so invasive because its leaves and stems contain chemicals that inhibit the growth of native plants, a phenomenon known as *allelopathy*.

Common Sow Thistle, *Sonchus oleraceus*, with its 10-in. (25-cm)-long leaves was a source of greens that were boiled for food. Similarly the mustards are another group of European natives that have been introduced for their edible greens. Not only does Black Mustard, *Brassica nigra*, have edible leaves, but commercial mustard is prepared from its seeds. Field Mustard, *Brassica rapa*, has edible leaves, flowers, and turniplike roots, and rapeseed oil is prepared from its seeds. Mustards seem to dominate once they become established because they too appear to inhibit the growth of native plants.

Legend has it that Gaspar de Portolá, the Spanish adventurer, introduced mustard to California in 1769. With his mules and soldiers, de Portolá explored the interior of California from San Diego to San Francisco Bay. His route took him far from the coastline, and he was gone for many months. It is said that he sprinkled mustard seeds along his route, so that, when the time came to return to his ship, he could simply follow the trail of bright yellow flowers.

Who knows which plants were introduced to the islands by Native Americans? Certainly they have had an influence on native vegetation. They selectively harvested some plants, encouraged the growth of others by setting fires, altered natural communities around their villages, and transported plant materials from the mainland and between islands. Plants with underground storage organs (*geophytes*), such as Mariposa or Sego Lilies, *Calochortus* spp., and Blue Dicks, *Dichelostemma capitatum,* were harvested for their edible bulbs. Seeds of Chia, *Salvia columbariae,* are rich in protein and were gathered by all coastal peoples. Various parts of the tarweeds (*Hemizonia* spp.) (Fig. 138) were also eaten, either boiled or raw. Not only were these plants transported back and forth from the mainland, but coastal grassland areas were deliberately burned to encourage growth of this species, which is one of the first to return in areas damaged by fire.

Acorns were also widely harvested, and Native Americans may have deliberately planted oak trees in suitable habitats on the islands. The peculiar assemblage of oak species on Santa Cruz Island may be the result of early introductions.

Native Americans also ate the fruit of the Prickly-pear Cactus (*Opuntia* spp.) (Fig. 51; Plate 8C) and doubtless encouraged its growth in certain areas. An indirect effect of the heavy yet selective grazing by introduced herbivores was the spread of the native prickly-pears. The nonnative Mission Cactus, *Opuntia ficus-indica,* with edible fruits and edible young pads (nopales), has become naturalized on Anacapa, San Clemente, San Nicolas, and Santa Catalina Islands.

At least two plants associated with Native American ceremonies are associated with shell middens and former villages. These are Jimson Weed, *Datura wrightii,* a hallucinogen, and Wild Tobacco, *Nicotiana clevelandii.*

Some plants were introduced for ornamental purposes. Many of these, such as the garden plants in Avalon, are recent arrivals. On Santa Catalina, the Tree-of-Heaven, *Ailanthus altissima,* is considered an attractive ornamental by some, but biologists on the island consider it an invasive weed and have undertaken an extensive effort to eliminate it. On the other hand, the beautiful Malva Rosa, *Lavatera assurgentiflora* (Plate 6B), native to Anacapa, San Clemente, San Miguel, and Santa Catalina Islands, has been widely planted on other islands and the mainland, and it is considered an attractive addition to urban gardens.

During the ranching days on the islands many agricultural plants—including garden vegetables, fruit trees, grains, and grapes—were introduced. A variety of ornamental trees also sprang up. For example, Peruvian Pepper, *Schinus molle,* was reported growing wild and untended on Santa Cruz Island as early as 1875. Other commonly introduced trees, mostly on

Santa Catalina and Santa Cruz Islands, include Blackwood Acacia (*Acacia melanoxylon*), Monterey Pine (*Pinus radiata*), Italian Stone Pine (*Pinus pinea*), and Monterey Cypress (*Cupressus macrocarpa*) (Fig. 122).

Gum trees (*Eucalyptus* spp.), native to Australia, were planted all over California, including the islands. There is some controversy regarding the purpose of the introductions and when they actually took place, but it appears that the first ones occurred in northern California in the early 1850s. Trees were used for firewood and as windbreaks, and the Southern Pacific Railroad planted them in groves, hoping to use the wood for railroad ties. *Eucalyptus* leaves also produce a medicinal oil, used in such products as Vicks VapoRub.

The most common species, Tasmanian Blue Gum, *Eucalyptus globulus,* is found on all of the Channel Islands except San Miguel and Santa Barbara. For reasons that are not clear, the planting of this species on Santa Barbara Island did not take. *Eucalyptus* groves on Santa Cruz Island were well established by 1885. Groves at Smugglers' Cove and Scorpion Ranch and the large grove in the Central Valley are today well-known landmarks, treasured for the shade they provide on hot days.

On some islands the Blue Gums are the most conspicuous trees. On Santa Catalina Island, about 90 percent of the nonnative trees are Blue Gums. Ironically a nonnative beetle, one associated with the Blue Gum in its native range, has invaded the trees on Santa Catalina. The Eucalyptus Longhorn Borer, *Phoracantha semipunctata,* was first discovered in California in 1984, and now it is threatening the trees on the island; it prefers to attack drought-weakened trees, and the trees on Santa Catalina receive no irrigation.

On San Clemente Island, at the height of the devastation caused by introduced animals, the healthiest plants on the island seemed to be those in a *Eucalyptus* grove along the ridgeline. A dirt road passed through the grove, and Navy personnel with a sense of humor erected a sign—complete with a hand-painted version of Smokey the Bear—at one end that read, "Entering San Clemente Island National Forest." At the other end, about 100 yards down the road, another sign read, "Leaving San Clemente Island National Forest." The grove has since been removed, but the "Entering" sign still remains.

The largest grove of Blue Gum trees on the California islands covered about 90 acres (35 ha), over 10 percent of the land on Angel Island in San Francisco Bay. This grove, originally planted for shade by soldiers in the 1920s, was removed by the California State Park system in 1996 as part of a program to restore native plants to the region.

Whether by direct habitat destruction or the impact of introduced animals and plants, human activities have caused a significant change in the biota of California's islands. As a result, in 1997 thirteen of the endemic plant species on the Northern Channel Islands and three of those on the Southern Channel Islands were added to the federal list of endangered or threatened species.

Yet the negative impact of humans on island communities, although considerable, cannot spoil the tremendous natural history resource that they present. Scientists at the University of Southern California's Wrigley Institute of Marine Science at Big Fisherman's Cove on Santa Catalina Island have been able to study the island's rich marine environment, and students from numerous other colleges and universities also use the center. The University of California has a field station on Santa Cruz Island, administered by the Santa Barbara campus. The Nature Conservancy also has a facility there, and researchers based there have conducted numerous terrestrial studies on this large island. Cooperation with personnel from the U.S. National Park Service and the U.S. Navy and with private owners has allowed scientists to carry out numerous investigations throughout the islands, and many of these studies continue to this day.

A series of symposia on the Channel Islands has been sponsored by the Santa Barbara Museum of Natural History, offering further proof of the range of studies now in progress and confirming the California islands as an important resource for all naturalists. The islands continue to serve as field laboratories for the study of geology, botany, zoology, and anthropology, as well as ecology, evolution, and biogeography.

CHAPTER TWO

GEOLOGICAL HISTORY OF THE ISLANDS

The bedrock formation of the California islands is very complex, particularly on Santa Catalina and Santa Cruz Islands. Most of the islands are largely volcanic in origin. However, sedimentary sandstones and mudstones also commonly occur, indicating shallow-water deposition of materials moved by freshwater streams. Several of the islands feature discontinuous masses of marine sedimentary rocks, which may contain such fossils as sharks' teeth and whale bones. Marine deposits also often contain large concentrations of fossil glass (silicon dioxide) "skeletons" from plankton known as *diatoms*. This material, *diatomite,* is white with a chalky appearance; its presence indicates a deep-water origin for a land mass. The islands have many marine terraces or wave-cut benches, ranging in elevation up to 2000 ft (610 m). Such terracing seems to indicate an emergence of the islands, associated with simultaneous fluctuations in sea level, during the last million years or so. The youngest deposits on the islands are sand and alluvial fan materials formed during the last 10,000 years.

Recent geological evidence suggests that the continental shelf and slope off southern California began transforming into a landscape of basins and ridges (Fig. 6) about 30 million years ago. The islands are thus considered to be part of a continental borderland, formed by upward faulting of the earth's crust (the old continental shelf and slope). Because southern California is located at the convergence of two great plates separated by the San Andreas fault, considerable tectonic forces coupled with a right-lateral shear (a movement of the land to the right) caused the sea bottom to be thrust upward in a series of offshore ridges. The tops of these ridges are the Channel Islands, formed as mountains rising above the floor or valleys of the marine basins.

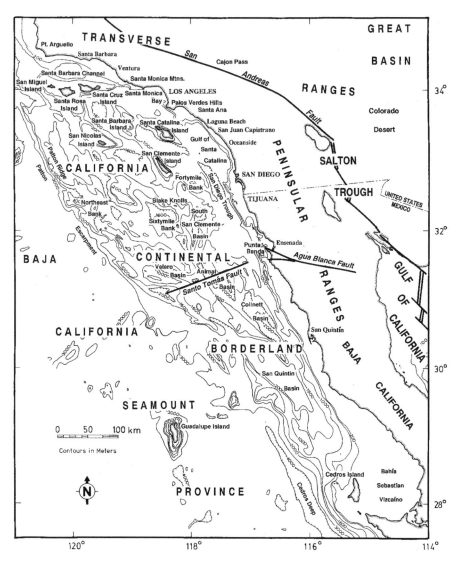

Figure 6. California borderland, showing undersea topography and locations of islands of southern California and adjacent Baja California. Contours in meters. (From Legg 1991.)

   The rocks on California's islands today are the product of a long and complicated history that cannot be understood without considering some of the basic principles of geology and the geological history of the west coast of North America in general. No other concept in geology is as important to understanding the geological complexity of California's coastline as that of *plate tectonics,* the movement of massive plates that slide about on the surface of the earth. The continental margins mark the region where two or more plates interact, but the nature of their inter-action is not always the same. Two plates may converge on each other, but their speed of convergence or the relative directions in which they move may differ. Each of these types of relative motion produces a different topography, which is reflected in the appearance of the coastline and the offshore islands.

The United States from the Rocky Mountains westward was almost com-pletely inundated by seawater for hundreds of millions of years. About 400 million years ago (during the Devonian period) North America began moving westward. The floor of the Pacific Ocean slid under the advancing edge of the North American plate in a process known as *subduction*. Heat and pressure caused by the subducting Pacific plate led to the formation of an offshore series of volcanic islands or island arcs similar to those found today off the east coast of Asia in the vicinity of Japan. At this time an inland sea covered most of California, and the islands lay at approximately the position of the present coastline. As subduction continued, these vol-canic islands became attached (*accreted*) to the western margin of the con-tinent; by means of these accreted terranes the continent began to grow westward. (The term *terrane* refers to a unit of land that has a similar geo-logical composition and origin.)

About 210 million years ago (during the Jurassic period) the speed of convergence on the west coast increased rapidly, creating a deep pool of melted rock or magma that upon cooling would become the plutonic rocks that now make up much of the Sierra Nevada, the mountains of southern California, portions of the southern Coast Ranges, and the Farallon Islands. When magma cools slowly deep within the earth, the result is coarse-grained rocks such as granitics, diorites, and gabbros that differ in color based on the ratio of silica to iron. Masses of these *plutonic rocks* are called *batholiths* (from the Greek for "deep rocks"). Intrusion of the magma, with its associated heat and pressure, deformed adjacent rock lay-ers into the metamorphic complex that makes up the submarine bedrock underlying most of southern California's inner borderland. This meta-morphic complex—including blueschist, greenschist, amphibolite, and serpentinite—is exposed on Santa Catalina Island and a small part of the Palos Verdes Peninsula.

A deep trench formed offshore west of the zone of subduction. Sedi-ments from this trench, now known collectively as *Franciscan rocks* (Fig. 7), include shales, diatomite, and serpentinite, which are now uplifted and exposed in the Coast Ranges, the islands in San Francisco Bay, and some of the Channel Islands. During this time the west coast of North America resembled the west coast of South America as we know it

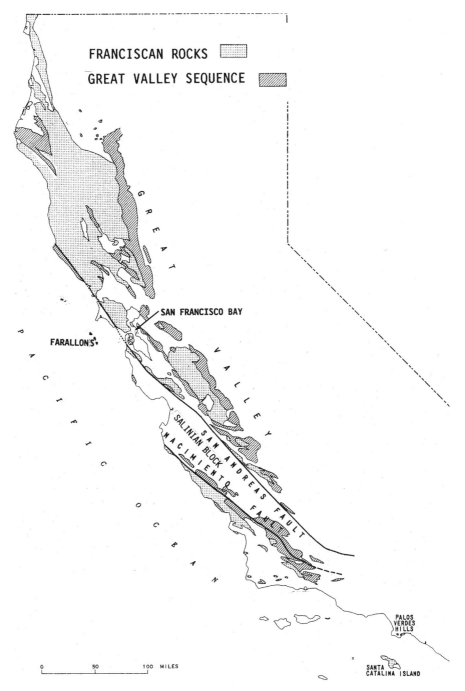

Figure 7. Generalized distribution of major rock types along the California borderland, showing the location of Franciscan rocks and granitics of the Salinian Block. (After Bailey et al. 1964.)

today. There was a large, mostly volcanic, mountain range, similar to the Andes, in the vicinity of the present Sierra Nevada. A narrow continental shelf extended steeply to a deep submarine trench approximately in the vicinity of today's Coast Ranges and offshore islands.

The onset of the Cenozoic era about 65 million years ago marked the beginning of roughly 40 million years of erosion from the highlands, which promoted deposition of sediments over most of the western half of California. Among these sediments are siltstones and sandstones that are found all along California's coastline and islands.

Overlying the marine sediments in southern California is a sequence of nonmarine beds of terrestrial origin. These redbeds were deposited under fresh water from about 37 million to 24 million years ago (Eocene to Miocene epochs). Island deposits can be correlated with the Sespe formation found along the southern California coastline. This formation, outcropping at various localities from Ventura County to Orange County, offers proof that at the time of deposition the area was part of a huge river mouth, a floodplain across which a large river meandered back and forth. Cobbles deposited in this formation can be matched up with source material that today is located in Sonora, Mexico, indicating that at the time of deposition our present coastal region was located perhaps as far as 300 miles (480 km) farther south.

The rifted California borderland as we know it today (Fig. 8) had its beginnings about 29 million years ago, about the middle of the Oligocene epoch. Over the course of some 10 million years the relative motion of the two plates changed from a head-on convergence to a sideways motion, creating what is known as a *transform system.* Deep cracks or faults began to form in the earth's crust, dividing the borderland into a series of blocks; some of these sank while others rose to become fault-block mountains or islands. Some of the blocks rotated in the process. For example, Santa Catalina may have rotated about 60° clockwise, and the Northern Channel Islands, which now lie on an east-west line, are on a block that rotated 90° clockwise. Santa Cruz Island, which today has a fault down its central valley, was previously two islands that became juxtaposed by sideways movement along the fault.

During this time, about 20 million years ago, the metamorphic complex that now makes up a portion of Santa Catalina Island was exposed as a large offshore terrane that was many times larger than the present-day island. Apparently this highland, occupying the area where Santa Catalina and San Clemente are now located, was breached by a submarine canyon into which sediments from the Poway River were dumped (Fig. 9). Evidence of a large submarine fan of Poway River gravels and cobbles to

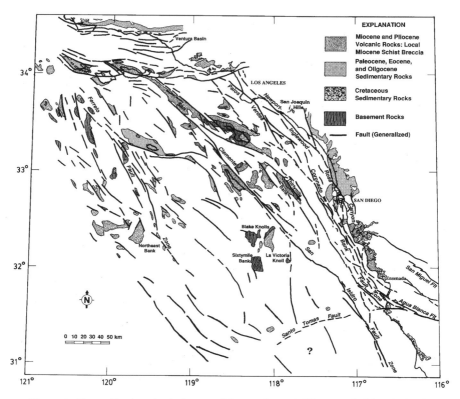

Figure 8. Generalized geological map of the southern California rifted borderland, showing location of the islands with respect to distribution of pre-Miocene rocks and major faults. (From Legg 1991, after Vedder et al. 1974.)

the west of Santa Catalina is provided today by a conglomerate rock made of these components that is found on San Miguel, San Nicolas, and Santa Rosa Islands. To account for the distribution of Poway River cobbles (and age-equivalent sediments on Santa Cruz Island), it has been proposed that the Northern Channel Islands were aligned just to the west of present-day Santa Catalina Island. Such an alignment would imply that the entire island complex has been dragged about 100 miles (160 km) north of its former position next to the mouth of the Poway River, now in San Diego County. Matching the cobbles now found on the islands with source material presently in Sonora, Mexico, seems to place the entire complex, including the mouth of the Poway River, an additional 200 miles (320 km) farther south. Presumably all this movement has occurred on a series of parallel faults west of and including the great San Andreas. Thus all of the present-day Channel Islands originated a good deal farther south than their present locations, and they owe their uplift to motion along the faults.

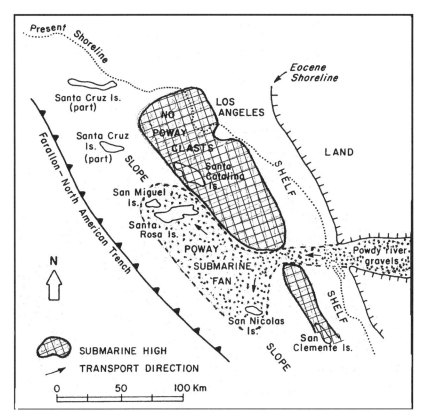

Figure 9. Reconstructed Eocene paleogeography, showing the position of islands, the Eocene shoreline, and the deposition of Poway River gravels. (From Rowland 1984, after Howell et al. 1974.)

The southern Coast Ranges west of the San Andreas fault have also experienced a significant amount of northern translocation (Fig. 7). The granitics west of the San Andreas apparently originated south of the present Sierra Nevada. This terrane, known as the Salinian Block, includes the Farallon Islands. The granitics of South Farallon Island, therefore, were formerly located at about the present latitude of Los Angeles.

Also of interest is a formation known as the San Onofre Breccia (Plate 4C). A *breccia* is a conglomerate rock made up of cobbles of varying sizes in which the cobbles are angular, indicating that they were not river washed prior to becoming cemented together. Analysis of the cobbles in the San Onofre Breccia indicates that they came from the large upland of Catalina schist that lay offshore (Fig. 10). It has been proposed that landslides from the island, perhaps in association with large earthquakes, poured into the sea and later became cemented into the breccia, which is now found on

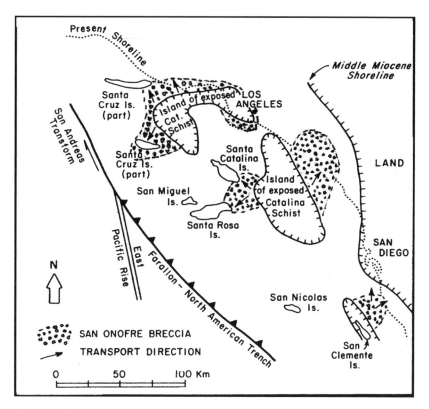

Figure 10. Reconstructed paleogeography of the southern California borderland during deposition of the San Onofre Breccia (Lower and Middle Miocene). Locations of present-day islands are shown for reference; they were not all islands at the time. (From Rowland 1984, after Howell et al. 1974.)

the mainland at scattered localities from the Santa Monica Mountains south to San Diego County, including Santa Catalina, Santa Cruz, and Santa Rosa Islands. This breccia, containing angular cobbles of blueschist, greenschist, and serpentine, has the appearance of wave-washed concrete. Presumably this large island source of schist, vestiges of which are still found on present-day Santa Catalina Island, is now all but gone.

During the Miocene epoch, from about 20 to 5 million years ago, many changes shaped the appearance of the California islands. Volcanism, which is frequently associated with faulting, was widespread during the time, and volcanic rocks, mostly 12–15 million years old, form substantial components of most of the California islands. Volcanic rocks cover about one-quarter of Santa Catalina Island (Plate 4B); San Clemente Island is composed almost entirely of volcanic rocks. In the Northern Channel Islands, correlated with the Conejo volcanics of the Santa Monica

Mountains, the thickness of volcanic rocks totals about 8000 ft (2440 m) on Santa Cruz Island and 2400 ft (730 m) on San Miguel Island. Lesser amounts occur on Santa Rosa Island. Anacapa and Santa Barbara Islands are small, but they too are almost entirely volcanic. The sea caves that are major tourist attractions on Anacapa and Santa Cruz Islands (Plate 4A) are formed by wave action on the volcanic rocks. In addition, the youngest pluton in California, dated to 19 million years ago, is exposed throughout most of the eastern end of Santa Catalina Island.

Since Miocene time, for the last 5 million years or so, the geological picture has largely been one of sedimentation. Marine and nonmarine sediments are found on all of the islands. Sediments on Santa Catalina Island are particularly interesting because they document what some geologists call "rollercoaster tectonics." Fossils of microscopic marine organisms known as foraminiferans indicate a subsidence of the Santa Catalina structural block from near sea level to a depth of at least 3000 ft (1000 m), and perhaps twice that depth, within a few million years. Subsidence was followed by a period of uplift, so that vertical elevation changes occurred at rates as rapid as 3 ft (1 m) per thousand years. Fossiliferous limey sandstone from late Miocene time is now found on Mount Banning at 1734 ft (559 m) elevation.

The great ice ages, an epoch known as the Pleistocene, began about 2 million years ago. During that time at least four major glacial episodes and many minor episodes occurred. During glacial episodes, so much water become bound up in ice that sea level was significantly lowered. Conversely, during interglacial intervals, episodes of global warming caused sea level to rise. It is the fluctuation of sea level, coincident with uplift of the west coast, including California's islands, that has produced the stair-step appearance of coastal topography. These flattened steps are known as *Pleistocene coastal terraces.*

Coastal terraces are formed by the action of surf on rocky headlands (Fig. 11; Plate 14A). Surf, with its load of sand, can be highly abrasive, cutting at right angles into the rock along the shore. The outcome of this action is a relatively flat, wave-cut bench or reef with a steep cliff on the shoreward side. Uplift by tectonic activity elevates old wave-cut terraces above sea level. Most of the terrace deposits on the islands occur between 20 and 100 ft (7–30 m) above present sea level. Terraces between 600 and 900 ft (200–300 m) above sea level are found on some islands. The uppermost (oldest) terrace on San Miguel is found at 600 ft (200 m); that on Santa Cruz, at 700 ft (225 m); and those on San Clemente and San Nicolas, at 900 ft (300 m).

Sediments on the terraces include sandstones, siltstones, and mudstones,

Figure 11. Coastal terraces on the west side of San Clemente Island, a product of crashing surf and fluctuating sea levels.

some of which yield fossils that tell us a great deal about climate and ocean temperatures during various glacial and interglacial episodes. Fossil remains in embayments are primarily foraminifera and ostracods, planktonic forms indicating that moderately deep water once covered the basins. Data on present-day distributions of comparable microorganisms indicate that water depths over these basins probably reached about 600 ft (180 m). Other comparative data for the fossil remains indicate that the minimum temperature of the sea in the vicinity of the Channel Islands during the late Pliocene was at least 3°F (2°C) warmer than it is today. Larger fossils, such as echinoderms, molluscs, and crustacea, also suggest an intertidal depositional environment for most of the terrace deposits.

From the mainland in Orange County, Santa Catalina Island is easily visible on a clear day. The stepped appearance of the southeastern end of the island in silhouette is the result of these terraces. The most spectacular development of Pleistocene terraces, however, is on San Clemente Island to the south. On the outboard or western side of San Clemente the land rises from the sea in a magnificent series of steps that reach to the summit of the island. The fact that Santa Catalina Island has minimal terracing compared with San Clemente Island to the south and the Palos Verdes Peninsula to the north (where thirteen terraces are visible) is a testament to the "rollercoaster tectonics" of Santa Catalina Island. Whereas San Clemente and the adjacent mainland appear to have been rising gradu-

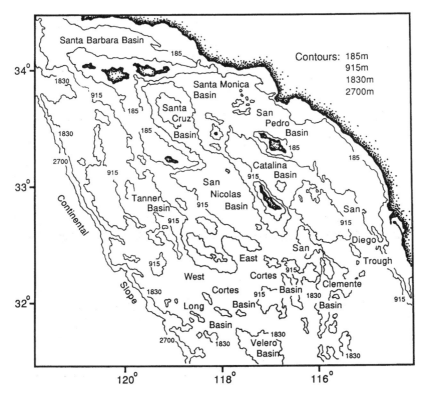

Figure 12. Ocean depths and location of basins around the California Channel Islands. Contours in meters. (From Dailey et al. 1993.)

ally from the sea, Santa Catalina has also experienced subsidence, which served to obliterate former terraces.

The appearance of the bottom topography in the Southern California Bight confirms that variations in sea level could cause the emergence of islands where they do not exist today, or flood existing islands (Fig. 12). At a time of higher sea level, the Palos Verdes Peninsula would be an island. Variations in sea level also influence the size of islands, the shape of islands, and the distance of islands from the mainland. During at least one of the interglacial episodes it appears that, among the Channel Islands, Anacapa, San Miguel, San Nicolas, and Santa Barbara were completely under water. Similarly all of the islands in San Francisco Bay as well as the Farallons and Año Nuevo were completely inundated. Large areas on San Clemente, Santa Catalina, Santa Cruz, and Santa Rosa have been continuously above sea level for at least the last 500,000 years. If one were to suppose that these islands could once have been connected to the mainland near present-day Mexico, and that they have since been carried farther north along fault systems, one could explain how extremely sedentary animals, such as the Island Night Lizard, *Xantusia riversiana,* and slender salamanders, *Batrachoseps* spp., were carried to their present locations like passengers on a huge ferry.

During the time of probable minimum sea levels, about 17,000–18,000 years ago, the four present-day Northern Channel Islands were all part of one large land mass, approximately 724 square miles (1874 km^2) in area, sometimes referred to as Santa Rosae. A question of long standing is whether this land mass, an apparent extension of the present Santa Monica Mountains, was ever connected to the mainland. The east end of Anacapa Island is separated from the mainland today by a narrow channel that is 750 ft (230 m) deep. During the Pleistocene epoch, when great ice sheets were present in the northerly latitudes, sea level was no more than 395 ft (120 m) below its present level. Seismic data obtained offshore of Oxnard do not indicate subsequent erosion of a submarine ridge connecting the mainland to Anacapa Island. Because nonmarine sediments on San Miguel, Santa Cruz, and Santa Rosa Islands have yielded fossils of the pygmy Exiled Mammoth, *Mammuthus exilis,* it was once assumed that Santa Rosae would have had to be connected to the mainland. It is now known that elephants can swim quite well and that the proposed minimum distance of 4.5 miles (7 km) from the mainland would likely not have been a barrier for them. The distance, however, is sufficient to explain why other vertebrate animals, such as rabbits, Mule Deer, Coyotes, or large skunks are common on the mainland but are absent from the islands.

Details of the geology of each of California's islands will be provided in subsequent chapters along with discussions of other characteristics of these islands.

CHAPTER THREE

EARLY HUMAN POPULATIONS ON THE CALIFORNIA ISLANDS

Californians are proud of their superlatives. The state has the largest living organisms in the huge Sierra Redwood or Giant Sequoia (*Sequoiadendron giganteum*), the tallest living organisms in the Coast Redwood (*Sequoia sempervirens*), and the oldest living organisms in the Bristlecone Pine (*Pinus longaeva*). It is thus only fitting that we should also attempt to lay claim to the earliest humans. Of the thirteen New World sites once purported to possess human bones much older than 11,000 years, all but two are in California. Ten of them are in southern California.

EVIDENCE FOR EARLY HUMAN SETTLEMENTS

One of the California skeletons, a skull and some other fragments found during road construction near Laguna Beach in 1933, was once dated at 17,000 years B.P. (before present), and a skull found near Del Mar in 1929 was dated at a startling 48,000 years B.P. These and other dates were established using a technique known as *amino acid racemization*. Amino acids are the building blocks that make up proteins. As proteins get older, their constituent amino acid molecules gradually rotate from one form to another, like a mirror image, and the ratios of the two forms can thus be used as a measure of the age of a fossil. However, the accuracy of the process was found to vary with certain environmental conditions, such as temperature.

Other techniques involving radioactive rates of decay were used to redate these and other remains, finally coming up with dates no older than 11,000 years. It is beyond the scope of this book to describe the details of radioactive dating, but the process depends on the fact that radioactive isotopes are unstable. They tend to decay to a stable configuration at a fixed rate and thus give rise to the characteristic known as a *half-life:* the length of time required for half of a radioactive material to decay. Trace amounts of radioactive materials are incorporated into living organisms while they are alive, and the process ceases when they die; thus the ratio between the amount of the radioactive isotope and that of the stable one can be used to determine how many years ago the organism died. For example, radioactive potassium-40 decays to argon-40 with a half-life of 1.3 billion years, which means that the potassium-argon ratio of a fossil helps scientists determine how many years ago an ancient fossil was a living organism. Different isotopes decay at different rates, and for organisms that were living in recent times carbon-14 (with a decay rate of 5730 years) is the preferred isotope for which to assay. The fact that it loses half its radioactivity every 5730 years means that the limit of accuracy for carbon-14 dating is about 40,000 years. Thus for human remains and human artifacts such as wood, bones, and shells in the Americas, radiocarbon dates have become the preferred tool for establishing age.

This archaeological "dating game" has led to numerous claims of the oldest signs of human habitation. Among these are at least 110 sites on Santa Rosa Island that were interpreted as human fire pits. These were brick red, crescent-shaped clay deposits that were found in association with inferior chipped stones that could be interpreted as resulting from early attempts to make tools. Radiocarbon dates of bones and other organic material from the sites ranged from about 11,000 years B.P. to beyond the limit of the radiocarbon dating method (about 40,000 years). Scientists studying the sites became convinced that early humans living there during the Pleistocene were hunting dwarf mammoths and cooking the meat over fires, as well as harvesting abalone from the coast.

A fossil wood locality on Santa Cruz Island was responsible for a new interpretation of the Santa Rosa Island fire pits. It was found that percolation of ground water through wood could leach out iron compounds and stain the surrounding sediments red. Scientists respond that, even if the staining were due to wood becoming soaked by ground water, the close association of bones, chipped stones, and charcoal at the Wooley site on Santa Rosa Island dates it to at least 43,000 years B.P. There are, unfortunately, no human bones at the Wooley site, but human remains that have been radiocarbon dated at 10,000 years B.P. are found on Santa Rosa Island, making it the site of very early human habitation nevertheless.

Perhaps the most significant site for archaeological and paleontological remains is Daisy Cave on San Miguel Island. At this site, dated at 11,700 years B.P., scientists have located the oldest coastal shell midden in North America. Evidence of five periods of habitation extending back 700 years makes up the most complete record of California island inhabitants anywhere on the coast. Among the artifacts found in the cave are burned mammoth bones, primitive circular fishhooks, bead-making kits, a bird-bone pan pipe, a fragment of a wooden plank boat, and tarred baskets and cordage made of sea grass. All of these ancient items, their age verified by carbon-14 dates, paint a picture of a Chumash culture, dependent on marine resources, that flourished since the end of the ice ages (Pleistocene).

Confounding the picture of humans in the New World is a 1996 fossil find in the state of Washington. The human bones making up the find known as "Kennewick Man," possessing what appear to be Caucasoid features, have been dated at 9600 years B.P. Some scientists, after comparing them with other fossils, hypothesize that at least some of the ancient humans in the New World were of "European" ancestry. Nevertheless, the characteristics of most of the California fossils seem to imply that early humans had features that linked them with Asians.

HISTORY OF EARLY HUMAN HABITATION

Thus we are left with the most generally accepted interpretation, namely that, at the end of the Pleistocene around 12,000 years ago, early humans crossed the Bering Strait on a land bridge and moved from Asia into North America. Within a thousand years these aboriginal hunters and gatherers moved across North America and reached the tip of South America. The great glaciers that covered much of the northern part of North America and filled many mountain valleys began to melt, and sea levels gradually rose. About 18,000 years ago all of the Northern Channel Islands were still joined into one land mass, separated from the mainland by a narrow channel. By 15,000 years ago, San Miguel Island was separated from Santa Rosa, and by about 11,500 years ago all of the Northern Channel Islands were separated. There is no evidence that the islands to the south were ever joined together.

The islands in San Francisco Bay were all attached to the mainland during periods of lowered sea level. Angel, Brooks, East Marin, and Yerba Buena Islands all have shell middens, indicating habitation by Native Americans.

As the first humans migrated into coastal California, they encountered a region undergoing great environmental changes associated with the advent of a warmer, drier climate and rising sea levels. They probably observed the last phase of the sea level rise and the accompanying flooding of coastal beach areas. In fact, many of the earliest settlements of these first Californians may now be under water. By drilling cores into sediments off Vancouver Island, scientists in Canada found plant remains proving that sea level was 300 ft (100 m) lower as recently as 10,500 years ago.

As discussed in Chapter 2, during the Pleistocene the present-day

Northern Channel Islands were connected as one large island separated from the mainland by a narrow, deep-water channel that would have been relatively easy for humans in boats to cross. We know that large mammals such as mammoths successfully crossed over to this large island and that mammoths evolved into the distinct, dwarf species known as the Exiled Mammoth, *Mammuthus exilis*. By the time early humans arrived, they probably had to cross a considerably larger expanse of water to get to the islands, perhaps on primitive rafts. The earliest, noncontroversial refuse mound or midden on any of the California islands indicating aboriginal habitation dates from 11,700 years B.P. It was found in Daisy Cave on San Miguel Island, the northernmost of the group. By about 7000 years B.P., sizable human populations were present on all of the larger islands. Archaeologists are not sure if human hunters were responsible for the extinction of the Exiled Mammoth, or if its extinction, along with that of the rest of the Pleistocene mammals so well represented in the Rancho La Brea deposits in Los Angeles, was due to other causes.

We do know that soon after their arrival in southern California humans were able to colonize almost all of the California islands. Because most of the islands are visible from shore on clear days during the fall and winter months, it would have been reasonable for hunting and gathering peoples of the coastal areas to attempt to reach them. An abundance of intertidal marine invertebrates, such as abalone and mussels, along with reef fishes, large rookeries of marine birds, and marine mammals made the islands valuable hunting and fishing grounds.

In 1542, 50 years after the arrival of Columbus in the New World, Juan Rodríguez Cabrillo "discovered" these islands and the rest of California, claiming them for Spain. During the next few centuries the islands were occasionally visited by European explorers, including Sebastián Vizcaíno, who mapped and named the islands and the adjacent coast in 1602.

When the first European explorers arrived in the sixteenth century, sizable aboriginal populations were still present on all of the larger islands. The ship's logs for Cabrillo's and Vizcaíno's voyages record considerable information on the habits and culture of these earliest Californians. As these explorers sailed up the coast of California, they stopped at good anchorages along the way. Both Cabrillo and Vizcaíno apparently visited Santa Catalina Island, where plank canoes filled with as many as thirteen men were launched to meet the newcomers from small settlements in cove areas along the leeward shore of the island. The Europeans went ashore for brief periods, and their descriptions form the basis for much of our historical information on aboriginal life on the Channel Islands.

A few other records of Native American life on the islands exist from the California mission period in the late eighteenth and early nineteenth centuries. Some information was passed down as oral history to descendants of island inhabitants. All other information on the development of the human populations on the islands and their subsequent culture comes from archaeological investigations of prehistoric settlement areas. Fortunately most of the islands contained at least a few relatively intact sites. By contrast, early coastal settlements along the mainland have been destroyed by urban development.

On all of the larger islands, mounds or middens of material appear in numerous localities; these represent prehistoric garbage dumps. Careful examination of these refuse mounds (such as those at Daisy Cave, described earlier) yields information on the density of human populations, the kinds of foods eaten, and the types of tools used. Shell middens also supply information on the origin and relationships of various tribes. Radioactive dating methods can be used to determine the time span of human occupation.

NATIVE TRIBES

Historically the Native American tribes of the California islands essentially belonged to three linguistic families or language groups. Those in the San Francisco Bay area were part of the Penutian linguistic family. Members of this group were spread widely across the West from northern British Columbia to southern Mexico. In the Bay area several tribal groups—such as the Wintun (Patwin), Costanoan (Ohlone), and Miwok—overlapped. The tribe most frequently associated with the islands of San Francisco Bay, including the Farallon Islands, was the Coast Miwok. They harvested the same kinds of foods as southern California Native Americans, deriving most of their sustenance from the sea. Unlike the southerners, however, they constructed canoes from the stems of tules or bulrushes (*Scirpus* spp.) rather than wooden planks.

When they first arrived on the Channel Islands of southern California, Europeans discovered Native Americans from two other language groups. The Hokan language was spoken by the Chumash tribe, which ranged along the southern coast from about San Luis Obispo to Malibu and also occurred on the Northern Channel Islands. This language was associated with tribes that were also widely distributed in California, from the Shasta and Modoc areas to San Diego. More specifically, the Island Chumash were known to the early Europeans as the Canaliño. The Diegueño of the San Diego area also spoke the Hokan language.

Surprisingly the language of the Native Americans on the Southern Channel Islands and in the adjacent Los Angeles Basin was different from that of the Chumash and Diegueño. These people, known as the Tongva or Gabrielinos, were speakers of the Uto-Aztecan (Shoshonean) language associated primarily with tribes of the Great Basin and Mojave Desert. The Indians of San Nicolas Island were also known as Nicoleños.

Displacement and separation of the Hokan tribes into Chumash and Diegueño by Uto-Aztecan peoples migrating from the desert is usually interpreted as a relatively recent event, having occurred as recently as 1000–2000 years ago. However, recently discovered artifacts, dated to 5000 years B.P., may indicate that the Uto-Aztecan (Shoshonean) tribes were on the islands much earlier. This evidence is based on collections of "puka shells," decorative beads made from the shells of a common intertidal snail, the Purple Olive Snail, *Olivella biplicata*. Although many shells from these snails have holes drilled in them naturally by an octopus, many were also drilled by Native Americans, presumably so that the shells could be strung together to make necklaces. Most of the shells were perforated by simple drills or punches, but some of them, usually unearthed in clusters, had been punctured by someone who scratched or sawed at the curved surface to produce a hole. These shells, dated at 5000 years old, are known as "Olivella grooved rectangle beads." They have been unearthed at Little Harbor on Santa Catalina Island, on San Clemente Island, on San Nicolas Island, at Newport Beach, and at various sites in the Great Basin, including eastern Oregon, northwestern Nevada, and southeastern California. This evidence links the Native Americans of the Southern Channel Islands with other Shoshonean tribes. If these 5000-year-old beads—as well as several other artifacts such as obsidian blades of similar age—are evidence of an ancient Shoshonean trade system, it may mean that the sophisticated culture of local Native Americans is much older than had previously been thought.

Although anthropologists have divided the aboriginal inhabitants of the southern California area into a series of groups based on customs and language, by about 2500 years ago all of the islands appear to have been populated by peoples of a maritime culture, and religious or linguistic differences do not appear to have limited trade or altered the life-styles of the islands' inhabitants. In comparing sites on the northern and southern islands with respect to the mollusc species eaten or the tools used, some differences exist, but both groups were probably very similar in customs and culture.

The Chumash culture (maritime hunters and gatherers) present at the time of the arrival of the first European explorers had probably developed over a period of several thousand years. Some chronological changes are evident from the excavation of middens, such as the greater dependence upon fishing beginning about 2500 years ago. But it is otherwise difficult to determine precisely how the culture evolved over time.

The islanders usually lived in small villages or groups at the mouths of canyons that contained water. They wore very simple clothes made of animal skins or bird feathers and lived in dome-shaped houses, thatched with surf-grass or rushes. Most of their refuse mounds or middens yield metates, which were probably used to grind acorns, cherry pits, and dried meat. They had many types of bowls, ollas, and effigies made of steatite soapstone (Fig. 13), all of which was apparently mined from a few out-croppings on Santa Catalina Island. Steatite is a relatively soft rock that is easy to carve, and it does not crack when heated. At least one steatite quarry can be seen on Santa Catalina Island just east of the Airport-in-the-Sky, where large, partially carved bowls were never removed and can be observed still embedded in the outcrop. The steatite vessels were found on most of the islands and on the mainland, a fact that supports the notion that the early islanders enjoyed considerable mobility and traded regularly. Collections of good steatite ollas and many other implements can be seen at the Avalon Museum on Santa Catalina Island and at the Natural History Museum in Santa Barbara.

Perhaps one of the most unfortunate interactions of New and Old World cultures occurred soon after California was settled by Spanish mission-aries. Although the California islands and their inhabitants were discov-ered in 1542, they were granted another two centuries of relative peace, free from intrusion before the major immigration of Europeans. The early European contacts, although brief, undoubtedly introduced some diseases, weeds, and pests that were new to the islands. However, in the latter part of the eighteenth century Spanish missions were established along the Cal-ifornia coast, and seal and sea otter hunters also came into the area at this time. During the 50 years after the founding of San Juan Capistrano Mission in 1776, the island villages were for the most part abandoned.

Otter hunters were probably to blame for much of the rapid decline of the island populations. The hunters were of English, American, and Russ-ian nationality and brought Aleuts with them as they worked their way down the Pacific coast, hunting the valuable sea otters wherever they could find them. As the hunters made camp on the islands, they introduced com-mon viral and bacterial diseases to which the islanders had no immunity. The aggressive Aleuts apparently fought with and killed many of the natives, and by 1812 the island populations had been greatly reduced. Dur-ing that year a tremendous earthquake (with an epicenter near Santa Cruz Island) destroyed most of the coastal missions. The temblor apparently convinced the islanders to leave their homes and accompany the mission fathers back to the mainland. By the 1820s the last few Native Americans had been removed from the southern islands, with the exception of one inhabitant on San Nicolas Island. The lone woman of San Nicolas Island is a remarkable story of abandonment and survival. This woman, who somehow was left on the island when the rest of the inhabitants were evacuated by mission fathers, survived alone for a period of 18 years. Her survival experience is discussed in detail in Chapter 7.

Thus, over a period of only 50 years, all of the island natives vanished. After thousands of years of continuous existence, the native human populations of the California islands had become extirpated in less than a century.

POPULATION DENSITIES

From studies of Island Chumash baptisms and marriages in registers kept by early Franciscan missionaries, it has been estimated that Santa Cruz Island had ten villages; Santa Rosa Island, eight; and San Miguel, two. The total human population of the Northern Channel Islands during the late 1700s is estimated to have been about 3000. Anacapa and Santa Barbara Islands have little or no permanent water sources and were probably not inhabited for long periods of time, although small middens on these islands indicate they were often used as fishing and hunting campsites.

San Clemente and Santa Catalina Islands probably supported population densities similar to those of Santa Cruz and Santa Rosa, whereas more remote San Nicolas Island appears to have had an aboriginal population density similar to that of San Miguel.

FOOD

There is considerable evidence to indicate that the Northern Channel Islands were used as hunting and fishing areas by mainland Chumash populations. These Chumash apparently lived in villages along the coast between what is now the city of Ventura and Point Conception. All of the coastal Chumash peoples constructed sturdy canoes of narrow wooden planks, and these craft were able to move quickly over the often choppy waters of the Santa Barbara Channel. Those living on the islands also had canoes, from which they fished and hunted marine mammals. However, these island residents had to rely on additional, more consistent, sources of food, because marine mammals such as California Sea Lions and Northern Elephant Seals only establish onshore rookeries for breeding, and large migratory fishes such as Pacific Bonito, *Sarda chiliensis,* and Pacific Barracuda, *Sphyraena argentea,* probably were present only during the summer months.

Middens on the islands indicate that the California Mussel, *Mytilus californianus,* and various species of Abalone, *Haliotis* spp., were other important food sources. Also present in considerable numbers are shells of the Black Turban Snail, *Tegula funebralis,* and skeletons or tests of the sea urchin, *Strongylocentrotus* spp., along with bones of fishes, mammals, and birds.

Fishes, especially resident reef-dwelling species such as California Sheephead, *Pimelometopon (=Semicossyphus) pulchrum,* and various rockfish, *Sebastes* spp., were probably always an important food source for island inhabitants. However, beginning about 2500 years ago, and perhaps due to increasing population size and hence the need for new food resources, fishing apparently became more important. The earliest fishhooks were simple bone hooks, dated to between 5000 and 4000 years B.P., from the Little Harbor village site on Santa Catalina Island. Subsequently more sophisticated hooks of bone, wood, and abalone shell were used (Fig. 13C).

From analyses of radiocarbon-dated faunal remains obtained from layered samples on Santa Cruz Island, it appears that shellfish were an important part of the diet for over 7000 years of occupation. After 2600 years B.P., however, marine mammals and fishes increased in importance, and fishes became the most important food as of 800 years ago.

Birds were used as a source of food and feathers. Bones of ducks, geese, and such sea birds as cormorants, *Phalacrocorax* spp., are common in middens on the islands. Evidence of butchering and charring indicates that some species were roasted for food. Other bird skeletons show no such evidence, and these birds could have been used as sources of feathers for clothing.

Marine mammals also were important food sources for even the earliest inhabitants; mammal bones dating back to 7000 years B.P. have been found in middens on Santa Cruz Island. Extensive seal and sea lion (pinniped) rookeries exist today on San Miguel and San Nicolas Islands, and midden remains on these islands indicate that marine mammals provided an important source of food throughout the time that hunters and gatherers lived there. Seals and sea lions were probably easy to kill at their rookeries by clubbing, especially at night. Stalking them by canoe seems unlikely, but spears (Fig. 13F), clubs, or harpoons may have been used to kill them on beaches.

LAND-BASED FOOD SOURCES

Numerous types of plant food were gathered on the southern California mainland by prehistoric humans. Acorns, berries, cactus fruit, and portions of other edible plants were abundant. These plants were less abundant on the islands, however, because of the generally reduced numbers of organisms associated with islands. Acorns, pine seeds, berry-producing

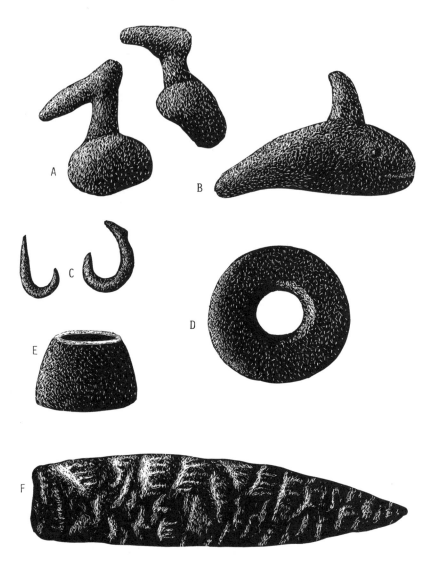

Figure 13. Examples of early American artifacts found on the Channel Islands.
(A) Pelican effigies. (B) Killer whale effigy. (C) Abalone shell fishhooks.
(D) Unidentified circular artifact (possibly a net weight or a pounding stone
for a digging stick). (E) Pestle. (F) Spear point.

shrubs, and cactus pads and fruit were present on many islands, and seeds,
roots, and tubers of many herbaceous plants were also gathered from extensive grassland habitats. Digging stick weights or pounding stones (round,
doughnut-shaped stone objects) (Fig. 13D) are more common in midden
sites on the islands than in those on the mainland, indicating that plant
roots (bulbs and tubers) were relatively important to the diet of islanders.

TRADE

There was probably considerable trading for food between island populations and those on the mainland. From oral histories obtained from natives who were descendants of Chumash from the Northern Channel Islands, we know that when certain fruits and nuts were ripe, many islanders came to the mainland to trade for acorns and the fruits of Catalina Cherry (*Prunus ilicifolia* ssp. *lyonii*). Seeds of Chia (*Salvia columbariae*), Red Maids (*Calandrinia ciliata*), and California Buckwheat (*Eriogonum fasciculatum*) were also obtained. Indian Hemp, *Apocynum cannabinum,* was bartered for and used to make a tough cord that served to lash planks together in constructing canoes.

Otter skins, butchered marine mammals, and other game obtained on the islands were traded for plant foods that were more rare on the islands. The "puka shells" mentioned earlier were probably the basis for a shell-money industry in which chert bladelets were used to cut shells and chert drills were used to make small holes to complete the beads. Abalone and mussel shell materials were also worked to make pendants, fish-hooks, and other items. There is some evidence that certain Santa Cruz Island villages became specialized in bead-making and regularly traded with villages on the mainland. The industrious islanders from these villages probably made an economic breakthrough in discovering that bartering for food with shell-money they had manufactured was superior to hunting and gathering, especially as the human population on the islands gradually increased or the marine food resources were eventually depleted.

CHAPTER FOUR

MARINE LIFE

Although the nature and composition of the marine biota of the California islands have not been thoroughly investigated, the studies that have been conducted indicate that the marine life is very similar to that of the mainland. In a book of this nature it is impossible to cover marine life in detail, but readers interested in a full description of intertidal plants and animals of the California coast may refer to many books written on the subject. Portions of this chapter have been excerpted from *A Natural History of California* by Allan A. Schoenherr (University of California Press, 1992).

Differences in distribution of plants and animals along the coast seem to be a function primarily of water temperature. Ocean water along the California coast is generally cold. Off the northern California coast, winter water temperature averages 50°F (10°C). On its journey southward the water warms about 7–8°F (3–4°C). During summer it is only 8–10°F (5–6°C) warmer.

The region south of Point Conception and extending to a point just south of the United States–Mexico border is known as the Southern California Bight. (*Bight* is a term used by geographers to refer to a bend in a coastline, river, or mountain range.) The general southward trend of the cold California Current is altered by the bight, and an eddy pattern is developed in which the water swings inward toward the coast between San Diego, California, and Punta Colnett, Baja California. The result is that within the bight the average surface flow is northward up the coast, forming the Southern California Countercurrent. This flow, substantially blocked by the Northern Channel Islands, is diverted westward to merge with the California Current west of San Miguel Island (Fig. 14).

Most species of the intertidal zone are widespread, occurring all along the coast. For those that show a variation in distribution, Monterey Bay

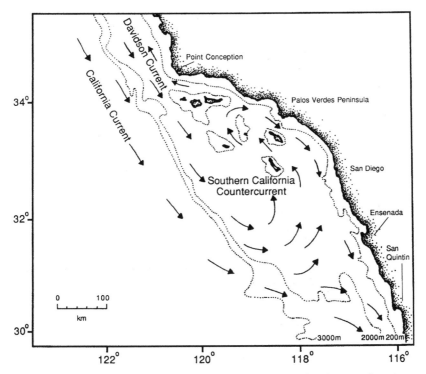

Figure 14. Surface circulation in the Southern California Bight, showing direction of the major currents. Bottom contours in meters. (From Dailey et al. 1993.)

seems to be a dividing line. Many northern species go no farther south and many southern species go no farther north than the bay. A second, less pronounced, break occurs at Point Conception, north of Santa Barbara. There the coastline makes a dramatic change in direction to form the Southern California Bight. South of Point Conception the coast forms a nearly east-west line, and there is also a tendency of some northern species of intertidal fishes to move into colder, deep water offshore.

Because of the overlap between northern and southern species, there is greater species diversity south of Monterey, especially around the Palos Verdes Peninsula. This pattern is reflected in the distribution of marine algae as well, with the greatest diversity occurring in the red algae (Rhodophyta).

An important source of cold water and nutrients is upwelling from the deep ocean. During the summer months, associated with a persistent high-pressure system over the north Pacific, the prevailing wind blows southward along the coast. Because of the so-called Coriolis force, wind in the Northern Hemisphere tends to turn to the right and surface water is effectively blown away from the coast, causing an upwelling of cold water near shore. The major beneficiary of the nutrients thus brought up from the depths is the oceanic ecosystem at the edge of the continental shelf, although some nutrients are carried to intertidal areas by waves and currents. In southern California this upwelling occurs from about 55 to 125 miles (90–200 km) offshore. Another upwelling occurs in the Southern California Bight in late summer and autumn, when winds blow offshore. Nutrients for the intertidal region come primarily from outwelling of rivers and estuaries.

The shape of California's coastline is a product of geological activity and erosion. California has an *emergent* coastline: most of the rocks distributed along the coast were formerly on the ocean floor. North of San Francisco, coastal rocks are mostly Franciscan sediments 100–150 million years of age. South of San Francisco, most of the rocks are sediments no older than about 60 million years. Most of these sedimentary rocks are relatively soft. The action of the surf has cut into them, forming flat benches backed by sea cliffs, and uplift of the shoreline has elevated these wave-cut benches into a series of terraces (Fig. 11; Plate 10A). For a more detailed description of the geology of the coastline, the reader should consult Chapter 2.

At various points the cliffs are broken by canyon mouths. Most of these are relatively narrow, as is typical of an emergent coastline. San Francisco Bay, however, has a different shape. It was the product of downcutting by large rivers during a period of lower sea level, presumably hundreds of thousands of years ago, during the Pleistocene epoch. At the present time, an elevated sea level has drowned the old river mouths, forming the bay. The islands in the bay, formerly part of the mainland, are hilltops projecting above the water surface.

Where the coastline is formed of hard rocks such as granitics or basalts, the land is more resistant to erosion, and rocky headlands jut into the Pacific. At the base of these headlands, tide pools, visible only at low tide, abound in marine life. Between the rocky headlands are beaches and coves of various sizes. The sands that make up these beaches are carried to the ocean by rivers and deposited by the action of waves.

The most powerful force responsible for erosion along the coast is wave action. Waves are generated by winds associated with storm fronts; since most of these storms form over the north Pacific, most waves hit the coast from the northwest. In much the same manner as a pool ball bounces off a cushion, waves bounce off the coastline. Those arriving from the northwest are reflected southwest, and this action carries sand off the beach in a southwesterly direction. The next wave carries it back toward the coast in a southeasterly direction. Thus the flow is always southward, forming a "river of sand" that migrates down the coast. This southerly flow of water,

Figure 15. Energy that promotes erosion is directed by the bending of waves to all sides of a rocky headland.

known as the *longshore current,* lies just outside the surf line. It carries sand southward until it reaches a submarine canyon, where the sand is drained off to the ocean floor. If the supply of new sand is interrupted by dams on the rivers leading to the coast, beaches will continue to erode, becoming smaller each year. Construction of seawalls to protect coastal buildings merely redirects the energy of waves to unprotected stretches of beach, causing increased erosion there.

As waves move into shallow water, friction with the bottom causes them to slow down. When the depth of the water is about half the distance between successive waves (the wave length), a wave becomes steeper. It finally breaks when its height reaches 1.3 times the water depth. The energy of the wave is directed forward as the water rushes up the beach; this is known as the *swash.* Water that flows back again is the *backwash.*

Where waves strike the coast at an angle, they are bent in the process, so that they tend to become oriented parallel to the coastline. Where rocky headlands project into the surf, wave energy becomes concentrated on all sides of it, causing the headland to erode (Fig. 15). Softer rocks erode first, shaping typical coastal formations known as *arches* and *stacks,* such as those at the eastern end of Anacapa Island (Fig. 74). Stacks are small, steep-sided rock islands that may be the remains of collapsed arches. Regardless of their relative hardness, all of these rock formations are doomed eventually to become victims of the energy of wave action.

In coves or recessed areas, the energy of the waves is intercepted so that sand accumulates and beaches form. The net result is that the coastline is constantly being straightened. Rocky headlands erode while the beaches between them become larger. Where the longshore current carries sand away from the beach, it may be deposited at the mouths of bays, parallel to the coast, forming so-called *bay-mouth bars,* which in turn help to shelter the bays from the action of the surf.

INTERTIDAL ECOSYSTEMS

The region where the land and sea overlap is known as the *intertidal* or *littoral zone.* This region, influenced by the daily ebb and flow of tides, is one of the best examples of *edge effect* in the world. Because the area retains characteristics of both the ocean and terrestrial habitats, it is home to organisms associated with both regions. Thus the diversity of species and habitats within 10 vertical feet is greater in the intertidal zone than in any other habitat on earth.

Ecosystems contain three general kinds of organisms. *Producers* are usually photosynthetic and produce the food for the other organisms in the system. The total amount of food produced by photosynthesis per year is known as *primary production. Consumers* are the animals that eat the photosynthetic organisms as well as each other. *Decomposers* (actually the terminal consumers) are the microorganisms, including bacteria and fungi, that recycle nutrients in the system by decomposing the *detritus* (organic debris) that results from biological processes such as death and defecation. In intertidal ecosystems, there are also many kinds of detritus feeders or scavengers that play an intermediate role between the decomposers and the other consumers.

The producers of the intertidal zone include floating photosynthetic microorganisms generally called *phytoplankton.* These smallest "plants" are not readily seen by visitors to islands, and a detailed description of them is not included here. Most important in this group are the *diatoms,* which probably contribute more primary production to the planet than any other group of organisms. Diatoms are single-celled, photosynthetic organisms that possess an external skeleton of glass (silicon dioxide), and they contain a tiny drop of oil that keeps them floatng near the surface.

Also of significant interest are the dinoflagellates *Gonyaulax* and *Noctiluca.* During summer months *Gonyaulax polyhedra* may undergo tremendous blooms under certain nutrient and temperature conditions to create a condition known as *red tides. Gonyaulax catenella* contains certain amounts of a neurotoxin that can be concentrated by filter-feeding shell-fish such as clams and mussels. From May 1 to October 31 in most years, a mussel quarantine is posted. Another dinoflagellate, *Noctilucal scintilans,* produces bioluminescence under mechanical stimulation. When abundant in the phytoplankton, this species puts on a spectacular nighttime per-formance. Waves breaking on a beach and the bow wave of a ship take on a beautiful white-green glow. Small fish can be observed from a moving boat to burst into light as the pressure wave of the boat excites them. Dol-phins appear to be glowing torpedoes as they streak toward a moving ship to ride the bow wave. This natural light show appears to occur only in cer-tain years and then is best experienced on dark, moonless nights after 10:00 P.M. Apparently *Noctiluca* undergoes a daily vertical migration, rising to the surface several hours after dark. Plankton samples taken from surface waters just at dusk produce few *Noctiluca,* but by 10:00 P.M. large num-bers are observed.

Of great importance to the productivity of the intertidal zone are the kelps, brown algae (Phaeophyta) that are conspicuous components of rocky intertidal zones, particularly on the islands. California's kelp forests are constantly changing. The abundance of kelp itself undergoes dramatic fluc-tuations, particularly on the mainland. In southern California, when kelp forests disappear it is considered by many to be an ecological disaster. In many areas the absence of kelp has contributed to beach erosion, because without the kelp beds to absorb some of the wave energy, the surf pounds on the beach without interference and washes away the sand. Loss of kelp also causes a coincident loss of all the associated animal species.

No doubt an assortment of factors contributes to the decline in the abundance of kelp. In part, loss of kelp up and down the coast has been attributed to increases in temperature associated with periodic El Niño conditions. Warming of coastal waters occurred in the 1950s, 1960s, 1980s, and 1990s, and each time there was an associated loss of kelp.

The influence of temperature is not understood thoroughly, but it has been demonstrated that the giant kelps (*Macrocystis* spp.) (Fig. 26) can-not survive long if water temperature exceeds 58°F (14.5°C). During an El Niño episode, water temperature of 70°F (20°C) or higher is common. Furthermore in areas where seawater is used to cool electrical power plants, the temperature near the outflow is often warmer than that tol-erated by many kelp communities. For example, near the outflow of the nuclear power plant at San Onofre, the temperature commonly ranges above 70°F (20°C). Nuclear power plants produce a great deal of heat, and they require more water for cooling than do fossil fuel plants; consequently they emit more heat to the sea.

Another factor associated with loss of kelp has been the increase in the number of sea urchins in the subtidal zone, particularly in the vicinity of sewer outfalls. Their mode of feeding, which includes scraping of the hold-fast or stipe of the kelp, increases the amount of kelp that is carried away by the surf. It appears that grazing by sea urchins has kept the kelp from returning long after the warming effect of an El Niño episode.

Feeding of sea urchins has been studied thoroughly. In addition to grazing, sea urchins are able to absorb dissolved organic matter from seawater. The additional load of such water-soluble nutrients in the vicinity of sewer outfalls encourages the growth of the sea urchin population, which in turn exerts increased grazing pressure on the kelp.

The natural order of things should encourage a corresponding increase in the population levels of sea urchin predators. However, two of the primary predators of sea urchins, California Spiny Lobsters, *Panulirus interruptus,* and Sea Otters, *Enhydra lutris* (Fig. 36), are victims of human interference. Lobsters cannot be counted on to limit the number of sea urchins because cropping of lobsters of legal size by commercial fishermen is nearly complete. The Sea Otter (which will be discussed later in this chapter) was all but eliminated by the 1800s, the victim of fur hunters. Today Sea Otters range regularly from about Pismo Beach north to Santa Cruz, and often to Año Nuevo. The magnificent kelp forests of the islands, however, are helped by the lobsters because lobsters prey on young mussels, and this process tends to keep rocky areas clear for the attachment of kelp.

Humans must also be considered predators on sea urchins. The industry that harvests sea urchins for their edible gonads is now having an impact on sea urchin populations. How this industry will fare in the face of intensive cropping, and whether the kelp will return, remain to be seen. What is certain is that the species composition and abundance of California's kelp forests have changed over the years, as the result of a complex of natural environmental changes influenced by the activities of humans.

CAUSES OF INTERTIDAL ZONATION

Although a complex of abiotic and biotic factors is responsible for intertidal zonation, certain generalizations may be made. The upper limit of distribution of most species is regulated by their tolerance of such physical factors as heat, light, and desiccation. Lower limits tend to be established by biological interactions such as predation and competition. Distribution on outer, more exposed sites is limited by tolerance of wave shock and/or the typical extent of colonization by larvae. The opportunity for larvae to become established is in turn directly related to the abundance of organisms. Appropriate bare space on hard surfaces must be available, and larvae must be able to reach the site. In protected areas, the accumulation of sediment on rocky surfaces also becomes a problem.

The outcome of all of these interactions is that drought- and/or heat-tolerant species such as small snails and barnacles occur in the upper intertidal zone. They are prevented from inhabiting lower zones by competition with larger or faster-growing species. Similarly, mussels inhabit the middle intertidal zone. The extent of their upper distribution is limited by their tolerance for desiccation and that of their lower distribution by starfish predation. Within mussel beds, two species will be segregated by their respective abilities to tolerate wave shock or sedimentation. If an offshore reef intercepts larvae, mussels and/or barnacles may be less common than one would expect. In this case other species may seem unusually common. Thus juvenile rockfishes (Scorpaenidae) in offshore kelp beds prey on the larvae of intertidal invertebrates; one study on Monterey Bay found that predation by juvenile rockfishes reduced recruitment of barnacles to one-fiftieth the level in the absence of the fish.

Predatory birds, particularly oystercatchers (Plate 3C), are also important in limiting the upper distribution of certain organisms, such as barnacles and/or mussels. In some areas, cropping of attached intertidal animals is so complete that the oystercatchers become a major factor contributing to the creation of the bare space necessary for colonization by new organisms.

The distribution of algae is regulated by the same sorts of constraints. Most photosynthesis takes place while the tide is in, and therefore different varieties of algae are sorted into distributional belts based on their abilities to tolerate heat and desiccation as well as depth of water (Fig. 20).

Water is a very effective filter for light. Wavelengths penetrate to different depths: shorter wavelengths, such as blues and violets, penetrate more deeply, whereas longer wavelengths, such as reds and oranges, are eliminated near the surface. Various pigments within plants are associated with the absorption of assorted wavelengths of light; for example, chlorophyll absorbs red and blue light most readily, but obviously in deep water red light cannot be used effectively. As a result different kinds of aquatic plants live at different depths and make use of different assortments of pigments, with which they can make optimal use of the light available for photosynthesis at their particular depths. Green algae are the most similar to land plants; they grow in shallow water. Kelps are brown algae, and they are thus able to grow in deeper water. Their holdfasts may be quite deep, but photosynthesis in brown algae seldom occurs at depths greater than 50 ft (15 m). Red algae grow in the deepest water, up to 100 ft (30 m) down. The red pigment reflects red light and absorbs the other colors, but at the depth where these algae grow there is no red light. They must therefore photosynthesize with only the deeply penetrating blue light. Red algae are effectively black where they grow; this feature may also be an adaptation to conceal them from herbivores in the dim light.

Many seaweeds have defenses to prevent them from being eaten. For example, coralline algae are covered with a calcareous material that makes them difficult to eat. Chemical defenses are also employed; one of the most interesting is the gas bladder of the Bull Kelp, *Nereocystis luetkeana,* which contains about 10 percent carbon monoxide. Furthermore most kelps are poor food items because they contain toxic tannins and phenols. Another interesting adaptation may be seen in the subtidal kelp *Desmarestia.* This plant has small bubbles (vacuoles) of sulfuric or malic acid within its tissues, and these acids can dissolve the calcareous teeth of sea urchins.

Succession is another feature that influences which organisms may be seen at any given time. Disturbances cause bare areas, and the sequence in which organisms reappear in these areas is determined by succession. A typical situation would be for a large object such as a floating log to be bashed against the rocks during a storm, cleaning the rocks locally of such organisms as mussels by the force of its impact. The reestablishment of mussels and goose barnacles would take about a year. Early successional stages would include filamentous and sheetlike green algae. These are heavily grazed by limpets and crabs, but they are soon followed by forms that resist grazing, such as crustose and coralline algae, with their calcareous coatings. These forms may in turn be replaced by acorn barnacles, which physically pry off the algae as they grow. Mussels and goose barnacles eventually overtop the acorn barnacles. If the water is too deep, predators such as starfish and dogwinkles will soon eliminate the mussels and goose barnacles. In the long run they will be replaced by thick, leathery, or coarsely branched kelps such as sea palms or rockweed. An interesting characteristic of sewer outfalls is that they tend to keep the intertidal zone in a juvenile state in which the dominant life forms include mostly filamentous and sheetlike green algae, or calcareous crustose and coralline algae. This phenomenon has been documented particularly for Wilson Cove on San Clemente Island.

There are also seasonal changes in the organisms that inhabit the intertidal zone, especially the algae. As might be expected, the early successional species dominate in summer and fall, but they are far less common in winter. They are primarily annual forms with a rapid turnover, typical of early successional species in any habitat. Perennial species such as surf-grasses and kelps dominate during winter. Although there is some variation in animal species, on a seasonal basis the variation is not obvious. There is a slight increase in the population levels of attached animals such as barnacles in the spring, coinciding with their reproductive cycles and probably reflecting attempts to colonize bare areas.

INTERTIDAL COMMUNITIES

Three major habitat types are influenced by the tides: sandy beaches, rocky headlands, and estuaries. (Because there are no substantial rivers on the islands, true estuarine habitats are absent, although Catalina Harbor on Santa Catalina, owing to its size and protection from the surf, possesses many of the qualities of an estuarine habitat.) Because San Francisco Bay, with its accompanying marshes, is a large estuary, characteristics of that community are discussed in Chapter 10.

Sandy Beaches

Because their substratum is always shifting, beaches are the most hostile of the three habitats. On beaches where the action of the surf has carried away the sand, there may be cobbles or shingles that roll and slide with every wave. Very few living organisms can tolerate the physical hazards posed by such an environment. Where there is abundant sand, however, there may be an assortment of creatures that tolerate or even require shifting sand.

The sands of beaches are derived primarily from weathering of rocks in the mountains. As we have already seen, the sand is delivered to the ocean by rivers and carried southward by the action of waves and currents. Additional materials are added to beaches by erosion of shoreline cliffs. The bulk of material in beach sand is quartz, a hard, insoluble mineral sorted into particles that usually range between 0.06 and 2 mm in diameter. Particle size determines the water-holding capacity of a beach, a feature that has a profound influence on the nature of the creatures that live there. Sands that remain soft, retaining moderate amounts of water, are in general the most habitable.

Food for sand-dwelling organisms comes primarily from planktonic or detrital particles suspended in seawater. Another important source of food is organic molecules that adhere to sand particles themselves. A third source is broken-up kelp and other debris washed up on the beach by high tides or storms. Of course, beach-dwelling organisms also eat each other.

One of the most common animals on sandy beaches is the Pacific Mole Crab or Western Sand Crab, *Emerita analoga* (Fig. 16A). This crustacean, about 1 in. (25 mm) in length, is shaped like a small, flattened egg; its small

A   B

Figure 16. Animals of sandy beaches. (A) Pacific Mole Crab or Western Sand Crab, *Emerita analoga*. (B) Lugworm, *Arenicola brasiliensis*. (From Hinton 1987.)

appendages can be used for swimming or digging. Mole Crabs move up and down the beach in the surf line, feeding on detritus and plankton. Every time a wave recedes, they burrow backwards into the soupy sand, so they are seldom seen; however, persons wading in the surf may feel them as a tingling sensation on their bare feet. Between molts, when their carapaces are soft, Mole Crabs are prized as bait by surf fishermen.

At the upper tide line on the beach, there is often a deposit of kelp and its associated organisms that has been washed ashore. A number of scavengers live among these piles of rotting kelp, the most common of which are amphipod crustaceans known as beach fleas or beach hoppers (*Orchestoidea* spp.). The Large Beach Hopper, *Orchistoidea californiana*, may reach 1 in. (25 mm) in length. Beach hoppers usually spend the daylight hours in burrows under the decaying kelp. After dark they come out by the thousands to feed on the kelp and other detritus. Southern California sunbathers are sometimes pestered by small beach hoppers. People who lie on the beach near piles of kelp often find the smaller species hopping onto their legs.

Isopod crustaceans also occur on beaches. These creeping, tank-shaped crustaceans, related to sow bugs, prefer to eat meat. On the mainland, one form, known as Harford's Greedy Isopod, *Cirolana harfordi*, occurs in swarms large enough to clean the skeleton of a dead fish within a matter of hours. A species found on some of the Channel Islands is *Excirolana chiltoni*.

Among the filter-feeding inhabitants of sandy beaches are several varieties of clams. When the tide is in, these organisms pass a current of water through their bodies, extracting small organisms and particulate organic matter from the water. A number of species—such as the thin, flat California Jack-knife Clam, *Tagelus californianus*, and the small, fragile Bent-nosed Clam, *Macoma nasuta*—are associated with beaches on the islands.

Blood worms (*Glycera* spp.), Lug Worms (*Arenicola brasiliensis*) (Fig. 16B), and Red Worms (*Euzonus mucronata*) also occur on sandy beaches. These segmented worms (Annelida) feed like earthworms on beaches with fine sand. They ingest sand, feed on the organic material suspended in it, and pass the rest of the undigestible mass through their bodies. These worms, belonging to the group known as polychaete worms, have small, bristly paddles on each segment. They are usually about 1 in. (25 mm) long, although in some habitats they may be much larger. The bright red color of these worms comes from hemoglobin, the same pigment that gives vertebrate blood its color. As in vertebrate blood, the pigment is used to carry oxygen, an important adaptation that helps the worms survive in the sand when the tide is out. At that time they feed actively near the surface of the sand. When the tide comes back in, they retreat to deeper sand so they are not carried away by the surf. Some Blood Worms and Red Worms are known to penetrate beach sands to a depth of 18 in. (45 cm).

Catalina Harbor has been found to have the greatest abundance of polychaete worms on the Channel Islands. Particularly notable is the presence of Capitella Worms, *Capitella capitata,* which are a notable indicator of septic conditions. In Catalina Harbor these worms are very common in association with deposits of fresh tar.

Perhaps the most conspicuous of the beach dwellers are the kelp flies (*Fucellia, Coelopa,* and others). Larvae of flies, known as maggots, can be seen in decaying piles of seaweed. Adults are small black flies that rise in swarms when people walk near the kelp.

Rocky Headlands

The rocky intertidal region of the ocean is one of the most fascinating habitats in the world. In spite of its harshness, many authorities believe that most higher animals evolved in the intertidal region and the tide pools of rocky headlands. Representatives of every major group, or phylum, of animals are found in this region.

Based on the length of time that the organisms in them are out of the water, the rocky intertidal region can be divided into five distinctive zones. From upper to lower, these zones are known respectively as the splash, upper intertidal, middle intertidal, lower intertidal, and subtidal zones (Fig. 17). Each zone is characterized by its own combination of stresses— including wave shock, exposure, temperature extremes, and predators— and adaptations to these stresses are diverse (Table 4). Each zone also has its characteristic organisms that are conspicuous at low tide. Although there is some controversy over the precise boundaries for each zone or the organisms that inhabit each, they do occur in distinct bands on the rocks. The reasons for this zonation, as explained earlier, draw upon some of the most interesting concepts in ecology.

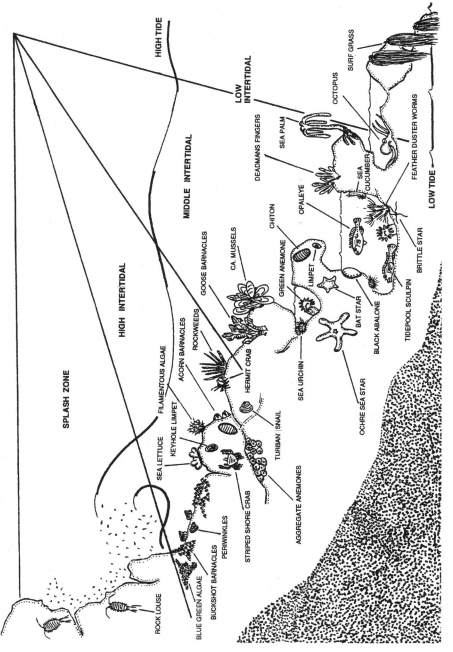

Figure 17. Zonation in the rocky intertidal region. (Drawing by Thomas Trooien.)

TABLE 4   EXAMPLES OF ADAPTATIONS TO STRESSES
OF THE ROCKY INTERTIDAL REGION

STRESS	ADAPTATION	EXAMPLE
Wave shock	Adherent threads	Mussels
	Stick tightly	Chiton, limpets
	Conical shape	Barnacles, limpets
	Flexible stalks	Goose barnacle, kelps
	Hide in cracks	Crabs
	Motility	Periwinkles
Dehydration	Motility	Starfish
	Operculum	Turban snails
	Stick tightly	Abalone, limpets
	Seal opening	Barnacles
	Valved shells	Mussels
Temperature extremes	Motility	Crabs
	Evaporative cooling	Mussels
	Tolerance	Barnacles
	Nocturnal behavior	Rock lice
Salinity extremes	Tolerance	Periwinkles
	Motility	Crabs
Feeding	Filter feeding	Mussels, barnacles
	Grazing	Chitons, limpets
	Detritus feeding	Sea hares, crabs
	Absorption of dissolved	Sea urchins
	organic matter	Octopus, starfish
	Predation	
Predation	Hard shells	Barnacles, mussels
	Motility	Crabs
	Toxins	Nudibranchs, kelps
	Protective coloration	Tidepool sculpin
Competition	Aggression	Crabs, octopus
	Rapid growth	Barnacles
	Opportunistic larval	Mussels, barnacles
	establishment	
	Large numbers of offspring	Sea urchins, barnacles
	Good dispersal	Planktonic larvae

Splash Zone The splash zone is primarily a terrestrial community that is wetted by surf spray during high tide. This is an extremely harsh habitat, and one subject to prolonged drying every time the tide is out. Photosynthetic organisms in this zone are drought-tolerant, crustose forms such as blue-green algae (Cyanophyta) and black-colored lichens.

Few species of animals can tolerate such harsh conditions; those that do either hide in cracks during daylight hours or take refuge in shallow tide pools. Most common among the dwellers in the cracks is an inch-long (25-mm) isopod crustacean known as the Rock Louse, *Ligia occidentalis*

Figure 18. Rock Louse, *Ligia occidentalis.*

(Fig. 18). The Rock Louse is seldom seen because it spends daylight hours in hiding and seldom ventures out until after dark. It feeds on attached algae or kelp that are deposited on rocks by the surf. Rock Lice exhibit a circadian (daily) rhythm in which they change color, from dark during daylight hours to lighter at night, and biologists have studied these small animals in an attempt to gain a better understanding of innate biological clocks.

In the shallow tide pools, the most common animals are small snails known as periwinkles (*Littorina* spp.). There are several species of these snails, but they have in common their ability to tolerate exposure. When the tide goes out they may seek refuge in cracks or gather in shallow tide pools, where they continue feeding. If the environment becomes too dry, they retreat into their shells, sealing the entrance with a circular bit of shell known as an *operculum*. When the tide is in, periwinkles creep about on the rocks, grazing on attached algae. These small snails are especially suited to life in the splash zone, for they can breathe either in or out of water, and they can tolerate submersion in fresh water, a common occurrence in the rainy Northwest.

One of the hazards of life in the intertidal zone is the awesome power of a crashing wave. Snails are well equipped to stick tightly to the rocks on which they anchor themselves and resist the force of most waves. Even so, they may occasionally be knocked off their perches and carried by the backwash into deeper water. Periwinkles have an interesting set of reflexes that instinctively brings them back to their normal habitat in the splash zone. When they are under water they respond negatively to gravity, a behavioral response known as *negative geotaxis*. This instinct causes them to crawl upward, toward the surface. If a snail crawls into a crack, when it is right side up it has a negative reaction to light, but if it is upside down it has a positive reaction to light. These instincts are known as *positive and negative phototaxes*. The result is that cracks pose no problem for a snail:

it crawls into the crack and back out again, always moving upward. Once the snail emerges from the water it knows it is "home." As long as it remains moist it will move only to feed.

Upper Intertidal Zone The upper intertidal zone is covered by nearly every high tide and exposed by most low tides. This area is characterized by attached green algae (Chlorophyta), such as sea felt (*Enteromorpha* spp.) and sea lettuce (*Ulva* spp.). These algae are found in intertidal zones all over the world; in California they are often quite similar in appearance. Sea felt is thin and fragile, whereas sea lettuce is usually larger, up to 4 in. (10 cm) in length, and has a wavy margin. These forms of algae are heavily grazed upon by the animals of the rocky intertidal zone. Sea lettuce gets its name from the fact that humans also gather it for food: dried sea lettuce, supposedly rich in vitamins and minerals, is sold under the names Iceland Sea Grass or Green Laver.

Most animals of the upper intertidal zone (Fig. 19) are grazers and filter feeders. Periwinkles will move into this zone to feed, but the more common grazers are limpets and chitons, which are flattened marine snails (Gastropoda).

Limpets, of which there are many species in the rocky intertidal zone, appear circular when viewed from the top, but in side view it can be seen that the shell has the form of a flattened cone. This is an ideal shape to disperse the energy of wave shock. During low tide this shape also helps to seal in water under the edge of their shells. Like periwinkles, limpets stick tightly to rocks, and studies of these grazers show that they too have instinctive patterns of behavior. They feed when the tide is in, but they have "home" depressions to which they return to wait out the low tide. Limpets follow slime trails back to the same depressions from which they started. Since they must return in time to settle down tightly before the tide goes out, their internal clock causes them to move away from home when the tide first comes in, but back toward home when the tide starts to go out.

Chitons belong to a group of molluscs known as the Polyplacophora. This name signifies that they bear many plates, and it specifically refers to their hinged shell, which is made up of eight plates. The advantage of the hinged shell is that chitons are able to bend as they move over irregularities on rocks. Furthermore, if one becomes dislodged, it is able to roll up to protect its vulnerable underside from drying or predators.

Filter feeders of the upper intertidal zone include mostly small barnacles. There is some confusion regarding the common names for these barnacles, but the name *buckshot barnacles* seems to suit them as well as any.

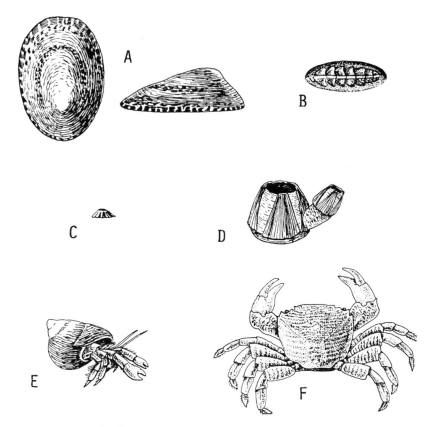

Figure 19. Animals of the upper intertidal zone. (A) Owl Limpet, *Lottia gigantea*. (B) Troglodyte Chiton, *Nuttalina fluxa*. (C) Buckshot Barnacle, *Chthamalus* sp. (D) Red-striped Acorn Barnacle, *Megabalanus californicus*. (E) Hairy Hermit Crab, *Pagurus hirsutiusculus*, in the shell of a Black Turban, *Tegula funebralis*. (F) Striped Shore Crab, *Pachygrapsus crassipes*. (From Hinton 1987.)

Most common are the Brown Buckshot Barnacle (*Chthamalus fissus*) and the White Buckshot Barnacle (*Balanus glandula*). These are small crustaceans that live in volcano-shaped shells. When the tide is in, they feed with feather-like hind appendages. When the tide goes out their shells, made of several plates, contract to seal in the water. In the upper intertidal zone, they may be so common as to coat the rocks in a nearly solid band of gray volcanoes about a quarter of an inch (6 mm) high. Of all the species of barnacles, these are able to tolerate desiccation for the longest period of time. The upper limit of their range is heavily influenced by the activities of predatory birds, such as the oystercatchers described later in this chapter.

At the lower margin of this zone is a belt of larger barnacles known as Acorn Barnacles (*Megabalanus californicus*). These barnacles are usually about 1 in. (25 mm) in height. They are unable to tolerate desiccation as well as buckshot barnacles, so they are unable to live higher on the rocks. On the other hand, they grow faster and larger than buckshot barnacles, and this rapid growth enables them to pry the smaller species off the rocks by growing under them. This type of zonation among barnacle species is found all over the world.

Hundreds of snails may occur in tide pools of the upper intertidal zone. Many of these are the periwinkles mentioned previously, but there are also other species. One common type is the Black Turban, *Tegula funebralis.* When the tide is in, turbans move about, grazing on algae; when the tide is out, they retreat to the tide pools.

A person peering into these upper tide pools will note that many of the turban shells appear empty. It may also come as a surprise to see some of these shells lurching along in a most un-snail-like fashion. Closer inspection will reveal that the shell is actually inhabited by a small crab. Hermit crabs, the most common of which is the Hairy Hermit Crab, *Pagurus hirsutiusculus,* commonly occupy empty turban shells, although they will use any hollow container that is of an appropriate size, perhaps even a discarded lipstick tube or film can. In southern California, these crabs seldom reach over an inch (25 mm) in length, but to the north they may reach lengths of 4 in. (10 cm). As they grow, they must find a succession of larger containers. Life for a hermit crab is characterized by incessant scavenging—either for food or for a home with the proper fit.

The most conspicuous crab that inhabits the upper tide pools is the Striped Shore Crab, *Pachygrapsus crassipes.* Many children delight in chasing these squarish, flattened crabs with big claws. Their flattened shape is ideal for enabling them to cling within a shelter to resist wave shock. For the most part they are nocturnal, seeking shelter in cracks during the daytime. In the tide pools, however, any bit of food, animal or vegetable, that becomes available will lure them out of hiding. Battles between rival crabs are common, with the larger crab usually winning.

Middle Intertidal Zone The middle intertidal zone is uncovered by many, but not all, low tides. Conversely, it is covered by every high tide. This is a zone of filter-feeding animals and highly resilient attached algae. Among the attached algae are small kelps or brown algae (Phaeophyta), principal among them rockweeds (*Pelvetia, Pelvetiopsis, Hesperophycus*). These are small kelps, seldom over 4 in. (10 cm) in height, that grow in clumps in exposed rocky areas (Fig. 20).

Northern Sea Palm, *Postelsia palmaeformis,* is one of the most conspicuous organisms of this zone from Morro Bay northward, including Año

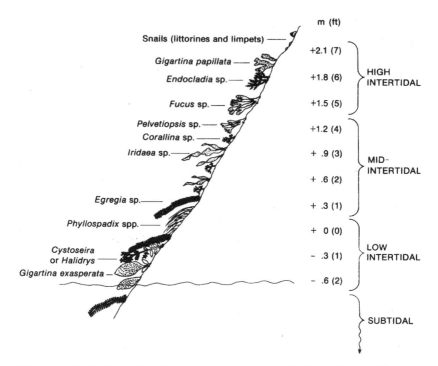

Snails (littorines and limpets) —

Gigartina papillata —

Endocladia sp. —

Fucus sp. —

Pelvetiopsis sp. —

Corallina sp. —

Iridaea sp. —

Egregia sp. —

Phyllospadix spp. —

Cystoseira or Halidrys —

Gigartina exasperata —

m (ft)

+2.1 (7)

+1.8 (6)

+1.5 (5)

+1.2 (4)

+ .9 (3)

+ .6 (2)

+ .3 (1)

+ 0 (0)

− .3 (1)

− .6 (2)

HIGH INTERTIDAL

MID-INTERTIDAL

LOW INTERTIDAL

SUBTIDAL

Figure 20. Vertical zonation of some common seaweeds in the rocky intertidal region. (From Dawson and Foster 1982.)

Nuevo and the Farallon Islands. They are particularly common in zones buffeted by high surf. This distinctive kelp looks like a palm tree about 2 ft (60 cm) tall. It is an annual species that is torn loose by the surf during fall and winter. Each year, usually in February, a new forest of Sea Palms grows on bare surfaces produced by disturbance. In this sense it competes with other attached organisms, particularly mussels. This yearly turnover makes the middle intertidal zone one of the most productive ecosystems in the world. Many people consider Sea Palm a delicacy. The stemlike stipe and blades may be washed in fresh water, steamed, and eaten with lemon juice and soy sauce; sweet pickles may also be made from the stipes.

On the Channel Islands, there is a different sea palm. The Southern Sea Palm, *Eisenia arborea,* forms a dense, low-growing marine forest in many areas, and it commonly occurs in deeper water than its northern counterpart.

The most conspicuous animals of the middle intertidal zone are the mussels (*Mytilus* spp.). Mussels are bivalve molluscs (Pelecypoda); they are black-colored clams that adhere to the rocks by means of strong tendrils known as *byssal threads.* When the tide is in, they feed on plankton and

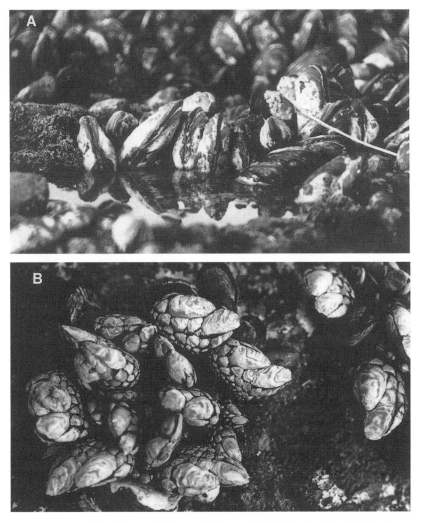

Figure 21. Animals of the middle intertidal zone. (A) California Mussels, *Mytilus californianus.* (B) Goose Barnacles or Leaf Barnacles, *Pollicipes polymerus.*

perhaps dissolved organic matter by passing a current of water through their bodies. When the tide is out, they close up in order to prevent dehydration. If they become exposed on hot days, they may remain partially open so that evaporation of water from the inside will help to cool them.

Throughout California, there are two species of mussels. The smaller Bay Mussel, *Mytilus edulis,* is more resistant to desiccation, and thus it most commonly occurs on the upper fringes of mussel beds; it is also dominant in protected areas. The larger mussel is the California Mussel, *Mytilus californianus* (Fig. 21A), and it dominates in regions of stronger wave shock.

The byssal threads of the Bay Mussel are thinner, and Bay Mussels are thus more easily knocked off rocks. On the other hand, Bay Mussels are better able to tolerate quiet water because they are motile. Their ability to grow new byssal threads and detach the old ones enables them to move upward out of potential sedimentation that would clog their filter-feeding systems.

These various adaptations also mean that there may be seasonal changes in dominance within the same "wads" of mussels. During periods of quiet surf, usually in the summer, Bay Mussels are more common because they are able to move to the outer edges of the mussel clumps. During winter, when the pounding of the surf is more severe, Bay Mussels are carried away and the California Mussels with their stronger byssal threads prevail.

Mussels are common intertidal organisms throughout the world. Because they grow so rapidly, mussels are one of the world's most important cultured seafoods, and in many nations they may be the most important cultured source of protein. In Spain, they are grown abundantly on floating rafts. In this way, kept full time under water, mussels feed continuously and grow rapidly. Where they are not cultured, they are knocked from the rocks with a chisel. Mussels formed a significant portion of the diet of the Native Americans who lived on the islands of California, and to this day, where it is legal, they may still provide an impromptu and memorable beach meal. They should first be allowed to feed in a bucket of clean seawater for a few hours in order to clear out the grit from their bodies. Then they should be steamed until they open, dipped in garlic butter, and served with hot French bread and cold white wine. Caution should be exercised not to eat local mussels during summer months, when they could potentially cause mussel poisoning. This disorder results from the mussels' ingesting large numbers of dinoflagellates, particularly during episodes of red tide. Local authorities usually post mussel quarantine signs for this reason.

Unfortunately, in some parts of California, many mussel beds are now threatened by overharvesting. This is in part a consequence of the influx into the state of new residents from regions in which harvesting of intertidal animals for food is routine. The problem is particularly severe in many of the coastal marine life refuges, where any form of harvesting is illegal.

Clam Worms, *Neanthes brandti,* are seldom seen by visitors to the tide pools because they remain hidden among the mussels during low tide. These polychaete worms may grow to a length of 3 ft (1 m), although those that are observed are frequently much smaller. One "monster" specimen from Santa Catalina Island was reported to be 6 ft (1.8 m) long. These omnivores eat all kinds of small prey and algae, which they locate by squirming over the mussel beds when the tide is in. They are notable for their breeding swarms, during which they swim to the surface and shed their eggs and sperm while gyrating in a writhing, seething mass. Afterward the spent males and females sink to the bottom and die.

Other animals that commonly occur in mixed colonies with the mussels include Goose Barnacles or Leaf Barnacles, *Pollicipes polymerus* (Fig. 21B). These barnacles occur on flexible stalks, and the arrangement of their enclosing plates resembles a goose in profile. In Europe, the Goose Barnacle is the subject of an ancient legend. In the North Atlantic, along the west coast of Europe, lives a bird known as the Barnacle Goose, *Branta leucopsis,* which resembles the Canada Goose, *Branta canadensis,* of North America. As the story goes, the leaves of certain trees fall into the sea and become barnacles. After a time the barnacles fall off rocks, logs, or ships' timbers and become Barnacle Geese. In the thirteenth century Irish priests believed that Barnacle Geese arose from Goose Barnacles. Thus they considered them seafood, not fowl, and the geese were considered acceptable to eat during Lent. But Pope Innocent III was not convinced, and he issued a decree in 1215 that forbade the eating of Barnacle Geese during Lent. Meanwhile, a prominent rabbi in France concluded that if Barnacle Geese arose from Goose Barnacles, Jews could not eat them because they were shellfish, which were forbidden under religious dietary laws.

The Black Oystercatcher, *Haematopus bachmani* (Plate 3C), frequents the rocky intertidal region of all the islands. Because it is a motile animal it cannot be considered a member of any particular intertidal zone, but because it feeds primarily in mussel beds it should be mentioned here. Oystercatchers are not common birds where humans are abundant, but on the islands, with their inaccessible, rocky shores that can be approached only by boat, these interesting birds may readily be observed at work. They are bizarre-looking creatures that look as if they have been assembled from spare parts. They are completely black except for pink legs and a bright red bill. The long bill, which is compressed laterally, is used to open mussels and barnacles with a swift peck, so that the meat can be plucked out. Oystercatchers also feed heavily on juvenile mussels and other sedentary prey species. As such, their activity, along with that of gulls or other predatory birds, is important for the formation of bare areas that are necessary for the establishment of new colonies. A related bird, the American Oystercatcher, *Haemotopus palliatus,* is resident on Santa Cruz Island. Of more southern affinities, it differs from the Black Oystercatcher by having a white belly and white wing patches. It is an occasional visitor to the other Channel Islands but has become an established breeder on Santa Cruz.

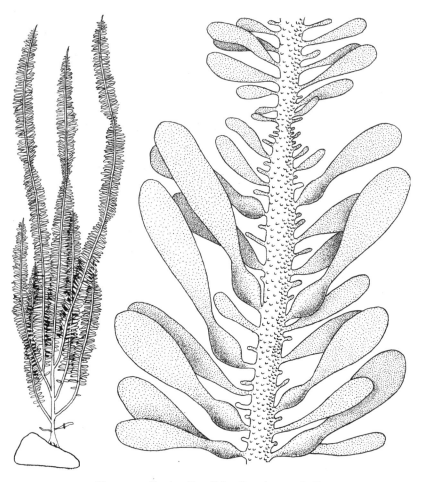

Figure 22. Feather Boa Kelp, *Egregia menziesii.*

Lower Intertidal Zone The lower intertidal zone is exposed only by the lowest of low tides, the spring tides. Its upper margin is considered to be the average sea level, the line from which the height of a tide is measured. A low tide that drops below this line is called a *minus tide.* During a 6-ft tide, this line would be 6 ft under water.

This zone is characterized by the presence of a number of species of kelp, such as the Feather Boa Kelp, *Egregia menziesii* (Fig. 22) and, farther north, the Sugar Wrack, *Laminaria saccharina.* Also found here are the seed plants known as Eel-grass, *Zostera marina,* and surf-grasses (*Phyllospadix* spp.) (Fig. 23). This family of plants (Zosteraceae) is unique in that its members are terrestrial plants—complete with roots and flowers—that are adapted to living under water. Eel-grass is most often associated with quiet

Figure 23. Low tide in the rocky intertidal zone, exposing the surf-grass, *Phyllospadix* spp., and a variety of kelp species.

water, as in bays, but surf-grasses are the conspicuous, bright green plants that seem to form meadows when they become exposed by the low tides. Usually the roots are anchored in the sand, but the tough, fibrous, rootlike stems (rhizomes) may become anchored to solid rock. Surf-grasses produce millions of filamentous pollen grains that are shed into the water. These microscopic, slimy threads become entangled in the stigmas of the flowers on female plants. The stigmas in turn produce a sticky secretion that adheres to the pollen and holds it in place in the surf. The stigma-pollen bond will only form with pollen of the correct species, and this specificity prevents hybridization when more than one kind of pollen is shed simultaneously into the surf.

A very common brown alga seen around the Channel Islands is an introduced species called Sargasso Weed, *Sargassum muticum*. This species of kelp has been carried all over the world attached to ships. It appears to have fine or feathery branches made up of clusters of branchlets with tiny floats. The dense, conical plants may be 3–5 ft (1–2 m) in length. This species is common in protected water, and by blocking light needed for photosynthesis by smaller attached algae, it may actually provide too much shade for the tide pools.

Most of the animals of the lower intertidal zone take refuge in or attach to these abundant kelps. Included in this group are many species of worms, snails, and limpets. The "spiny-skinned" animals (Echinodermata) constitute

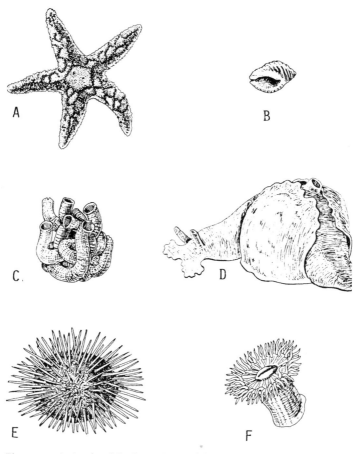

Figure 24. Animals of the lower intertidal zone. (A) Ochre Sea Star, *Pisaster ochraceus.* (B) Rock Thais, *Nucella (=Thais) emarginata.* (C) Scaly Tube Snail, *Serpulorbis squamigerus.* (D) Brown Sea Hare, *Aplysia californica.* (E) Red Sea Urchin, *Strongylocentrotus franciscanus.* (F) Solitary Green Anemone, *Anthopleura xanthogrammica.* (From Hinton 1987.)

a purely marine phylum, unique among animals in that they circulate seawater through their bodies. Perhaps the most familiar of these animals are the sea stars or starfishes (Asteroidea). The most common California island starfish is the Ochre Sea Star, *Pisaster ochraceus* (Fig. 24A), although on the Channel Islands the Knobby Starfish, *Pisaster giganteus* (Fig. 28B), is also common. Starfishes can be seen clinging to rocks by means of hundreds of small hydraulic suction cups known as *tube feet.* On the mainland in southern California, they used to be one of the most conspicuous animals at low tide, but over the years curious children and collectors of memorabilia seem to have decimated the population. Another cause of starfish disappearance is a viral infection known as "wasting disease," associated with the warming of waters that occurs during El Niño episodes. These days, particularly in southern California, starfishes are seldom exposed by low tide. Their usual habit is to migrate during high tide into the middle intertidal zone in order to feed on mussels or acorn barnacles, and then to retreat before the tide goes out. Different species and/or sizes of sea stars feed on different kinds of prey. The lower limit of the mussel bed is regulated by starfish predation. The regulating factor is the length of time it takes for a starfish to digest the flesh of a mussel, dictated by the feeding style of the starfish. When a starfish feeds, it everts its stomach, inserting it between the mussel's shells through the small openings the mussel uses to siphon water. Digestive juices break down the soft body parts and the stomach is drawn back into the starfish to complete the process. The starfish must move onto the mussel bed during high tide, feed, and then move back into the lower intertidal zone before the tide exposes it: the length of time it takes to complete this process is the critical factor that enables mussels to dominate the middle intertidal zone.

Among the predatory snails of the lower intertidal zone are the unicorns (*Acanthina* spp.), dogwinkles, and moon snails (*Polinices* spp.). The Emarginate Dogwinkle or Rock Thais, *Nucella* (=*Thais*) *emarginata* (Fig. 24B), is about an inch and a half (37 mm) in length. These snails have a rasplike drill that they use to puncture holes in other shelled animals, such as mussels or limpets. However, when the Emarginate Dogwinkle attacks snails, such as periwinkles or turbans, the prey species have an unusual escape mechanism: they crawl on top of the dogwinkle so that they cannot be eaten. During the larval stage, these dogwinkles are cannibalistic; larvae eat each other within the egg capsules. Another name for this group of snails is the purple snails, a reference not to the color of the shell (which is white to pale brown), but instead to a purple dye that may be extracted from the flesh.

Moon snails are large carnivores, up to 5 in. (13 cm) across. They live on sand and mud bottoms, where they feed on clams in a manner similar to that of dogwinkles. Their light brown, highly polished shells are easily recognized, but in life the oversized body covers the lower part of the shell. They lay their eggs in distinctive flexible "sand collars," commonly found in sandy or muddy areas during summer low tides.

Filter-feeding animals of the lower intertidal zone are not particularly common because so much of the area is covered by kelps. However, in protected areas, out of the crash of the surf, may be found honeycombed masses of tubes that belong to polychaete worms known as Sand-castle Worms, *Phragmatopoma californica*. These worms possess an operculum with which they may close the entrances to their tubes when the tide is out. Their tubes, formed by cementing together many particles of sand, should not be confused with those of the Scaly Tube Snail, *Serpulorbis squamigerus* (Fig. 24C), a true snail that has taken up a filter-feeding way of life. These snails live in limey tubes about a quarter of an inch in diameter that are laid out on rocks like toothpaste in coiled piles. Their tubes are also common in the middle tide zone.

Grazers in the lower intertidal zone feed primarily on kelp and are seldom seen out of the water. During the low spring tides they will be found either in tide pools of the lower intertidal zone or in the subtidal zone. Studying tide pools of the lower intertidal zone thus provides a glimpse of what goes on when the tide is in, and also what the subtidal zone is like.

The Brown Sea Hare, *Aplysia californica* (Fig. 24D), is a sluglike mollusc. It is brownish-purple in color and has two longitudinal folds along its back. It may be up to 15 in. (35 cm) long and weigh 15 lb (6.8 kg). These creatures glide along the bottom of tide pools, grazing on attached kelp or bits of kelp that have broken off and floated to the bottom. When a Brown Sea Hare is disturbed, it emits a cloud of deep purple ink, which allows it to escape by obscuring the vision of, or at least distracting, the would-be predator.

Other grazers in this zone include three species of abalone (*Haliotis*). These are actually large, flattened snails (Gastropoda); a close look will reveal that the shell is spiral, but flat like a cinnamon roll. A number of open holes in the shell permit the passage of water that carries wastes away from the animal. The edible part of the animal, which brings a high price in gourmet restaurants, is its large, muscular foot. The three species of abalone are named by color: black, green, and red. Black Abalone, *Haliotis cracherodii,* is the most commonly seen. Small specimens live in the lower intertidal zone, where they graze on various kinds of algae, including kelp. Individuals of this species are seldom over 6 in. (15 cm) in diameter, and they have five to nine open holes. Green Abalone, *Haliotis fulgens,* is larger, averaging about 8 in. (20 cm) in diameter with five to seven open holes that are slightly elevated from the shell. It is less common than Black Abalone in the intertidal zone but fairly common in the subtidal zone. Red Abalone, *Haliotis refescens,* occurs in the deepest water, to depths of up to 500 ft (150 m). With individuals up to 11 in. (28 cm) in diameter, it is the most important species from a commercial point of view, and it has been harvested heavily by commercial fishermen. It has only three to four open holes, which are raised from the shell into small tubes. The Red Abalone is rarely found in the intertidal zone.

Tide pools of the lower intertidal zone are often coated with red algae

(Rhodophyta) known as coralline algae (*Corallina* spp.). These algae are short, seldom over 4 in. (10 cm) high, and they resemble coarse, pinkish lace. The coarse texture is caused by a coating of calcium carbonate that is secreted by the plant. This hard coating serves as a deterrent to grazing by most herbivores.

Sea urchins and sand dollars (Echinoidea) are in the same phylum as the starfishes (Echinodermata). The Common Sand Dollar, *Dendraster excentricus,* occurs in sand beyond the surf line or on sand flats in protected bays. When alive, Common Sand Dollars are covered by a ruglike mat of soft spines, but when they are dead and have washed up on the beach, the spines are usually gone and all that is left is the flattened, calcareous skeleton or test. The off-center, flowerlike pattern on the back of the test is formed by holes through which tube feet protrude.

Two common species of sea urchin are residents of the intertidal zone. The smaller, the Purple Sea Urchin, *Strongylocentrotus purpuratus,* is the more common. The Red Sea Urchin, *Strongylocentrotus franciscanus* (Fig. 24E), is not well represented in the intertidal zone of the islands. Although its body may reach 5 in. (13 cm) in diameter, the spines extend well beyond that distance, and the animals resemble pincushions with long, moveable spines. Careful inspection of sea urchins will reveal extended, flexible tube feet between the spines. If a sea urchin is turned over, it can right itself in minutes using its tube feet. Purple Sea Urchins rest, protected from wave shock, in depressions that they enlarge by frequent gnawing. Sea urchins are grazers and scavengers. They have five jaws that form a structure known as Aristotle's lantern, used also to gnaw on kelp or carrion. Gnawing by a sea urchin on the holdfast that anchors a kelp can cause the kelp to be carried away by the surf. Predators such as sea otters that keep sea urchins under control therefore help to maintain kelp beds. Fresh water is also lethal to sea urchins. Following heavy storms, when the intertidal zone becomes flooded by fresh water, over 90 percent mortality of Purple Sea Urchins has been recorded. When a sea urchin dies, its mouth parts and its internal skeleton (test), resembling a hollow pincushion, often remain in the intertidal zone for many years.

As mentioned earlier in this chapter, in recent years a market for sea urchin gonads has developed. Since 1970, when the industry was born, the harvest has grown into a multimillion-dollar industry. The gonads of the Red Sea Urchin are more valuable. Sold as "uni" or "frutta del mare," they are considered a delicacy in Japan, Italian markets, and some American sushi bars. In Japan customers are quite willing to pay the equivalent of $85.00 for a sushi tray of the finest uni. American divers receive up to $1.00 a pound for their catch. It is now profitable to harvest sea urchins, remove the gonads—a mere fraction of the total body mass—and discard the rest of the animals. The present abundance of sea urchins near sewer outfalls makes this a profitable venture, but if overfishing decimates the population (as it is likely to do), the industry may kill itself.

By 1997 overfishing had all but eliminated Red Sea Urchins from the kelp beds on the south side of San Miguel Island. In an attempt to restore the species to that site, a two-day translocation program was funded by the California Department of Fish and Game's Sea Urchin Advisory Committee. In this process, divers succeeded in harvesting several thousand juvenile Red Sea Urchins from a site near Prince Island, from water that was considered less than optimal for the species, and in transplanting them to the kelp beds of their former abundance. It remains to be seen if the experiment has been successful.

One has only to search beneath rocks in the tide pools to discover still other forms of animal life. Brittle stars or serpent stars (Ophiuroidea) are starfish without tube feet that travel by moving their serpentlike arms. They feed on fine, particulate organic matter that collects between sand grains. Sea Bats, *Patiria miniata,* are small red starfish with webbing between their arms. They feed, in typical starfish fashion, on small mussels and barnacles. Careful inspection of the grooves, lined with tube feet, on the underside of these animals will reveal the presence of a small polychaete worm, *Ophiodromus pugettensis.* This worm lives on the "table scraps" left over from the feeding of the starfish. It thus benefits from the actions of the starfish but does not harm it, a type of symbiosis known as *commensalism.*

Flatworms (Platyhelminthes) are primitive animals that have a saclike digestive cavity with but one opening. Many members of this group, including flukes and tapeworms, are parasitic. Under rocks in the lower tide pools are found free-living flatworms known as planarians. They creep about on ciliated bellies, looking more like gray shadows than animals. Their flattened body form enables them to get oxygen and nutrients to their cells by simple diffusion, without the need for a circulatory system. They are equipped with a pair of light receptors on their heads that enable them to tell when it is day or night: at night they creep over the rocks, feeding on detritus, and during the day they remain under the rocks. There are two common species of flatworms on the mainland, although there is some controversy as to how common they are on the islands. One, the Common Flatworm, *Notoplana acticola,* looks like a one-way sign— a fat arrow, seldom over a half inch (12 mm) in length. The other type is known as the White Flatworm, *Pseudoceros luteus.* It is roughly circular and may be up to an inch and a half (37 mm) in length. This form is able to swim gracefully with lateral undulations of its body, looking like a minia-ture bat ray.

Among the most conspicuous inhabitants of these tide pools are the sea anemones (Anthozoa) (Fig. 24F). These are classified in the phylum of hollow-bodied animals (Coelenterata or Cnidaria), which also includes jellyfishes and corals. The body plan of these animals is a two-layered bag with a single opening into the digestive cavity. A ring of tentacles around the mouth gives them a flowerlike appearance. The tentacles bear tiny sting-ing cells known as *nematocysts*. Any small object that touches the tentacles is instantly pierced by toxic barbs; the tentacles fold toward the mouth and cilia carry the object inward until it drops into the mouth. Digestion is rapid, and undigestible matter is regurgitated within a surprisingly short time. Sea anemones are opportunistic predators. They lie in wait with their tentacles open wide, catching materials that drop in or small organisms that carelessly walk across them. Among the food items that might drop in are pieces of mussel or barnacle that during high tide escape from a sloppy eater in the mussel bed above.

The most common anemone species on the islands, especially abun-dant on steep, rocky slopes facing the sea, is the Aggregate Anemone, *Antho-pleura elegantissima*. It is called *aggregate* because it occurs in clusters; these anemones reproduce asexually, and therefore all the members of a par-ticular cluster are clones. The expanded size of the largest individuals in a group is rarely over 2.75 in. (7 cm). The largest of the anemones is the Green Anemone, *Anthopleura xanthogrammica*. It may reach 10 in. (25 cm) in diameter, although specimens half that size are more usual. This species has a bright green color owing to the presence in the tissues of a single-celled, photosynthetic alga. These algae use the anemone for sup-port and protection but apparently contribute nothing in return—another form of commensalism.

A large grazing mollusc often observed in lower tide pools is the Giant Keyhole Limpet, *Megathura crenulata,* which gets its name from a large opening at the apex of the shell. It has a large, muscular, bright yellow foot, but a part of its soft body, the mantle, extends beyond its shell and curves back over the top to nearly cover the shell. It ranges in color from a light tan to black.

Among the carnivores of these lower tide pools is a group of sluglike molluscs known as nudibranchs. These are shell-less snails with exposed gills; the name *nudibranch* is derived from Latin roots meaning "naked gills." Nudibranchs are often brightly colored, but most are smaller than 2 in. (50 mm) in length, so they are seldom conspicuous. One interesting species, *Phidiana* (=*Hermissenda*) *crassicornis,* is white with bright blue

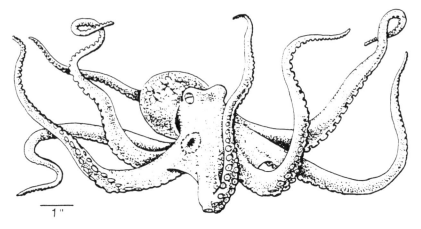

Figure 25. Two-spotted Octopus, *Octopus bimaculatus.* (From Hinton 1987.)

lines along the center of its back. This species feeds on sea anemones and their relatives. The anemones' sting cells are ingested intact, and they are translocated to the tips of the exposed gills, where they provide protection for the slow-moving but brightly colored mollusc. Nudibranchs are good examples of a phenomenon known as *warning coloration,* in which a brightly colored animal need not fear predators.

The largest predator of these lower tide pools is the Two-spotted Octopus, *Octopus bimaculatus* (Fig. 25). Individuals may measure up to 3 ft (1 m) across, but more likely they will be about half that size. An octopus grasps its prey with its tentacles and immobilizes it with venomous saliva. The saliva may be emitted into the water, in which case it affects the prey like an anesthetic; crabs are trapped and eaten in this way. The octopus can also drill a hole into an abalone shell with its filelike radula and inject the venom. The Two-spotted Octopus is capable of producing a painful bite when grabbed by a human, but this occurs only rarely. The octopus is famous for its ability to change color instantly. In the tide pools it usually remains out of sight under an overhanging ledge, but even when it is in the open it is difficult to see because its color so perfectly matches that of the background.

Octopus is considered a delicacy when properly prepared, but the animals are not easy to catch. Unfortunately, people have been known to attempt to bring an octopus out of hiding by pouring bleach into the water of a tide pool. This illegal practice causes great harm to all the animals in the intertidal system.

Fishes of the lower tide pools are usually kelplike in appearance and marvelously colored to remain nearly invisible. The most common is the

Wooly Tidepool Sculpin, *Clinocottus analis* (Fig. 32C), sometimes known as the Tidepool Johnnie. These fish remain motionless on the bottom most of the time. When they move, they often crawl, using their large pectoral fins; when they swim, it is only in a short burst. These sculpins feed primarily on detritus that accumulates in the tide pools.

Superficially similar to the Wooly Tidepool Sculpin is the California Klingfish, *Gobiesox rhessodon*. This little fish has an adhesive sucker on its underside that enables it to cling upside down under rocks of the low tide zone. Among the kelps, a diligent observer may notice the Spotted Kelpfish, *Gibbonsia elegans*. This is an elongated, kelp-colored fish with a long dorsal fin running almost to its tail and a prominent, eyelike spot above and behind the gill cover (operculum). This shy little fish resembles so well the kelp in which it hides that it is seldom seen. The Rockpool Blenny, *Hypsoblennius gilberti,* and its relative the Bay Blenny, *Hypsoblennius gentilis,* resemble the kelpfishes, but they are rounded rather than flattened in cross section. They have a short, stubby nose and a long, continuous dorsal fin. They are common in the lower intertidal zone, but they are seldom seen because they also hide in the kelp.

Subtidal Zone Offshore, beyond the influence of tides, is a zone where wave surge carries away fine sediments, such as silts or muds, leaving a rocky or sandy bottom. Anchored to rocks or sand by their large, rootlike holdfasts, huge kelps may grow in forests in water up to 100 ft (30 m) deep. Because of their flexible nature, kelps play an important role in moderating wave action, and this dispersal of wave energy helps to protect beaches from erosion.

In southern California the most common kelp is the Giant Bladder Kelp, *Macrocystis pyrifera* (Fig. 26). It is the largest of all known species of algae, and individual plants have been recorded at up to 200 ft (60 m) in length. Furthermore it is the fastest-growing kelp known: individual fronds can grow over 14 in. (35 cm) per day. Long, intertwined, stemlike stipes of giant kelp extend to the surface, where a canopy of wrinkled, leaflike blades is kept afloat by gas bladders located at the base of each blade.

On the outer fringe of the kelp beds of southern California, another species of giant kelp is usually seen only by scuba divers because it occurs at depths of about 100 ft (30 m). This is Elk Kelp, *Pelagophycus porra* (Fig. 27). It has a single, very long stipe that terminates at the surface in a gas bladder that may be 6 in. (15 cm) in diameter. This large kelp has blades about 1 m wide, which often lay upon the substrate like carpet runners. The blades attach to two branches that protrude like antlers from the bladder and give the plant its name. If storms break the slender stipe,

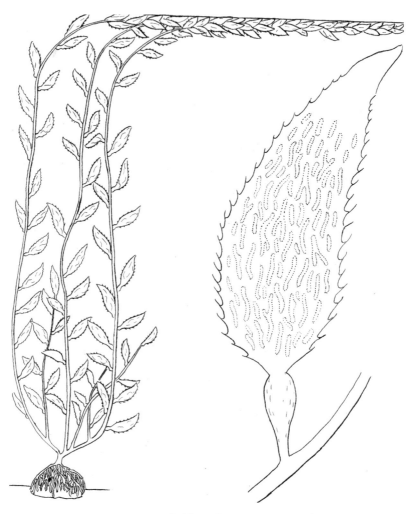

Figure 26. Giant Bladder Kelp, *Macrocystis pyrifera.*

the bladder will float away, and eventually the blades will break off, leaving only the large bladder and a portion of the stipe. Early Spanish seamen recognized the appearance of these bladders at sea as a sign they were approaching land. They called them *porra* ("club"), descriptive of the appearance of the bladder attached to a short section of stipe.

A low-growing, common brown alga known as Bladder-chain Kelp, *Crystoseira osmundacea,* occurs on rocky bottoms, usually in areas where kelp beds are not well developed. It has small, fernlike blades on the lower portion and delicate higher branchlets with four to ten bladders.

Red algae (Rhodophyta) grow in the deepest water. The red pigment reflects red light and absorbs light of other wavelengths, but at the depth

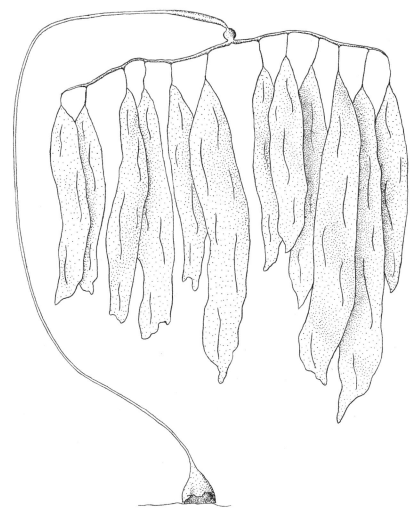

Figure 27. Elk Kelp, *Pelagophycus porra.*

where they grow there is no red light. They must therefore photosynthesize using only the deeply penetrating blue light. Red algae are effectively black where they grow, and this coloration helps to conceal them from herbivores in the dim light. Nevertheless, the Sea Hare, *Aplysia californica,* feeds heavily on a common and beautiful red alga known as *Plocamium cartilagineum. Plocamium* has a feathery or bushy appearance and a deep red or purplish-red color.

Other red algae that grow in deep water include agarweeds (*Gelidium* spp., *Pterocladia* spp.). These algae are sources of agar, a gelatin that is used as a culture medium for microorganisms and for making casts such as dental impressions. Because they live in deep water where there is a limited amount of illumination, agarweeds do not grow rapidly. Thus harvesting them shows only limited economic promise in California, although some are harvested from the waters around Santa Catalina. Visitors to the Isthmus sometimes see agarweeds drying on the beach before being baled. Nevertheless most commercial U.S. agar is imported from Japan.

From about Pismo Beach northward, Bull Kelp, *Nereocystis luetkeana,* becomes the dominant seaweed. This massive species has a long, hollow, hoselike stipe up to 115 ft (35 m) long, which ends in a single gas bladder. Above the bladder, long, flat, straplike blades up to 3 ft (1 m) in length extend into the water. As unlikely as it may seem, this is an annual species, attaining its enormous size within one year. Bull Kelp was an important food item for the Native Americans of the Pacific coast. They also made musical instruments from the hollow stipes and bladders; for example, a trumpet of sorts can be fabricated from a section of stipe and half a bladder.

Kelp beds provide a variety of habitats for animals. More than 750 species of fish and invertebrates live in these underwater forests. Among the invertebrates that inhabit the subtidal zone, none is more important commercially than the lobster. Lobsters are found in kelp forests, reefs, and tide pools from Point Conception southward. The California Spiny Lobster, *Panulirus interruptus,* lacks the large pincers of the Atlantic lobster—although it is by no means defenseless. If a lobster is grabbed barehanded, it can saw its antennae, with their spines, across the wrist of its captor. Furthermore the captive lobster will slap its tail back and forth vigorously, causing more sawteeth on the lower margin of the abdomen to cut like a mechanical hedgeclipper. Lobsters up to 3 ft (1 m) in length and weighing almost 30 lb (14 kg) have been captured, although today such monsters appear to be a thing of the past. In many areas, intensive fishing seems to crop them rapidly as they reach legal size.

Lobsters can move in any direction by walking. When they are in a hurry, however, they swim backwards with rapid flips of their muscular tails.

Lobsters feed on practically anything; in turn they are fed on by fishes and octopuses. They are omnivorous scavengers, feeding on dead or living plants and animals, and they are particularly important as predators of sea urchins and juvenile mussels. In fact, one of the mysteries of intertidal ecology was solved by underwater observations of nocturnally active Spiny Lobsters at Santa Catalina Island. A dense mat of kelp forms a conspicuous, unbroken belt along the shores of the Channel Islands. Why does a similar mat not occur on the nearby mainland? Many hypotheses had been proposed, relying on such causes as pollution, sea urchins, Santa Ana winds, and warm water temperatures. It turns out that on the islands, where the lobsters are extremely abundant (probably because of reduced fishing pressure), they feed heavily on juvenile mussels. Given enough time, adult, fully grown California Mussels are capable of occupying so much space on intertidal rocks that all other competitors are unable to become established on the bare spaces. On the islands, the nocturnal feeding forays of the abundant Spiny Lobsters effectively remove the juvenile mussels from the rocks, enabling the kelp to become established. Apparently, north of Point Conception, the Ochre Sea Star performs the same task.

A number of species of crabs are also characteristic of the subtidal zone. California's largest crab, the Sheep Crab, *Loxorhynchus grandis*, lives at the bottom of kelp beds, where it feeds on attached invertebrates or carrion. This member of the spider crab family (Majidae) may attain a legspread of 38 in. (96 cm). Similar to the Masking Crab, *Loxorhynchus crispatus*, with which it may coexist, a young Sheep Crab has a habit of camouflaging itself by covering its back with a variety of living invertebrates and algae. An adult Sheep Crab has very few enemies, and therefore large specimens are not decorated with camouflage.

Sea cucumbers (Holothuroidea) are other members of the phylum that includes starfish and sea urchins (Echinodermata). They are most common on sandy bottoms, where they mop up organic matter with their tentacles. In southern California, the Common Sea Cucumber, *Parastichopus californicus* (Fig. 28A), is an orange, pickle-shaped member of the subtidal community. In northern California, two species may be encountered: a large orange species, *Cucamaria miniata*, which is found subtidally, and a small black cucumber, *Cucamaria curata*, which is about an inch (25 mm) long and occurs in the mussel beds. A sea cucumber maintains its body shape by filling itself with seawater, utilizing a so-called *hydrostatic skeleton*. Its tube feet are reduced to a ring of tentacles around the mouth that are used to gather detritus. Sea cucumbers move around on the floor of kelp beds, where they feed heavily on broken pieces of kelp. They do not have many enemies, but when they are disturbed they eviscerate themselves, expelling most of their internal organs through the anus. It has been proposed that this habit is so disgusting that a would-be predator moves off in revulsion. A new set of internal organs can be regenerated in about six weeks.

On the rock faces a diver also often observes the Knobby or Giant Starfish, *Pisaster giganteus* (Fig. 28B), which may measure 18 in. (46 cm) across. In crevices a sea urchin, *Centrostephanus coronatus*, is common. This long-spined black urchin is inactive by day but forages away from its protective shelter during the night.

Many sheer rock faces around the islands are covered with Pink

Figure 28. Animals of the subtidal zone. (A) Common Sea Cucumber, *Parastichopus californicus*. (B) Knobby Starfish, *Pisaster giganteus*. (C) Wavy Top-shell, *Astraea undosa,* with hitchhiking gorgonian.

Anemones, *Corynactis californica*. Around the Channel Islands, these anemones occur in the subtidal zone to depths of 100 ft (30 m), whereas in the northern parts of their range in Sonoma County they are intertidal species. This is another small, aggregating anemone species in which the members of each cluster are clones. They are very beautiful, varying in color from pale yellow through deep orange-red. An unusual feature of their coloring is that they appear red even at depths of 100 ft (30 m), where red light is unable to penetrate. The color is due to fluorescence: the blue and ultraviolet light that penetrates to this depth is absorbed by the anemones and reemitted as red light, just as certain minerals fluoresce in ultraviolet light.

Two species of gorgonians or sea fans are commonly seen in the subtidal region, often attached to rocks or the shells of large snails such as the Wavy Top-shell, *Astraea undosa* (Fig. 28C) (this is another form of commensalism, in which the "hitchhiking" sea fan seems not to disturb the snail). *Muricea californica* has yellow polyps and *Muricea fructicosa* has red polyps. These colonial cnidarians are related to corals and feed on small planktonic organisms. Another filter feeder is a rock scallop, *Hinnites multirugosa*. This bivalve mollusc is usually firmly attached to a rock and often may be encrusted with algae or other invertebrates, such as sea fans. *Hinnites* is most readily observed when the shells (valves) are partially gaped, when the orange color of the mantle is readily visible. When the rock scallop is disturbed, the valves come together and the scallop seems to disappear.

A large, colorful snail found on Giant Kelp and the Southern Sea Palm is the Smooth Brown Turban, *Norissia norrisi.* The flesh of this snail is bright orange-red, and its rich brown shell has a bright green depression on the underside. A small species of snail known as the Turban Slipper Shell, *Crepidula norrisiarum,* is often found "hitchhiking" on the shell of the Brown Turban, in yet another example of commensalism. The Brown Turban appears to move up the kelp plant, grazing as it goes, until it reaches the surface. Once there it releases its hold on the plant, falls to the bottom, and begins its upward climb again. If by chance the Brown Turban becomes exposed to the air, it withdraws its soft parts into the shell and covers the opening with an *operculum,* a circular bit of shell attached to the top of its foot.

One of the most spectacular examples of the subtidal community in the Southern California Bight is that on Farnsworth Bank, a submarine pinnacle located off the southern shoreline of Santa Catalina Island. On this pinnacle, which has recently been designated a biological preserve, there are numerous species of invertebrates, including the Purple Coral, *Allopora stylantheca.* This species is also found along the mainland, but it reaches its most beautiful growth form on offshore pinnacles.

Once into the cool, clear waters of protected coves and bays, a diver will see a myriad of colorful fishes of many shapes and sizes. Since water visibility is often 50 ft (16 m) or more, observation of a wide spectrum of marine life is possible, and fishes are the most visible portion of the marine fauna in these clear waters.

Rocky bottoms are usually covered with seaweed or kelp that attracts the greatest number of fishes. Some, however, are only seen on sandy substrates, and several are common in small midwater aggregations as well as large schools.

There are more than 150 species of fishes along the California coast. Nearly all of them can be found at one time or another in the kelp beds, and some fifteen to twenty species are regularly found in the beds. Fishes are attracted to the kelp beds because of the abundant food supply; there they feed on invertebrates as well as each other. Small fishes such as Topsmelt, *Atherinops affinis* (Fig. 29A), use the kelp for refuge, feeding largely on plankton. These fishes, similar in appearance to Grunion, *Leuresthes tenuis,* are also in the silversides family (Atherinidae).

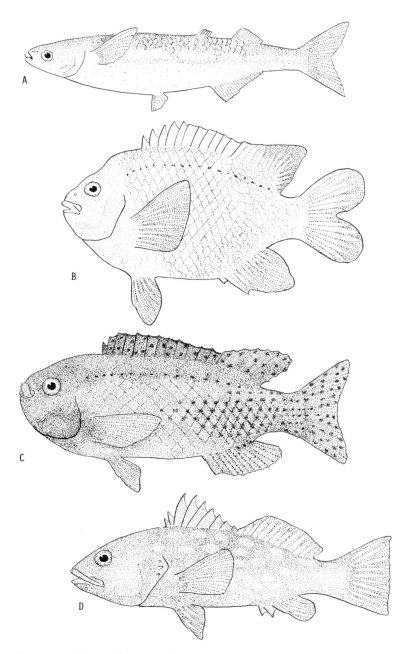

Figure 29. Fishes of the kelp beds. (A) Topsmelt, *Atherinops affinis*. (B) Garibaldi, *Hypsypops rubicundus*. (C) Blacksmith, *Chromis punctipinnis*. (D) Kelp Bass, *Paralabrax clathratus*. (E) California Sheephead, *Pimelometopon* (=*Semicossyphus*) *pulchrum*. (F) Señorita, *Oxyjulis californica*. (G) Rock Wrasse, *Halichoeres semicinctus*. (H) Opaleye, *Girella nigricans*. (I) Halfmoon, *Medialuna californiensis*.

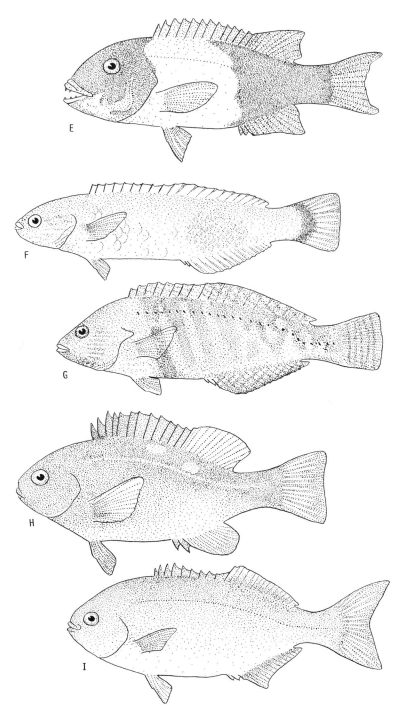

Figure 29. (*Continued*)

The Garibaldi, *Hypsypops rubicundus* (Fig. 29B), is the official state marine fish. Juveniles are sometimes seen in tide pools, particularly in the spring and early summer. Garibaldis are members of the tropical damselfish family (Pomacentridae). As juveniles these fish are a bright reddish-orange with very brilliant blue spots. As adults they are brilliant orange without the blue color, although there may be some blue on the edges of the fins. It is illegal to harm or capture them at any age. Adults reach about a foot (30 cm) in length. They are seldom seen in tide pools, but they are so common offshore that from any number of viewpoints above the sea they may be seen as glints of gold in the water. Indeed Goldfish Point in La Jolla gets its name from this phenomenon. The bright orange color is an advertisement, warning any other fish that it is in for a fight if it tries to invade the Garibaldi's territory, which is usually an offshore rock crevice or cave. Adults also seem curious, often bumping into a diver or swimming into the field of view as a diver attempts to take a photograph. The name *Garibaldi* is probably a reference to a loosely fitting red garment by that name that was popular in the 1890s; the garment was named for Giuseppe Garibaldi, an Italian patriot, who wore such a red shirt as a uniform.

Also in the damselfish family (Pomacentridae) is the Blacksmith, *Chromis punctipinnis* (Fig. 29C). This blunt-nosed fish, about the same size as the Garibaldi, is blue-black with black spots on its upper surface and dorsal fin. Blacksmiths swim in swarming schools at the upper edge of the kelp beds. Their upturned mouths are useful for feeding at the surface.

Blacksmiths often occur with brightly colored Señoritas, *Oxyjulis californica* (Fig. 29F). These are members of the large, mostly tropical, wrasse family (Labridae). Señoritas are long, thin fishes up to 10 in. (25 cm) in length, bright yellow with a black tail. They are the "cleaners" of the kelp beds, another example of commensalism. Señoritas pick parasites off other fishes, particularly the Blacksmiths and Garibaldis. Their bright color is an advertisement, and because their feeding activity is beneficial, other fishes seldom prey on them. In fact, "customers" may wait in line to be cleaned! When they are not cleaning, their preferred food is kelp blades covered with a mosslike animal (bryozoan) of the phylum Ectoprocta (*Membranipora membranacea*).

Another conspicuous member of the wrasse family is the California Sheephead, *Pimelometopon* (=*Semicossyphus*) *pulchrum* (Fig. 29E). Typical of many wrasses, the Sheephead has large, doglike teeth that are used to feed on starfish, sea urchins, lobsters, crabs, and many varieties of molluscs. When the tide is in, the California Sheephead is a major predator in the intertidal zone; lobster fishermen often describe how a sheephead will enter a lobster trap and destroy the catch. A male California Sheephead is a brightly colored fish with a black head and tail, a bright white chin, and a brick red midsection. The juvenile is a long, thin, fluorescent green fish with a bright yellow stripe down the lateral line. Young adults are all females, reddish brown all over. When they reach the age of seven to eight years they change sexes: females become males.

A smaller wrasse that is common above sandy bottoms near kelp beds is the Rock Wrasse, *Halichoeres semicinctus* (Fig. 29G). It is greenish brown, and the male has a vertical dark blue bar under the pectoral fin. Its general shape is similar to that of the Señorita, but it is usually much larger, reaching a length of up to 15 in. (37 cm).

The Opaleye, *Girella nigricans* (Fig. 29H), is a common fish often seen near shore. It can be distinguished by its dark olive green color with one or two white or yellow spots at the base of the dorsal fin; the eyes are opal blue. Young fishes frequent tide pools, whereas larger individuals usually occur at depths of 25 ft or less in kelp forest and rocky bottom areas, where they feed mainly on kelp. In certain areas around Avalon, such as the dock and Pebbly Beach, these fish will voraciously feed on bread crumbs thrown onto the water's surface.

A fish sometimes mistaken for Opaleye is the Halfmoon, *Medialuna californiensis* (Fig. 29I), often called the Blue Perch or Catalina Perch by fishermen. Halfmoons usually occur in groups of two or three individuals around kelp in midwater. Halfmoon, like Opaleye, feed mainly on kelp, but larger individuals, up to 19 in. (48 cm), will take most baits.

The surfperch family (Embiotocidae) is also well represented in the subtidal zone. One of the commonest fishes around rocky bottoms where attached algae are available is the Black Surfperch, *Embiotoca jacksoni* (Fig. 30A). This black or brown to reddish fish has dark vertical bars on its sides and a yellowish belly. Its length is up to 15 in. (38 cm) but most individuals measure half that. Another common surfperch is the Walleye Surfperch, *Hyperprosopon argenteum* (Fig. 30B), a silver surfperch often seen in schools over sandy bottom areas. Specimens grow to 12 in. in length and can be distinguished by their shape and large eyes. Around docks and pilings one often observes the Shiner Surfperch, *Cymatogaster aggregata* (Fig. 30C). This small surfperch is gray-green above and silver below and has three vertical yellow bars down its sides. In terms of sheer numbers, the Kelp Surfperch, *Brachyistius frenatus* (Fig. 30D), is one of the most abundant fish. This small golden surfperch occurs in dense schools in the kelp forest. It grows to 8 in. in length but is often only 3–5 in. long. A somewhat larger and more solitary fish is the Pile Surfperch, *Damalichthys vacca* (Fig. 30E), a silvery surfperch that reaches 17 in. (43 cm) in length and has a dark vertical bar at midbody and a long dorsal fin ray.

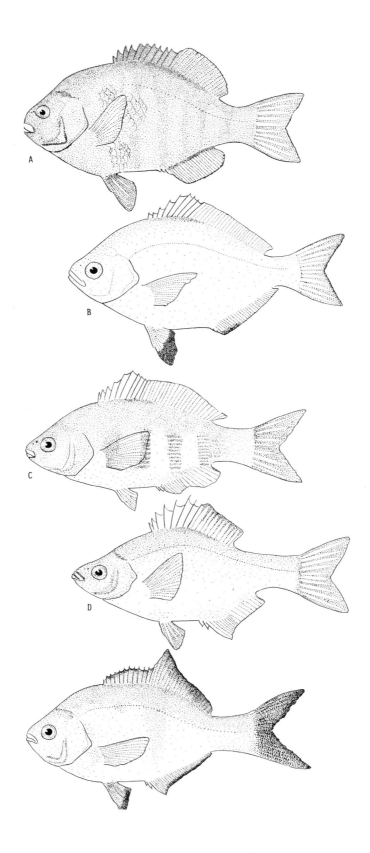

The fish probably most often observed by divers is the Kelp Bass, *Paralabrax clathratus* (Fig. 29D), which may be seen swimming among the stipes of the kelp along with the brightly colored Garabaldi. This distinctly colored fish forms a significant part of the sportfishing catch. Young Kelp Bass spend the fall and winter months in the kelp canopy, where they are well camouflaged. Similar in appearance, but more common in sandy areas, is the Barred Sand Bass, *Paralabrax nebulifer*. As is the case for the California Sheephead, many basses are females when they are young and change sexes when they are older.

Not to be confused with the basses of the family Serranidae, which they superficially resemble, the most common fishes of the California coast belong to the scorpionfish or rockfish family, Scorpaenidae. Many of these fishes forage on the bottom. Of particular interest in this niche is the California Scorpionfish, *Scorpaena guttata* (Fig. 31A). This fish is also known to many as a sculpin, but it is not a member of the sculpin family (Cottidae). California Scorpionfish are common in lower tide pools, where they lie motionless, concealed by their coloration, waiting for prey. Scorpionfish derive their name from the venomous spines on all of their median fins, which are designed to discourage predators. Fishermen who grab a scorpionfish without taking care to avoid the fins may receive a painful sting. The severity of individual reactions varies, but most describe a deep, numbing pain and a sensation of heat. Swelling may be extensive. Much to the dismay of lobster fishermen, scorpionfish also invade lobster traps.

The Cabezon, *Scorpaenichthys marmoratus* (Fig. 31B), superficially resembles the California Scorpionfish, and both fishes occur in the same habitat. The Cabezon, however, is smooth skinned, whereas the California Scorpionfish is scaly. The Cabezon is in the sculpin family (Cottidae). Although a common name for the California Scorpionfish is *sculpin,* it is not in the sculpin family, and furthermore the scientific name for the Cabezon means "scorpionfish." No wonder there is confusion! In Spanish, the name *Cabezon* means "big head." The diet of the Cabezon includes almost any animal of the right size that moves; it is also considered to be an important predator of abalones. The Cabezon moves in and out with the tides, migrating from kelp beds to the intertidal zone when the tide is in. It is not uncommon for a Cabezon to become trapped in a lower tide pool when the tide is out. It is capable of changing color to mimic its sur-

Figure 30 (*opposite*). Surfperches of the subtidal zone. (A) Black Surfperch, *Embiotoca jacksoni*. (B) Walleye Surfperch, *Hyperprosopon argenteum*. (C) Shiner Surfperch, *Cymatogaster aggregata*. (D) Kelp Surfperch, *Brachyistius frenatus*. (E) Pile Surfperch, *Damalichthys vacca*.

Figure 31. Rockfish of the California coast. (A) California Scorpionfish, *Scorpaena guttata*. (B) Cabezon, *Scorpaenichthys marmoratus*. (C) Kelp Rockfish, *Sebastes atrovirens*. (D) Treefish, *Sebastes serriceps*. Note: The Cabezon, a rockfish look-alike is actually in the sculpin family (Cottidae).

roundings so that it can lie in a crevice, where its mottled color makes it nearly invisible.

Several other species of rockfish are commonly observed by divers. The Kelp Rockfish, *Sebastes atrovirens* (Fig. 31C), is a mottled brown fish that attains a length of 16 in. (40 cm). It is seen most frequently in rocky habitats in ledges and crevices, feeding at night and remaining inactive during the day. This fish can often be closely approached by divers.

The Treefish, *Sebastes serriceps* (Fig. 31D), is usually seen in groups of six to eight near kelp beds, midway between the surface and the bottom. This rockfish is olive brown with light areas under the dorsal fin and reaches a maximum length of 24 in. (60 cm), although those fishes commonly seen around the islands are usually only 6–8 in. (20 cm) in length.

The Giant Kelpfish, *Heterostichus rostratus* (Fig. 32A), is relatively large (measuring up to 24 in. [60 cm]) and light brown to greenish in color, with white mottling. As do all members of the Kelpfish family (Clinidae), this fish has large fins that make it appear to be a piece of kelp. It is often camouflaged in the kelp and surf-grass, where it hides and stays quite still unless it is touched.

Similar in appearance to the "kelp-shaped" fishes already mentioned as residents of the lower intertidal zone are a series of well-camouflaged fishes that live farther offshore in the kelp beds. Among these is another member of the sculpin family (Cottidae), the Lavender Sculpin, *Leiocottus hirundo* (Fig. 32B), a distinctive fish that inhabits rocky bottoms in the kelp beds. This olive-green fish with blue shading is often mottled with red. It may reach a length of 10 in. (25 cm) and can always be distinguished by its elongated first dorsal spine.

The goby family (Gobiidae) is a group of generally bottom-dwelling fishes that superficially resemble the sculpins. Unlike the sculpins, however, these fishes have a peculiar suction cup formed by fusion of the pelvic fins on the front half of their undersides. A small goby (up to 6 in. [15 cm]), usually found resting on sand bottoms under protective rocks, is the Bluespot or Blackeye Goby, *Coryphopterus nicholsii* (Fig. 32D). It can readily be distinguished by its large black eyes and very light-colored body. One of the most beautiful fish observed by divers is the Catalina or Bluebanded Goby, *Lythripnus dalli* (Fig. 32E). This small, 2-in. (5-cm) fish is a bright orange-red with blue bands. Bluebanded Gobies are most often seen along rocky walls or near crevices, where they remain still. If approached too closely they immediately disappear into a hole or crack.

Also found on the bottom, among the stipes, is the California Moray, *Gymnothorax mordax* (Fig. 33A). It ranges from the Santa Barbara area south to Baja California. In spite of its large size (specimens up to 5 ft [1.5 m]

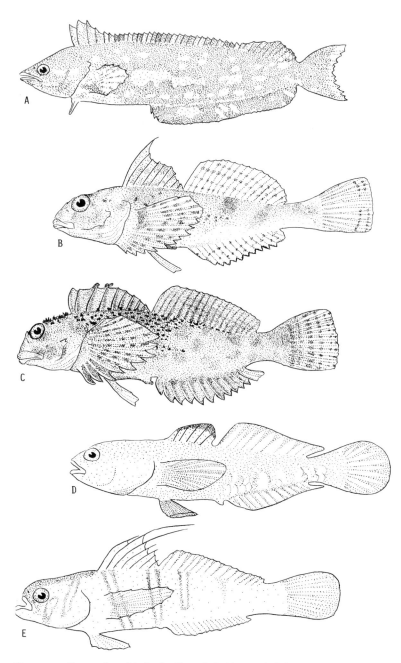

Figure 32. Camouflaged kelp dwellers. (A) Giant Kelpfish, *Heterostichus rostratus*. (B) Lavender Sculpin, *Leiocottus hirundo*. (C) Wooly Tidepool Sculpin, *Clinocottus analis*. (D) Bluespot or Blackeye Goby, *Coryphopterus nicholsii*. (E) Catalina or Bluebanded Goby, *Lythripnus dalli*.

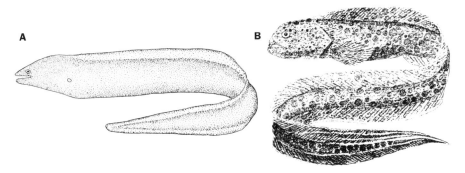

Figure 33. Eel-like fishes of California coastal waters. (A) California Moray, *Gymnothorax mordax*. (B) Wolf-eel, *Anarrhichthys ocellatus*. (Illustration B from Fitch and Lavenberg 1975.)

long have been reported), this eel-like fish is well adapted for swimming among tangled kelp stipes or for wriggling into cracks and hollows in the rocks. Morays spend the daylight hours among the rocks and forage for crabs, shrimps, and lobsters among the kelps during the night. Among divers, morays have a reputation for being aggressive. It is true that morays will bite divers, and it is true that the bite may require stitches, but the moray does not attack unless provoked. A moray protects its territory within the rocks, usually remaining in its crevice with only its head and jaws, armed with large teeth, visible at the entrance. Should a diver unwittingly put a hand into the home of a moray—for example, while feeling about in the cracks for lobsters—a painful bite will almost certainly be the result. A red shrimp, *Hippolysmata californica*, lives in similar areas, usually in association with the moray. The shrimp apparently clean parasitic copepods from the morays and probably also share some of their meals, another example of commensalism.

From about Point Conception northward, the Wolf-eel, *Anarrhichthys ocellatus,* a California Moray look-alike, lives in shallow, rocky areas. It seems to replace the California Moray in northern waters. South of Point Conception to San Diego County, this fish occurs farther offshore in deeper, colder water. It is not really an eel, but rather a member of the wolf-fish family (Anarhichadidae), closely related to the blennies; the Wolf-eel is the only member of this family that occurs in the eastern Pacific Ocean. The Wolf-eel provides an example of *parallel evolution.* It has moraylike habits and body shape, and it eats mostly crabs, sea urchins, snails, and abalone. It differs from the California Moray in having large, eyelike spots all over its body. The nose of the Wolf-eel is blunter (like that of a large blenny), and its eyes are larger and situated higher on its head.

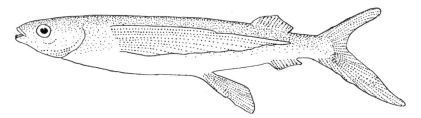

Figure 34. California Flying Fish, *Cypselurus californicus.*

The California Flying Fish, *Cypselurus californicus* (Fig. 34), is often associated with Santa Catalina, although it is found in open water throughout the Channel Islands. Earlier passengers on the big white steamship to Avalon would often see large numbers of them as the boat approached the island, and a launch equipped with a powerful spotlight allowed viewing at night. Although no longer as numerous, they may still be seen attracted to lights on summer nights and occasionally gliding along the surface during daylight hours. These fish are metallic blue above and silver below, and they reach a length of about 20 in. (45 cm). Their "flight" is made possible by long, winglike pectoral fins that allow gliding, and by the large caudal fin, which propels the fish to velocities that allow flight.

Sharks and rays (Chondrichthyes) are also frequently observed by divers. These "denizens of the deep" differ from the bony fishes (Osteichthyes) mentioned previously by having skeletons made of cartilage rather than bone, and by passing water over their gills by means of individual slits, rather than a single opening covered by an operculum. In general, sharks differ from rays because they propel themselves with their tail fins, whereas rays propel themselves with their expanded pectoral fins and steer with their tails.

Although the Great White Shark, *Carcharodon carcharias,* has a fearsome reputation that is deserved, it is not actually a commonly observed fish along the California coast. In recent years there has been an increase in the number of documented shark attacks on humans off the central California coast. Of particular concern are deaths caused by attacks of the Great White Shark. The cause of this increase is not certain, but some authorities relate it to the resurgence of marine mammal populations, particularly those of the Northern Elephant Seal. Others relate the attacks to the increased number of surfers riding small surfboards, the silhouettes of which, when viewed from below, might resemble a juvenile Northern Elephant Seal or sea lion.

During a period of continuous observations that documented many shark attacks off the Farallon Islands (see Chapter 9), one encounter between a Great White Shark and a human, an abalone diver, was recorded. The attack began like many of those on pinnipeds. The diver was about 650 ft (200 m) from shore in about 20 ft (6 m) of water, pausing to equalize pressure in his ears. The shark swam up underneath him, seized him by the leg, pulled him down for 5–7 sec, and then suddenly let go and swam off. The diver bled profusely while in the shark's grasp. He was able to hit the shark with the butt of a metal bang-stick at least three times, and that may have been the reason the shark did not return. There is other evidence to indicate that humans and other prey that have bodies consisting mainly of muscle may not be as desirable to sharks as pinnipeds, with their high fat content. Sea Otters, Brown Pelicans, and even fat-free sheep carcasses have not been as attractive to sharks as whales and seals.

The Horn Shark, *Heterodontus francisci* (Fig. 35A), is frequently sighted on sandy bottoms with scattered rocks. This small shark grows up to 4 ft (3.1 m) in length; it is gray-brown with dark speckling on the body, and a large spine occurs in front of each dorsal fin. Young sharks develop in a large (5- to 6-in. [15-cm]), screw-shaped egg case, which is often found lodged in a rocky crevice. Another shark often encountered by divers is the Swell Shark, *Cephaloscyllium ventriosum* (Fig. 35B). It rests on rocky ledges or crevices during the day and can be easily approached by a diver. This shark, which grows up to 3.5 ft (1 m) in length, is brownish with dark spotting. Its name refers to its ability to greatly inflate its body with water when harassed by a predator. The egg case of the Swell Shark is called a mermaid's purse, a name that well describes its shape.

The Pacific Angel Shark, *Squatina californica* (Fig. 35C), is a flat, gray to light brownish shark seen on sandy bottoms, where it settles into the sand for concealment. It reaches 5 ft (1.5 m) in length and has a skatelike body with gills located in a notch behind the head. Angel Sharks can be somewhat hostile when harassed and should be left alone.

One of the largest sharks around the Channel Islands is the Blue Shark, *Prionace glauca* (Fig. 35D), which is often seen by passengers on boats crossing the channel to Santa Catalina. It inhabits open, blue-water areas and is usually 3–6 ft (1–2 m) in length, although its maximum length is 13 ft (4 m). Although this shark is potentially dangerous to divers, it does not usually come into shallow-water areas.

The Leopard Shark, *Triakis semifasciata* (Fig. 35E), is commonly seen on the bottom in both kelp beds and sandy-bottom areas. It grows to over 6 ft (2 m) in length and is a dusky gray with heavy black mottled bars and spots on the body.

Rays are cartilaginous fishes whose pectoral fins are flattened into large wings. Rays propel themselves with their pectoral fins and steer with their

A

B

C

D

E

F

G

tails. The Round Stingray, *Urolophis halleri,* probably stings more humans than any other marine vertebrate. It is most common on sandy bottoms in lagoons and river mouths and off sandy beaches, places of the sort frequented by human swimmers. The venomous spine is located on top of the long, whiplike tail at the base of the terminal caudal fin. The attack is a defensive maneuver by the fish, usually occurring when the ray is stepped on. The animal reacts by whipping its tail reflexively, thrusting the serrated spine into its victim. Severe pain usually lasts for an hour or so but may continue for an entire day. The best treatment for the pain seems to be to soak the injured limb in a pan of hot water. A doctor's inspection is always advisable.

One of the most impressive fishes inhabiting the kelp forest community is the Bat Ray, *Myliobatis californica* (Fig. 35G). This large ray, with a "wingspread" of up to 4 ft (1.3 m), is very dark brown above and white below and is usually seen resting on sandy bottoms. The head and eyes are anterior to the large pectoral fins, and there is a venomous spine at the base of the small dorsal fin on the tail. Bat Rays are important predators on bottom-dwelling invertebrates. They have been observed to feed by constructing feeding pits about a foot (30 cm) deep in soft sediment. Apparently these large bottom-feeders migrate to deeper water during winter and return to shallow water during spring and summer; spawning in estuaries occurs during that time.

The Shovelnose Guitarfish, *Rhinobatos productus* (Fig. 35F), is actually a sharklike ray. This rather large fish is usually seen on sandy bottoms, where it conceals itself by settling into the sand. The head is longer than it is wide, a feature that readily distinguishes it from the Angel Shark. The Shovelnose Guitarfish usually reaches a size of up to 5 ft (1.5 m) and is a brownish gray.

MARINE MAMMALS

Mammals are air-breathing, fur-bearing animals. Because marine mammals have interacted with humans along the California coast for over two centuries, and because they are so conspicuous they deserve special mention. Seals and sea lions range out to sea to feed, but they return to the land to reproduce; therefore, they can be considered members of both the

Figure 35 (*opposite*). Sharks and rays of California coastal waters. (A) Horn Shark, *Heterodontus francisci.* (B) Swell Shark, *Cephaloscyllium ventriosum.* (C) Pacific Angel Shark, *Squatina californica.* (D) Blue Shark, *Prionace glauca.* (E) Leopard Shark, *Triakis semifasciata.* (F) Shovelnose Guitarfish, *Rhinobatus productus.* (G) Bat Ray, *Myliobatis californica.*

Figure 36. Sea Otters, *Enhydra lutris*.

intertidal and oceanic zones. The Sea Otter is a legitimate permanent resident of the subtidal zone. Whales, on the other hand, are oceanic species, but because travelers to and from the islands are likely to view them on occasion, a few comments about them are also in order.

Sea Otters

The Sea Otter, *Enhydra lutris* (Fig. 36), is a member of the weasel family (Mustelidae). Males are slightly larger than females, reaching lengths of over 4 ft (120 cm), including their 10- to 12-in. (25- to 30-cm) tails. Although large males have been recorded as weighing up to 86 lb (39 kg), average weights range from 44 to 64 lb (20–29 kg).

Sea Otters live in a cold environment. Their beautiful, fine fur has been prized for years. Yet in spite of the insulating qualities of this fur, Sea Otters must eat a remarkable amount of food in order to keep warm: they consume about 25 percent of their body weight each day.

These comical animals are truly a delight to watch. They float on their backs in the kelp beds, and they seem to feed constantly. Their preferred food items are sea urchins, crabs, and abalone; in sandy beach areas they also eat clams. A Sea Otter swims to the ocean bottom, where it uses a rock to dislodge its prey. Back on the surface it swims on its back with the rock on its chest, using the rock to crack the shells. The Sea Otter's prodigious appetite has become the basis for a new controversy, for shellfish fishermen now fear that the otter will put them out of business.

In fact the history of Sea Otters in California has always been closely tied to the activities of humans. At one time, otters ranged in a continuous arc from Japan to Baja California. Biologists estimate that 200 years ago the California herd numbered about 20,000. By the turn of the twentieth century hunters had reduced the otter herd to perhaps fourteen animals that lived near Point Sur. Hunting was outlawed in 1911 by the Fur Seal Treaty with Russia, Japan, and Great Britain, and in 1913 otters were further protected in California by state law. Nevertheless the species was feared to be extinct in California until a group of about a hundred animals was "rediscovered" in 1938 during construction of Highway 1 along the coast. In 1941 a California Sea Otter Game Refuge was established, and in 1959 it was enlarged to include the area from the mouth of the Carmel River south to the mouth of Santa Rosa Creek near Cambria. Sea Otters responded well to their new level of protection, and by 1976 the Sea Otter herd had increased to an estimated 1700 individuals. In 1977 the federal government listed the Sea Otter as a threatened species and outlawed the use by commercial fishermen of gill nets in shallow coastal water. Nevertheless, the herd has failed to expand significantly since the 1970s. Carrying capacity of the refuge may have been reached, pollution in the Southern California Bight may be a problem, or perhaps the cause remains incidental catch in gill nets set near Sea Otter habitats.

In recent years there has been a dramatic increase in offshore drilling and tanker transport of oil along the California coast. Experts fear that an oil spill could threaten the Sea Otter herd because the insulating and buoyancy-promoting properties of Sea Otter fur could be lost if it were soiled with oil. Authorities propose that, as a buffer against catastrophe, a portion of the herd should be moved to a second locality. In order to reduce economic impacts to a minimum, the U.S. Fish and Wildlife Service proposed translocating about 250 otters to San Nicolas Island, where they would be released in a region known to be within their historic range and also rich in shellfish.

Commercial fishermen countered that about 11 percent of Santa Barbara's abalone and lobster catch comes from San Nicolas Island, and that introduction of the Sea Otter would certainly put them out of business. In support of their case they also implicated the Sea Otter in the disappearance of the Pismo Clam, south of the present refuge. Some biologists responded to that claim by explaining that it was in fact the extermination of Sea Otters from the area that had kept the abalone, lobster, and clam populations artificially large, and that commercial fishermen had simply been lucky to have had it so good all those years. Starting in 1987 and for a period of three years, a total of 139 Sea Otters were captured off the mainland, flown to San Nicolas Island, and released. The biggest unforeseen problem was that most of the Sea Otters chose not to remain near the island. As of 1995, the total population on the island numbered only ten to fifteen Sea Otters, although reproduction was taking place and biologists have determined that these animals use the island as their home site.

Seals and Sea Lions

There are six species of seals and sea lions along the California coast, and it has been claimed that the California islands support a more varied population of seals and sea lions than any other area in the world that is conveniently accessible by humans. These marine mammals are grouped into two families. Although they superficially resemble each other, they are easy to tell apart if one knows what to look for. Earless seals or true seals (Phocidae) have no visible external ears. Eared seals (Otariidae), including sea lions, have small, visible, external ears. Furthermore earless seals swim in a fishlike manner with a side-to-side motion of the torso and hind flippers. Eared seals swim with a birdlike flapping of their front flippers and steer with their hind flippers. When any of these animals is on land, anatomical differences associated with these two modes of swimming are obvious. Earless seals have small, clawed front flippers; on land their hind flippers project backward, so they move themselves by lurching wormlike on their bellies. Eared seals have large, winglike front flippers, and they can bring their hind flippers forward to support their weight. On land they walk on all fours with a side-to-side, swinging motion.

Earless seals include hair seals and elephant seals. Worldwide there are seven species of hair seals (*Phoca*). In general, these are the animals whose babies are born on the ice in polar latitudes. They have received worldwide attention because of the demand for their fine white fur, which has led to the clubbing to death of the babies while they are on the ice. The local Harbor Seal, *Phoca vitulina* (Fig. 37; Plate 2C), is the only member of the group that routinely does not have babies with white fur; the white fur is lost either while the young are still in the uterus or shortly after birth. However, the Harbor Seal has not escaped notoriety, for it has been suggested that its feeding habits pose a threat to commercial fisheries. In northern latitudes Harbor Seals feed heavily on small fishes, and in California waters they also feed on octopus.

Biologists estimate that there are about 18,000–20,000 Harbor Seals in California. The seals are so named because they are frequently observed in protected inlets, bays, or river mouths. They seem not to tolerate human disturbance, and they will flee to deeper water when approached by a boat. Harbor Seals also haul out on rocks or reefs, or in waterline caves, where

Figure 37. Harbor Seal, *Phoca vitulina.*

they may feel secure. They haul out on all of the California islands through-out the year, although the largest populations are on San Miguel, Santa Cruz, and Santa Rosa, where numbers up to 1200 have been counted. Typ-ically they occur in groups of a few dozen or so, although they may aggregate in groups of over a hundred at certain preferred sites.

Males and females are similar in appearance. They are mottled, with numerous small black and white spots. The color darkens considerably when they are wet. Males are slightly larger (up to 6 ft [2 m] in length) and weigh up to 300 lb (136 kg).

Unlike other seals and sea lions, Harbor Seals seem not to have an elab-orate social structure, nor do they maintain breeding harems. They are some-times described as monogamous, but they are actually promiscuous: males will mate with any female that is in heat, and females may mate with more than one male. There is some evidence of a dominance hierarchy among males. The male will only defend the female if he has not yet mated. Mat-ing usually takes place in the water, and the female is left to fend for her-self after copulation is accomplished. A female gives birth to a single pup in the spring, between February and May. Young are precocial: they are able to swim as soon as they are born, and they nurse for only about four weeks.

Harbor Seals are well adapted for diving. They can dive to depths of 1000 ft (300 m) and remain submerged for up to 23 min. As do other seals, they exhale before diving; thus only a small amount of air is carried below, enabling them to dive deeply and surface rapidly without experiencing the bends. (The *bends* is the informal name for the decompression sickness that results from the presence of nitrogen bubbles in the blood of humans when they return to the surface too quickly after breathing compressed air.) Instead, oxygen is stored in the seals' blood and tissues. Their blood volume is large, and when they dive their spleen and liver are capable of storing the oxygenated blood. While they are under water their heart rate drops from about 55 to 15 beats per minute. In the absence of oxygen their tissues accumulate lactic acid, tripling the concentration of lactic acid in their blood. When they surface and breathe again, they metabolize this lactic acid rapidly in their heart, lungs, and brain.

The Northern Elephant Seal, *Mirounga angustirostris,* is the largest seal in the Northern Hemisphere. A large male (Fig. 167) may attain a length of 16 ft (5 m) and weigh up to 5000 lb (2200 kg). Females are about two-thirds the size of males. Adult males may be distinguished by their bizarre foot-long (30-cm) snouts, which they use as resonating chambers to amplify their vocalizations.

The former distribution of the Northern Elephant Seal extended from Baja California to Point Reyes, north of San Francisco. However, because of their valuable blubber they were hunted nearly to extinction. One 16-ft male reportedly would yield 245 gallons (925 liters) of precious oil, which was used as a lamp fuel. By 1892 the population was estimated to number less than 100 individuals. Hunting stopped in the late 1800s when the animals became so scarce that it required too much effort to locate them, and as petroleum products began to replace seal oil as fuel for lamps. Hunting was prohibited altogether by the 1911 Fur Seal Treaty. In 1930 a small colony of Northern Elephant Seals was discovered on Guadalupe Island, 157 miles (252 km) from the Baja California mainland, and from that group of seals the population has made a remarkable recovery. At the present time it has rebounded to more than 90,000 individuals, and it is still increasing. The largest breeding colonies (rookeries) are on San Miguel, Santa Barbara, and San Nicolas Islands, but now the seals also reproduce on the mainland at Año Nuevo near Santa Cruz and as far north as the Point Reyes Peninsula. Favorite viewing points include Año Nuevo and the Farallon Islands.

Elephant seals practice a type of polygamy known as *polygyny,* in which males keep a harem. Males engage in fierce battles in order to establish dominance and maintain access to females. They face each other on land or in shallow water (Fig. 38) and then raise their chests, throw back their heads, and make loud clapping noises with their snouts extended

Figure 38. Male Northern Elephant Seals, *Mirounga angustirostris*, battling for dominance.

into their open mouths. If such a threat does not settle the matter, they press against each other chest to chest and lash downward at each other's necks with their upper canine teeth. The necks and chests of elder males are covered with thick, scarred skin, presumably the result of many such encounters, which helps to protect them during these fights. Once dominance has been established, a male inseminates a harem of ten to a hundred females. Subdominant males tend to remain on the periphery of a breeding colony. Sometimes a subdominant male will be able to copulate with one of the females, but about 85 percent of the females are fertilized by only 4 percent of the males. Nevertheless the contribution of these so-called "sneak males" is important in maintaining genetic variation in the population.

Aggregations of breeding seals on beaches are called *rookeries.* Rookeries begin to form in December, and mating and childbirth take place during winter. Some authorities contend that the only factor limiting the population size of these huge mammals is the amount of space available on the beach for childbirth. Females begin to appear on the beach first. As soon as males arrive, the fights begin. Once a harem has been formed the male will defend his access to the females in his harem whether it is in water or on land. Males defend access to the females themselves, not to the space they occupy on land. Throughout most of the winter months, elephant seals remain in or near the rookeries. During this time they molt, and when they haul out on the beach they spend most of their time sleeping.

The value of basking and/or sleeping by large mammals is subject to some debate. Studies of their physiological state during basking show that heart and breathing rates diminish considerably and that body temperature drops 10–15°F (5–9°C) during this time. Conservation of energy seems to be the primary value of this behavior: for every 16°F (10°C) drop in body temperature, metabolic rate is cut in half. Other studies imply that basking by elephant seals is necessary to stimulate hair growth during this period of molting. It is hypothesized that the basking activity warms the skin, enhancing the blood flow to the surface that is necessary for the growth of new hair. Although their fur probably plays a minimal role in keeping these animals warm, its principal value must be for purposes other than thermoregulation, for the most effective insulation is the thick layer of subcutaneous blubber.

The growth rate of young Northern Elephant Seals is remarkably rapid. At birth, they are not very much larger than Harbor Seal pups. They nurse for about four weeks, during which time their mothers lose about 30 percent of their body weight. Juveniles drink about a gallon (4 liters) of milk a day. The milk is very rich, containing about 45 percent fat; in comparison, cow's milk is only about 4 percent fat, and human milk is slightly lower in fat. During the first few weeks of life, pups remain on the beach. Later they enter the water from time to time. Once they are weaned, mother-child interactions are minimal. By this time the pup has become remarkably fat, its weight having usually quadrupled.

Where Northern Elephant Seals go after they leave their rookeries is poorly understood, but they are known to travel great distances. Young animals, three to four months old, are known to migrate from Guadalupe Island to San Miguel Island in the Channel Island group, a distance of nearly 600 miles (950 km). Apparently Northern Elephant Seal herds disperse, to spend most of their time at sea. During spring and summer, they are constantly at sea. Females seem to go to the open sea to feed in deep water. Males appear to feed along the continental shelf near the Aleutian Islands, some 1800 miles (3000 km) north of their northernmost breeding ground.

Several females equipped with recording instruments were found to spend up to 90 percent of their time under water during the time they were at sea, an interval that averaged 72 days. Little is known of their eating habits, but based on their behavior in very deep water, it appears that

Figure 39. California Sea Lion, *Zalophus californianus.*

they feed on squid and other organisms that inhabit the oceanic zone at the lower reaches of light penetration. They have very large eyes, a characteristic that implies that they see well in the dim light of deep water. They are also capable of diving deeply and remaining under water for up to 45 min: individuals equipped with recording devices routinely dive to depths in excess of 3000 ft (900 m), and one dive estimated to have reached a depth of at least 4650 ft (1500 m) has been reported.

The California Sea Lion, *Zalophus californianus* (Fig. 39; Plate 2C), is the most common eared seal on the California coast. These are the trained "seals" that perform in the circus. The name *sea lion* refers not only to the animals' breeding and social behavior, in which males fight for dominance and keep a harem of females, but also to the appearance of the dominant male, which in some species has a large, thick mane of yellowish hair on his neck and chest, somewhat like that of a male African Lion. Male sea lions maintain a territory primarily on land, fighting to keep the area clear of subdominant males. Dominant males are conspicuously larger than females: they may attain a length of 8 ft (2.5 m) and weigh 600 lb (280 kg); females grow to a length of 6 ft (2 m), but they seldom weigh over 200 lb (90 kg). An adult male, with his huge chest and large head, may appear quite regal as he maintains a position on a high perch amid a harem of ten to twenty females and juveniles. Adults are tan when they are dry, but dark brown to black when they are wet.

California Sea Lions are not as well insulated as seals or Sea Otters, having neither thick fur nor a thick layer of blubber. Consequently they tend to remain in tropical and subtropical areas of the world. Subspecies of the California Sea Lion also occur in Japan and the Galápagos Islands, but distribution of the species does not extend northward beyond Vancouver Island in British Columbia. About 90 percent of the population of the California subspecies breeds on San Miguel and San Nicolas Islands, with the remainder on San Clemente and Santa Barbara Islands, although individuals will haul out at various times of the year on all of the Channel Islands.

Even though they do not have the insulation of seals, it appears that the high metabolic rate of sea lions more than compensates for that deficiency. Their body temperature is not known to fall when they are basking; in fact it appears that they are more concerned about keeping cool. On warm days they frequently wet themselves in tide pools or roll in wet sand, behaviors that increase evaporative cooling. After a period of exercise in the water, they float on their sides with one front and one hind flipper out of the water, a behavior that also assists in evaporative cooling. Where the water is cold, sea lions apparently are able to reduce heat loss by holding dry flippers out of the water. Fur seals also do this, and sometimes they grasp their front and hind flippers together in a position that reminded sailors in olden times of a jug handle. Thus the behavior became known as "jugging."

Breeding aggregations of California Sea Lions begin to form in May. Unlike elephant seals, sea lions breed and give birth in the spring. As with elephant seals, mating and birth take place on land. Pups nurse for about four months on milk that is nearly 16 percent fat. Each female knows her own pup and keeps track of it by its odor and vocalizations. At first, newborn pups have black pelage, which may enhance heat absorption on land; by the end of the first year the hair has taken on the tan color of the adult. After the breeding season, about mid-August, California Sea Lions disperse up and down the coast from their rookeries, appearing along the coast singly or in small groups. There is some evidence that males tend to go northward and females southward.

Sea lions are thought to feed primarily at night. They have been known to dive to a depth of over 900 ft (300 m), although they probably feed closer to the surface than most of the earless seals. Their eyes are relatively large, a trait that seems to indicate that they use vision to locate prey. In addition, the movement and sounds of prey are picked up by their whiskers (vibrissae) as vibrations in the water. Experiments have indicated that sea lions' whiskers are about 10,000 times more sensitive than their ears. They prey upon schooling animals such as anchovies, squid, and shrimp. Estimates of the amount of food eaten per day vary from 2 to 30 lb (1–14 kg). A 600-lb (280-kg) sea lion in a New York zoo was fed nearly 100 lb (45 kg) of fish each week, but this sea lion was no doubt relatively inactive and therefore required less food than would a free-ranging animal at sea.

A peculiar feature of sea lions is that many have been found with rocks in their stomachs. One specimen in a zoo had 69 lb (31 kg) of stones in its stomach! Theories regarding the function of these stones vary considerably. It has been suggested that sea lions use the stones as a ballast or to suppress appetite. It also has been proposed that the stones aid in breaking up fish bones or at least in their defecation. Perhaps the stones help to grind up the parasitic worms that often plague sea lions.

The actual number of sea lions along the California coast is subject to some controversy. Commercial collectors began capturing sea lions for zoos, circuses, and aquaria in 1878, taking most of the animals from Anacapa, San Miguel, and Santa Cruz Islands. Perhaps 3000 had been taken for that purpose by 1955. Since that time, hunting has ceased and the numbers of sea lions in the wild have increased. Estimates of the total number today vary from about 50,000 to 200,000. Since the late 1970s consistently conducted population surveys seem to have produced a reliable estimate of population numbers. According to personnel at the National Marine Fisheries Service, as of 1996 the total number of California Sea Lions in the United States was around 200,000 and increasing by about 6–8 percent per year.

Mortality of California Sea Lion pups is usually fairly high, with about 45 percent of the newborns dying of natural causes in any given year. During El Niño years, however, the number is inordinately high. The problem, it seems, is that the forage fishes and squid disappear with the warming of the water, but the marine mammals still breed on the same beaches. Invasions of the pelagic Red Crab, *Pleuroncodes planipes,* also eaten by many sea birds, seem not to help the marine mammals, because large concentrations of these crabs seldom reach all the way to the outer islands. Consequently females, which require a steady food supply in order to produce sufficient milk, are unable to do so, and the pups die by the thousands. This trend was documented during the El Niño of 1982–83, but it was particularly severe during the winter of 1997–98. Precise mortality records were tracked only on San Miguel Island, but of the 23,000 California Sea Lions born that year, about 70 percent died of starvation. A similar trend was observed for Northern Fur Seals, in which an estimated 75 percent of the 2000 pups were found dead.

Interactions between sea lions and fishermen in California have been controversial since the early 1920s. The population was provided protection by the state in the 1930s and by the federal government with the passage of the Marine Mammal Protection Act in 1972. In recent years the number of sea lions hauling out on local beaches has increased. By 1996, to the delight of tourists but the exasperation of fisherman, up to 400 young male California Sea Lions at a time had begun hauling out in the harbor at Monterey Bay.

The increase in the number of sea lions and fishermen has resulted in increasing conflicts. Before 1994 commercial fishermen could obtain a permit allowing them to take necessary measures, including killing, in order to protect their gear and catch. Since then they have been permitted only to scare sea lions away using loud firecrackers and other nonlethal means. Sportfishermen were not permitted even to take those steps, but in 1986 the federal government began permitting operators of sportfishing boats to use nonlethal harassment to keep sea lions away from the fishing lines of their customers. Various government agencies are cooperating in studies to devise methods to reduce the number of interactions between sea lions and fishermen.

The Northern Sea Lion or Steller's Sea Lion, *Eumetopias jubatus* (Fig. 40; Plate 2D), occurs from San Miguel Island northward. This is a large, tawny-colored sea lion; a large, breeding male possesses a tawny golden mane like that of an African Lion, hence the name *sea lion* (Plate 2D). The range of the California Sea Lion overlaps that of the larger Northern Sea Lion as far north as Vancouver Island. During summer, however, most adult California Sea Lions move southward to their rookeries. Northern Sea Lions usually occupy remote, rocky coasts, so they are not conspicuous to humans. They can, however, be observed at Sea Lion Caves in Oregon or on Año Nuevo Island, or sometimes at Seal Rocks by the Golden Gate.

Populations of Northern Sea Lions off the southern California coast have diminished since the 1930s. Data are inconclusive, but during the late 1920s it appears they were more common than California Sea Lions. The decline on the Channel Islands began about 1938, when the population was estimated to number about 2000 during the summer on San Miguel, Santa Cruz, and Santa Rosa Islands. The cause of the decline is not well understood, but it may have been related to a gradual warming of the water.

Figure 40. Northern Sea Lions, *Eumetopias jubatus*.

Other possible causes include competition from expanding populations of California Sea Lions and the effects of pesticides such as DDT. By 1976 the population on the Channel Islands, particularly San Miguel, had dropped to about fifty animals, and it has not recovered significantly since. The last Northern Sea Lions on the Channel Islands were seen on San Miguel in 1984. Yet the Channel Islands represent the southernmost portion of the range, and large population fluctuations are not uncommon at the periphery of an animal's range. On the Farallon Islands, the mortality of Northern Sea Lion pups has increased markedly: by 1982 two-thirds of the pups were dying. Perhaps slight changes in the environment or food supply are able to stress them in the southern portion of their range. Throughout their entire range, including most of the north Pacific, there are about 250,000 of these majestic animals, including about 1600 individuals in northern California.

The male (bull) Northern Sea Lion can reach a length of 13 ft (4 m) and a weight of 2000 lb (900 kg)—over twice the size of a male California Sea Lion. A female Northern Sea Lion is about the size of a male California Sea Lion. The social behavior of Northern Sea Lions is similar to that of

California Sea Lions. They can dive to a depth of 600 ft (190 m), and they feed on such prey as squid and herring.

The other two species of eared seals that occur off California are known as fur seals. Northern Fur Seals, *Callorhinus ursinus,* are primarily winter visitors, although a small colony is present year-round on San Miguel Island. Most of the time Northern Fur Seals will be seen in a small group in the open ocean 10–50 miles (16–80 km) offshore. They can be distinguished from sea lions by their short gray noses, long flippers, and thick fur. These southern migrants are usually females and juveniles; males tend to remain in northern waters. Major breeding rookeries are on the Pribilof Islands in the Bering Sea, and adults return each year to their place of birth. Their round-trip migrations of 6000 miles (9600 km) are among the longest of any mammal species.

In common with other fur-bearing mammals, Northern Fur Seals were hunted almost out of existence for their high-quality fur. It was only treaties regulating the killing of fur seals that enabled them to rebound. In the 1960s a breeding colony of the seals was discovered on San Miguel Island, and within twenty years its size had increased to almost 4000 animals; however, as of 1986 the number of births in this species was again in decline. There are now about a million Northern Fur Seals in U.S. waters; up to 11,000 of them breed on San Miguel Island, producing about 2000–3000 pups per year. As mentioned previously, during the El Niño episode of 1997–98 some 75 percent of the year's pups died of starvation.

Perhaps the species will return in abundance to southern waters. In 1996 a Northern Fur Seal bull, three females, and a pup were discovered on the Farallon Islands, and winter sightings at sea indicate that at least some animals are apparently not migrating to the Arctic. Archaeological excavations indicate that Northern Fur Seals historically occurred on the Channel Islands. It thus may be that this rise and fall in numbers is part of the normal population fluctuations of the species.

The Guadalupe Fur Seal, *Arctocephalus townsendi,* originally inhabited a range that extended from Monterey Bay to the Revillagigedo Islands of Mexico; the northernmost breeding rookeries were likely on San Miguel Island. These seals also resemble sea lions, but they can be distinguished by their long, collie-like muzzle; long, narrow flippers; and thick, dark fur. They were once hunted ruthlessly for their fur, and by 1895 were thought to be extinct. In 1926 a few were reported on Guadalupe Island off Baja California. In 1928, two males from Guadalupe Island were collected for the San Diego Zoo. They died in captivity, and the species was once again thought to be extinct. In 1949 a lone male was reported on San Nicolas Island, but it was not until 1954 that a small breeding colony, consisting of fourteen animals in a cave, was once again discovered on Guadalupe Island. Since that time, the population has grown to over 1600 animals, and their range appears once again to be expanding northward. Lone males have been observed as far north as San Miguel and San Nicolas Islands, and a few individuals have been seen on San Clemente and Santa Barbara Islands.

Most likely it was not the fur treaties that protected Guadalupe Fur Seals. They were saved by their very rarity, which by the turn of the century made it unprofitable to hunt for them. The seals were provided protection in 1928, when Guadalupe Island was designated a nature preserve by Mexico. Hunting was banned outright by Mexico in 1966, and the species was afforded protection by the United States with the passage of the Marine Mammal Protection Act in 1972. Additional protection was provided in 1985, when the species was listed as threatened by the federal government. Population recovery was also facilitated by the seals' habit of hauling out in dark, inaccessible caves. Perhaps continued protection will enable them to reestablish a breeding population on the Channel Islands.

The question of how it is possible for all these marine mammals seemingly to coexist on a few beaches along the California coast is a legitimate one. It is particularly perplexing when one realizes how many of them haul out on only two islands, San Miguel and San Nicolas. Recent studies on diet, diving, and migration reveal that their coexistence represents a classic case of niche partitioning. Sea Otters forage close to shore, primarily on shellfish. Northern Elephant Seals are only in California waters for a few months, primarily to breed. During this time, with the exception of lactating females, they do very little feeding; after the breeding season they move to the north Pacific, where, for most of the year, they feed at great depth, primarily on squid. Harbor Seals feed primarily on octopus and fish, which they harvest at medium depths. California Sea Lions and Northern Fur Seals feed mostly at night, waiting for the nocturnal migration of fishes to depths nearer the surface. Furthermore they tend to feed offshore, in the vicinity of upwellings. Northern Fur Seals and Northern Sea Lions feed farther north, and there is some evidence that Northern Fur Seals tend to feed farther out at sea. Furthermore the peak abundance of each species does not occur at the same time. Numbers of Northern Elephant Seals peak first, followed by those of Harbor Seals, California Sea Lions, and Northern Fur Seals in that order. So, by reducing overlap in foraging niches, large populations of marine mammals coexist in California waters while simultaneously seeming to overwhelm the unique and limited terrestrial habitats of the offshore islands.

When we view the conflict between humans and marine mammals, we realize that humans' view of the animals depends on whether or not they are attempting to make a living from the harvesting of marine life. Many would like to see marine mammals harvested for their fur, blubber, or meat. Others would like to reduce their numbers because they compete with humans for fish, clams, abalone, or lobsters. There is no question that unregulated hunting at one time decimated the number of marine mammals, and that since they have been provided protection their numbers have increased. If they eventually become so abundant that they do interfere with the natural order of things, it is possible that they could be hunted in a regulated way, as are such terrestrial game animals as deer. Critics of this idea contend that the economic importance of seals, sea lions, and sea otters is trivial compared with the stabilizing effect they exert as top carnivores in the coastal ecosystem. Another benefit that is often overlooked is that these animals, by feeding in deep water and returning to the surface to eliminate wastes, actually perform an important function in bringing nutrients to surface waters. The maintenance of ecological equilibrium in the ocean benefits all of mankind. Killing sea otters, seals, and sea lions in order to assure the economic protection of a few hundred fishermen makes very little sense.

Whales

There are two kinds of whales: toothed whales and baleen whales. Toothed whales include Sperm Whales (*Physeter macrocephalus*), Killer Whales (*Orcinus orca*), and porpoises or dolphins. Sperm Whales and Killer Whales are not frequently sighted near the islands of southern California: about 95 percent of the sightings occur north of Monterey Bay, although during the winter of 1996 Killer Whales made a well-documented appearance in the Southern California Bight. The reason for this appearance is unknown, but Killer Whales seem to prefer cold water in the vicinity of abundant food, which for them includes seals, sea lions, and larger fish species.

Porpoises and dolphins are merely smaller versions of the toothed whales. The difference between a porpoise and a dolphin is the source of ongoing controversy. In general, a dolphin has an extended beak, whereas a porpoise has a bluntly rounded snout. Using these criteria, a Killer Whale would be considered a large porpoise, but it is in the dolphin family (Delphinidae). The only true porpoise (family Phocoenidae) occasionally seen in California waters is the small Harbor Porpoise, *Phocoena phocoena*. Three species of dolphins are common enough to merit description here. The Common Dolphin, *Delphinus delphis,* is the most frequently seen, often riding the bow waves of boats. This small species, about 8 ft (1.5 m) long, is black or brownish on top and lighter on its sides. A distinctive identifying mark is a narrow, dark line that runs from the corner of its mouth to the base of its flipper on each side. Its dorsal fin is sickle-shaped (falcate) and colored. The White-sided Dolphin, *Lagenorhynchus obliquidens,* may at first appear to be a porpoise because its beak is small and may not be visible as the animal leaps acrobatically from the water. At 6 ft (2 m) in total length, the White-sided Dolphin is a bit larger than a Common Dolphin, and its sickle-shaped dorsal fin is frequently whitish. In addition, its white sides are conspicuous when it leaps. These dolphins frequently occur in large numbers, but they are more commonly viewed away from the islands in the open sea. The Bottlenose Dolphin, *Tursiops truncatus,* is a dull-colored dolphin with a stout, distinctive beak. At sea, members of the species usually travel in small groups. At about 14 ft (4 m) in length, this is the largest dolphin likely to be seen in California waters. This and the White-sided Dolphin are the species that are frequently trained to perform tricks at marine amusement parks and aquaria.

The local baleen whales are also known as *rorquals.* A rorqual has a series of brushlike strainers known as baleen or whalebone in the roof of its mouth; in addition the underside of its throat is pleated to allow the mouth to expand and fill with water. Rorquals feed by filtering large volumes of water and trapping organisms in the baleen. Any of five species of baleen whales might be spotted by visitors to the California islands. Although none of these is actually resident in local waters, all pass through on their annual migrations between productive feeding grounds in the Arctic and calving grounds in the tropics.

The Minke Whale, *Balaenoptera acutorostrata,* is the smallest of the local baleen whales, and also one of the fastest. It is about 35 ft (10 m) in length and has a small, sickle-shaped dorsal fin. A Norwegian whaler named Minke once harpooned one of these little whales, thinking it was a great Blue Whale. Other whalers, amused by his mistake, began to refer to this species as Minke's whale, and it still carries his name. It is one of the whales that may frequently be attacked by Killer Whales, and it is the only species that is still hunted in large numbers by humans. Minke Whales are most likely to be seen during the spring and autumn, when the population off the California coast may reach about sixty individuals. They are most frequently sighted in the western Santa Barbara Channel.

Fin Whales, *Balaenoptera physalus,* are observed during migration from March to October. About seventy of these whales may be present in local waters during June. They are most frequently sighted along the Santa Rosa–San Nicolas Ridge and inshore toward Anacapa and Santa Catalina. These are large rorquals, sometimes reaching 85 ft (27 m) in length; only Blue Whales are larger.

The largest animal that has ever lived is the Blue Whale, *Balaenoptera musculus.* A true highlight of a summer whale-watching trip in the vicinity of the Northern Channel Islands is the opportunity to view one of these behemoths. About fifty Blue Whales may congregate in June to feed in the productive waters of the Santa Barbara Channel. Imagine an animal 100 ft (31 m) long, weighing 150 tons (136 metric tons), surfacing within a few feet of your boat and passing by quietly for what seems to be an eternity before its disproportionately small fluke breaks the water. Very little is known about the movements of these whales, but it is believed that fewer than 2000 of them remain in the north Pacific. Their disappearance from the Santa Barbara Channel during the late 1990s was associated with the El Niño condition, during which squid and forage fishes declined in abundance, to the detriment of several species of marine mammals.

In contrast, the Humpback Whale, *Megaptera novaeangliae,* has huge fins and flippers (Plate 2B). Humpbacks are half the size of Blue Whales, but their fins are so large and they so frequently reveal them that they appear larger than they are. Humpback Whales are the most acrobatic of the rorquals, leaping clear of the water and landing on their backs or sides with a resounding splash. They occur in the Southern California Bight during their spring and autumn migrations, when sightings are widespread but sparse. Most of the Humpback Whale population migrates between Hawaii and the Gulf of Alaska, where they feed on shrimplike plankton (krill) and small, schooling fishes. During the summer, however, about 300 of them feed off the coast of central and northern California.

The 6000-mile (9600-km) migration of the California Gray Whale, *Eschrichtius robustus,* between calving lagoons in Baja California and feeding grounds in the Bering Sea is one of the most significant events in California's coastal waters. Mating and birthing take place in the warm, nutrient-rich lagoons on the Pacific side of the Baja California peninsula. Pregnancy lasts about a year, and young whales (Plate 2A) stay with their mothers for about a year, so that females mate and give birth every other year. Baby whales are fed the richest milk known of any mammal species: it is 40 percent fat and nearly 40 percent protein. In spring the whales make their journey northward along the coast to feed in the Bering Sea during the summer, when continuous light promotes the production of tremendous amounts of food.

California Gray Whales are the most primitive of the baleen whales, having coarse, widely spaced baleen plates and only two pleats in their throats. They are about the same size as Humpback Whales, approximately 50 ft (15 m) long, and they have no dorsal fins. They feed primarily on the bottom by stirring up the mud and sifting it for crustaceans. Their gray color results from scars all over their bodies, caused primarily by barnacles that attach to their skin and are subsequently scraped off. It is believed that California Gray Whales are more susceptible to barnacle infestations because they spend so much time in shallow coastal waters. The patterns of scarring are unique to each whale, a characteristic that has enabled scientists to track the progress of individuals from the air, and in so doing learn a great deal about the migratory routes of the species.

The passage of the California Gray Whales can be observed all along the coast of California, but in the Southern California Bight whale-watching has become a favored winter pastime for tourists. The whales begin to appear in November as they move southward, and the northbound whales, including newborn calves, pass between February and May. The whales may be seen up to 125 miles (200 km) offshore, but at least 50 percent of the sightings occur within 9 miles (15 km) of the mainland. In some localities the whales routinely pass so close to shore that watching from land has also become popular. Point Loma in San Diego County, Dana Point in Orange County, Davenport Landing near Santa Cruz, and Point Reyes in Marin County are prime whale-watching promontories. While traveling through the Channel Islands the whales follow three primary routes: one close to shore, one between San Clemente and Santa Catalina, and one outside the islands. There is some evidence that in recent years more and more of the whales have begun taking the outside route, and some scientists suspect that the large number of whale-watching boats is causing this shift in migration pattern. North of Point Conception most of the whales seem to follow a similar course, relatively near the coast. Most sightings along the central and northern coast are within 5 miles (9 km) of the shore, except when crossing the Gulf of the Farallons off San Francisco Bay.

The recovery of the California Gray Whale population is often touted as an example of the importance of managing endangered species. In 1946 total protection of the California Gray Whale was initiated by international agreement. From dangerously depleted numbers in the early 1900s, the population has now recovered to more than 21,000 animals, a population size probably equivalent to preexploitation levels. In 1978 the International Whaling Commission reclassified the California Gray Whale from "protected" to "sustained-management" status, which allows a noncommercial quota to be set each year. Then, on June 15, 1994, the U.S. Fish and Wildlife Service officially removed the California Gray Whale from the endangered list, as one of a package of sixteen "delistings."

SEA BIRDS

The greatest concentration of nesting sea birds on the California coast occurs on the Farallon Islands. During the breeding season in spring, up to 250,000 nesting birds occupy these islands—a number that represents about two-thirds of all breeding sea birds north of Mexico. In southern California, the largest colonies of nesting sea birds occur on Castle Rock and Prince Island, offshore islets of San Miguel Island. Next in importance are Santa Barbara and Anacapa Islands.

Nesting sea birds can be divided into five groups: pelicans (*Pelecanus* spp.), cormorants (*Phalacrocorax* spp.), gulls (*Larus* spp.), storm-petrels (*Oceanodroma* spp.), and alcids (family Alcidae). The auk family (Alcidae) on the California islands includes the Common Murre (*Uria aalge*), Tufted Puffin (*Fratercula cirrhata*), Pigeon Guillemot (*Cepphus columba*), Xantus' Murrelet (*Synthliboramphus hypoleucus*), and Cassin's Auklet (*Ptychoramphus aleuticus*).

Pelicans and Cormorants are related birds. They both have webbed feet with four toes in the web; a long, hooked beak; and a membranous throat (gular) pouch. The gular pouch is the trademark of the pelicans: it enables them to catch and hold large fish.

The Brown Pelican, *Pelecanus occidentalis* (Fig. 192J; Plate 3A), is one of California's most familiar sea birds. What is more admirable than the flight of a Brown Pelican? It glides just above the surf, with its wingtips so close to the water that it seems it will surely crash. When it spots food, it seems to put on brakes, halting abruptly in midair and crashing into the water. Its gular pouch acts like a parachute to stop it at the surface with such abruptness that it seems the bird will break its neck. Some authorities contend that this feeding behavior creates a shock wave that stuns the targeted fish so that it can be retrieved easily by the bird.

Historically Brown Pelicans bred on all of the Channel Islands and as far north as Bird Island, at Point Lobos near Monterey. The bulk of the population, however, occurs in Mexican waters. In the late 1960s, this symbol of California's beaches had all but disappeared. At its height, the population numbered 5000 breeding pairs on Anacapa Island alone. By 1968 only 100 breeding pairs were left on Anacapa; in 1969, of 1125 nests, only 12 contained intact eggs, and no more than four birds fledged that year. The culprit, it seemed, was DDT. The pesticide was causing birds to lay eggs with shells too thin to support the weight of the nesting adults. The Brown Pelican was added to the federal and California lists of endangered species.

In 1972 use of DDT was banned in the United States, and the birds slowly returned. Yet despite the 1972 ban, the pesticide persisted in the environment for many years. In the 1980s widespread reports of DDT and PCB residues in fish livers implicated the Southern California Bight as one of the most polluted bodies of water in the world. Finally, in the 1990s, although samples of sediment showed DDT and PCBs still present, repeated tests of fish livers revealed the concentrations of these chemicals to be about 5 percent of the levels measured during the previous decade.

By 1987 the number of nesting Brown Pelicans on the Channel Islands had increased to 7300 pairs, but the number inexplicably dropped again in following years, hovering in the late 1990s at about 5000–6000 pairs, most of them on West Anacapa Island. Some estimates indicate that the birds have returned to only about 10 percent of their former numbers on Anacapa Island. During the El Niño years of 1983, 1990, 1992, and 1998, only a few hundred nesting pairs used the Channel Islands. A factor implicated in the decline was the collapse of the Northern Anchovy population, which represented 92 percent of the bird's food during the breeding season; this collapse was particularly evident during warm-water intervals associated with El Niño. Commercial overfishing also appeared to have been an important factor in the overall decline of the Northern Anchovy population.

Cormorants are large black birds that fly and swim with their bills uptilted. They hunt for fish while swimming, and they dive to catch them. Unlike those of most water birds, to decrease buoyancy and facilitate underwater pursuit of prey, the outer feathers of cormorants are wettable. The birds spend so much time under water that their feathers sometimes become waterlogged. Thus it is not uncommon to see them perched in a "spread-eagle" position with their wings outstretched to dry. Three species of cormorant nest on the California islands. Brandt's Cormorant, *Phalacrocorax penicillatus,* is the most common, nesting on seven of the Channel Islands; it can be recognized by the blue color of its gular pouch. The Double-crested Cormorant, *Phalacrocorax auritus* (Plate 3B), is the species most commonly observed along the coast and inland. Its gular pouch is orange-yellow. It has experienced a severe decline in numbers in recent years. Although nesting colonies are today still located on San Miguel, Santa Barbara, and West Anacapa Islands, as they were historically, numbers have decreased considerably. Indeed there may be as few as 150 pairs of breeding birds left on the Channel Islands. The Pelagic Cormorant, *Phalacrocorax pelagicus,* is a smaller bird, and its red gular pouch can be seen only at close range. Nesting colonies on the Northern Channel Islands, particularly San Miguel, represent the southern limits for the species. It is the least common of the Southern California cormorants, but thousands of individuals nest on the Farallon Islands.

How do these apparently similar birds partition their resources? As do marine mammals, they feed in different places, at different times, and on different food items. Research on these birds on the Farallon Islands in the 1970s revealed that Double-crested Cormorants fed over 90 percent of the time on Shiner Surfperch, *Cymatogaster aggregata* (Fig. 30C), a schooling species typical of quiet, shallow, inshore waters. Brandt's Cormorant fed primarily on Rockfish, mainly *Sebastes flavidus* and *Sebastes jordani,* as well as Pacific Tomcod, *Microgadus proximus.* These prey species are typical of muddy-bottomed estuarine habitats. In contrast, Pelagic Cormorants fed primarily on fish that hide in submerged, rocky reefs. Depending on the abundance during different years, the preferred prey species were either sculpins (Cottidae) or juvenile rockfish (*Sebastes* spp.).

The decline in the numbers of cormorants and pelicans is probably related to a combination of factors in addition to the use of DDT in the 1960s. The range of the Double-crested Cormorant near the coast and inland has been affected by development. On the islands, increased human activity has also had an effect, although it is not uncommon to see the birds roosting on the rocks at the south side of Avalon Cove on Santa Catalina Island within a few feet of pedestrians and vehicles. It remains to be seen if increased visitation in Channel Islands National Park will have an effect on the numbers of breeding birds there. Finally, the disappearance of fishery-depleted forage species such as the Pacific Sardine, *Sardinops sagax,* and the Pacific Herring, *Clupea pallasi,* has doubtless had an effect on the numbers of pelagic (surface-feeding) birds. Additional evidence from the last three decades of monitoring indicates a rise in water temperature of about 2°C and that the pattern of yearly upwelling of cold, nutrient-rich water near the Channel Islands seems to have subsided.

Numerous species of gulls winter along the coast of California. Perhaps the most familiar are the Ring-billed Gull, *Larus delawarensis,* and the California Gull, *Larus californicus.* The Ring-billed Gull has a black ring around its bill and yellow feet. The California Gull looks like it except that it lacks the dark ring and has a red spot on the lower part of the bill. For breeding, both of these species migrate to various lakes of the Great Basin in the United States and Canada. The California Gull has a breeding population at Mono Lake, where it has been threatened in recent years by lowering of the water level. But whatever its fate there, the California Gull has already been immortalized in Salt Lake City. A statue there commemorates an incident in which a flock of California Gulls arrived in time to consume a swarm of Mormon Crickets, *Anabrus simplex,* that threatened the Mormon settlers' first crop.

The Western Gull, *Larus occidentalis* (Fig. 192A; Plate 3D), remains along the coast and is the most common, widespread breeding bird on the California islands. The Western Gull differs from the California Gull mentioned previously in having dark gray wings and pinkish feet. The world's largest colony of Western Gulls, estimated at some 25,000 birds, occurs on the Farallon Islands (Fig. 172). This is probably the only breeding sea bird that has increased its numbers in recent years, perhaps because it feeds in refuse dumps along the coast. The remains of gull meals, including chicken and turkey bones, often litter the nesting areas.

Storm-petrels are small, dark birds that are seldom seen. They feed at sea on small fish and crustaceans, usually at dusk, by flying low over the water, frequently in wave troughs. Petrels nest on San Miguel, Santa Barbara, Santa Cruz, and the Farallon Islands. Adults feed at sea for several days, and each member of a breeding pair takes turns on the nest incubating the eggs. After the eggs have hatched the adults visit their nests on the islands at night. A nest may lie in a crevice, or if there is enough soil the adults may build a burrow up to 3 ft (1 m) deep. Leach's Storm-Petrel, *Oceanodroma leucorhoa*, is the most widespread storm-petrel on the Pacific coast; it commonly nests on the Farallon Islands, but only a few nesting pairs have been observed on San Miguel Island, and none on any of the other Channel Islands. Ashy Storm-Petrels, *Oceanodroma homochroa* (Fig. 174), are the most common storm-petrels nesting on the California coast. At one time they were the most common nesting bird on the Farallon Islands. Hundreds of pairs still breed on San Miguel and Santa Barbara Islands, and perhaps thirty pairs are known to breed on Santa Cruz Island. Least common of the breeding storm-petrels is the Black Storm-Petrel, *Oceanodroma melania*. These birds commonly nest on the islands of Baja California, but in the Channel Islands they are known to breed only on Santa Barbara Island. Ironically, the increase in the number of Western Gulls seems to have taken its toll on some of the other bird species. One study on the Farallons indicated that about 2.5 percent of the storm-petrels were killed each year by gulls.

The family Alcidae represents the northern counterparts of the penguins, except that alcids can fly. They have short necks and stubby beaks. They are expert divers, and they nest in great numbers on sea cliffs. Cassin's Auklet, *Ptychoramphus aleuticus* (Fig. 171), is a short, stubby black bird with a white belly. It is the most common nesting species on the California islands. In the 1990s, an estimated 50,000 pairs nested on the Farallon Islands, but that number is declining. About 10,000 pairs nested on San Miguel Island, and perhaps a hundred pairs each nested on Santa Barbara and Santa Cruz Islands. Like the storm-petrels, auklets are seldom seen because they travel to and from the islands under cover of darkness and they nest in cracks or burrows. Auklet chicks take about 40 days to fledge from their burrows, during which time the adults must make repeated trips out to sea to find food.

Common Murres, *Uria aalge* (Fig. 173), are also black with a white belly, but they are about the size of a duck, twice the size of Cassin's Auklet. This is a common species in the north Pacific, but the southernmost breeding colonies are on the Farallon Islands, where there are about 75,000 birds. Their numbers have also declined. Formerly they bred as far south as San Miguel Island, but the species has not been recorded there since 1912. In addition to the threats mentioned earlier, egg collectors formerly raided the nests of these birds, particularly on the Farallon Islands. Also possibly contributing to the decline in the population on the Farallons have been oil spills during the late 1980s. Evidence indicates that the preferred prey of Common Murres used to be the Short-belly Rockfish, *Sebastes jordani;* now they feed mostly on other species.

Using funds obtained from oil companies in oil spill litigation, in 1996 an experiment was begun to lure Common Murres back to one of their former breeding sites on Devil's Slide Rock near Half Moon Bay, about 25 miles (40 km) south of the Farallon Islands. Several hundred decoys, accurate models of Common Murres, were placed on the cliffs of the island in the hope that live birds could be tricked into joining the colony and nesting there. The first decoys placed there were inundated with the droppings of other birds, so to improve the system, mirrors with pointed tops were also installed. The mirrors were to provide an animated image for the birds, and the pointed tops were to discourage birds from perching on the mirrors. In addition, recordings of murre calls were broadcast over solar-powered outdoor speakers. Some initial success has been reported, but only time will tell if the system really works.

The Tufted Puffin, *Fratercula cirrhata* (Fig. 176), is the clown prince of sea birds. Its stubby, thick, red and yellow bill is distinctive, if not humorous. Tufted Puffins also have curved yellow ear tufts arranged like racing stripes on the sides of their heads. Sometimes they seem ill equipped to fly: individuals will run across the water with their wings flapping and fail to get airborne, perhaps because of the added weight of their last meal. Tufted Puffins are also birds of the north Pacific, and their disappearance from the Channel Islands parallels that of the Common Murre. The Farallon Islands are home to the southernmost of the breeding colonies today, but only a few pairs have been observed there recently.

Pigeon Guillemots, *Cepphus columba* (Fig. 175), look like black pigeons with a white shoulder patch and red feet. They are completely absent from the Southern California Bight in the fall and early winter, but they return

Figure 41. The Osprey, *Pandion haliaetus,* a fish-eating hawk, no longer nests on the California islands, but proposals to reintroduce it have been put forward.

to breed in the spring, when they nest in damp sea caves. They breed throughout the north Pacific, and their southernmost breeding colonies are on Santa Barbara Island. Hundreds of pairs are also found on San Miguel, Santa Cruz, and Santa Rosa Islands. Major breeding colonies also occur on the Farallon Islands, although reduction of the local population of rockfish species has caused a decrease in their numbers similar to that of the Common Murre mentioned previously.

The entire breeding range of Xantus' Murrelet, *Synthliboramphus hypoleucus* (Fig. 164), occurs between central Baja California and Point Conception. The northernmost colony occurs on San Miguel Island, where there are about 75 pairs. The greatest number of them occur on Santa Barbara Island, where there are about 1500 pairs of breeding birds. The murrelets formerly bred on Anacapa Island as well.

Bald Eagles, *Haliaeetus leucocephalus* (Fig. 65), and Ospreys, *Pandion haliaetus* (Fig. 41), technically are not classified as sea birds, yet they nest along the coast and feed primarily on fish. Both of these beautiful raptors have been all but eliminated from the California islands, victims of pesticides and predation by feral cats. In the late 1990s attempts have been made to reintroduce the Bald Eagle to Santa Catalina, but breeding success has been limited, perhaps owing to the lingering effects of pesticides. Ospreys have not nested on the Channel Islands for many years, yet they are still relatively abundant on the islands off Baja California and may be observed fishing in estuaries on the California mainland. Reintroduction of these fish-eating hawks to the islands has also been proposed.

Peregrine Falcons, *Falco peregrinus,* formerly extirpated from the islands, have made a remarkable comeback on the Northern Channel Islands. Birds released in the early 1980s on San Miguel Island have established a breeding population. Those released by wildlife experts have been joined by natural colonizers. As of 1998 there were fourteen nesting pairs that have produced about seventy offspring on the five islands in Channel Islands National Park.

Thus it can be seen that nesting sea birds on the California islands represent a mixture of northern and southern species. The Farallon Islands have the greatest abundance of nesting sea birds, but most of the species are of northern affinity. In the Channel Islands most of the nesting sea birds occupy the outer, smaller islands, particularly San Miguel. Southern species that reach the northernmost limits of their distribution mix with northern species that reach the southernmost limits of their distribution to create a diverse sea bird fauna of twelve different species on San Miguel Island, eight of which are more numerous there than on any of the other Channel Islands. In general, if it were not for the islands, where nesting birds can find refuge from terrestrial predators, sea birds would be absent from the California coast.

Marine life of the California coast is rich and diverse, and the islands represent jewels of unspoiled coastline. Serious divers who explore the coves and inlets of California's islands are familiar with its marine treasures, but even casual beach-walkers delight in exploring remote island tidepools. Boatloads of passengers are often followed by seabirds in effortless flight, and the sighting of whales or dolphins may be the highlight of the trip.

CHAPTER FIVE

SANTA CATALINA ISLAND

Santa Catalina Island (Fig. 42) is by far the best-known island within California, although Alcatraz Island may have better name recognition outside the state. Of the southern group of Channel Islands, it is the closest to the coast, located about 20 miles (32 km) south of Point Vicente on the Palos Verdes Peninsula. The island has an area of about 76 square miles (122 km^2); it is about 21 miles (34 km) long and 8 miles (13 km) wide near its center. At Two Harbors the land narrows to form the Isthmus, where the island is less than half a mile (1 km) in width.

Santa Catalina Island has the most visitors of all the California islands—up to a million persons a year—with daily ferry and air transportation to the communities of Avalon and Two Harbors. It is also the most populous island. The resort city of Avalon (permanent population 3000) is located on a broad, semicircular bay near the east end of the island; it remains a popular destination for summer visitors, who may number 10,000 on a busy day. The smaller community of Two Harbors (permanent population 200), always popular with yachting enthusiasts, is located at the Isthmus, about 14 miles (23 km) by water or 23 miles (37 km) by road from Avalon. Catalina Harbor, on the south side of the Isthmus, is the only natural, deep, all-weather harbor between San Diego and San Francisco. In addition to the towns, attractions on Santa Catalina include 54 miles (86 km) of coastline punctuated by numerous coves and inlets, and a rugged interior well suited for camping and hiking.

The climate of the island is mild and dry; infrequent storms occur mainly between November and April. Over a 32-year period the total annual precipitation at Avalon averaged 12.35 in. (314 mm). Summer temperatures at Avalon average 74°F (23°C) in the daytime and 59°F (15°C)

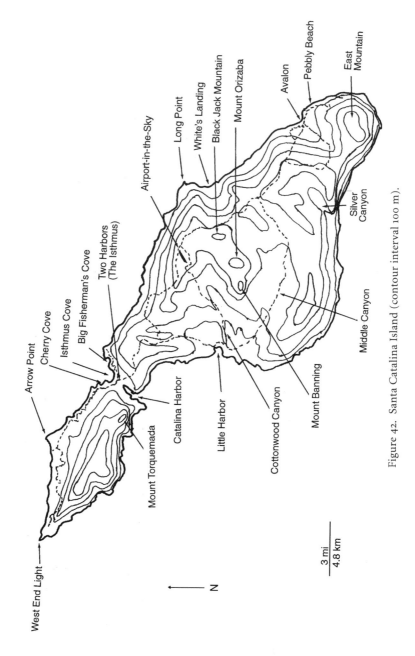

Figure 42. Santa Catalina Island (contour interval 100 m).

West End Light

Arrow Point

Cherry Cove

Isthmus Cove

Big Fisherman's Cove

Two Harbors (The Isthmus)

Airport-in-the-Sky

Long Point

White's Landing

Black Jack Mountain

Mount Orizaba

Avalon

Pebbly Beach

East Mountain

Silver Canyon

Middle Canyon

Mount Banning

Cottonwood Canyon

Little Harbor

Catalina Harbor

Mount Torquemada

3 mi
4.8 km

N

at night. Winter temperatures drop to a daytime average of 63°F (17°C) and 49°F (9°C) at night.

The island is quite mountainous, with a high central ridge running its length. Narrow canyons drain steep slopes on both sides of this ridge, and small coves with mainly cobblestone beaches lie at the canyon mouths. A few sandy beaches are found below the larger canyons. Mount Orizaba, at an elevation of 2097 ft (670 m) near the island's center, is the highest point on Santa Catalina Island. Nearby, at 2010 ft (648 m), is Black Jack Mountain, the site of a vigorous lead and silver mine in the 1920s. On the southern or windward side the coastline is exposed to the pounding Pacific surf. The northern or leeward side faces the California coast and is usually calm. Here good anchorages in secluded coves are avidly sought by the boating public, and the clear waters attract skin and scuba divers.

The subtidal marine habitats of Santa Catalina are rich and diverse (see Chapter 4). Many colorful species of invertebrates, fishes, and seaweeds can easily be observed with mask and snorkel or from the glass-bottom boat that operates out of Avalon. Both sandy and rocky reef-type habitats are common around the island, with dense forests of Giant Bladder Kelp, *Macrocystis pyrifera* (Fig. 26), and Southern Sea Palm, *Eisenia arborea.* Some mud-flat habitat is present in Catalina Harbor, but overall this habitat is poorly represented on the island. Rocky intertidal pools are difficult to find except in a few locations on the windward side of the island.

HISTORY

The history of Santa Catalina Island is well documented. Ernest Windle, editor of the local newspaper, the *Catalina Islander,* first published his account in 1931, then updated it in 1940. However, the most thorough account was published in 1997 by longtime residents Bill White and Steve Tice.

The island has played an important role in the history of California, from its first settlement by Native Americans, to its discovery by Cabrillo in 1542, through the Spanish mission period of the late 1700s to the early 1800s, and on through the "Wrigley" era of the early twentieth century. Otter hunters and miners were attracted to the island along with smugglers and pirates. The land boom of the 1880s provided the impetus for the establishment of the town of Avalon, which became world renowned as a retreat for the rich and famous in the 1920s and 1930s. The settlement has had many names: Rousillon Bay, Timm's Landing (after a shipping magnate), Shatto (after a real estate speculator), and finally Avalon (after the mythical paradise to which King Arthur was taken after his death).

The Native Americans of Santa Catalina Island were part of the

Gabrielino group, which was descended from the Shoshonean peoples of the Great Basin. They called the island Pimu or Pemú'nga. Other names included Pimurit or Pipimar, and they called themselves Pimugnans or Pipimares. The Gabrielinos lived in several villages along the shore as far back as 500 B.C. They navigated back and forth in plank canoes up to 28 ft (9 m) in length and survived on natural plant foods and marine life. Soapstone from an area near the present-day Airport-in-the-Sky was carved into various objects, such as bowls, jars, and ornaments, which were apparently traded to tribes on the mainland for necessities not present on the island. The largest villages were at the Isthmus and at the present-day sites of Little Harbor and Avalon. The island's oldest Indian village site is at Little Harbor on the southwestern shore.

The story of Juan Rodríguez Cabrillo and his role in the discovery of the Channel Islands has been the subject of some controversy. According to early documents, his mission was to sail from the Mexican port of Naavidad and to explore the coastline northward "until its end and secret" were known. However, Lois J. Roberts of Carmel, California, has reinterpreted and clarified some of the early records. First, even though most records indicate that Cabrillo was Portuguese, in reality he was Spanish. Second, even though some historical records note that Cabrillo only spent half a day on Santa Catalina, he actually overwintered there in 1542–43 and died there following an accident that shattered his shinbone. This incident has apparently been recorded incorrectly as having occurred on San Miguel Island, and thus the monument to Cabrillo that is now on San Miguel Island is in the wrong place (see Chapter 6).

Nevertheless Cabrillo is given credit for discovering Santa Catalina in 1542, and he also gave the island its first official name: San Salvador, the name of his flagship. Apparently he also named the entire group of islands the San Lucas Islands, and from time to time in his log he referred to both Santa Catalina and San Miguel as Isla de Posesión or La Posesión. It was this latter reference that apparently led to the misinterpretation of just where his accident and subsequent death actually occurred.

In 1553 Sebastián Rodríguez Cermeño passed the island in his ship the *San Augustín* but did not land. After a long trip from Manila he managed to obtain food from the Gabrielinos on the island. Europeans did not visit the island again until 60 years after Cabrillo, when Sebastián Vizcaíno arrived on the feast day of Saint Catherine of Alexandria, at which time he named the island Santa Catalina in honor of the martyred saint.

Spanish colonization of California began in 1769, but Santa Catalina was not to become a part of the presidio-mission-rancho system. Nevertheless the indirect influences of new diseases, destruction of the hunting-trading way of life, and incursions by Aleut otter hunters eventually led to the demise of Santa Catalina's Native American population (see Chapter 3).

During the Spanish-Mexican period and on into the era of early statehood, Santa Catalina functioned primarily as a center for smuggling. Richard Henry Dana, in *Two Years Before the Mast,* mentions the island's importance as a way station for smugglers: American traders would avoid payment of customs duties by hiding their cargo on the island. Smuggling continued after statehood, with Santa Catalina being used to hide all sorts of contraband, including Chinese immigrants in the 1850s and liquor during Prohibition.

In 1848, under the Treaty of Guadalupe Hidalgo, Mexico released the southwestern United States, including California, to the United States. However, when the boundary descriptions were prepared, the islands off the coast of California—including the Channel Islands and the Farallons—were inadvertently overlooked; thus ownership was technically never transferred to the United States. Mexico has never attempted to regain control of the islands, but as recently as 1972 protestors raised a Mexican flag on Santa Catalina Island.

The last Mexican governor, Pio Pico, ceded the island in 1846 to Thomas Robbins of Santa Barbara, and title to the island changed hands many times during the ensuing years. The town of Avalon was founded as a potential resort in 1887, but the developers ran out of money. The Banning family then bought the island, formed the Santa Catalina Island Company, and completed work on Avalon, which they promoted as a fishing resort. In 1915 a fire whipped through Avalon, all but destroying the nascent resort. William Wrigley, Jr., of chewing gum fame, purchased a majority interest in the Santa Catalina Island Company in 1919, the same year he purchased the Chicago Cubs. He built a mansion on Mount Ada, overlooking Avalon, that is still in place today. The Wrigley family was to remain in control of development on the island for the next 56 years.

Another famous resident of Santa Catalina Island was Zane Grey, a writer of novels about the old west. In 1926 he moved into a large adobe home that he had built on the island. About his refuge on Santa Catalina Grey wrote, "It is an environment that means enchantment to me. Sea and mountain! A place for rest, dream, peace, sleep." The home is now a hotel.

In 1972 the Santa Catalina Island Conservancy, dedicated to preservation of open space and native plants and animals, was established. The Santa Catalina Island Company entered into an agreement with Los Angeles County in 1974 that gave the county control of more than three-quarters of the island for recreation and conservation. The company retained ownership of most of Avalon and the Two Harbors area, as well as a horse ranch (Rancho Escondido) in the interior. The Conservancy gained control of most of the rest of the Island Company property in 1975. Thus, after nearly 90 years of private ownership, the Conservancy's management now ensures that at least 86 percent of the island will be maintained as an undeveloped preserve.

A truly unique facility on Santa Catalina Island is the seawater desalination plant at Pebbly Beach, south of Avalon. Southern California Edison owns and operates the facility, but it was built with private funds under a unique public-private partnership. Faced with a major deterrent to the development of condominiums at Hamilton Cove, north of Avalon, the developer entered into an agreement under which it would underwrite the construction of the $3 million facility in exchange for access to half of the water produced. The plant went on line in 1991. Using the reverse osmosis process, in which seawater is forced through a membrane under high pressure, the facility produces about 132,000 gallons (4.8 million liters) of fresh water a day, providing roughly one-third of the island's supply.

GEOLOGY

The northwestern part of Santa Catalina Island consists mainly of crystalline metamorphic rocks—such as blueschist, greenschist, and garnet-rich amphibolite—that have been altered by heat and pressure from their original state (Fig. 43). They tend to be old, dating back about 200 million years to the Jurassic period, when they were components of a deep marine trench that lay off the California coast. These rocks, which make up a large proportion of the inner continental borderland, are exposed on Santa Catalina Island and a small part of the Palos Verdes Peninsula. A number of them—such as serpentine (=serpentinite), the state rock—are part of a group of rocks that are abundant in the Coast Ranges but primarily under the sea off Southern California. Serpentine is a waxy green material associated with what is known as the Franciscan Formation, a group of metamorphic trench rocks named for San Francisco. Many of them are remnants of what was once a large upland of metamorphic rocks that lay offshore about 20 million years ago. Good exposures of these rocks are visible at Little Harbor and along the road between the Airport-in-the-Sky and the Isthmus. A spectacular outcrop of garnet amphibolite lies on a hilltop near the airport.

Exposed over an area of about 20 square miles (50 km^2) on the southeast third of the island is a massive pluton of quartz hornblende diorite porphyry, which intruded into the metamorphic rocks. This deposit of Miocene age, dated at 19 million years B.P., is the youngest pluton in

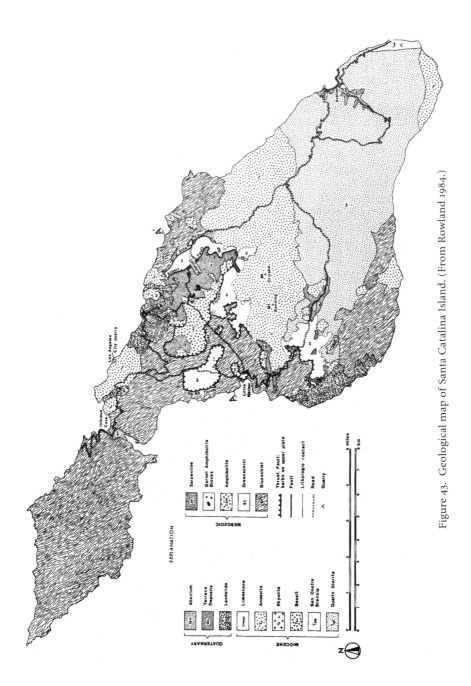

Figure 43. Geological map of Santa Catalina Island. (From Rowland 1984.)

California. Good exposures are visible in roadcuts between Avalon and the airport.

Volcanic flows of late Miocene age cover about a quarter of the island, particularly near the center and highest points of the island, and extend over 13 square miles (33 km^2). These andesitic lavas are also found in small, isolated areas at other localities, for example, Big Fisherman's Cove southeast of the Isthmus. Of particular interest here are the spectacular layered ashfalls (Plate 4B).

Although not abundant on Santa Catalina, late Miocene sedimentary strata are found at surprisingly high elevations on Cactus Peak and Mount Banning. In particular, the fossiliferous limey sandstone on Mount Banning is indicative of 1800–2100 ft of rapid uplift in just a few million years. Other sedimentary strata occur in the lower reaches of Cottonwood and Middle Canyons and at Big Fisherman's Cove. The southern portion of this cove is bounded by white cliffs composed of diatomite. There are numerous large landslides south of the Isthmus and along the southern cliffs. Recent alluvial deposits may be seen in the valley bottoms, including sand in some of the coves, and gravel or cobble beaches are scattered around most of the island, especially at the mouths of canyons. Because of rapid uplift, Pleistocene marine terraces are few in number and remarkably high in elevation.

Outcrops of steatite (soapstone) occur at several places on the island. These areas were utilized as quarries by island natives, who formed bowls, pipes, and other objects from the steatite (Fig. 13). Such a steatite quarry can be seen near the Airport-in-the-Sky, where partially finished bowls protrude from the outcrop. Other minerals mined periodically on Santa Catalina Island have included gold, silver, lead, and zinc, primarily extracted from Black Jack Mountain.

TERRESTRIAL VEGETATION

A number of people have studied the flora of Santa Catalina Island, including Robert Thorne of the Rancho Santa Ana Botanic Garden. The most comprehensive listing of the plants of all the Channel Islands, however, was compiled by Gary Wallace in 1985. A total of 606 kinds of plants have been found growing wild on Santa Catalina: 421 are indigenous and 185 were introduced. Since the geology of the island indicates total submergence sometime during the Pleistocene (circa 300,000 years ago), it appears that the native plants present today have arrived by over-water dispersal. The island today supports seven endemic plants: four fully endemic species and three subspecies. In addition about thirty species, subspecies, and varieties are represented on Santa Catalina that survive only on this and other Channel Islands (Table 5). A few other plants

TABLE 5   ENDEMIC VASCULAR PLANTS
OF SANTA CATALINA ISLAND

Dicots
  Asteraceae (sunflower family)
    Nevin's Eriophyllum (*Eriophyllum nevinii*)—Rare
    Island Tarweed (*Hemizonia clementina*)
  Brassicaceae (mustard family)
    Santa Cruz Island Rock Cress (*Sibara filifolia*)—Endangered
  Cistaceae (rockrose family)
    Island Rush-rose (*Helianthemum greenei*)—Threatened
  Convolvulaceae (morning-glory family)
    Island Morning-glory (*Calystegia macrostegia*)
  Crassulaceae (stonecrop family)
    Santa Catalina Island Live-forever (*Dudleya hassei*)[a]
    Bright Green Dudleya (*Dudleya virens* ssp. *insulare*)
  Crossosomataceae (crossosoma family)
    Catalina Crossosoma (*Crossosoma californicum*)
  Ericaceae (heath family)
    Santa Catalina Island Manzanita (*Arctostaphylos catalinae*)—Rare[a]
  Fabaceae (pea family)
    Southern Channel Island Bird's-foot Trefoil (*Lotus argophyllus* var. *argenteus*)
    Island Deerweed (*Lotus dendroideus* var. *dendroideus*)
    Island Pinpoint Clover (*Trifolium gracilentum* var. *palmeri*)
  Fagaceae (oak family)
    MacDonald Oak (*Quercus* ×*macdonaldii*)
    Island Scrub Oak (*Quercus pacifica*)
    Island Oak (*Quercus tomentella*)
  Hydrophyllaceae (waterleaf family)
    Lyon's Phacelia (*Phacelia lyoni*)
  Malvaceae (mallow family)
    Southern Channel Island Malva Rosa (*Lavatera assurgentiflora* ssp. *glabra*)
  Papaveraceae (poppy family)
    Channel Island Tree Poppy (*Dendromecon harfordii*)
    Island Poppy (*Eschscholzia ramosa*)
  Polemoniaceae (phlox family)
    Island Gilia (*Gilia nevinii*)
  Polygonaceae (buckwheat family)
    Santa Catalina Island Buckwheat (*Eriogonum giganteum* var. *giganteum*)[a]
    Island Buckwheat (*Eriogonum grande* var. *grande*)
  Rhamnaceae (buckthorn family)
    Feltleaf Ceanothus (*Ceanothus arboreus*)
    Island Ceanothus (*Ceanothus megacarpus* var. *insularis*)
    Big-pod Ceanothus (*Ceanothus megacarpus* var. *megacarpus*)
    Island Redberry (*Rhamnus pirifolia*)
  Rosaceae (rose ramily)
    Prostrate Chamise (*Adenostoma fasciculatum* var. *prostratum*?)
    Catalina Island Mountain Mahogany (*Cercocarpus traskiae*)—Endangered[a]
    Santa Catalina Island Ironwood (*Lyonothamnus floribundus* ssp.
      floribundus)—Rare[a]
  Rubiaceae (madder family)
    Santa Catalina Island Bedstraw (*Galium catalinense* ssp. *catalinense*)[a]
    Nuttall's Island Bedstraw (*Galium nuttallii* ssp. *insulare*)

(*Continued*)

TABLE 5   *(Continued)*

Dicots *(Continued)*
    Saxifragaceae (saxifrage family)
      Island Jepsonia *(Jepsonia malvifolia)*
    Scrophulariaceae (figwort family)
      Santa Catalina Figwort *(Scrophularia villosa)*—Rare
      Santa Catalina Island Monkeyflower *(Mimulus traskiae)*—Extinct(?)[a]
    Solanaceae (nightshade family)
      Santa Catalina Island Desert-thorn *(Lycium brevipes* var. *hassei)*—Extinct(?)
      Wallace's Nightshade *(Solanum wallacei)*[a]
Monocots
    Poaceae (grass family)
      California Dissanthelium *(Dissanthelium californicum)*—Extinct(?)

[a]Single-island endemic.

are near-endemics, occurring on very restricted coastal areas of the mainland.

The flora of Santa Catalina today is far from what Cabrillo saw when he first sailed along its coast. Not only have introduced animals altered the natural scene, but many of the conspicuous plants on the island have been introduced. As will be discussed later, nonnative Mediterranean weeds, associated with introduced livestock, dominate the grasslands. In the vicinity of Avalon, Two Harbors, and the interior ranches, many of the trees and shrubs are introduced. The most common trees on Santa Catalina are Blue Gums, *Eucalyptus globulus;* they are particularly conspicuous where they line the road from Avalon to the airport and around the ranches. The Tree-of-Heaven, *Ailanthus altissima,* a native of China characterized by long compound leaves and handsome clusters of red-brown fruit, has invaded many canyons in the Avalon area, and biologists on the island have now undertaken a program to eliminate it.

Near the ranches along the summit of the island are mixed groves of introduced pine trees. Santa Catalina has no native pine trees. Most of the introduced pines are Monterey Pines, *Pinus radiata,* native to the mainland but not the islands. The large, long-needled pines are Coulter Pine, *Pinus coulteri,* similarly native to the adjacent mainland. The fine-needled, wispy pine with its needles in clusters of two is Aleppo Pine, *Pinus halepensis,* which is native to the Mediterranean area.

The palm trees that are so conspicuous at Twin Harbors and the campground at Little Harbor are also introduced. There are no native palms on the islands of Alta California. Guadalupe Island, off the coast of Baja California, has its native Guadalupe Island Palm, *Brahea edulis,* which has been used as a horticultural variety throughout southern California, but most of the palms on Santa Catalina are the Mexican Fan Palm, *Wash-*

ingtonia robusta. A legacy of the early days of moviemaking, many of the fan palms were planted in 1935 during the filming of *Mutiny on the Bounty.* The short, heavy-trunked palm trees with long, feathery fronds are Canary Island Date Palms, *Phoenix canariensis.*

The most invasive shrubs on Santa Catalina are the brooms, which have overgrown and replaced many of the native Coastal Sage Scrub species on the slopes around Avalon. French Broom, *Genista (=Cytisus) monspessulanus,* and Narrow-leaf Broom, *Genista linifolia,* bloom in great profusion during the spring, when the slopes turn bright yellow with the attractive blossoms of these members of the pea family (Fabaceae). It is unfortunate that they so effectively replace the native flora, much of which can be similarly attractive.

Domestic goats (*Capra hircus*) (Fig. 5A) were introduced to the island about 1800, and they have since destroyed or altered much of the original vegetation. The legacy of former resident Zane Grey remains on the island in the form of a "buffalo" herd. American Bison (*Bison bison*) (Fig. 5C) were introduced in 1924 during the filming of the John Ford movie *The Vanishing American,* based on the novel of the same title by Grey. The Bison have had a further impact on the native vegetation. There are now about 500 individuals, and the herd is maintained at that level by capturing surplus individuals and exporting them to the mainland.

Pigs (*Sus scrofa*) (Fig. 5D) were introduced in the 1930s, and they have added to the damage caused by goats and Bison. Large feral populations of these species are still present, perhaps numbering 3000 in the area near Avalon. The natural distribution and species composition of the island's plant communities prior to their introduction is unknown, although they may have been instrumental in the disappearance of forty-eight indigenous and eighteen introduced species from the island's flora. For example, the Santa Cruz Island Rock Cress, *Sibara filifolia,* which was federally listed as endangered in 1997, has not been seen on Santa Catalina since 1973 and may have been extirpated. (This species is also believed to be gone from Santa Cruz Island but was recently rediscovered on San Clemente Island.)

Some plants exist only in small, protected populations on steep cliffs or on offshore rocks, areas inaccessible to introduced herbivores. For example, on Santa Catalina, natural populations of Malva Rosa, *Lavatera assurgentiflora* (Plate 6B), are restricted today to two isolated rocks near the Isthmus (Bird Rock and Indian Rock). A few planted populations can also be seen in the Avalon area. Similarly the Island Rush-rose, *Helianthemum greenei,* recently federally listed as a threatened species, is known primarily from fourteen sites on Santa Cruz Island and also has a single population on the northeast side of Black Jack Mountain.

Some of the island's endemic species are extremely rare. One species, a small annual known as the Santa Catalina Island Monkeyflower, *Mimulus traskiae,* which has white flowers stained with wine color, has not been reported since 1901 and is presumed extinct. Another species, the Catalina Island Mountain Mahogany, *Cercocarpus traskiae,* occurs only in one arroyo near the southernmost point of the island, where only seven known shrubs still exist. The species was listed as endangered in September 1997, and several specimens of this exceedingly rare plant can now be seen in the Wrigley Memorial Botanical Garden near Avalon. Another rare endemic is the Santa Catalina Island Ironwood, *Lyonothamnus floribundus* ssp. *floribundus* (Fig. 2A; Plate 5A), which exists only in several steep canyons on the channel side of the island.

The naming of plant communities has been in a state of flux, with philosophies ranging from the very general to the highly specific. In 1995 the California Native Plant Society, in conjunction with the California Department of Fish and Game's California Natural Diversity Data Base, published a new system that is intended to become the standard. That system, authored by John Sawyer and Todd Keeler-Wolf, recognizes about 280 units called *series.* In the same year V. L. Holland and David Keil published a system that classified plants into some 80 communities. In contrast, Phillip Munz and David Keck published a system in 1959 that included only 28 categories. In this book an attempt will be made to use community names that communicate effectively a grouping of plants that is easily recognizable and meaningful to lay persons. Widely used names, based on the Munz and Keck system, will be used, with some attention to the newer systems.

Coastal Sage Scrub

Coastal Sage Scrub is the dominant plant community seen over much of the island, especially on the south- and west-facing slopes (Fig. 44; Plate 7A). Some authors object to this name because there are some versions of the community, particularly on islands, in which sages are not dominant; hence the name Coastal Scrub appears in some of the literature. Irrespective of the name chosen, in this community, moisture rapidly evaporates and the soil is shallow and rocky. The community is best established where fog and temperatures above the freezing point are the rule. Several of its components are not frost tolerant. Coastal Sage Scrub is characterized by low-growing, drought-deciduous shrubs and succulents such as cacti.

Among the most common shrubs are two members of the sunflower family (Asteraceae). California Sagebrush (*Artemisia californica*) (Fig. 45A), is a low-growing plant that covers large areas of the island, especially along the central ridge. Its leaves are brushlike; they are a gray-green color in

Figure 44. Coastal Sage Scrub on a hilltop overlooking Isthmus Cove.

Figure 45. Indicator species for Coastal Sage Scrub. (A) California Sagebrush, *Artemisia californica*. (B) Coyote Brush, *Baccharis pilularis*.

Figure 46. Coast Brittlebush or California Encelia, *Encelia californica.*

the spring and early summer but soon dry or fall off for the remainder of the dry season. This plant has a distinct, pungent, sagebrush odor when crushed. Coast Brittlebush or California Encelia, *Encelia californica* (Fig. 46; Plate 7B) has a more typical sunflower blossom. This colorful plant forms patches that can be identified by the abundant yellow blooms in the spring and early summer.

Two other members of the sunflower family, commonly found in Coastal Sage Scrub, have flowers that lack the ring of petal-bearing ray flowers. Saw-toothed Goldenbush, *Hazardia squarrosa,* is a small, resinous shrub with saw-toothed leaves and whitish flowers, tinged with red. Coyote Brush, *Baccharis pilularis* (Fig. 45B), is a larger shrub up to 10 ft (3 m) in height. Its leaves and flowers resemble those of Saw-toothed Goldenbush, but close inspection will reveal that the leaves of Coyote Brush have three main veins instead of one.

The figwort or snapdragon family (Scrophulariceae) is renowned for its beautiful flowers, and several members of this family are important components of the Coastal Sage Scrub community. The monkeyflowers (*Mimulus* spp.), so named because some members of the group seem to resemble the face of a monkey, include herbaceous species and small shrubs. The Orange Bush Monkeyflower, *Mimulus aurantiacus* (Fig. 47), is a drought-deciduous species that usually has orange flowers, although there is great deal of variation in coloration, ranging from white to yellow to red. These monkeyflowers are inconspicuous most of the year because they are small and may be leafless. In the spring, however, when they come into

Figure 47. Orange Bush Monkeyflower, *Mimulus aurantiacus.* Note that the stigma lobes are closed in the flower on the right.

bloom, entire hillsides are colored by their blossoms. Typical of the family, the flowers of these plants are fused into a two-lipped tube, and the tip of the pistil (stigma) is divided into two conspicuous lobes. When a pollinator, such as a bee, visits the flower, it touches the stigma lobes, causing them to fold together. This change in appearance is a signal to later would-be pollinators that the flower has already been visited, and in this way the efficiency of the pollinator and the plant is optimized.

Although there is technically only one species of Bush Monkeyflower today, not all authorities agree with the lumping of these monkeyflowers into one species, and therefore it is common to see references to other species, even in recent publications. Formerly several species were identified, including the beautiful, scarlet-flowered Red Bush Monkeyflower, *Mimulus puniceus,* that occurs along the coast from Laguna Beach southward and on Santa Catalina Island. Another species, formerly known as Southern Bush Monkeyflower, *Mimulus longiflorus,* occurs on Santa Cruz Island, Santa Rosa Island, and the adjacent mainland. Another red-flowered form, the Island Monkeyflower, formerly *Mimulus flemingii* (Plate 6C), was considered to be an endemic species of special concern that occurred only on the Northern Channel Islands and San Clemente Island. Because it is still recognized by reputable botanists, *Mimulus flemingii* is included here as an island endemic.

Two other shrubs in this family have island populations. Showy Island Snapdragon, *Galvezia speciosa,* is an island endemic with beautiful tubular

Figure 48. Climbing Penstemon, *Keckiella cordifolia.*

red flowers that are pollinated by hummingbirds. It is a sprawling, almost viney species that occurs most commonly on cliffs of the Southern Channel Islands (except San Nicolas). On the Northern Channel Islands, in canyon bottoms and on north-facing slopes, is found Climbing Penstemon, *Keckiella cordifolia* (Fig. 48). This species has dark green oval leaves and long, tubular red flowers, and it is also pollinated by hummingbirds. Flowers from this plant were used medicinally by Native Americans.

There are also many herbaceous species in this family. Paintbrushes (*Castilleja* spp.) (Plate 7B), for example, are bright red wildflowers familiar to many. Paintbrushes are *hemiparasites;* that is, they are partially parasitic. They are photosynthetic and produce their own food, as does any free-living plant, but in addition, paintbrushes tap into the root systems of nearby shrubs to enhance their absorption of water and minerals. Therefore they are able to grow vigorously, even when the surface layers of the soil become too dry for most small plants. One species, *Castilleja affinis,* is widespread in California, including Santa Catalina and the Northern Channel Islands, and it is the paintbrush most likely to be seen. Its foliage is greenish to purple and frequently quite bristly; its flowers vary from yellow to red. Woolly Paintbrush, *Castilleja foliolosa,* is a small (1- to 2-ft) dark green plant that occurs in dry, rocky areas and has a bright red paintbrush flower. It is found on the mainland in chaparral communities, but Santa Catalina is the only island on which it is found.

Owl's Clovers are related to paintbrushes. They were formerly grouped in the genus *Orthocarpus* but are now included with the paintbrushes. Purple Owl's Clover, *Castilleja exserta* (=*Orthocarpus purpurescens*) (Plate 10B), is common in grassland and Coastal Sage Scrub communities on the mainland as well as Santa Catalina and the Northern Channel Islands. These flowers superficially resemble paintbrushes, but the color of the petals is pinkish purple. The name Owl's Clover refers to the owl-like appearance of some of the blossoms, which are white tipped. Close inspection and a bit of imagination reveal the images of perched owls in some of the flower clusters. Two other species of Owl's Clover are endemics on the Northern Channel Islands (Chapter 6).

There are also wildflowers in this family that are known as Snapdragons (*Antirrhinum* spp.). Nuttall's Snapdragon, *Antirrhinum nuttallianum*, is found in coastal areas on the mainland as well as the islands. It is a tall, slender ephemeral with small lavender to blue-purple flowers. Members of the southern Diegueño tribe apparently boiled the flowers of these snapdragons and used the brew medicinally. The Climbing Snapdragon, *Antirrhinum kelloggii*, is a fire follower: it is most common in disturbed sites, particularly those that have recently been subject to fires, and can be found all along the coast as well as on Santa Catalina and Santa Cruz Islands. This is a slender, almost vinelike species that may have stems up to 3 ft (1 m) long. It is capable of growing erect but nevertheless often clings to other plants or objects.

The broom-rape family (Orobanchaceae) is a family of truly parasitic plants in which the flowers resemble those of the figwort family. These fleshy herbs, lacking chlorophyll, have yellow to brownish stems with scale-like leaves. The two-lipped flowers are often purplish in color. These plants tap into the root systems of nearby plants and parasitize the photosynthetic product of the host plant. Five species of these interesting plants, none of which is common, are found on the Channel Islands. Perhaps the most common is the Clustered Broom-rape, *Orobanche fasciculata*, which tends to parasitize California Sagebrush or various buckwheats (*Eriogonum* spp.). It appears in the spring, when several fleshy stems erupt from the earth and grow about 4–7 in. (10–18 cm) high. This species is found on all the Channel Islands except San Clemente and Santa Barbara. Apparently Native Americans ate entire plants. The Bulbous Broom-rape, *Orobanche bulbosa*, is found on Santa Catalina, Santa Cruz, and Santa Rosa Islands, where it parasitizes Chamise, *Adenostoma fasciculatum*. The rarest of these species (even though it is found on several islands) is the

Short-lobed Broom-rape, *Orobanche parishii* ssp. *brachyloba* (Fig. 154). It inhabits sandy areas on San Miguel, San Nicolas, Santa Catalina, Santa Cruz, and Santa Rosa Islands, where it parasitizes the low-growing Coast Goldenbush, *Isocoma menziesii.*

The mallow family (Malvaceae) is also noted for its beautiful flowers. The hibiscuses make up a well-known group of cultivated plants in this family. Perhaps one of the most beautiful of all the island endemic shrubs is the Southern Channel Island Tree Mallow or Malva Rosa, *Lavatera assurgentiflora* ssp. *glabra* (Plate 6B). This large shrub has large, palmate leaves and flowers about 3 in. (8 cm) across. The petals are white to pale purple and have purple veins. Numerous stamens are fused into the hibiscus-like pistil, producing a round, brushlike structure in the center of each flower. These beautiful shrubs are native to San Clemente and Santa Catalina Islands, but they have been planted on the mainland and many of the other islands, including the Northern Channel Islands, where the Northern Channel Island Tree Mallow, *Lavatera assurgentiflora* ssp. *assurgentiflora,* is native.

The Santa Catalina Island Bush Mallow, *Malacothamnus fasciculatus* var. *catalinensis,* is another attractive near-endemic that is a member of the mallow family. This shrub has tall, slender branches; smaller, palmate leaves; and rose-colored flowers. The flowers are smaller than those of Malva Rosa, but their sheer numbers make up for their reduced size. On the mainland, this variety is also found in Coastal Sage Scrub in northern Baja California, but it is not recognized as a distinct entity by all authorities. Other members of this species are fire-followers that become extremely abundant in the years following major fires in Coastal Sage Scrub. The similar Santa Cruz Island Bush Mallow, *Malacothamnus fasciculatus* var. *nesioticus* (Fig. 77), and the San Clemente Island Bush Mallow, *Malacothamnus clementina,* are so rare now, owing to introduced herbivores, that they have been classified as endangered by government agencies.

The Silver Bush Lupine, *Lupinus albifrons* (Fig. 49), is a large (2- to 4-ft) plant with a rounded and much-branched growth form. On other islands, this species seems more typically associated with sand dune habitats (see Chapter 6). The leaves are silvery in color, whereas the flowers are dark blue or purple.

Black Sage, *Salvia mellifera,* is common along with the California Sagebrush on dry hillsides. Its leaves are slightly elongate, oval shaped, and dark green. This plant is easily distinguished by its violet to white flowers, which are arranged in compact, whorled clusters spaced 3–4 in. (9–12 cm) apart on the erect stems.

One of the conspicuous endemic plants in the Coastal Sage Scrub

Figure 49. Silver Bush Lupine, *Lupinus albifrons.*

community is Santa Catalina Island Buckwheat or Saint Catherine's Lace, *Eriogonum giganteum* var. *giganteum* (Fig. 50). This large (1- to 4-ft [1-m]), whitish shrub is common along the ridge road and around Avalon. The leaves are oval, 1–2 in. long, and woolly. The flowers are grouped on stalks in tight bunches and remain dry, as in most buckwheats, allowing this plant to be distinguished easily.

A plant in the nightshade family (Solanaceae) that is considered by some authorities to be endemic to Guadalupe and Santa Catalina Islands is Wallace's Nightshade, *Solanum wallacei,* a spreading shrubby plant 2–4 ft (1 m) high. Its leaves are dark green, hairy, and 2–3 in. (5–8 cm) long; the flowers are dark blue; and the fruit is black and poisonous.

Several species of cacti occur in Coastal Sage Scrub (Fig. 44). The most common cactus on the island is the Coastal Prickly-pear or Tuna, *Opuntia littoralis* (Fig. 51A; Plate 8C). This low-growing or sprawling species is very common on the dry, grass-covered hillsides, where it sometimes forms large clumps. Large yellow flowers and round red fruits are present on this cactus through most of the year. Because it is lightly grazed by goats, it probably has become much more abundant in recent years. A taller, sometimes treelike, prickly-pear cactus is *Opuntia oricola* (Fig. 52). Less common than Coastal Prickly-pear, it can be recognized by its taller stature and large, round pads: pads of Coastal Prickly-pear are usually oval in shape. The Coastal Cholla, *Opuntia prolifera* (Fig. 51B; Plate 8A,B), is also a component of this community. Its striking, wine-colored flower is perhaps the most beautiful of those of all the species of cholla in California.

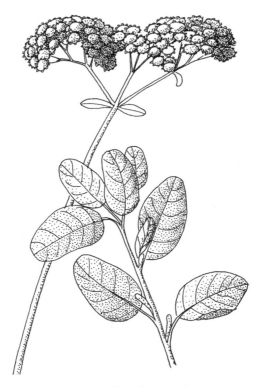

Figure 50. Santa Catalina Island Buckwheat,
Eriogonum giganteum var. *giganteum*.

These are the cacti that are sometimes called "jumping cactus" because the cylindrical joints seem to break off easily and become lodged in clothing or painfully attached to skin.

As one progresses southward toward Baja California, Coastal Sage Scrub becomes more and more characterized by succulent species. Maritime Desert Scrub (Figs. 143 and 147; Plate 8) is a community name used by some authors to characterize this variation on Coastal Sage Scrub. Of all the species that characterize Maritime Desert Scrub, perhaps the presence of Golden Cereus or Button Cactus, *Bergerocactus emoryi* (Fig. 146; Plate 8D), is most indicative. This is a clumped, cylindrical cactus with yellow spines. It enjoys limited distribution on Santa Catalina Island, but it is very common on the lower slopes of San Clemente Island.

The Maritime Desert Scrub community is present on the south- and west-facing slopes in a few localities. It is best seen on the southwest side of Indian Head Point. Here the succulent species are joined by common shrubs such as California Sagebrush and Coast Brittlebush, as well as those shrubs with more southern affinities such as Cliff Spurge, *Euphorbia mis-*

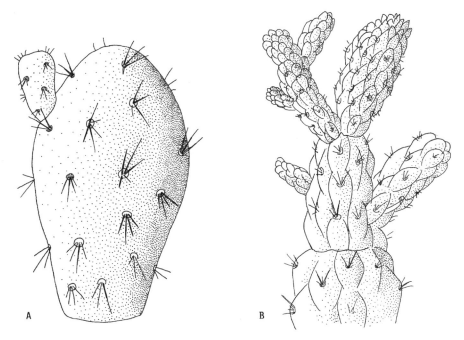

A

B

Figure 51. Common cacti of Coastal Sage Scrub. (A) Coastal Prickly-pear or Tuna, *Opuntia littoralis*. (B) Coastal Cholla, *Opuntia prolifera*.

Figure 52. *Opuntia oricola*, a tall prickly-pear with rounded pads.

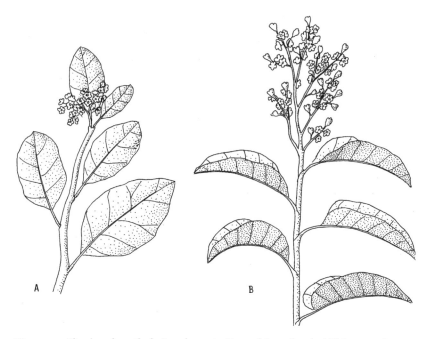

Figure 53. Shrubs of north-facing slopes in Coastal Sage Scrub. (A) Lemonade Berry, *Rhus integrifolia.* (B) Laurel Sumac, *Malosoma laurina.*

era (Fig. 145), a semisucculent, drought-deciduous member of the spurge family (Euphorbiaceae), and Box Thorn, *Lycium californicum* (Fig. 144), a thorny, drought-deciduous member of the nightshade family (Solanaceae). The Santa Catalina Island Desert-thorn, *Lycium andersonii* var. *hassei,* a similar species with small, succulent leaves, is now believed to be extinct. It also formerly occurred on San Clemente Island.

On north-facing slopes where Coastal Sage Scrub receives less direct sunlight, the plants tend to be larger, have larger leaves, and keep their leaves throughout the year. Perhaps the most common shrub in these cooler areas is Lemonade Berry, *Rhus integrifolia* (Fig. 53A; Plate 7C), a gray-green shrub with thick, oval leaves. It is one of the shrub species that can tolerate salt spray, and its growth form varies from a prostrate shrub on exposed, windward sea cliffs to a large, treelike plant in more moist areas. The berries have a sour taste, very much like that of a lemon, and they were used by Native Americans to make a drink. Another large, common shrub with a rounded growth form is Laurel Sumac, *Malosoma laurina* (Fig. 53B). The leaves of this common shrub are elongate and somewhat folded, like a taco. As the summer wears on, the leaves of these shrubs become more and more folded. Presumably the shrub reduces the leaf surface subject to evaporation in this manner. Laurel Sumac is a frost-sensitive plant. On those

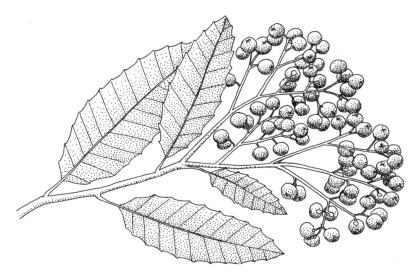

Figure 54. Toyon, *Heteromeles arbutifolia.*

occasions when the temperature drops below freezing, these shrubs seem to die back to the ground. The following spring, however, new growth occurs from the root stock, and the new shoots fill in to replace what appeared to be a dead plant.

Toyon, *Heteromeles arbutifolia* (Fig. 54), takes on treelike proportions in shaded canyons, where it may be intermixed with Catalina Cherry trees and Island Chaparral (which will be discussed later). This evergreen shrub is another of the large-leaved plants of north-facing slopes. Also called Christmas Berry or California Holly, it has serrated leaves and bright red berries that develop during the winter. This is the shrub for which Hollywood was named.

Coastal Bluff Scrub

On the steep sea bluffs, which afford exposure to coastal fog and protection from grazing goats, a variation of the Maritime Desert Scrub community develops. This community, known as Coastal Bluff Scrub, is characterized by a number of distinctive island species. Several of the species already discussed, such as Showy Island Snapdragon, are also found on these cliffs, but in this section we will discuss only those plants that seem to be limited to this sea bluff portion of the community.

It is here that Sea Dahlia or Giant Coreopsis, *Coreopsis gigantea* (Plate 9), occurs. This large, attractive sunflower has a succulent stem and a cluster of fernlike leaves near the top. As are many members of Coastal Sage Scrub, it is drought deciduous. The species is a frequently cited example of island gigantism, for its mainland relatives are significantly smaller in stature.

Another sunflower, known as Nevin's Eriophyllum or Island Dusty Miller, *Eriophyllum nevinii,* is a small, hairy, whitish shrub with intricately lobed leaves. This rare island endemic is also found on San Clemente and Santa Barbara Islands. It is seriously threatened by the grazing of non-native animals.

Catalina Crossosoma or California Thorn Apple, *Crossosoma californicum* (Plate 6D), also found on these dry bluffs is a drought-deciduous shrub that has white, roselike flowers. Its only close relative in California is a desert species, Ragged Rock-flower, *Crossosoma bigelovii,* which is found on rocky slopes at the edge of the Colorado Desert. Catalina Crossosoma is an island endemic, found also on Guadalupe and San Clemente Islands and the Palos Verdes Peninsula, a former island.

Coastal Bluff Scrub is also the preferred habitat for the succulent members of the stonecrop family (Crassulaceae), which commonly are known as live-forevers or dudleyas. The Santa Catalina Island Live-forever, *Dudleya hassei* (Fig. 55A), is endemic to Santa Catalina, and the Bright Green Dudleya or Green Live-forever, *Dudleya virens* (Fig. 55B), is also found on the Southern Channel Islands as well as a few locations on the mainland in Los Angeles County. Although both live-forevers seem to be significantly different in appearance and they co-occur on Santa Catalina Island, one authority has recently reduced the Santa Catalina Island Live-forever to a subspecies of the Bright Green Dudleya.

Island Chaparral

Chaparral is a community of plants with small leaves that have hard, waxy, or resinous coatings. Such leaves are said to be *sclerophyllous,* which means hard leafed. The plants making up this community are all evergreen and are adapted to long, dry summers. They also tolerate colder temperatures than Coastal Sage Scrub. The Chaparral community on Santa Catalina is present on the north and east slopes of the channel or the leeward side of the island, generally at higher elevations than Coastal Sage Scrub (Plate 11B,C). Here the waxy-leaved, gray-green vegetation covers the ravines and hillsides with a velvetlike cover, which in some areas is so dense it can only be penetrated on one's hands and knees. Good examples of chaparral can be seen in upper Avalon Canyon and on the slopes of Black Jack Mountain, where many species take on treelike proportions. The most important species in the Chaparral community on Santa Catalina are Chamise (*Adenostoma fasciculatum*) (Fig. 88; Plate 11C), Island Scrub Oak (*Quercus pacifica* [=*berberidifolia*]) (Fig. 87; Plate 11C), Island Ceanothus (*Cean-*

Figure 55. Live-forevers of Coastal Bluff Scrub. (A) Santa Catalina Island Live-forever, *Dudleya hassei*. (B) Bright Green Dudleya or Green Live-forever, *Dudleya virens* ssp. *insulare*.

othus megacarpus var. *insularis*) (Fig. 84A), Big-pod Ceanothus (*Ceanothus megacarpus* var. *megacarpus*), Feltleaf Ceanothus (*Ceanothus arboreus*) (Fig. 84B), and Island Mountain Mahogany (*Cercocarpus betuloides* var. *blancheae*) (Fig. 85), not to be confused with the endangered Catalina Island Mountain Mahogany (*Cercocarpus traskiae*), which has white wooly hairs beneath its leaves.

Manzanitas, so common on the northern Channel Islands, are rare on

Figure 56. Santa Catalina Island Manzanita,
Arctostaphylos catalinae.

Santa Catalina. The endemic Santa Catalina Island Manzanita, *Arcto-staphylos catalinae* (Fig. 56), is a rare treelike shrub with white bristles on its twigs. This member of the heath family (Ericaceae) is restricted to the upper slopes of volcanic outcrops.

Natural fires are an important part of a typical Chaparral community. On the mainland, these fires historically were caused by lightning. Surprisingly, however, there have been only three documented lightning-caused fires on the islands during the last 140 years. Nevertheless plants of the Chaparral community possess various mechanisms that ensure their return after a fire. For example, Chamise and Island Scrub Oak have a root-crown burl that resprouts after a fire, and various species of Ceanothus produce a tremendous number of seeds that require heat to stimulate germination. Similarly many short-lived herbaceous species such as Chia (*Salvia columbariae*) and California Poppy (*Eschscholzia californica*) also require the presence of ashes, which dissolve in the runoff of the first rains after a fire. This *leachate* or *charate* is as important to stimulate germination as the heat. Recent research also indicates that smoke stimulates germination of many of these species. Native Americans deliberately set fires to stimulate the growth of plants such as Chia because they harvested them and ate the seeds.

For a more thorough discussion of Island Chaparral see Chapter 6.

Island Woodland

What appears to be woodland on north-facing slopes and canyon bottoms is in reality an example of gigantism that is frequently encountered on islands. Most of the "trees" in these groves are unusually large specimens of common shrubs, such as Toyon and Island Scrub Oak.

However, Island Woodland and Riparian Woodland communities are present in certain canyons where more moisture collects and is retained. The community known as Southern Oak Woodland on the mainland corresponds roughly to Island Woodland; however, Coast Live Oak, *Quercus agrifolia,* which is considered an indicator for Southern Oak Woodland, is not present on Santa Catalina Island. Nevertheless, three species of oaks occur in scattered localities on Santa Catalina. Valley Oak, *Quercus lobata* (Fig. 93B), has limited distribution on Santa Catalina, as does its hybrid descendent, MacDonald Oak (*Quercus ×macdonaldii*). Middle Canyon has some fine specimens of this hybrid species. The endemic Island Oak, *Quercus tomentella* (Fig. 92), occurs in upper Gallagher's Canyon. For a complete discussion of oaks on the islands, see Chapter 1.

One indicator species of Island Woodland is a good example of a shrub that appears to be a tree. Catalina Cherry, *Prunus ilicifolia* ssp. *lyonii* (Plate 5C,D) in several valleys near the Isthmus is a treelike relative of Holly-leafed Cherry, a component of Chaparral on the mainland. The Catalina Cherry has large, glossy leaves with variable amounts of serration along the margins and small clusters of tiny white flowers in the spring. The large red cherries appear in the fall. They are delicious to eat, but they have a very large seed that contains cyanide. These cherries are an important autumn food for animals on the islands; they swallow the seed whole, without releasing its poisonous load. Native Americans ate the seeds, too—after leaching out the cyanide in the same way they leached the tannins from acorns.

Santa Catalina Ironwood, *Lyonothamnus floribundus* ssp. *floribundus* (Fig. 2A; Plate 5A), also appears to be a shrublike tree in growth habit. Groves of these trees may be present in areas that may appear to be quite dry but actually have seepages to supply moisture, as is the case in upper Swain's Canyon and on the north slope of Black Jack Mountain. They can best be seen just above the road near Black Jack Mountain or by a short hike up the canyon above Goat Harbor. The trees occur in small, dense groves and are 20–50 ft (6–16 m) tall and up to 18 in. (46 cm) in diameter. Very few seedlings of this rare tree have been observed on the island for many years owing to heavy grazing by goats and rooting by pigs. Another subspecies (*Lyonothamnus floribundus* ssp. *aspleniifolius*) (Fig. 2B; Plate 5B), occurs on San Clemente, Santa Cruz, and Santa Rosa Islands. This subspecies differs from *floribundus* by having slender, fernlike (pinnately compound) leaves that are dissected with many lobes on either side, whereas the Santa Catalina Ironwood has entire leaves with wavy margins and no such dissection (Fig. 2). Although some Santa Catalina Ironwoods have been propagated, the other subspecies is more commonly planted in southern California. Mature specimens of both subspecies grow together at the Rancho Santa Ana Botanic Garden in Claremont, where they hybridize quite freely.

Riparian Woodland

In Cottonwood and Middle Canyons, small, permanent streams support Riparian Woodlands. Native trees present in these wet areas include Black Cottonwood (*Populus trichocarpa*), Blue Elderberry (*Sambucus mexicana*), and Red Willow (*Salix laevigata*). Also present are vines and shrubs that form dense thickets along the stream banks, including California Wild Rose (*Rosa californica*) (Fig. 57A), Poison Oak (*Toxicodendron diversilobum*) (Fig. 58), California Blackberry (*Rubus ursinus*) (Fig. 57B), Douglas Mugwort (*Artemisia douglasiana*), Coyote Brush (*Baccharis pilularis*) (Fig. 45B), Giant Rye Grass (*Leymus condensatus*), and a rush (*Juncus acutus* ssp. *leopoldii*). The conspicuous pines near Middle Ranch are not native to Santa Catalina.

Coastal Grassland

Because of shallow soils and low rainfall, many ridgetops and southwest-facing slopes support a sparse to dense grassland community of mainly introduced grasses and weeds. Many northeast-facing slopes are also totally covered by nonnative grasses and weeds. Crisscross trails occur every few feet down these slopes, indicating heavy use by nonnative grazers. Common grass species include Wild Oats (*Avena fatua*) (Fig. 59A), California Brome (*Bromus carinatus*), Ripgut Brome (*Bromus diandrus*), Red Brome (*Bromus madritensis* ssp. *rubens*) (Fig. 59D), Italian Ryegrass (*Lolium multiflorum*) (Fig. 59C), Meadow Barley (*Hordeum brachyantherum*) (Fig. 59B), and Foxtail (*Hordeum murinum*). The introduction of these nonnative species is a phenomenon that has occurred all over California. The grasses are frequently native to the Mediterranean area of Europe, where the climate is similar, and most were introduced to California in the feed, fur, and intestinal tracts of domestic livestock.

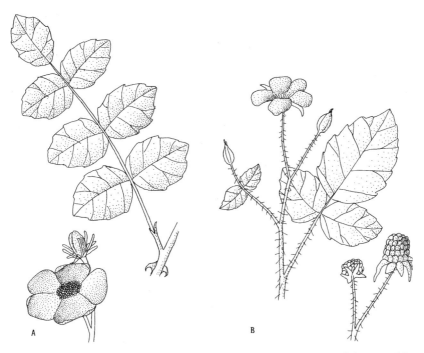

Figure 57. Shrubs of the rose family that occur along streams. (A) California Wild Rose, *Rosa californica*. (B) California Blackberry, *Rubus ursinus*.

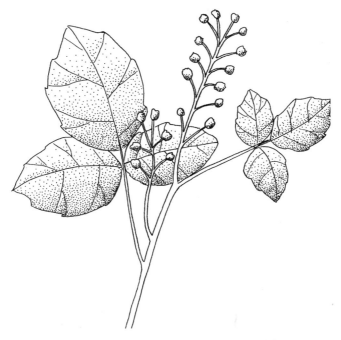

Figure 58. Poison Oak, *Toxicodendron diversilobum*.

Figure 59. Common introduced grasses. (A) Wild Oats, *Avena fatua.* (B) Meadow Barley, *Hordeum brachyantherum.* (C) Italian Ryegrass, *Lolium multiflorum.* (D) Red Brome, *Bromus madritensis* ssp. *rubens.* (Illustrations A–C from Hitchcock 1950. Illustration D from Robins et al. 1970.)

In the spring months many grasslands become covered with wildflowers, especially on the channel slope. For the most part these are ephemeral or annual herbaceous species, many of which are fire-followers. Some of the more common are Goldfields (*Lasthenia californica*) (Plate 10B), Tidy Tips (*Layia platyglossa*), fiddlenecks (*Amsinckia* spp.) (Fig. 155), lupine (*Lupi-*

nus sp.), popcorn flower (*Cryptantha* spp.), California Poppy (*Eschscholzia californica*), Island Poppy (*Eschscholzia ramosa*) (Fig. 163), shooting star (*Dodecatheon clevelandii* ssp. *insulare*) (Plate 10D), Parry's Larkspur (*Delphinium parryi*), Catalina Mariposa Lily (*Calochortus catalinae*) (Plate 10C), and Blue Dicks (*Dichelostemma capitatum*) (Fig. 198). The latter two return each year from bulbs. These wildflowers are particularly susceptible to devastation by pigs, which uproot them relentlessly for food.

Other communities present on Santa Catalina Island are Salt Marsh and Freshwater Pond, but both are so poorly represented that they will not be described here.

TERRESTRIAL ANIMALS

Santa Catalina Island has considerable diversity of land animals (Table 6), equivalent only to that of Santa Cruz Island. Its relatively large size and close proximity to shore allow for a higher probability of colonization. The Los Angeles, San Gabriel, and Santa Ana Rivers are potential sources of colonizers after heavy floods, which occur every 30–50 years. Since these rivers enter the ocean just across the channel from Santa Catalina Island, the probability of a lizard, snake, or small mammal rafting to the island is relatively high.

Invertebrates

Island invertebrates have not been studied thoroughly, but land snails, flying insects, and those arthropods associated with human habitation are present on Santa Catalina. A total of 370 species of moths and butterflies, 10 of which are island endemics, have been recorded for Santa Catalina Island (Table 3). Of particular interest is the Avalon Hairstreak, *Strymon avalona,* which may have the smallest distribution of all the butterflies in California. This small, gray butterfly, with a wingspread of about 1 in. (25 mm), can be recognized by a thin, taillike extension on each of its hind wings. Its nearest relative, the Common Hairstreak, *Strymon melinus,* is common on the other islands and the mainland.

A unique katydid of Santa Catalina Island is Propst's Shield-back Katydid, *Neduba propsti.* This peculiar member of the grasshopper and katydid group (Orthoptera) has an enlarged shield over its thorax that covers its wings, and unlike most katydids it is not bright green, but rather a dull brown with greenish mottling.

Amphibians and Reptiles (Herpetofauna)

For the reasons mentioned earlier, a surprising number of amphibians and reptiles occur on Santa Catalina Island, more than on any of the other

TABLE 6   VERTEBRATE ANIMALS OF SANTA CATALINA ISLAND

Amphibians
  Arboreal Salamander (*Aneides lugubris*)
  Garden Slender Salamander (*Batrachoseps pacificus major*)
  Pacific Treefrog (*Hyla* [=*Pseudacris*] *regilla*)
  Bullfrog (*Rana catesbeiana*)—Introduced
  Leopard Frog (*Rana pipiens*)—Introduced (not established)

Reptiles
  Side-blotched Lizard (*Uta stansburiana*)
  Western Skink (*Eumeces skiltonianus*)
  Southern Alligator Lizard (*Elgaria multicarinatus*)
  Desert Night Lizard (*Xantusia vigilis*)—One record
  Western Rattlesnake (*Crotalus viridis*)
  Common King Snake (*Lampropeltis getulus*)
  Mountain King Snake (*Lampropeltis zonata*)—Old record
  Western Ringnecked Snake (*Diadophis punctatus*)
  Gopher Snake (*Pituophis melanoleucus*)
  Two-striped Garter Snake (*Thamnophis hammondii*)—Unique color pattern

Birds: See Table 7

Native terrestrial mammals
  Ornate Shrew (*Sorex ornatus*)
  Santa Catalina Island Ground Squirrel (*Spermophilus beecheyi nesioticus*)
    —Endemic
  Woodrat (*Neotoma* sp.)—One record
  Santa Catalina Island Harvest Mouse (*Reithrodontomys megalotis catalinae*)
    —Endemic
  Santa Catalina Island Deer Mouse (*Peromyscus maniculatus catalinae*)
    —Endemic
  Santa Catalina Island Fox (*Urocyon littoralis catalinae*)—Endemic
  Long-eared Bat (*Myotis evotis*)
  California Bat (*Myotis californicus*)
  Townsend's Lump-nosed Bat (*Plecotus townsendii)*
  Pallid Bat (*Antrozous pallidus*)

Introduced mammals
  Domestic Goat (*Capra hircus*)
  Horse (*Equus caballus*)
  Cattle (*Bos taurus*)
  Pig (*Sus scrofa*)
  American Bison (*Bison bison*)
  House Cat (*Felis domesticus*)
  Domestic Dog (*Canis familiaris*)
  Black Rat (*Rattus rattus*)
  Norway Rat (*Rattus norvegicus*)
  House Mouse (*Mus musculus*)
  Mule Deer (*Odocoileus hemionus*)
  White-tailed Deer (*Odocoileus virginianus*)—Not established
  Black Buck Antelope (*Antelope cervicapra*)
  Barbary Sheep (*Ammotragus lervia*)—Not established

Marine mammals
  Harbor Seal (*Phoca vitulina*)
  California Sea Lion (*Zalophus californianus*)

islands. The native herpetofauna consists of five species of snakes, three species of lizards, a frog, and two species of salamanders. Two species of amphibians may have been introduced by humans.

Much of the island's herpetofauna is also well represented on the mainland. The conspicuous Side-blotched Lizard, *Uta stansburiana* (Fig. 60A), is the most common lizard on all the Channel Islands except San Miguel, Santa Barbara, and Santa Rosa, and a well-known colonizer on islands on both coasts of Baja California as well. The other two lizards, the Western Skink, *Eumeces skiltonianus* (Fig. 60B), and the Southern Alligator Lizard, *Elgaria multicarinatus* (Fig. 60C), are less conspicuous, commonly found under logs or rocks. Among the Channel Islands, the Western Skink is found only on Santa Catalina Island, although it is also present on Los Coronados and Todos Santos Islands, which are relatively close to the mainland off the coast of Baja California. There is one record of dubious validity of the Desert Night Lizard, *Xantusia vigilis.* The Island Night Lizard, *Xantusia riversiana* (Fig. 151; Plate 1C), is not known from Santa Catalina.

Of the eight Channel Islands, snakes are found only on Santa Catalina, Santa Cruz, and Santa Rosa. Surprisingly, on Santa Catalina the number of snake species (five) is greater than the number of lizard species (three). Santa Catalina is the only island that has a rattlesnake, the Western Rattlesnake, *Crotalus viridis* (Fig. 61), and it appears to be fairly common. The other three common species of snakes include the Common King Snake (*Lampropeltis getulus*), the Western Ringnecked Snake (*Diadophis punctatus*), and the Gopher Snake (*Pituophis melanoleucus*) (Fig. 106).

The Two-striped Garter Snake, *Thamnophis hammondii,* formerly known as the Santa Catalina Island Garter Snake (*Thamnophis couchi hammondi*) is rare. Prior to 1974 it was known from only two specimens. Currently it is known to occur only along a 1-mile (1.6-km) stretch of permanent flow in Cottonwood Canyon that includes a small reservoir. There is very little appropriate habitat for this semiaquatic snake on Santa Catalina, and it may be on the verge of extirpation. The total population may include no more than twenty-five to thirty individuals, and they are threatened by a variety of predators, including the introduced Bullfrog, *Rana catesbeiana.* The possible origin of this snake, with its peculiar stripeless color pattern, which resembles snakes from a population near Lompoc in Santa Barbara County, is discussed in Chapter 1.

Of the amphibians native to Santa Catalina Island, two are salamanders. The Arboreal Salamander, *Aneides lugubris* (Fig. 62), is extremely rare. On the mainland it usually is associated with oaks; that pattern seems to hold true for Santa Catalina, although there are no oak trees where it occurs on the Farallons. The other salamander, the Garden Slender Salamander,

Figure 60. Lizards of Santa Catalina Island. (A) Side-blotched Lizard, *Uta stansburiana.* (B) Western Skink, *Eumeces skiltonianus.* (C) Southern Alligator Lizard, *Elgaria multicarinatus.*

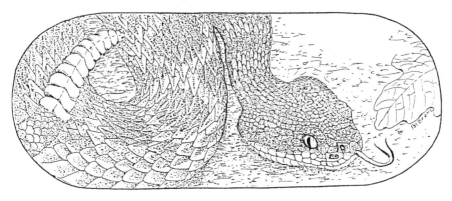

Figure 61. Western Rattlesnake, *Crotalus viridis*. (Drawing by Pat Brame. From Schoenherr 1976.)

Figure 62. Arboreal Salamander, *Aneides lugubris*. (From Stebbins 1951.)

Batrachoseps pacificus major, also occurs on Los Coronados and Todos Santos Islands off Baja California and on the adjacent mainland. This is the common salamander that occurs in moist habitats, including gardens at low elevations along the coast. It is not uncommon in Coastal Sage Scrub, and it is not the same subspecies that occurs on the four Northern Channel Islands. The possible transport of these sedentary salamanders to their present locations by translocation of the islands along fault systems is discussed in Chapter 1.

The only native frog on Santa Catalina is the Pacific Treefrog, *Hyla* (=*Pseudacris*) *regilla* (Fig. 63). Choruses of these diminutive frogs may be heard around Avalon, in particular at water hazards on the golf courses. The Pacific Treefrog is also found on Santa Cruz and Santa Rosa and on Cedros Island off Baja California. By virtue of its suction-cup-like toe tips, this species is able to cling to vertical smooth surfaces. It is therefore entirely possible that these small frogs could have rafted over to the islands in association with logs washed out to sea by a storm. It is interesting to note, however, that on the mainland this frog is usually not associated with trees; despite its name, it is chiefly a ground dweller. Its usual habitat is in low

Figure 63. Pacific Treefrog, *Hyla* (=*Pseudacris*) *regilla.*

vegetation along the borders of slowly moving water, although it is frequently found some distance from water in Coastal Sage Scrub, and therefore finds adequate habitat on islands.

Although Santa Catalina Island has good habitat for amphibians, lizards, and snakes, certain factors probably endanger them and restrict their distribution. Habitat destruction by goats and pigs may well limit the distribution of certain species. It is believed that pigs were originally introduced to Santa Catalina Island to control the rattlesnake population. Although pigs are indeed reported to eat snakes, they have also been observed turning over fallen vegetation to eat the salamanders that are thus exposed.

With the construction of reservoirs on the island, nonnative species such as the Bullfrog, *Rana catesbeiana,* and possibly the Leopard Frog, *Rana pipiens,* became established. Other than the Two-striped Garter Snake mentioned previously, no native animals appear to be threatened by these introduced species.

Birds

Thirty-seven species of land birds have been known to breed on Santa Catalina Island (Table 7). Of these, two species represent endemic races: the Catalina race of the California Quail (*Callipepla californica catalinensis*) (Fig. 64D) and a race of Bewick's Wren (*Thryomanes bewickii catalinae*)

TABLE 7   BREEDING BIRDS OF SANTA CATALINA ISLAND

Land birds
   Endemic to Santa Catalina
      California Quail (*Callipepla californica catalinensis*)
      Bewick's Wren (*Thryomanes bewickii catalinae*)

   Island endemics
      Loggerhead Shrike (*Lanius ludovicianus anthonyi*)
      Western Flycatcher (*Empidonax difficilis insulicola*)
      Rufous-sided Towhee (*Pipilo erythrophthalmus clementae*)
      House Finch (*Carpodacus mexicanus clementis*)
      Orange-crowned Warbler (*Vermivora celata sordida*)
      Allen's Hummingbird (*Selasphorus sasin sedentarius*)
      Horned Lark (*Eremophila alpestris insularis*)

   Nonendemics
      Bald Eagle (*Haliaeetus leucocephalus*)
      Red-tailed Hawk (*Buteo jamaicensis*)
      American Kestrel (*Falco sparverius*)
      Burrowing Owl (*Athene cunicularia*)
      Long-eared Owl (*Asio otus*)
      Northern Saw-whet Owl (*Aegolius acadicus*)
      Killdeer (*Charadrius vociferus*)
      Mourning Dove (*Zenaida aurita*)
      White-throated Swift (*Aeronautes saxatalis*)
      Anna's Hummingbird (*Calypte anna*)
      Northern Flicker (*Colaptes auratus*)
      Acorn Woodpecker (*Melanerpes formicivorus*)
      Black Phoebe (*Sayornis nigricans*)
      Barn Swallow (*Hirundo rustica*)
      Common Raven (*Corvus corax*)
      Swainson's Thrush (*Catharus ustulatus*)
      Phainopepla (*Phainopepla nitans*)
      Hutton's Vireo (*Vireo huttoni*)
      Western Meadowlark (*Sturnella neglecta*)
      Northern Mockingbird (*Mimus polyglottos*)
      Rock Wren (*Salpinctes obsoletus*)
      Hooded Oriole (*Icterus cucullatus*)
      Lesser Goldfinch (*Carduelis psaltria*)
      Chipping Sparrow (*Spizella passerina*)

   Introduced species
      Rock Dove (*Columba livia*)
      House Sparrow (*Passer domesticus*)
      European Starling (*Sturnus vulgaris*)
      Brown-headed Cowbird (*Molothrus ater*)

Sea birds
      Western Gull (*Larus occidentalis*)
      Black Oystercatcher (*Haematopus bachmani*)
      Brandt's Cormorant (*Phalacrocorax penicillatus*)—Extirpated(?)

Figure 64. Native land birds of California islands. (A) Burrowing Owl, *Athene cunicularia*. (B) American Kestrel, *Falco sparverius*. (C) Allen's Hummingbird, *Selasphorus sasin sedentarius*. (D) California Quail, *Callipepla californica*. (E) Horned Lark, *Eremophila alpestris insularis*. (F) Western Meadowlark, *Sturnella neglecta*. (G) Northern Mockingbird, *Mimus polyglottos*. (H) Rufous-sided Towhee, *Pipilo erythrophthalmus*. (I) Rock Wren, *Salpinctes obsoletus*. (J) Bewick's Wren, *Thryomanes bewickii*.

Figure 64. (*Continued*)

(Fig. 64J). A few other species that nest on Santa Catalina Island are island endemics, limited to Catalina Island and other nearby islands. These include races of the Loggerhead Shrike (*Lanius ludovicianus anthonyi*) (Fig. 111), Western Flycatcher (*Empidonax difficilis insulicola*), Rufous-sided Towhee (*Pipilo erythrophthalmus clementae*) (Fig. 64H), House Finch (*Carpodacus mexicanus clementis*) (Fig. 110), Orange-crowned Warbler (*Vermivora celata sordida*) (Fig. 109), Allen's Hummingbird (*Selasphorus sasin sedentarius*) (Figs. 64C and 113), and Horned Lark (*Eremophila alpestris insularis*) (Fig. 64E). Several other species may represent gene pools separate from mainland populations, but this possibility has yet to be confirmed.

For a more thorough discussion of island birds see Chapter 6.

The most conspicuous birds are the Western Meadowlark (*Sturnella neglecta*) (Fig. 64F), Horned Lark (Fig. 64E), Northern Mockingbird (*Mimus polyglottos*) (Fig. 64G), and Allen's Hummingbird (Figs. 64C and 113). Groups of California Quail (Fig. 64D) are often encountered, and a short quail-hunting season existed in past years.

Several birds that would be expected in Coastal Sage Scrub, Chaparral, and Oak Woodland habitats are not found on the island, notably the Wren-tit, *Chamaea fasciata,* and California Towhee, *Pipilo crissalis.* Both are common on the adjacent mainland but apparently are not good colonizers. Other species, such as the Rock Wren, *Salpinctes obsoletus* (Fig. 64I), and the Orange-crowned Warbler (Fig. 109) occur on the islands in greater abundance or occupy more habitats than their mainland equivalents.

Recently Bald Eagles, *Haliaeetus leucocephalus* (Fig. 65), have been reintroduced to the island, and they may often be seen flying above the cliffs high above Goat Harbor and other areas along the island's leeward shore. As of 1995, thirty-three birds had been placed on Santa Catalina Island, but reproductive problems seem to be preventing them from flourishing. The birds continue to lay thin-shelled eggs. In an attempt to prevent breakage by nesting adults, an artificial substitute egg is temporarily placed in the nest while the real egg is hatched in an incubator. The young eaglet is the returned to the nest to be reared by the parents naturally. It is believed that DDT, still present in local waters, continues to have deleterious effects on this species in the Southern California Bight. Nevertheless in 1994 the Bald Eagle in the lower forty-eight states was downlisted from endangered to threatened, and the federal government has proposed that it be removed entirely from the listing. The 1942 Bald Eagle Protection Act will, however, remain in effect, so it will still be illegal to kill this spectacular symbol of our country.

Other birds once resident but no longer present include the Osprey,

Figure 65. Bald Eagle, *Haliaeetus leucocephalus.*

Pandion haliaetus (Fig. 41), and Peregrine Falcon, *Falco peregrinus.* Predation by humans and the widespread presence of pesticides in ecosystems adjacent to large population centers are probably responsible for the demise of these magnificent predators on Santa Catalina Island. Raptors that are present and likely to be seen include the Red-tailed Hawk, *Buteo jamaicensis,* and the American Kestrel, *Falco sparverius* (Fig. 64B). Owls, inconspicuous because they are nocturnal and hide during the daytime, include the Long-eared Owl, *Asio otus,* and the Northern Sawwhet Owl, *Aegolius acadicus.* The Burrowing Owl, *Athene cunicularia* (Fig. 64A), is actually active during the day, but it is inconspicuous by virtue of its habit of remaining motionless near its burrow, commonly the abandoned burrow of a ground squirrel.

Nonnative birds associated with humans have also become established on Santa Catalina. Among these are the House Sparrow (*Passer domesticus*), the European Starling (*Sturnus vulgaris*), and the Brown-headed Cowbird (*Molothrus ater*). Some of these species can pose threats to native birds.

For example, European Starlings displace native cavity-nesting birds, and House Sparrows provide competition for native sparrows and finches. Brown-headed Cowbirds originally were associated with Bison on the Great Plains. They migrated westward in association with domesticated animals, hence the name cowbird. Ironically on Santa Catalina these birds have become reassociated with Bison, following Bison herds and feeding on insects in their hair and in their droppings. Unfortunately the cowbirds are nest parasites that lay their eggs in the nests of various native songbirds. It remains to be seen whether the Brown Cowbird will affect the abundance of native birds on the island, particularly those that nest in riparian habitats.

Santa Catalina is visited by many species of birds during spring and fall migrations. These birds may stop as part of their regular migration along the California coast or land, exhausted, after being lost at sea. Little is known about the needs of these migratory birds or the role the island plays as a stopover point during migrations.

Sea Birds

Santa Catalina Island supports fewer breeding sea birds than any other island in the Santa Barbara Channel. Most sea birds require secluded habitats, and it seems that the presence of humans causes them to leave their nests, subjecting their eggs to predation by gulls, to death by overexposure to the sun, or to both. Pigs and feral cats also destroy sea birds' nests and their young.

Because Santa Catalina Island's shores have been subjected to heavy use by humans since the 1840s, and because a significant Native American population was probably present for thousands of years, sea birds may have utilized Santa Catalina Island sparingly for breeding in historic times. Conspicuously absent, or at low population densities, are storm-petrels (*Oceanodroma* spp.), cormorants (*Phalacrocorax* spp.), the Brown Pelican (*Pelecanus occidentalis*) (Fig. 192J; Plate 3A), the Common Murre (*Uria aalge*) (Fig. 173), the Pigeon Guillemot (*Cepphus columba*) (Fig. 175), Xantus' Murrelet (*Synthliboramphus hypoleucus*) (Fig. 164), Cassin's Auklet (*Ptychoramphus aleuticus*) (Fig. 171), and the Tufted Puffin (*Fratercula cirrhata*) (Fig. 176). These species are known breeders on one or more of the other California islands, particularly farther north. With the removal of feral cats, it is hoped that many of these sea birds may colonize in the future. Even though they are not known to breed on Santa Catalina, Brown Pelicans and cormorants are frequently observed feeding in local waters. In fact, one of the few places where they may be observed easily is on the rock outcrop just south of Avalon Cove. Brown Pelicans, Double-crested Cormorants (Plate 3B), and Western Gulls (Fig. 192A; Plate 3D) perch on the rocks, seemingly oblivious to the stream of tourists walking or driving by. The population sizes of auklets, petrels, and murrelets seem to be on the increase in the area as well.

Currently the only breeding population of sea birds on the island is on Bird Rock, located 1 mile (1.6 km) north of Two Harbors at the island's isthmus. This small inlet supports a population of about fifty pairs of Western Gulls, *Larus occidentalis,* and an occasional Black Oystercatcher, *Haematopus bachmani* (Plate 3C).

Brandt's Cormorant, *Phalacrocorax penicillatus,* formerly bred on Santa Catalina, but disturbance by humans and egg predation by Western Gulls probably eliminated the species from the island.

Terrestrial Mammals

The native land mammals recorded on Santa Catalina Island consist of five species: three species of rodents, a shrew, and a fox. The Ornate Shrew, *Sorex ornatus,* is known from a single specimen taken from a spring above the town of Avalon, and this is the only specimen ever taken from a California island. This area has since been developed. Searches of the area and other portions of the island have not met with success in finding additional individuals. However, shrews are notoriously difficult to capture except by the use of pit traps, and an extensive effort to capture them on Santa Catalina Island has never been attempted. If this species still survives on the island, it probably would be located in wetter stream areas. Shrews are the only known venomous mammals, the venom being useful for subduing large prey. They are tiny carnivores famous for their voracious appetites and high metabolic rates, which certainly make them unlikely candidates for colonization of an island.

The Santa Catalina Island Ground Squirrel, *Spermophilus beecheyi nesioticus* (Fig. 66), is endemic to Santa Catalina Island. The squirrel is slightly larger than its mainland counterpart. It is not understood why it has not colonized the other islands, but it has long been on Santa Catalina, as evidenced by skeletal remains found deep within Indian midden deposits on the island. Apparently Native Americans ate the squirrels, and it has been hypothesized that they may have been brought deliberately to the island as a source of food—although, if that is in fact the case, it has not been explained why the squirrels were not transported to other islands for the same purpose.

There are two species of native mice on Santa Catalina. The Santa Catalina Island Harvest Mouse, *Reithrodontomys megalotis catalinae* (Fig. 67A), is an endemic subspecies on Santa Catalina Island. The species is also found

Figure 66. Santa Catalina Island Ground Squirrel, *Spermophilus beecheyi nesioticus.*

Figure 67. Native mice of Santa Catalina Island. (A) Santa Catalina Island Harvest Mouse, *Reithrodontomys megalotis catalinae.* (B) Santa Catalina Island Deer Mouse, *Peromyscus maniculatus catalinae.*

on Santa Cruz and San Clemente Islands, although the latter is the result of an inadvertent introduction along with a shipment of baled hay.

The Santa Catalina Island Deer Mouse, *Peromyscus maniculatus catalinae* (Fig. 67B), is the endemic subspecies of a mouse found on all eight of the Channel Islands. Each island has its own assigned endemic subspecies, although recent analysis suggests that subspecific status for the Santa Catalina Island Deer Mouse may be unwarranted. This is also the most common wild mouse on the mainland. Similar to other small island mammals, the deer mice are larger than their mainland counterparts.

Studies of the two mouse species on Santa Catalina have shown that they are widespread, occurring in nearly every plant community sampled. Deer mice were found in every habitat except Coastal Sage Scrub, and harvest mice were absent only from Coastal Grassland and Oak Woodland. Maritime Desert Scrub was the preferred habitat for both species.

There is a report of the trapping of a woodrat (*Neotoma* sp.) in Bulrush Canyon. There is no general evidence, however, of woodrats on any of the islands. A small, isolated population may occur on Santa Catalina, but this has yet to be confirmed.

The Island Fox, *Urocyon littoralis* (Fig. 4; Plate 1A), though not as numerous as on other islands, is occasionally observed near the Wrigley Memorial Botanical Garden, near Middle Ranch, and near Two Harbors. The foxes are apparently not as tame as those on Santa Cruz Island, and therefore they are not as easily approached. Many scientists are now convinced that Island Foxes from several sources were carried to Santa Catalina by Native Americans. For a complete discussion of the biogeography of this species see Chapter 1.

Of the seven species of bats found on the Channel Islands, four—the Long-eared Myotis (*Myotis evotis*), the California Myotis (*M. californicus*), the Lump-nosed Bat (*Plecotus townsendii*), and the Pallid Bat (*Antrozous pallidus*)—have been documented as occurring on Santa Catalina. Some were found roosting in abandoned mine shafts; others have been collected by mist netting. All represent species found on the mainland.

Introduced Animals of Santa Catalina Island

The introduction of feral animals to an island can cause severe disruption of the island's ecosystem and the extinction of many island organisms. Introduced predators have decimated land bird populations around the world. Herbivores such as sheep, goats, burros, and rabbits left on islands undergo population explosions in the absence of their natural predators and diseases. The result is overgrazing of the island's vegetation, causing the extinction not only of plant species but also of the birds and mammals that depend on them. Overgrazing may also result in severe erosion problems, especially in arid regions. The impact of introduced mammals on the various islands of California is discussed in Chapter 1.

On Santa Catalina Island the primary introduced nonnative mammals include feral goats, Bison, feral pigs, house cats, domestic rats, and mice. Among native California species, both the Mule Deer, *Odocoileus hemionus,* and the White-tailed Deer, *Odocoileus virginianus,* have been introduced to the island, where they formerly did not occur; however, it appears that the White-tailed Deer population did not persist.

Goats Goats, *Capra hircus* (Fig. 5A), were introduced to Santa Catalina Island around 1800, and their numbers increased to as many as 20,000 earlier in this century. The effect on the island has been severe overgrazing and the prevention of the reproduction of seedlings of many of the island trees.

When ownership of the island passed to William Wrigley in 1919, he recognized the problems resulting from overgrazing by goats and other species and instituted a control program to limit the damage done by grazing animals. Cattle, *Bos taurus,* were removed from the island, and, beginning in 1954, the goat population was reduced by sport hunting and reduction hunting by Santa Catalina Conservancy personnel until numbers reached 7000–10,000 animals. Hunting was carried out in areas where goat populations had caused noticeable damage to the vegetation. Fences were constructed to limit the movement of goats back into areas from which they had been removed. Currently the number of goats is down to near 1000 in the canyons and ravines near Avalon. A program involving helicopter-borne marksmen, begun in 1989, has systematically reduced their numbers so that they are all but gone from the west side of the island. Because goats cannot be tolerated by the island ecosystem, their continued control is considered essential.

Pigs Wild pigs or boars, *Sus scrofa* (Fig. 5D), introduced to Santa Rosa Island by early hunters or explorers, were transported to Santa Catalina in 1934 in the hope that they would act as a biological control agent for rattlesnakes. Although pigs do eat snakes, they are omnivorous and in fact consume a wide range of foods. On Santa Catalina Island they eat, in addition to snakes, small salamanders and lizards, bird eggs, and a variety of plant materials, including acorns and the seeds, roots, and seedlings of many plants, including rare and endemic species.

The size of the pig population on Santa Catalina Island is difficult to estimate owing to the animals' nocturnal habits. Each year about 500 pigs

Figure 68. Overgrazing on Santa Catalina Island. Bison graze on the left side of the fence, goats on the right.

are removed from the island by sport hunting, and the total population must be several times this figure. Continued efforts to reduce the pig population are under way.

Bison As mentioned previously, fourteen "buffalo" or American Bison, *Bison bison,* (Fig. 5C) were brought to Santa Catalina Island in 1924 for the filming of the movie *The Vanishing American.* Eleven more animals were added to the herd in 1934, and twenty-two bulls have recently been added to counteract the deleterious effects of inbreeding. The population of Bison on the island has been as high as 500 individuals, but it is near 300 at present. They are free ranging on the island and their number is controlled by selective removal.

Bison, along with other introduced herbivores, can overgraze stream areas and cause damage to such habitats through trampling, especially in times of drought. However, the impact of Bison on the island does not appear to be as severe as that of goats and pigs. Along fence lines where goats and Bison graze on opposite sides, the extreme degradation caused by the goats is particularly obvious (Fig. 68).

House Cats House cats, *Felis domesticus,* are present on the island as pets, principally in the town of Avalon and in the Isthmus area. Some cats have escaped from these areas and become feral, invading the interior of the island, where they represent a relatively new predatory force on birds and rodents. Santa Catalina Island Company personnel have attempted to limit their numbers by trapping and shooting. Although the number of feral cats is currently small (no population estimate is available at this time), they present a serious potential threat to the island's populations of small animals. The cats are in direct competition with the Island Fox for food.

Rats and Mice Black Rats (*Rattus rattus*), Norway Rats (*Rattus norvegicus*), and the House Mouse (*Mus musculus*) have all found their way to Santa Catalina Island. They live within human settlements, foraging the inhabited areas of the island, especially in the palm trees around Avalon.

Mule Deer Mule deer, *Odocoileus hemionus,* from the Kaibab Plateau of Arizona were introduced in the 1930s in an attempt to develop sport hunting on Santa Catalina Island. A hunting program has now been established, and the population of deer is estimated to be about 300, centered on the eastern end of the island. White-tailed Deer, *Odocoileus virginianus,* were also introduced, but they seem not to have persisted.

Marine Mammals

Santa Catalina Island is the most accessible of the Channel Islands from the mainland, and because of its fine harbors it hosts numerous boating visitors throughout the year. This intensive use of the island's shores by humans has undoubtedly been responsible for preventing most marine mammals from using Santa Catalina for breeding. Five species of seals and sea lions (pinnipeds) inhabit the waters of southern California. The numbers of all these species were severely reduced in the nineteenth century by hunting. Although they are protected today, their numbers have not returned to their former levels in Southern California owing to the lack of isolated beaches where they can breed without disturbance. Major breeding areas occur today only on such protected islands as San Miguel and San Nicolas Islands, both of which are owned by the U.S. Navy and are closed to the public, or on the more distant islands that are less frequently visited, such as Santa Barbara Island. The best area to observe these animals is Año Nuevo Island off central California.

Elephant Seals, *Mirounga angustirostris* (Figs. 38 and 167), may have once bred on sandy beaches of Catalina Harbor and Little Harbor. The Harbor Seal, *Phoca vitulina* (Fig. 37; Plate 2C), and the California Sea Lion, *Zalophus californianus* (Fig. 39; Plate 2C), are frequent visitors to the island, stopping to rest on its shores. Seal Rock, at the southeast end of the island, was once frequented by many sea lions, but their numbers have diminished in recent years.

Marine mammals in general are discussed in Chapter 4.

Marine Life

Among the most attractive aspects of Santa Catalina Island's natural history are the clear, calm waters and the beautiful subtidal plant and animal communities along its shoreline. Glass-bottom boats opened this submarine world to Avalon's visitors as early as 1896, and over the past 30 years the island has become extremely popular among scuba divers. Dense kelp beds and colorful fishes and invertebrates, found around most of the island, make it a beautiful place to dive.

The University of Southern California built the marine science center at Big Fisherman's Cove near Two Harbors in the late 1960s. Now known as the Wrigley Institute of Marine Science, it has served as the base for numerous scientific studies of Santa Catalina Island's marine life. A large decompression chamber was installed in 1974 in cooperation with the County of Los Angeles for the treatment of divers who experience decompression accidents.

Santa Catalina Island has also long been a favorite sportfishing locale. Charles Frederick Holder and five associates founded the Tuna Club in 1898, and tuna and marlin fishing soon transformed Avalon into a major gamefishing resort. Yellowtail, White Sea Bass, and Barracuda could be caught during the summer months from small skiffs very near shore. Most of these species are now rarely taken, but Kelp Bass (Fig. 29D) still abound along the island's windward shore. Many island residents prefer fishing for rockfish (Fig. 31) and sand dabs in favorite coves along the protected leeward shore, and these fishes are still quite numerous.

For a full discussion of marine life, consult Chapter 4.

CHAPTER SIX

THE NORTHERN CHANNEL ISLANDS

The Northern Channel Islands (Fig. 69) are among the most conspicuous landmarks in southern California. Unlike the Southern Channel Islands, each island in this group is visible from the mainland on clear days. Millions of travelers on U.S. Highway 101 in southern Santa Barbara and Ventura Counties are treated to a grand procession of islands paralleling the coast. From the vicinity of the University of California campus at Santa Barbara, all four islands can sometimes be seen stretching in a broken silhouette across much of the Pacific horizon. A magnet for local researchers, the islands remain a tantalizing mystery to the general public, although recent changes in ownership have made them more accessible.

The four northern islands are separated from each other by relatively narrow and shallow passages from 3 to 6 miles (5–9 km) wide (cover illustration). Because of their shared geological, biological, and human histories (as well as their geographic proximity), we can readily examine patterns of variation in the group as a whole rather than treat each island as a special case. Although the islands have been intensively studied, more work of a synthetic nature concerning their ecology is in order, and topics for new studies are constantly being suggested by research in various fields.

INTERISLAND GEOGRAPHIC PATTERNS

From west to east, the four Northern Channel Islands are San Miguel Island, Santa Rosa Island, Santa Cruz Island, and Anacapa Island. Except for Anacapa Island, at the eastern end of the chain, this is also the order of increasing size. Small, dry, and rocky, Anacapa (Fig. 70 and cover illustration; Plate 13A) supports relatively few species of plants and animals. Next in size is San Miguel Island (Plate 13C), the outermost of the group, which receives the full force of the cold California Current. The island is low and sandy,

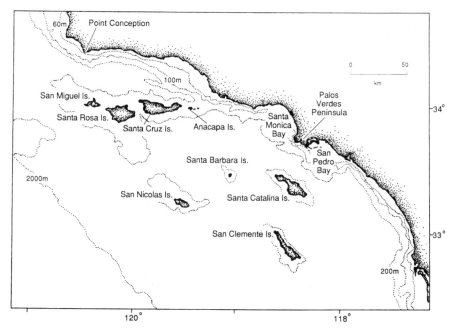

Figure 69. The Channel Islands, showing 100-m and 200-m bottom contours. (From Dailey et al. 1993.)

Figure 70. East end of Anacapa Island, showing steep southern scarp and lighthouse.

supporting scrubby vegetation and spectacular colonies of sea birds, seals, and sea lions. Santa Rosa Island (Plate 13B) is a large and somewhat dry island with grassy slopes dissected by precipitous, wooded canyons. Rugged Santa Cruz Island (Plate 12A-C) is the largest and most prominent of all of the California Islands and supports the greatest biological diversity.

A number of interesting comparisons can be made between the Northern and Southern Channel Islands. When the islands are listed in order of increasing area, as above, the general characteristics of the northern islands closely parallel those of the southern islands. Yet a number of differences between the northern and southern groups are also evident. The northern islands are less arid, closer to shore, and closer to each other than their southern counterparts. They are also generally larger and higher in elevation. Although the islands exhibit certain similarities, each also has its own unique characteristics, and these are emphasized in the discussion of the individual islands in this chapter.

Against the background of comparisons of the physical geography of the Northern and Southern Channel Islands, some interesting biogeographic trends may be noted in most groups of plants and animals. The most obvious trend is toward greater ecological diversity and increased numbers of species on the larger, wetter islands close to shore (see Chapter 1). The populations of many islands, especially those in the northern group, appear to be more closely related to populations found on the mainland to the north than to those along the drier, adjacent coast of southern California. In agreement with island biogeography theory, the Southern Channel Islands support proportionally more endemics than do the northern ones. Because the endemic plants and animals are the most distinctive features of the islands' natural history, and because some of them have figured prominently in scientific debates concerning the process of evolution in general, they are emphasized in this chapter.

Single-island endemics are especially interesting because they may focus attention on the unique qualities of an island's evolutionary history. The single-island endemics of the Northern Channel Islands are discussed as part of the coverage of the appropriate islands later in this chapter, whereas more wide-ranging endemics are described in the general discussion of the islands' plants and animals. Endemics too rare to be found without considerable difficulty have been treated briefly or not at all.

HISTORY

Although the earliest date of the arrival of humans on the Northern Channel Islands is not known with certainty (see Chapter 3), radiocarbon dates place humans on San Miguel Island as early as 11,700 years B.P., and by about 7000 years ago sizable populations inhabited all of the larger islands. The life-style and origins of these aborigines are largely matters of conjecture. By about 2500 B.P. the Chumash had diversified the existing, largely maritime, economy; their flourishing culture was among the most advanced in California. As did the natives of the southern islands, the Chumash traded heavily with mainland villages to offset the lack of resources imposed by island life, bartering shell beads for food and other items. It is highly probable that the early cultures had a profound impact on the ecology of the Northern Channel Islands through such agricultural practices as burning of native vegetation to encourage food production. They also engaged in hunting and gathering, as well as the accidental and purposeful transportation of plants and animals between the islands and the mainland. Consult Chapter 3 for a more thorough discussion of early humans.

The period of European influence, beginning with the discovery of the islands by Juan Rodríguez Cabrillo and extending through the Mission period, devastated the Native American culture (see Chapters 1 and 3). By the middle of the nineteenth century the native islanders and most of the sea mammals were gone and the two largest Northern Channel Islands were privately owned. After California joined the United States in 1850, the islands changed hands several times and were developed into farms and ranches. In 1938, with the establishment of the Channel Islands National Monument, Anacapa and Santa Barbara Islands became the first to receive protection. Then in 1976 the National Monument was declared an international biosphere reserve. In 1978, the western 90 percent of Santa Cruz Island came under the protection of The Nature Conservancy. In 1980 the National Monument was redesignated a national park, at which time San Miguel, Santa Cruz, and Santa Rosa were added to the unit; simultaneously the waters extending 6 nautical miles off the islands were declared a national marine sanctuary. All of the Northern Channel Islands were now incorporated into a new Channel Islands National Park, although Santa Rosa Island and the eastern 10 percent of Santa Cruz Island were still privately owned. Santa Rosa was purchased by the National Park Service in 1986, and in 1990 and 1992 a 75 percent interest in the eastern end of Santa Cruz Island was purchased. In 1997, with a controversial seizing of the remaining 25 percent under a federal law that permits "legislative taking," the National Park Service took full control of the eastern end of Santa Cruz Island, and ownership of the last remaining parcel of the California Channel Islands was resolved.

After the National Park Service took over management of the eastern end of Santa Cruz Island it eliminated the boat landing and camping fees.

Estimates of usage indicate that about 1100 boats visited the island during the summer of 1997—about a 400 percent increase in usage over the previous year. The number of visitors to Channel Islands National Park also increased, with about 40,000 people setting foot on one or more of the islands. The visitor center at Ventura Harbor on the mainland logged about 220,000 visitors. Compared with a park such as Yosemite, which has millions of visitors annually, these numbers are still low, but that is part of the charm of Channel Islands National Park.

The year 1997 also brought severe storms to the Channel Islands, a consequence of the El Niño condition. Unrestrained by the denuded landscape, torrents of water rushed down the canyons on the eastern end of Santa Cruz and washed away some of the historic buildings at the Scorpion Ranch. The century-old adobe endured, but the blacksmith shop and the barn were swept away.

THE PHYSICAL ENVIRONMENT

The Northern Channel Islands form a chain stretching about 60 miles (100 km) from east to west. The eastern end of the chain (Anacapa Island) is only 13 miles (20 km) from shore and the remainder averages about 25 miles (40 km) south of the east-west coastline. The islands are loosely strung along 34° N latitude, centered on 120° W longitude.

Considering the Northern Channel Islands as the exposed top of a single, dissected mountain range (Figs. 12 and 69) permits a more integrative discussion of their topography. The island ridge is lower at either end (San Miguel and Anacapa Islands) and highest in the center (western Santa Cruz and eastern Santa Rosa Islands). The degree of local relief correlates with size and elevation, being greatest on the larger islands. The straits between the islands may be thought of as broad, transverse valleys, which became exposed when lower sea levels connected the islands to each other. Higher sea levels resulting from ice melting during warm interglacial periods, combined with local deformations of the earth's crust, may have completely submerged the islands, except for the highest parts of Santa Cruz Island. The stepped series of marine terraces, conspicuous on most of the islands, suggest that most of the land was covered by water from time to time.

The climate of the Channel Islands is largely controlled by the oceanic currents that bathe southern California (see Chapter 4). The California Current sweeps southward past Point Conception, where the coast veers sharply eastward. As the edge of the current strikes San Miguel Island, part of it often splits off and forms a counterclockwise eddy in the Santa Barbara Channel that cools the northern sides of the islands eastward to Santa Cruz Island, at which point the eddy loses momentum and becomes warmer. The main part of the flow continues south past San Nicolas Island and forms another, larger eddy, the inshore arm of which is the Southern California Countercurrent. Bringing relatively warm water up from the south, the countercurrent affects the southern sides of the northern islands (east from Santa Rosa), but it has a stronger influence on the Southern Channel Islands. These currents and eddies determine the distribution and mixing of temperature and salinity gradients, sediments, nutrients, and pelagic forms of marine life. They also have a profound effect on the distribution of terrestrial organisms, primarily through climatic factors but also by promoting the dispersal of rafting organisms from north of Point Conception to the Northern Channel Islands. The same currents might carry organisms from the northern to the southern group of islands.

The California Current system (Fig. 14) is driven by prevailing northwesterly winds that interact with local topography to produce the climate characterizing each island. Along with the marine currents, these winds tend to turn eastward and diminish in intensity as they encounter the barrier of the islands. San Miguel and Santa Rosa Islands are almost constantly whipped by strong winds, which are also prevalent at the western end of Santa Cruz Island. As these winds are forced upward by the mountains on Santa Cruz and Santa Rosa Islands, they encounter cooler air, and greater precipitation occurs on the western side of the highlands. Water shortages are most critical when strong desert winds (Santa Anas) bring dry, hot air from the northeast, most frequently in autumn.

The climate of the islands is much like that of the adjacent mainland. On Santa Cruz Island, areas with south-facing exposure and elevation similar to those on the mainland near Santa Barbara have nearly the same range of temperature and rainfall. The island sites tend to have more fog and periods of low cloud cover during the summer and slightly higher humidity owing to the persistence of an atmospheric marine layer below 1000 ft (300 m). Since the region is subject to seasonal and periodic droughts, the slight increase in available moisture on the islands is probably instrumental in maintaining some of the differences observed between the plants and animals on the island and those on the mainland. Moisture is the principal limiting factor in determining the distribution of terrestrial organisms on the islands; temperature is relatively unimportant. Temperatures below freezing and above 100°F (38°C) are largely nonexistent, except rarely in the Central Valley of Santa Cruz Island and perhaps in sheltered areas on Santa Rosa Island. To the west, the islands have a cooler, moister, and more uniform climate, similar to that of the central California coast. As described in Chapter 4, the marine life of the Northern Channel Islands reflects these temperature relationships.

TERRESTRIAL VEGETATION

Although many botanists have studied the Northern Channel Islands, most of the recent information on the plants of the islands was compiled by Peter Raven and Ralph Philbrick. The listing published by Gary Wallace in 1985 was the most comprehensive one available until 1995, when *A Flora of Santa Cruz Island* by Steve Junak, Tina Ayers, Randy Scott, Dieter Wilken, and David Young of the Santa Barbara Botanic Garden was published. This volume, technically relevant only to Santa Cruz Island, is actually a compendium of the climate, geology, and plants of all of the Northern Channel Islands.

The flora of the northern islands is characterized by a high proportion of plant species that are also found on the mainland north of Point Conception. Many of them are found no farther south than Monterey or northern San Luis Obispo Counties. These disjunctions probably became established during the ice ages (Pleistocene), when northern species invaded southern California during glacial episodes and then retreated during warmer times. These relict populations are maintained largely by the cooling influence of the California Current. Although most of the northern species are not conspicuous members of the flora, a few—including the lavender-flowered Seaside Daisy, *Erigeron glaucus*—are readily observed on San Miguel Island and other islands. The majority of the northern species have developed no distinctive features in their southern outposts. The most distinctive endemics are apparently derived from a more southerly flora that occupied the mainland prior to the Pleistocene epoch, some 2–5 million years ago. Specimens closely resembling several endemic and near-endemic trees and shrubs, such as Island Ironwood (*Lyonothamnus floribundus*), have been found in fossil deposits dating from the Miocene and Pliocene epochs (2–20 million years B.P.). Such plants are almost certainly relicts of a warmer and more equable climate, with summer rainfall, that characterized the continent before the formation of deserts and the onset of glaciation. Many of the Northern Channel Island species have relatives on the Southern Channel Islands, along the mainland coast of northwest Baja California and San Diego County, and in the highlands of central and southern Mexico. Their continued presence on the islands suggests that their habitat has been more stable than that on the mainland for at least 2 million years.

The proportion of endemics in the native flora is much higher on the Channel Islands than on ecologically similar areas of the mainland, such as the Santa Monica Mountains in Los Angeles County. The percentage of endemic plants on the Northern Channel Islands ranges from about

5 to 7 percent, compared with about 0.3 percent in the Santa Monica Mountains. The Southern Channel Islands have 6–16 percent endemic species, and, for comparison, the Hawaiian Islands have about 95 percent (89 percent for flowering plants). Island endemism in general is discussed in Chapter 1.

Although the endemic species constitute a relatively small part of the total island flora, many of them are abundant and conspicuous. The common nonendemic species are typical members of corresponding mainland communities and are essentially the same on all of the Channel Islands (see Chapter 5); they are not discussed in detail in this chapter. The illustrations and descriptions provided here should be sufficient to identify many species, but others are so closely related to nonendemics that they must be distinguished with the use of identification manuals.

The distinctiveness of each endemic falls along a spectrum. Many island plants show very slight differences from mainland forms and have not been given formal taxonomic recognition. These include many dwarf and prostrate forms of nonendemic plants growing in windswept areas. Other endemics are considered varieties or subspecies of mainland plants. Still others are considered distinct species, but only one endemic plant, Island Ironwood, is in a unique genus (*Lyonothamnus*) (Fig. 2B; Plate 5B), although that genus did formerly occur on the mainland.

As is true for all of the Channel Islands, grazing by domestic and feral animals has seriously disturbed the native vegetation. As a result, in 1997 the U.S. Fish and Wildlife Service listed eleven plants from the Northern Channel Islands as endangered species and two more as threatened. Three additional species from the Southern Channel Islands were also listed as endangered.

Depending on the classification scheme used, numerous plant communities, representing a wide range of habitats, can be identified on the Northern Channel Islands. (The general nature of the common communities is discussed in Chapter 5.) The degree of local exposure to wind, fog, salt spray, rain, and sun is critical in determining the vegetation of particular areas, and soil type is also very important. The various types of vegetation are represented to differing degrees on the individual islands, because the conditions that determine their distribution vary in their geographic influence.

Coastal Sage Scrub

Coastal Sage Scrub is not as widespread on the Northern Channel Islands as on Santa Catalina or the adjacent mainland. Consisting of low, scrubby, drought-deciduous, aromatic shrubs interspersed with succulents such as cacti, this community occurs primarily on steep, rocky, south-facing slopes (Plate 7A), exposed ridges, and marine terraces. Like Coastal Bluff Scrub vegetation, the amount of Coastal Sage Scrub appears to have been greatly reduced on the islands by grazing, and recovery has been slow even when herbivores have been eliminated. Instead, nonnative grasses have replaced Coastal Sage Scrub in many locations.

On Santa Cruz Island, Coastal Sage Scrub is most noticeable on the south side and on south-facing slopes in the central and eastern portions of the Central Valley. On Santa Rosa Island it covers about 20 percent of the island. On coastal slopes it occurs at around 45 ft (15 m) in elevation, but inland it is found from 700 to 800 ft (215–245 m) in elevation. For a more thorough description of this community see Chapter 5.

The common drought-deciduous shrubs of Coastal Sage Scrub include California Sagebrush (*Artemisia californica*) (Fig. 45A), Coast Brittlebush (*Encelia californica*) (Fig. 46; Plate 7B), and Black Sage (*Salvia mellifera*). Of the evergreen species, the dominant one is Lemonade Berry, *Rhus integrifolia* (Fig. 53A; Plate 7C). Also present, particularly on north-facing slopes, is Toyon, *Heteromeles arbutifolia* (Fig. 54), although some authors consider this species a component of the Chaparral community. On the Northern Channel Islands it shows some characteristics, such as larger leaves, that differentiate it from the mainland populations. It produces masses of white flowers in the summer and bright red berries in the fall and winter. Laurel Sumac, *Malosoma laurina* (Fig. 53B), an important component on Santa Catalina Island, is conspicuously absent on the Northern Channel Islands. On the other hand Coyote Brush, *Baccharis pilularis* (Fig. 45B), is so common in some areas on the larger of the Northern Channel Islands that some authors relegate stands of this evergreen shrub to a community they call Coyote Brush Scrub. It is significant that Coyote Brush is a particularly important component of Coastal Sage Scrub on the mainland north of Point Conception. The absence of Laurel Sumac and the presence of Coyote Brush illustrate the northern affinities of this community on the Northern Channel Islands.

The succulent component of Coastal Sage Scrub on the Northern Channel Islands is represented by Coastal Prickly-pear or Tuna, *Opuntia littoralis* (Fig. 51A; Plate 8C), and its taller treelike cousin *Opuntia oricola* (Fig. 52), with the latter species dominating in most situations. The nonnative Mission Cactus, *Opuntia ficus-indica,* is also found on Anacapa, Santa Catalina, and Santa Cruz Islands. This treelike species often has pads that are spineless. Where it has been introduced, its young pads, known as *nopales,* have been used as an edible component of salsas or mixed with scrambled eggs. The Coastal Cholla, *Opuntia prolifera* (Fig. 51B; Plate 8A,B), is also an important, though less common, cactus in Coastal Sage Scrub.

Plate 1. Endemic animals. (A) Island Fox, *Urocyon littoralis,* native to San
Clemente, San Miguel, San Nicolas, Santa Catalina, Santa Cruz, and Santa Rosa
Islands. (B) Island Scrub Jay, *Aphelocoma insularis.* Native only to Santa Cruz
Island, this is the only bird species that is a single-island endemic. (C) Island
Night Lizard, *Xantusia riversiana,* on a bed of lichens. This lizard is native to
San Clemente, San Nicoloas, and Santa Barbara Islands.

Plate 2. Marine mammals. (A) Young California Gray Whale, *Eschrichtius robustus*, rising to look around or "spy-hopping." (B) Humpback Whales, *Megaptera novae-angliae*, are the most acrobatic of our marine mammals. As it clears the water with its entire body, this breaching Humpback Whale reveals its enormous white pectoral fins. (C) California Sea Lions, *Zalophus californianus*, and Harbor Seals, *Phoca vitulina*, hauled out on San Miguel Island. (D) Northern Sea Lions, *Eumetopias jubatus*, on a typical haul-out station.

Plate 3. Frequently observed sea birds. (A) Brown Pelican, *Pelecanus occidentalis.*
(B) Double-crested Cormorant, *Phalacrocorax auritus.* (C) Black Oystercatcher,
Haematopus bachmani. (D) Western Gull, *Larus occidentalis.*

Plate 4. Distinctive rock formations. (A) Painted Cave, on western Santa Cruz Island, is one of many sea caves that have developed in volcanic rocks. (B) A layered ashfall at Fisherman's Cove near the Isthmus on Santa Catalina Island. (C) San Onofre Breccia, a solidified landslide deposit coated with bird guano on Santa Cruz Island.

Plate 5. Distinctive trees of the Channel Islands. (A) Santa Catalina Ironwood,
Lyonothamnus floribundus ssp. *floribundus,* endemic to Santa Catalina Island.
(B) Island Ironwood or Fern-leaved Ironwood, *Lyonothamnus floribundus* ssp.
aspleniifolius, native to San Clemente, Santa Cruz, and Santa Rosa Islands.
(C, D) Catalina Cherry, *Prunus ilicifolia* ssp. *lyonii,* native to Anacapa, San
Clemente, Santa Catalina, Santa Cruz, and Santa Rosa Islands.

Plate 6. Endemic wildflowers. (A) Channel Islands Tree Poppy, *Dendromecon har-fordii,* native to San Clemente, Santa Catalina, Santa Cruz, and Santa Rosa Islands. (B) Malva Rosa, *Lavatera assurgentiflora,* native to Anacapa, San Clemente, San Miguel, and Santa Catalina Islands. It has been planted widely on other islands and the mainland. (C) Island Monkeyflower, *Mimulus flemingii* (=*M. aurantiacus*), native to Anacapa, San Clemente, Santa Cruz, and Santa Rosa islands. This red-flowered shrub has been lumped with Orange Bush Monkeyflower, *Mimulus aurantiacus,* by some authorities. (D) Catalina Crossosoma or California Thorn Apple, *Crossosoma californicum,* native to San Clemente and Santa Catalina Islands, also has small populations on Guadalupe Island and the Palos Verdes Peninsula, a former island. (E) Cliff Aster, *Malacothrix saxatilis* var. *implicata,* native to the Northern Channel Islands and San Nicolas Island, is one of a complex of dandelionlike sunflowers that have evolved on islands.

Plate 7. Coastal Sage Scrub. (A) Typical undisturbed habitat showing the slope effect. Dark green shrubs are on the north-facing slopes. (B) Coast Brittlebush or California Encelia, *Encelia californica*, and associated paintbrush, *Castilleja* sp. (C) Lemonade Berry, *Rhus integrifolia*. This large shrub is common on north-facing slopes.

Plate 8. Maritime Desert Scrub. (A) Typical habitat dominated by Coastal Cholla, *Opuntia prolifera*. (B) Flower of Coastal Cholla, *Opuntia prolifera*. (C) Flower and pads of Coastal Prickly-pear cactus or Tuna, *Opuntia littoralis*. (D) Flower of Button Cactus, *Bergerocactus emoryi*.

Plate 9. Coastal Bluff Scrub. (A–C) Coastal bluff scrub on Santa Cruz Island, featuring Giant Coreopsis, *Coreopsis gigantea*.

Plate 10. Grassland. (A) Coastal terraces on west end of Santa Cruz Island with Goldfields, *Lasthenia californica*, in bloom. (B) Goldfields, *Lasthenia californica*, and Purple Owl's Clover, *Castilleja exserta*. (C) Catalina Mariposa Lily, *Calochortus catalinae*, returns from bulbs in years with adequate rainfall. (D) Shooting Star, *Dodecatheon clevelandii* ssp. *insulare*, returns from bulbs in years with adequate rainfall, particularly following fires.

Plate 11. Santa Catalina Island. (A) Avalon harbor. (B) East side of Santa Catalina showing Chaparral and Oak Woodland. (C) Island Chaparral near the isthmus, featuring Chamise, *Adenostoma fasciculatum,* and Island Scrub Oak, *Quercus pacifica* (=*berberidifolia*).

Plate 12. Santa Cruz Island. (A) Central Valley, associated with the Santa Cruz fault. Coastal Sage Scrub is in the foreground. (B) Bishop Pines, *Pinus muricata*, near Prisoners' Harbor. (C) Oak trees near Prisoners' Harbor showing the effects of salt spray.

Plate 13. Northern Channel Islands. (A) Anacapa Island: view westward from East Anacapa showing Middle and West Islands. (B) Torrey Pines, *Pinus torreyana*, on Santa Rosa Island. Santa Cruz Island is in the distance. (C) San Miguel Island showing recovery of native vegetation since the elimination of nonnative animals.

Plate 14. Outer Southern Channel Islands. (A) West side of San Clemente Island showing coastal terraces. (B) Sand Dunes on San Nicolas Island. (Photograph by William Mautz.) (C) Santa Barbara Island showing clusters of Sea Blite, *Suaeda californica,* and nesting Western Gulls, *Larus occidentalis.*

Plate 15. Islands in San Francisco Bay. (A) Yerba Buena Island showing forest of introduced trees. The Oakland Bay Bridge is in the background. (B) Treasure Island as seen from Yerba Buena Island. (C) The Brothers as seen from Point San Pablo. The old lighthouse on East Brother Island is now a bed-and-breakfast. The Marin Islands are visible in the distance to the left.

Plate 16. Angel Island. (A) North side of Angel Island. Northern Coastal Scrub is dominated by Coyote Brush, *Baccharis pilularis*, visible in the foreground. Mixed Evergreen Forest is seen on the lower slopes. Tiburon Peninsula and Raccoon Strait are in the background. (B) Mixed Evergreen Forest on the north side of Mount Livermore. Introduced Scotch Broom, *Cytisus scoparius*, is visible in the foreground. (C) Pacific Madrone, *Arbutus menziesii*, a common member of Mixed Evergreen Forest on Angel Island.

In recent years prickly-pears and Coastal Cholla have become infested with the parasitic Cochineal Scale Insect (*Dactylopius* sp.), which was successfully introduced on Santa Cruz Island in 1951 and later spread to Anacapa and Santa Rosa Islands. The subsequent degradation of cactus patches has increased the vulnerability of several native plants and animals to grazing and predation by reducing an important natural deterrent to marauding herbivores.

In areas where grazing pressure is not too great, several endemics may be found. Perhaps the most conspicuous of these are two species of buckwheat. Santa Cruz Island Buckwheat, *Eriogonum arborescens* (Fig. 71) is an attractive, pale bush forming large mounds up to 6 ft (2 m) tall. It has narrow leaves and tiny white flowers massed into flat, interconnecting clusters that turn pink and finally brown in the summer. Although most abundant on Santa Cruz Island, this species also occurs on Anacapa and Santa Rosa Islands. In certain locales on Santa Cruz Island it has hybridized with Santa Catalina Buckwheat or Saint Catherine's Lace, *Eriogonum giganteum* (Fig. 50), a closely related (but very different) "giant" endemic of Santa Catalina Island that was introduced as an ornamental and then escaped. Recent attempts to eradicate the escapees and hybrids in order to preserve the native gene pool appear to have been successful. The other endemic buckwheat is a second "giant" known as Island Buckwheat, *Eriogonum grande* var. *grande* (Fig. 72). This species, also up to 6 ft (2 m) in height, has rosettes of heart-shaped leaves that are white below; its flowers are arranged in tall, round, branching clusters.

Also abundant in the Coastal Sage Scrub of the islands is the endemic Island Deerweed, *Lotus dendroideus* (Fig. 73), a small, twisted shrub with frondlike branches and compound leaves with three small, oval leaflets. Its abundant yellow flowers are typical of the pea family or legumes (Fabaceae). Older flowers that have already been pollinated take on a reddish hue, alerting pollinators and thus improving the efficiency of pollination for the pollinators and the plant. After they are pollinated the flowers give rise to dark, hornlike pods. As is true of many members of the pea family, bacteria that inhabit the plant's roots have the ability to convert nitrogen gas to amino acids, critical components of proteins. Many herbivorous animals therefore seek out legumes as important items in their diets, hence the common name Deerweed.

The genus *Malacothrix* of the sunflower family (Asteraceae) is a good example of *autochthonous evolution*. A number of its members have evolved separately on the islands, and their evolutionary relationships have still not been sorted out completely.

A common island endemic shrub that inhabits coastal bluffs, rocky

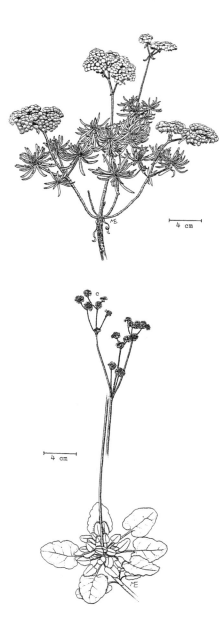

Figure 71. Santa Cruz Island Buckwheat, *Eriogonum arborescens.*

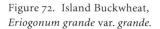

Figure 72. Island Buckwheat, *Eriogonum grande* var. *grande.*

slopes, and canyon walls is the Cliff Aster, *Malacothrix saxatilis* var. *implicata* (Fig. 74; Plate 6E). This member of the *Malacothrix* group can be recognized by its reddish stems arising from a woody base, finely divided leaves, and large white flower heads, which are yellowish toward the center and purple around the edges. A number of species related to Cliff Aster are rare on the Northern Channel Islands. These other species superficially resemble dandelions, and one of them, *Malacothrix incana*

Figure 73. Island Deerweed, *Lotus dendroideus.*

(Fig. 75), often associated with coastal dunes, goes by the name Dunede-lion. Dunedelion is a perennial herb that often grows in mounds. The other species, like dandelions, are *ephemeral* or *annual* species, which means that they return each year from seeds that germinate after the winter rains. Snakes-head, *Malacothrix coulteri,* which is also found in the San Joaquin Valley, has not been seen on the Northern Channel Islands since the 1930s. It is presumed to have been extirpated.

Island Malacothrix, *Malacothrix squalida,* and Santa Cruz Island Mala-cothrix, *Malacothrix indecora,* are Northern Channel Island endemics that are federally listed as endangered. The existing populations are so local-ized or small in number that they are in danger of extinction, by either habitat loss or such random events as storm, drought, or fire. Island Mala-cothrix is a species of rocky coastal bluffs known only from Middle Anacapa Island and two localities on the north shore of Santa Cruz Island. It has not been seen on Santa Cruz Island since 1968. Santa Cruz Island Malacothrix is currently known from one locality at Black Point on the west end of Santa Cruz Island. Its former occurrence on the northeast shore of San Miguel Island has not been verified recently. Unfortunately for these

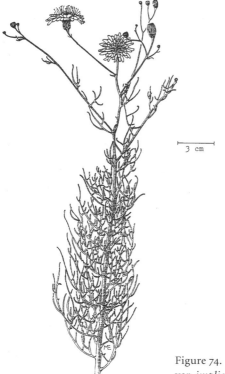

3 cm

Figure 74. Cliff Aster, *Malacothrix saxatilis*
var. *implicata.*

Figure 75. Dunedelion, *Malacothrix incana.*

4 cm

Figure 76. Island Hazardia, *Hazardia detonsa.*

two species, their favored habitat, particularly that on offshore islets, is also the nesting place for numerous cormorants and gulls.

Relationships of the different races of Leafy Malacothrix (Fig. 137) have only recently been untangled. Four subspecies have been described. These small spring ephemerals, resembling dandelions, may be found on Anacapa Island as well as San Clemente, San Nicolas, and Santa Barbara Islands (the outer Southern Channel Islands).

Another endemic member of the sunflower family is an unusual species of goldenbush known as Island Hazardia, *Hazardia detonsa* (Fig. 76). It is a species of special environmental concern, found at scattered locations and habitats throughout the Northern Channel Islands, although it is now most common on bluffs. It is a whitish bush with large, soft, toothed leaves and small yellow flowers. This endemic bears conspicuous yellow flower bracts on San Miguel, Santa Cruz, and Santa Rosa Islands, and red bracts on Anacapa and Santa Cruz Islands. The species is a close relative of the common Saw-toothed Goldenbush, *Hazardia squarrosa,* that is a component of Coastal Sage Scrub on the islands and on the mainland. An indirect threat to the continued existence of Island Hazardia as a distinct species is its tendency to hybridize with Saw-toothed Goldenbush.

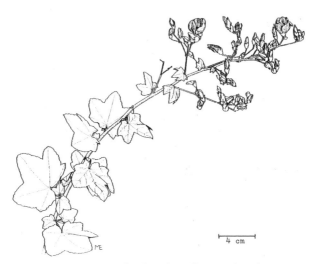

Figure 77. Santa Cruz Island Bush Mallow, *Malacothamnus fasciculatus* ssp. *nesioticus.*

A rare endemic shrub known as Santa Cruz Island Bush Mallow, *Malacothamnus fasciculatus* ssp. *nesioticus* (Fig. 77), is now officially listed as a federal and state endangered species. It is known from only two small populations on Santa Cruz Island, one along the west shore near the historic Christy Ranch and the other in the Central Valley near the University of California field station. This tall shrub has slender branches and palmate leaves. The rose-colored flowers, about 1.5 in. (38 mm) wide, are scattered along the branches. Typical of the mallow family (Malvaceae), the numerous stamens are fused with the pistil, producing a brushlike structure in the center of the flower. Commercial hibiscus flowers are also members of this family. On the mainland, Bush Mallows are notable as fire-followers, covering many acres in years after major conflagrations in Coastal Sage Scrub. The Santa Catalina Island Bush Mallow, *Malacothamnus fasciculatus* var. *catalinensis,* occurs in similar habitats on Santa Catalina Island and in northern Baja California. The similar San Clemente Island Bush Mallow, *Malacothamnus clementinus,* is also classified as an endangered species.

Another rare member of the Mallow family, the Northern Channel Island Tree Mallow or Malva Rosa, *Lavatera assurgentiflora* ssp. *assurgentiflora,* is perhaps one of the most beautiful of the island endemics. This large shrub, also with palmate leaves, has flowers 3 in. (8 cm) across. The petals are purple to white and have purple veins. The species is native to San Miguel and Anacapa Islands, but it has been planted on other islands as well. Similarly, the Southern Channel Island Tree Mallow, *Lavatera assur-*

gentiflora ssp. *glabra* (Plate 6B), also known as Malva Rosa and native to San Clemente and Santa Catalina Islands, has been planted in a variety of island and mainland localities.

The bedstraws represent another group of plants with a significant number of endemics on islands; seven species are found on California's islands. These usually herbaceous plants often have squarish stems and leaves arranged in whorls. Their name comes from the habit in certain parts of the world of stuffing mattresses with the dried foliage. Bedstraws belong to the widespread madder family (Rubiaceae), which includes a number of plants from which such commercially important products as quinine and coffee are produced.

Narrow-leaved Bedstraw, *Galium angustifolium* ssp. *foliosum,* is a common endemic on Anacapa, Santa Cruz, and Santa Rosa Islands. A related subspecies, *Galium angustifolium* ssp. *angustifolium,* is found on Santa Catalina as well as the adjacent mainland. Altogether there are eight different subspecies of this widely distributed plant in southern California.

Sea-cliff Bedstraw or Box Bedstraw, *Galium buxifolium,* is a shrubby form that grows to 4 ft (1.2 m) in height, rendered distinctive by its large, hairy leaves and fruits. It is only known from a few populations on San Miguel and Santa Cruz Islands, where it occurs on north-facing sea cliffs. It was federally listed as an endangered species in 1997 along with twelve other species from the Northern Channel Islands. This species is closely related to Santa Catalina Bedstraw, *Galium catalinense* ssp. *catalinense,* and San Clemente Island Bedstraw, *Galium catalinense* ssp. *acrispum.* Neither of these is common, and the latter is classified by the state as endangered.

The figwort or snapdragon family (Scrophulariaceae) includes several interesting plants found on the Northern Channel Islands. The paintbrush, *Castilleja affinis,* is a common wildflower on the mainland and the northern islands, but the Island Paintbrush, *Castilleja lanata* ssp. *hololeuca* (Fig. 78), is endemic to the four Northern Channel Islands. It is a subspecies of special environmental concern that tends to occur in scattered colonies on north-facing slopes. It is less abundant, and as is true of paintbrushes in general, it is hemiparasitic on the roots of other plants. The Soft-leaved Indian Paintbrush, *Castilleja mollis,* is a yellow-flowered species that is endemic to Santa Rosa Island, where it is known from only two localities, Carrington Point in the northeast corner and west of Jaw Gulch on the north side of the island. This species is associated with the Coastal Sand Dune habitat, where, as a hemiparasite, it appears to tap into the root system of Coast Goldenbush, *Isocoma menziesii.* This rare paintbrush was listed as endangered by the federal government in 1997.

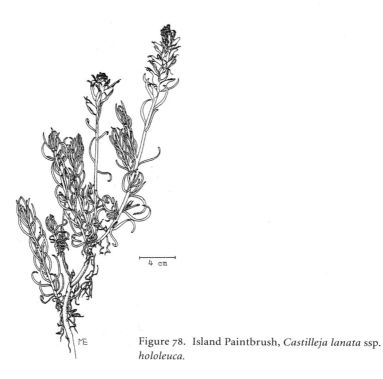

Figure 78. Island Paintbrush, *Castilleja lanata* ssp. *hololeuca.*

All of the snapdragons that occur on the Northern Channel Islands are annuals or ephemerals (see Chapter 4). Nuttall's Snapdragon, *Antirrhinum nuttallianum,* is the most common, and the Climbing Snapdragon, *Antirrhinum kelloggii,* is a fire-follower that appears in disturbed areas, particularly after burns. The Sticky Snapdragon, *Antirrhinum multiflorum,* also occurs along the mainland coast, but on Santa Cruz Island it is occasionally found on the north side between Lagunitas Secas and Cañada del Puerto and in the island's Central Valley between Picacho Diablo and Cañada de la Siesta.

Coastal Bluff Scrub

Nearly instantaneous runoff occurs on the steep faces of sea cliffs. Salt spray also increases the effect of drought on the few plants of Coastal Bluff Scrub that manage to find soil there. Despite these limitations, this variant of depauperate Coastal Sage Scrub reaches its fullest expression on the Channel Islands, undoubtedly because the islands support the only significant north- and east-facing sea cliffs on the California coast, where shade and fog augment the moisture available for growth. On the mainland and the south-facing slopes of the islands, Coastal Bluff Scrub blends imperceptibly into Coastal Sage Scrub. Point Mugu, at the western end of the Santa Monica Mountains, supports a community resembling that of the islands in some respects. Yet no place on the adjacent mainland achieves the unique aspect of cliffs such as Hoffmann Point on San Miguel Island, where luxuriant hanging gardens bloom in a profusion of colors in the spring.

Species richness, especially of endemic forms, is greatest on the steep, north-facing cliffs of these islands. Coastal Bluff Scrub vegetation consists mainly of lichens and low, perennial succulents, many of them endemic. The plants form a complex mosaic covering the rocks and terraces below 1000 ft (300 m). This community abuts all of the other island plant communities where cliffs break the landscape, and members of the other vegetation types have invaded the cliffs to some extent (especially away from the immediate coast). The cliff environment provides certain species with their final refuge from grazing pressures, and some of the supposedly extinct plants of the islands may someday be discovered clinging to precipitous cliffs. Coastal Bluff vegetation as a whole is highly sensitive to grazing, and thus it may formerly have been more extensive on the islands. As might be expected, the character and composition of the vegetation vary considerably from coastal to interior sites, north- to south-facing slopes, cliff faces to marine terraces, and island to island.

The present discussion deals primarily with the endemics found mainly in Coastal Bluff vegetation on all of the Northern Channel Islands. One of the most characteristic and unusual plants of this community on the islands is Giant Coreopsis, *Coreopsis gigantea* (Plate 9A–C), a near-endemic found in scattered colonies on the mainland coast from San Luis Obispo to Torrey Pines State Park in northern San Diego County. The plant is readily identified by its thick, succulent stems up to 10 ft (3 m) high, often branched like a candelabra and topped with summer-deciduous, carrotlike foliage and clusters of sunflowerlike blossoms appearing from February to April. This plant reaches its greatest density on the Northern Channel Islands, where it often forms miniature forests on marine terraces (Fig. 161) and may also be found on rocky interior slopes.

Also conspicuous on these bluffs are the often-endemic live-forevers (*Dudleya* spp.) of the stonecrop family (Crassulaceae). The important endemic live-forevers are discussed more thoroughly in Chapter 1, but it should be noted here that Santa Cruz Island alone is home to four different species. The Santa Cruz Island Live-forever, *Dudleya nesiotica* (Fig. 79A), is known from only one population, occupying less than 10 acres (4 ha) near Fraser Point on the west end of Santa Cruz Island. This rare species was officially listed as threatened by the federal government in September 1997. Greene's Live-forever, *Dudleya greenei* (Fig. 79B), is a whitish or green succulent that forms clumps of leafy rosettes with stalks bearing small

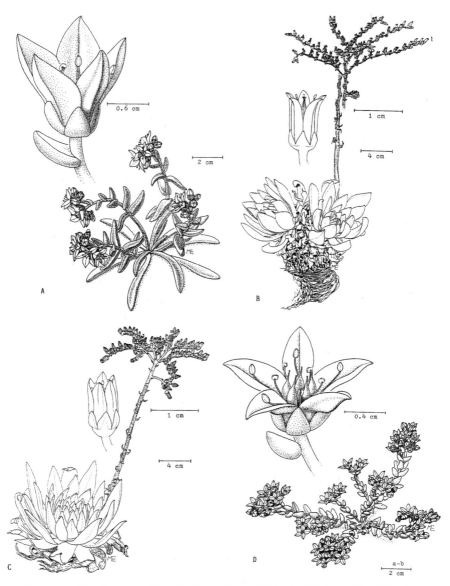

Figure 79. Live-forevers of the Northern Channel Islands. (A) Santa Cruz Island Live-forever, *Dudleya nesiotica.* (B) Greene's Live-forever, *Dudleya greenei.* (C) Candleholder Dudleya, *Dudleya candelabrum.* (D) Santa Rosa Island Dudleya, *Dudleya blochmaniae* ssp. *insularis.*

yellow flowers in early summer. This species is highly variable and only weakly differentiated from *Dudleya caespitosa,* a nonendemic that also occurs on Anacapa Island. Both of these species are unique in that they have arisen by a form of hybridization that involves the incorporation of all of the chromosomes of the parental types, producing multiples of the standard number of chromosomes. These *polyploid* species are typical of the other endemic species of this genus. The fourth species of live-forever found on Santa Cruz Island is known as Candleholder Dudleya, *Dudleya candelabrum* (Fig. 79C). It has a whorl of succulent leaves about 7 in. (17 cm) long and it produces a series of branching flower stalks, so that, as its name implies, the plant resembles a good-sized candelabrum. It is also found on San Miguel and Santa Rosa Islands.

Santa Rosa Island has three species of live-forever, including Greene's Live-forever, mentioned above. The species is also found on Anacapa, San Miguel, and Santa Catalina Islands. A newly recognized dwarf version of Greene's Live-forever is known as Dwarf Greene's Live-forever or Munchkin Dudleya, *Dudleya nana.* This species is known only from a single population composed of three colonies located near East Point. The other Santa Rosa Island endemic is Santa Rosa Island Dudleya, *Dudleya blochmaniae* ssp. *insularis* (Fig. 79D). It occurs only on the east end of the island in a 2-acre (1-ha) area near Old Ranch Point (Marsh Point). Its habitat consists of an ancient marine terrace with a cobbly surface. Associated species include Purple Owl's Clover, *Castilleja exserta,* and Goldfields, *Lasthenia californica* (Plate 10B).

Also found abundantly in Coastal Bluff Scrub is a near-endemic shrub known as Seaside Woolly Sunflower, *Eriophyllum staechadifolium* (Fig. 80). This species is common on all of the Northern Channel Islands and around Point Conception on the mainland. It is a low perennial with thick, lobed leaves that are felty white below, and it produces clusters of small, daisylike yellow flowers in spring. The related species known as Golden Yarrow, *Eriophyllum confertiflorum,* is a common member of the Coastal Sage Scrub community on the mainland and all of the islands except San Nicolas and Santa Barbara. It differs from the Seaside Woolly Sunflower in having much finer leaves.

The morning-glory family (Convolvulaceae) is characterized by vines that have trumpet-shaped flowers with pleats that remain after they unfold. The endemic Island Morning-glory, *Calystegia macrostegia* ssp. *macrostegia* (Fig. 81) has big, thick leaves and white, funnel-shaped flowers with a purple tinge. This large vine commonly drapes the rocks, slopes, and plants of the coastal bluffs, though it is found in other communities as well. It should not be confused with Bindweed, *Convolvulus arvensis,* a European

Figure 80. Seaside Woolly Sunflower, *Eriophyllum staechadifolium.*

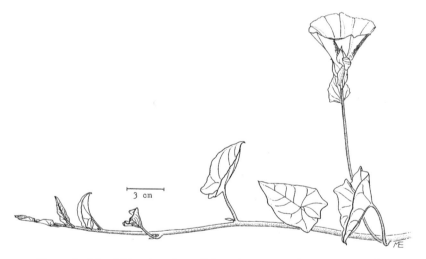

Figure 81. Island Morning-glory, *Calystegia macrostegia* ssp. *macrostegia.*

introduction that has become a noxious weed in many habitats on the mainland. It has been introduced to Catalina, Santa Cruz, and Santa Rosa Islands. Bindweed can be distinguished from the native Island Morning-glory by its smaller leaves and flowers and by the purple color that frequently occurs along the outside of the folds on the petals. Another morning glory that is rare on Santa Cruz and the Southern Channel Islands is a native annual species. *Convolvulus simulans* occurs on heavy clay soils; it has small, linear leaves and its flowers are only about a quarter inch (5–6 mm) long.

Island Chaparral

Island Chaparral is found only on the two largest of the Northern Channel Islands (Santa Cruz and Santa Rosa), mainly on steep, rocky, north-facing slopes. The community differs from mainland Chaparral both structurally and floristically; the more open, woodland aspect of Island Chaparral and its greater height are probably due in part to the islands' history of intense grazing and the low incidence of fires, resulting in older stands. Climate may also be important in encouraging arborescent growth, as opposed to the dense, uniform, and scrubby aspect of mainland Chaparral. Island Chaparral consists mainly of evergreen shrubs and small trees (Plate 11B) with fairly stiff, broad leaves. It differs from mainland Chaparral in that endemics, particularly manzanitas and oaks, dominate on the islands. Although browse-sensitive, Island Chaparral has suffered only gradual attrition during the past century because of its longevity and large size, which prevents the browsing of upper branches.

Another important characteristic of Chaparral communities is that they are subject to frequent fires. Historically, lightning would cause many of these fires, but it is also believed that Native Americans deliberately set fires to encourage the growth of early successional edible species. For a more thorough discussion of fire ecology, see Chapter 5.

Among the most abundant and conspicuous Chaparral plants on the Northern Channel Islands are several species of manzanita, all of them endemic (Fig. 82). Manzanitas produce small red berries, hence their name, which means "little apple" in Spanish. Manzanitas are members of the heath family (Ericaceae). On the mainland, members of this family are often associated with areas that receive significant snowfall or abundant fog. In particular, manzanitas are often associated with upper-elevation Chaparral, and it is therefore interesting that they should be such an important component of the vegetation on these islands.

An important characteristic of manzanitas is that their leaves are vertically oriented on the branches; that is, the leaves tend to grow straight up from the stem. Associated with this arrangement is the ability of the

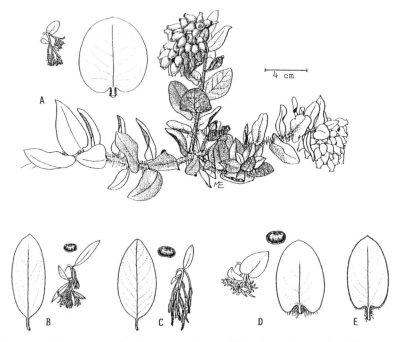

Figure 82. Manzanitas of the Northern Channel Islands. (A) Subcordate Manzanita, *Arctostaphylos tomentosa* ssp. *subcordata*. (B) Island Manzanita, *Arctostaphylos tomentosa* ssp. *insulicola*. (C) Santa Cruz Island Manzanita, *Arctostaphylos insularis*. (D) McMinn's Manzanita, *Arctostaphylos viridissima*. (E) Santa Rosa Island Manzanita, *Arctostaphylos confertiflora*.

plant to move its leaves so that they are oriented toward the sun for maximum temperature control and photosynthesis. When it is cold or cloudy, the leaves are turned flat toward the sun, and when it is hot, the plant orients the leaf edges toward the sun. This ability is called *sun tracking*.

Three manzanitas are restricted to Santa Cruz Island, one is restricted to Santa Rosa Island, and another occurs on both islands. It is also notable that only one species of manzanita occurs on any of the Southern Channel Islands, and that is the endemic Santa Catalina Island Manzanita, *Arctostaphylos catalinae* (Fig. 56).

Some of the manzanitas are restricted to particular soil types. Although manzanitas are readily identified as a group by their smooth, peeling, reddish bark and clusters of urn-shaped white or pink flowers, individual species are not so easily distinguished. Some reliable field characteristics used in identifying the various species include the overall shape of the plant (either branching from the base or forming a single trunk), the leaf shape (which is variable but tends toward characteristic modes), twig pubescence or hairiness (varying in density, length, and structure), and the developing flower clusters (inflorescences) found at the branch tips throughout most of the year.

The one manzanita that is not restricted to a single island is Island Manzanita, *Arctostaphylos tomentosa* ssp. *insulicola* (Fig. 82B). This form is generally uncommon and may be identified by its bushy shape and the feltlike, nonglandular hairs (pubescence) on its twigs; the leaves are narrow and smooth on the underside. In contrast, the Subcordate Manzanita, *Arctostaphylos tomentosa* ssp. *subcordata* (Fig. 82A), occurs on rocky slopes and ridgetops only on Santa Cruz Island. This subspecies has sticky, glandular hairs on its twigs, and its larger, rather heart-shaped leaves have small bumps (papillae) on their undersides.

The most common species on Santa Cruz Island, occurring on coastal bluffs, rocky slopes, and canyon walls, is Santa Cruz Island Manzanita, *Arctostaphylos insularis* (Fig. 82C), which is readily identified by its single trunk and threadlike nascent flower clusters (inflorescences). In addition, its fruit, sometimes over a half inch (15 mm) in diameter, is much larger than that of the other two species. Santa Cruz Island Manzanita is often found on soils derived from igneous rocks (volcanics or granitics). On the other hand, McMinn's Manzanita, *Arctostaphylos viridissima* (Fig. 82D), the only other tree-sized species, is common only on Monterey shale, particularly along the ridgelines and the isthmus. It also has large fruits; crowded, broad leaves; and long, nonglandular white hairs on its twigs.

A fifth Manzanita species is the officially endangered endemic Santa Rosa Island Manzanita, *Arctostaphylos confertiflora* (Figs. 82E and 123). It can be differentiated from Subcordate Manzanita and Island Manzanita, which also occur on Santa Rosa Island, by the absence of a burl at ground level.

Summer Holly, *Comarostaphylis diversifolia* ssp. *planifolia,* is a manzanita look-alike: a large shrub that grows on north-facing canyon walls of Anacapa, Santa Catalina, Santa Cruz, and Santa Rosa Islands. It differs from the manzanitas in having shiny leaves that may be serrated on the edges. Furthermore the bright red fruit is small, only about a quarter inch (5 mm) in diameter, and has small bumps (papillae) on it.

Another island endemic that is a Chaparral shrub with red berries (in this case borne singly in the summer) is the Island Redberry, *Rhamnus pirifolia* (Fig. 83). It is found on San Clemente, Santa Catalina, Santa Cruz, and Santa Rosa Islands, and it was last seen on San Miguel Island in 1886. A related species, known as California Coffeeberry, *Rhamnus californica,* occurs on the mainland and on Santa Cruz Island, where it is of scarce occurrence in canyon bottoms. Whereas Island Redberry has rounded leaves, flattened at the tip, California Coffeeberry has elongated leaves nearly 2 in. (5 cm) long.

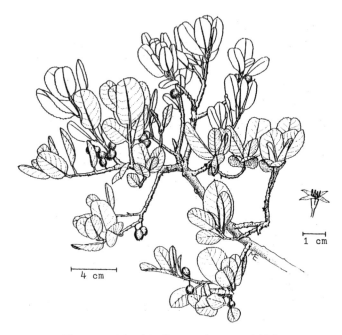

Figure 83. Island Redberry, *Rhamnus pirifolia.*

Also in the buckthorn family (Rhamnaceae) are two common species of California lilac (*Ceanothus* spp.). The many species of California lilac found in the state are important successional species after disturbance. One of the few examples of nonlegumes that have nitrogen-fixing bacteria in their roots, they are therefore a good source of protein for browsers. Island Ceanothus, *Ceanothus megacarpus* var. *insularis* (Fig. 84A), is endemic to Anacapa, San Clemente, Santa Catalina, Santa Cruz, and Santa Rosa Islands, where it is abundant on drier slopes. It has not been seen on San Miguel Island since 1886. It is inconspicuous except in late winter and spring, when it is covered with fragrant masses of tiny white flowers with dark purple centers. Once its seeds have matured and fallen, the empty capsules have a distinctive, three-lobed structure. Feltleaf Ceanothus, *Ceanothus arboreus* (Fig. 84B), is endemic to Santa Catalina, Santa Cruz, and Santa Rosa Islands. It is a larger species and occurs in moister habitats. Large, three-veined leaves and abundant, pale blue spring flowers distinguish this shrub.

An abundant near-endemic of the Island Chaparral is Island Mountain Mahogany, *Cercocarpus betuloides* var. *blanchae* (Fig. 85). It is found on Santa Catalina, Santa Cruz, and Santa Rosa Islands and in the Santa Monica Mountains. A shrub or small tree with whitish bark, it becomes con-

Figure 84. California Lilacs of the Northern Channel Islands. (A) Island Ceanothus, *Ceanothus megacarpus* var. *insularis*. (B) Feltleaf Ceanothus, *Ceanothus arboreus*.

spicuous in the summer because of its masses of seeds, each of which ends in a pale, feathery, curved tail. Similar to those of the manzanitas, its leaves tend to be vertically oriented and track the sun. Like the California lilacs, it is equipped with nitrogen-fixing bacteria in its roots and therefore attracts browsers.

The Channel Island Tree Poppy, *Dendromecon harfordii* (Fig. 86; Plate 6A), is an island endemic found on San Clemente, Santa Catalina,

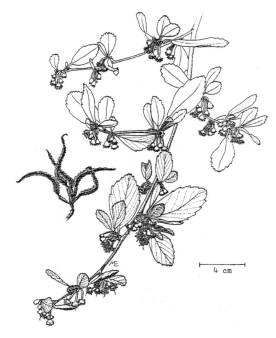

Figure 85. Island Mountain Mahogany, *Cercocarpus betuloides* var. *blanchae.*

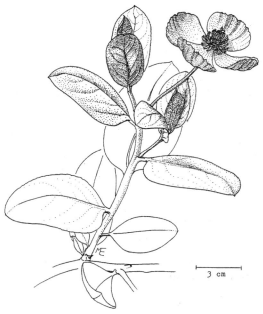

Figure 86. Channel Island Tree Poppy, *Dendromecon harfordii.*

Figure 87. Island Scrub Oak, *Quercus pacifica* (*=berberidifolia*).

Santa Cruz, and Santa Rosa Islands. It is readily identified by its large, four-petaled, yellow flowers that bloom primarily in the spring but appear almost throughout the year. The populations on the Southern Channel Islands, characterized by pale green leaves, were formerly assigned to a different subspecies. Recent analysis shows that the island forms in general are a distinctive species that is different from the related Bush Poppy, *Dendromecon rigida,* a fire-following shrub that is common on the mainland.

Scrub oaks are another important component of Island Chaparral. As discussed in Chapter 1, the evolution and differentiation of oaks make up an important part of the story of California flora. Eleven different kinds of oaks have been reported on Santa Cruz Island alone, and five from the Northern Channel Islands in general.

Three kinds of scrub oaks have been reported from the Northern Channel Islands. The most common is Island Scrub Oak, *Quercus pacifica* (*=berberidifolia*) (Fig. 87), which is endemic to Santa Catalina, Santa Cruz, and Santa Rosa Islands. This species has rounded leaf tips and small hairs on the undersides of the leaves. Santa Cruz Island Oak, *Quercus parvula* var. *parvula,* is found only on Santa Cruz Island. It differs from Island Scrub Oak in having a shiny green color on both sides of its leaves. The third kind of scrub oak, Nuttal's Scrub Oak (*Quercus dumosa*), is known from only one collection made in 1893 on Santa Cruz Island. Where it occurs on the mainland, it is associated with Coastal Sage Scrub, although it is not common.

Perhaps the most common plant in Chaparral on the mainland is Chamise, *Adenostoma fasciculatum* (Plate 11C). It is found in isolated locations on San Clemente, Santa Catalina, Santa Cruz, and Santa Rosa Islands. On the Northern Channel Islands it can be found in two growth forms: an erect, shrublike form that is typical of those found on the mainland, and a prostrate, moundlike shrub (Fig. 88A) that is found on some exposed ridges on Santa Cruz and Santa Rosa Islands. This latter form is probably a consequence of strong winds, but some authorities consider it to be a distinct variety, *Adenostoma fasciculatum* var. *prostratum*. Regardless of its growth habit, Chamise can be recognized by its tiny, waxy leaves that grow in clumps (Fig. 88B).

Island Woodland

Island Woodland occurs in areas similar to Chaparral habitat, but generally in moister sites such as in valleys and at higher elevations. It also occurs marginally on West Anacapa Island. Reaching its fullest expression on the northern slopes of Santa Cruz Island (Plate 12C), Island Woodland differs from Southern Oak Woodland in the dominance of island endemics rather than Coast Live Oak, *Quercus agrifolia*. Probably the best indicator of this community (and perhaps the most interesting plant on the islands) is the Island Ironwood, *Lyonothamnus floribundus* ssp. *aspleniifolius* (Figs. 2B and 89; Plate 5B). Representing the only endemic genus of organism on the Northern Channel Islands, this tree is not related to several other plants that are also called "ironwoods," nor does it closely resemble any other member of the rose family, to which it belongs. The Island Ironwood is easily identified as a slender tree more than 50 ft in height with reddish, shredding bark fading to gray. It has elaborately divided, fernlike leaves and, in the summer, large, flat clusters of tiny white flowers that ultimately become dry brown capsules. This graceful tree rarely produces seedlings in the wild (where grazing is at least partly responsible for their absence), but rather spreads by means of underground runners, forming dense groves with almost no undergrowth.

There is no good reason to believe that Island Ironwood and California Laurel, *Umbellularia californica* (Fig. 180), are involved in an unusual case of competitive exclusion. Although the two trees apparently grew together on the mainland several million years ago, they no longer do. They occupy similar habitats, but Ironwoods are restricted to the Channel Islands and California Laurel is absent there. The most likely explanation for the present distributions of these trees relies on differences in their modes of reproduction

Figure 88. Chamise, *Adenostoma fasciculatum*. (A) Prostrate growth form typical of exposed sites on Santa Cruz and Santa Rosa Islands. (B) Small, waxy leaves arranged in bundles (fascicles).

Figure 89. Island Ironwood, *Lyonothamnus floribun-dus* ssp. *aspleniifolius.*

in relation to the ecological changes that have affected the region during the past few million years. Island Ironwood may have reached the islands before California Laurel owing to the ease with which its tiny seeds can be dispersed by wind. It is unlikely, however, that the seeds of California Laurel have been completely incapable of bridging the Santa Barbara Channel, since other large-seeded forest trees (including close relatives of the California Laurel) have reached much more remote islands elsewhere in the world. Having reached the islands, Island Ironwood probably spread rapidly through suitable habitats by means of vegetative reproduction, making it more difficult for California Laurel to colonize the islands. Progressive drying in the region undoubtedly increased the incidence of fires on the mainland, perhaps gradually eliminating the susceptible Ironwood. California Laurel, with its fire-resistant basal burl, was able to persist on the mainland, while the Island Ironwood thrived on the Channel Islands, where extensive fires are rare thanks to the surrounding water and moist climate.

The Catalina Cherry, *Prunus ilicifolia* ssp. *lyonii* (Plate 5C,D), is another important indicator of the Island Woodland community. It sometimes forms small groves along washes. This tree was apparently replaced on the mainland by the Holly-leafed Cherry, *Prunus ilicifolia* ssp. *ilicifolia,* a few million years ago. Today Catalina Cherry survives only on the Channel Islands and in a few canyons in the mountains of central Baja California. Specimens on the northern islands show signs of intergradation with the mainland subspecies, perhaps because birds regularly transport the seeds of the latter to the islands during migration.

Southern Oak Woodland

On the mainland Southern Oak Woodland is dominated by the Coast Live Oak, *Quercus agrifolia* (Fig. 183A), but on the Channel Islands this species is present on only Santa Cruz and Santa Rosa Islands. The most complete expression of this community is on Santa Cruz Island, where it dominates many canyon bottoms on the island's north side, including sites that would tend to have Riparian Woodland on the mainland.

Common understory species in Southern Oak Woodland include Toyon, *Heteromeles arbutifolia* (Fig. 54), and Western Poison Oak, *Toxicodendron diversilobum* (Fig. 58). Western Poison Oak is not a member of the oak family (Fagaceae), but it is in the sumac family (Anacardiaceae) along with species such as Lemonade Berry and Laurel Sumac, which are characteristic of the Coastal Sage Scrub community. It is present on all of the Channel Islands (except Santa Barbara Island), where it is most common on north-facing slopes. Its characteristic shiny, bright green, compound leaves with three-lobed leaflets are familiar to many. In autumn, the leaves turn a bright red, adding a beautiful touch of fall color to locations where the plant is common. Oils produced by this species can cause severe contact dermatitis. The leaves fall off in late autumn and throughout most of the winter the leafless stems are not conspicuous, but they are still capable of producing a rash in sensitive people.

Island Jepsonia, *Jepsonia malvifolia* (Fig. 90), is an inconspicuous but interesting little perennial herb that is endemic to all of the Channel Islands except San Miguel and Santa Barbara. This species in the saxifrage family (Saxifragaceae) was named for one of the most famous botanists in California, Willis Jepson, who wrote the first comprehensive manual on wild plants in California. The *Jepson Manual,* in its most recent revision edited by J. C. Hickman, is the basic reference book for the botanical nomenclature of California plants (including terms used in this book). Island Jepsonia is a low-growing herb with basal leaves that arise from a swollen, rootlike base. It is locally common in moist areas of various habitats, including stream banks. It sends up a small stalk with whitish flowers from an underground stem in late fall, followed in winter and spring by two or three nearly circular, wrinkled leaves that wither in the

Figure 90. Island Jepsonia, *Jepsonia malvifolia.*

summer. The plant occurs in two forms that differ in flower structure; the two forms must cross-pollinate in order to reproduce. Island Alumroot, *Heuchera maxima* (Fig. 91), is a similar but larger plant in the saxifrage family, but it is a species of special concern. It also grows in moist habitats, but it is known from only four locations on Santa Rosa Island, eleven locations on West Anacapa Island, and twelve locations on Santa Cruz Island. Each of these populations is characterized by a small number of plants that are susceptible to extirpation by the usual threats.

Various other oak species are common on the Channel Islands (see Chapter 1), but Santa Cruz Island has the greatest variety. The most distinctive and widespread is the island endemic known as Island Oak, *Quercus tomentella* (Fig. 92). Some authorities include Island Oak as a component of Island Woodland, whereas others, citing nearly pure stands of this tree, place the species in a unique community known as Island Oak Woodland. Island Oak is a fairly large tree with big, dark green leaves ribbed with deep veins. The leaf margins may be smooth or serrated. Although it is not a common species on any island, groves are present in suitable habitat on all of the Channel Islands except San Miguel, San Nicolas, and Santa Barbara. It is also found far to the south on Guadalupe Island. On the Northern Channel Islands, Island Oak is most conspicuous on the high-

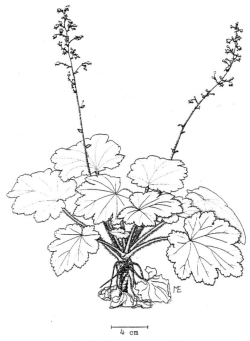

4 cm

Figure 91. Island Alumroot, *Heuchera maxima.*

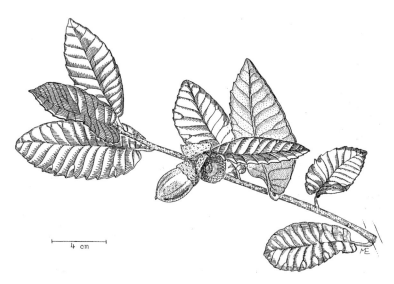

4 cm

Figure 92. Island Oak, *Quercus tomentella.*

lands of Santa Rosa, where it occurs as solitary individuals on the barren peaks, particularly Soledad Peak and Black Mountain. On West Anacapa Island two small stands are located in Oak Canyon. On Santa Cruz Island the species is found mostly in canyons and on high, north-facing slopes.

Nonnative herbivores have had a significant impact on Island Oak stands. On Santa Rosa Island, recruitment of Island Oak is virtually absent. The understory has been denuded, leaf litter is absent, and root buttresses are exposed by erosion. On Santa Cruz Island, damage has not been as severe, but continued pig rooting has reduced the recruitment rate of seedlings.

Canyon Live Oak or Golden-cup Oak, *Quercus chrysolepis,* is the most widely distributed oak in California. It is found on San Clemente, Santa Catalina, and Santa Cruz Islands. This species is easily recognized by the gray undersides of its leaves; the leaf margins on a single tree vary from smooth to serrated. On the islands where this species grows in association with Island Oak, it shows signs of hybridization. Canyon Live Oak is more common on Santa Cruz Island than on the other islands, but even so its distribution is spotty: it occurs occasionally on exposed, north-facing slopes above 1500 ft (500 m). It can be seen between Peak 1848 West and Red Peak, on El Montañon Ridge, and on El Tigre Ridge.

Of the deciduous oaks, Blue Oak, *Quercus douglasii* (Fig. 93A), and Valley Oak, *Quercus lobata* (Fig. 93B), enjoy limited distribution on Santa Catalina and Santa Cruz Islands. A hybrid species that resembles Valley Oak is known as MacDonald Oak, *Quercus ×macdonaldii;* it is also found on Santa Rosa Island. These three species have lobed leaves and differ from each other in the degree of lobing and the size of the leaves. Blue Oak has the smallest leaves, usually about an inch (2.5 cm) long. The other species may have leaves up to 4 in. (10 cm) in length. Reflecting their origin as hybrids between Valley Oak and Island Scrub Oak, Macdonald Oaks have leaves almost as large as those of Valley Oak, but with much shallower lobes. The species is also characterized by hairy twigs. Macdonald Oak is common only on Santa Cruz Island, where it occurs in canyons and on sheltered slopes up to 1400 feet (430 m) in elevation.

Closed-Cone Pine Forest

Pine diversity is also an important characteristic of the California flora (see Chapter 1). The pine forests of the Northern Channel Islands are of two types. The more widespread is Closed-cone Pine Forest, in which Bishop Pine, *Pinus muricata,* is the dominant tree (Plate 12B). Some authorities therefore call this community Bishop Pine Forest and distinguish it from similar assemblages dominated by a different species of closed-cone

Figure 93. Winter-deciduous oak trees. (A) Blue Oak, *Quercus douglasii.* (B) Valley Oak, *Quercus lobata.*

pine, such as Knobcone Pine, *Pinus attenuata,* or Monterey Pine, *Pinus radiata.* Although Closed-cone Pine Forest occurred extensively along the Pacific coast during the ice ages, it is now patchily distributed in coastal California, on the islands, and in northern Baja California, and where it occurs it is usually dominated by a single species of closed-cone pine.

Fossil trees found near the mouth of Cañada de los Sauces, on the west end of Santa Cruz Island, in sediments dated to 11,000 and 14,000 years

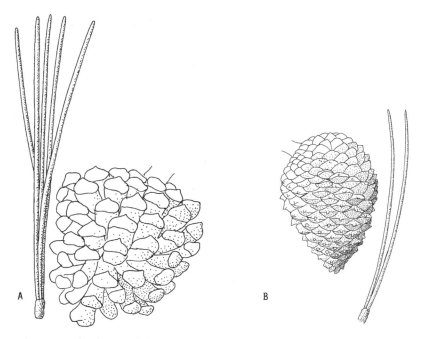

Figure 94. Island Pines. (A) Torrey Pine, *Pinus torreyana*. (B) Bishop Pine, *Pinus muricata*.

B.P. include Bishop Pine, along with Gowen Cypress, *Cupressus goveniana,* and Douglas Fir, *Pseudotsuga menziesii.* Gowen Cypress is found today on the mainland in association with Bishop Pine, but Douglas Fir is more often a component of Mixed Evergreen Forest, found along the north coast. For a discussion of this community see Chapter 10.

Bishop Pines today grow in three areas of Santa Cruz Island, primarily on north-facing slopes above the ocean (Plate 12B) and in canyons. Elsewhere they are scattered. Small populations occur at China Harbor and in the upper portion of Cañada de los Sauces on Sierra Blanca Ridge. The largest concentrations of Bishop Pines occur on north-facing slopes in the upper reaches of Cañada Christy and near Pelican Bay. The species is also found in a small grove on Black Mountain on Santa Rosa Island. The Santa Cruz Island populations are the most extensive and vigorous on the islands.

Bishop Pines are typically characterized by needles in clusters of two (Fig. 94B). The small, pointed cones generally occur in whorls on the stem; they remain on the tree in a closed state for many years. Heat from a fire will cause the cones to open and shed their seeds or, as is the case on most

Figure 95. Comparison of two types of closed-cone pines on Santa Cruz Island. (A) Typical Bishop Pine with reflexed cones. (B) Straight-cone type, sometimes called Santa Cruz Island Pine.

of Santa Cruz Island, where fire has been suppressed, the cones will open when the tree or limb dies.

Two races or forms of Bishop Pine have been recognized. On a typical Bishop Pine, the cones are asymmetrical, curving backward and downward (reflexed) along the stem toward the main trunk (Fig. 95A). On the other form, which formerly was known as Santa Cruz Island Pine (*Pinus remorata*), the cones are symmetrical and are borne at right angles to the stem (Fig. 95B). Both forms and their intermediates occur in the Santa Cruz Island populations.

Closed-cone pines in general (and Bishop Pine specifically) occur on habitat islands associated with depauperate fine-grained soils, frequent fog, and periodic fires. In this respect Bishop Pines occur on ecological islands within islands. Fog condenses on the needles, and the trees water themselves with fog-drip. This is an important adaptation, because the soil of the islands tends to repel water.

Many of the pines on Santa Cruz Island appear to be senile or dying, a situation that is believed to be the result of fire suppression. Although the cones on Bishop Pine also have a tendency to open with age, it appears that fire is an important component of a healthy forest. Whether or not the natural fire frequency on the Channel Islands has been altered significantly by humans is a controversial subject, for some scientists contend that fires on the islands have always been less frequent than those on the mainland. Nevertheless, scrub vegetation on the islands, including the closed-cone pines, shows the same suite of adaptations exhibited by plants on the mainland, and prescribed burning of the Bishop Pine forest is likely to be a routine in the future. For a more thorough discussion of fire adaptations in chaparral, see Chapter 5.

In areas where introduced sheep have been removed from Santa Cruz Island, Bishop Pine seems to be recovering remarkably, even in the absence of fire. Since the removal of sheep in 1985, the Pelican Bay population has demonstrated significant seedling germination and survival, and diversity of woody species has increased markedly. Another possible threat to Bishop Pines is the presence of Rust Gall, *Peridermium harknessii,* which (especially when followed by fungus infections) is taking its toll on Monterey Pines and Knobcone Pines on the mainland. The infection was found to be common in Bishop Pine stands on Santa Rosa Island.

Other trees that may occur in association with Bishop Pines on Santa Cruz Island are Island Ironwood, Coast Live Oak, and Island Oak. Understory species include Toyon, scrub oaks, and manzanitas. The rare endemic Island Barberry, *Berberis pinnata* ssp. *insularis* (Fig. 96), also occurs mostly in this community. This large shrub has spreading stems that are 5–25 ft (2–8 m) high, and its large leaves are each divided into five to nine glossy leaflets. Clusters of yellow flowers develop into blue berries that have a waxy whitish coating. The species is most common on Santa Cruz Island, although it has been reported from Anacapa and Santa Rosa Islands. Island Barberry has not been seen in Elder Canyon on Santa Rosa Island since 1930, and only dead, aboveground portions of this plant were found in Summit Canyon on West Anacapa Island in 1994. The species reproduces asexually from underground stems (rhizomes), so it may or may not have been extirpated from Anacapa Island. It was federally listed as endangered in 1997.

The other native pine on the Northern Channel Islands is Torrey Pine, *Pinus torreyana* (Fig. 94A; Plate 13B), which occurs only on sandstone bluffs near the northeast corner of Santa Rosa Island. A larger grove occurs on

Figure 96. Island Barberry, *Berberis pinnata* ssp. *insularis.*

coastal sandstone in a small area near Del Mar at Torrey Pines State Reserve in San Diego County. This is probably the smallest distribution of any pine species in the world. The island population has several characteristics that distinguish it from the mainland one: The cones are larger and the trees in general are smaller. On the island none of the trees is over 35 ft (11 m) in height, whereas on the mainland certain trees are over 100 ft (30 m) tall. Some authorities contend that the island version of Torrey Pine deserves its own name, Santa Rosa Island Pine, *Pinus torreyana* ssp. *insularis.*

Torrey Pine is related to Gray Pine (Digger Pine), *Pinus sabiniana,* and Coulter Pine, *Pinus coulteri,* long-needled species that are commonly associated with Chaparral on the mainland. These are the pines with large cones, although Torrey Pines have the smallest cones of the group. They are fire-adapted pines in the sense that the cones open only partially, releasing the seeds over a period of several years. Torrey Pines resemble Gray Pines with their candelabrum-like appearance, having many heavy branches in the crown. They resemble Coulter Pines in having very long, thick needles. However, unlike the other two species, which have needles in clusters of three, Torrey Pines have needles in clusters of five. The needles are grayish in color, similar to those of Gray Pine. The pines on Santa Rosa Island are blue-gray in color.

The mechanism by which a species could become distributed in such an odd manner has been the subject of much debate. It is possible that the former distribution was fairly continuous, and that the remaining trees are relics of that time. The distance between the mainland and the Northern Channel Islands was not great enough to have been a significant barrier to dispersal, because cones can float that far and birds such as Scrub Jays are noted for their ability to carry seeds or acorns in the their throats. On the other hand, right-lateral movement of fault systems has carried land segments hundreds of miles northward, including the land on which both populations of Torrey Pines now grow. There are at least two faults lying between the populations as they occur today, and it is entirely possible that ancestors of the present Santa Rosa Island population originated south of the present population near Del Mar.

If large cone size is an adaptation associated with drought conditions, it follows that the Torrey Pine would have smaller cones than its relatives, because of its more southerly and coastal origin. The fact that the island population has larger cones than those on the mainland also fits this hypothesis.

Because Torrey Pines occur in the absence of other tree species, and because they are not truly closed-cone pines, some authorities refer to the community in which they occur as Torrey Pine Woodland. Species associated with them on Santa Rosa Island include Chamise (Fig. 88) and Toyon (Fig. 54); the associated community on the mainland is primarily Coastal Sage Scrub, although Chamise is present there as well.

The Italian Stone Pine, *Pinus pinea,* has become established on parts of Santa Cruz Island. These large trees, native to the Mediterranean, are now expanding their range. They have a broad, rounded top and long needles in clusters of two. The large, round cones are wider than they are long. The main centers of distribution for the species at present are Pelican Bay and near Prisoners' Harbor on the north side of the island.

The other introduced conifer that has become established on several of the Channel Islands is Monterey Cypress, *Cupressus macrocarpa* (Fig. 122). These large, juniperlike trees may reach 50 ft (15 m) in height. They bear persistent, golf-ball-size, fleshy cones that resemble juniper berries. Their beautiful, irregular shape has made them a favored cultivar in many coastal areas, and they have been planted widely on the islands.

Marshes

The coastal salt marshes of the Northern Channel Islands are rather few and poorly developed, apparently owing to the scarcity of appropriate estuarine situations. The miniature salt marshes that do occur are at the mouths of canyons, and they are composed of salt-tolerant species of plants that are typical of estuaries on the mainland (Fig. 188). They range from salty tidal marshes on San Miguel and Santa Rosa Islands to the nearly freshwater marsh at Prisoners' Harbor on Santa Cruz Island. Most are located at the mouths of streams. There are no endemic plants commonly found in marshes on the islands. For a more thorough discussion of marshes see Chapter 10.

Coastal Strand

Coastal Strand is a community characterized by windblown sand that may or may not be stabilized with vegetation (Fig. 117). It is also known as the Coastal Beach and Dune community. Beach and dune vegetation on the Northern Channel Islands occurs mainly where the coast is exposed to the full force of the northwesterly winds. The Dune community is most extensive on San Miguel, where abundant sand and strong winds have caused the formation of more or less continuous dunes across large portions of the island. Similarly, the western third and the north coast of Santa Rosa Island have well-established dune systems. Patches occur on the eastern end of Santa Rosa Island, the western tip of Santa Cruz Island, and on isolated pocket beaches along the sheltered sides of all of the northern islands.

This is a terrestrial community of sandy beaches and dunes, the pioneer community of the coastline. It occurs where there are no sea cliffs. The water-holding capacity of sand is low, and the accumulation of sea salts (sodium chloride) is high, creating a stressful environment for plants. Plants that become established here have long tap roots, and they are commonly prostrate and succulent. The long tap root enables them to reach water that percolates deeply into the sand. Succulence enables them to cope with the salty soil in a manner similar to that of plants of the salt marsh: by storing water in their tissues, plants are able to dilute the concentration of salts.

Plants that are common on the Coastal Strand are often related to desert plants. Among these are Beach Ragweed or Beach-bur, *Ambrosia chamissonis* (Fig. 148), which is related to the desert Burro Bush. These low shrubs of the dunes have silvery herbage and grow in loose mats up to 10 ft (3 m) across. Also found on these sand dunes are plants related to those found on desert dunes. Among these is the Red Sand Verbena, *Abronia maritima*. Similar to the desert Sand Verbena, this viney species covers many dune areas, and during spring many clusters of reddish-violet flowers form a colorful carpet on the dunes. Another species with desert relatives, the Beach Evening Primrose, *Cammissonia cheiranthifolia* ssp. *cheiranthifolia,* is a prostrate evening primrose that bears bright yellow, four-petaled flowers on long, wiry stems that radiate from a central rosette. It is a conspicuous species all along the California coast.

Members of the ice plant family (Aizoaceae) occur on the beaches of the southern Coast Ranges and down to Baja California. These succulent plants are native to Africa, but they have colonized our beaches to the extent that they are often the most common species. One species is the familiar succulent ground cover known as Hottentot Fig, *Carpobrotus edulis,* which has been used to stabilize slopes in all forms of landscaping. It is found, where it has been planted, on Anacapa, San Clemente, San Nicolas, and Santa Rosa Islands. A related species is Sea Fig, *Carpobrotus chilensis,* which is common on all of the islands except Anacapa and Santa Barbara. Another member of the family, sometimes called Crystalline Ice Plant (Fig. 160), is a succulent ephemeral with tiny, water-filled blisters on its leaves. Its scientific name, *Mesembryanthemum crystallinum,* refers to the crystal-like appearance of the blisters. Apparently the blisters are related to the plant's attempt to excrete and concentrate salts outside its leaf tissues.

Many of the coastal species differ from their desert relatives in being perennial as opposed to ephemeral plants. The constant overcast along the coast limits light intensity so much that it is nearly impossible for annual plants to complete a life cycle in a single year.

Perhaps the most spectacular flower of the beach dunes is Beach Morning Glory, *Calystegia soldanella.* This species is a geophyte, returning each year from deep-seated, fleshy rootstock. It is not an annual, even though it may appear to be one. It produces a large rose to purple flower that looks like a typical morning glory, but it is not a vine. It is common on beaches from Washington to San Diego.

Hoffmann's Slender-flowered Gilia, *Gilia tenuiflora* ssp. *hoffmannii* (Fig. 97), is a slender, annual species that is only found in the sand dunes at East Point on Santa Rosa Island. It was federally listed as endangered in 1997. This little herb has a central stalk that grows from a rosette of densely hairy, strap-shaped leaves to a height of about 5 in. (12 cm). The flowers are purple in the center, fading to pink around the edges.

On the more stabilized dunes are two species of shrubby lupine—Silver Bush Lupine, *Lupinus albifrons* (Fig. 49), and Yellow Bush Lupine, *Lupinus arboreus* (Fig. 168)—that often dominate to such a degree that some authors have erected a community known as Lupine Scrub to describe the association. Although this association of plants is considered a subset of Dune habitat in this chapter, other authors regularly associate these species with Coastal Sage Scrub (see Chapter 5). Yellow Bush Lupine tends to be a large shrub that may assume treelike dimensions; it has lemon yellow

Figure 97. Hoffman's Slender-flowered Gilia, *Gilia tenuiflora* ssp. *hoffmannii.*

2 cm

flowers. Silver Bush Lupine is a low-growing, rounded shrub that has violet to lavender flowers. It is found on all of the Channel Islands except San Clemente and Santa Barbara. Yellow Bush Lupine, which is common on the coast north of Ventura, only occurs on San Miguel and Santa Rosa Islands, where the greatest development of the Coastal Dune complex occurs. Lupines are in the pea family (Fabaceae). As such, they are equipped with nitrogen-fixing bacteria in their roots, a characteristic that also helps them invade disturbed or uncolonized habitats. It is as if they make their own fertilizer! San Miguel Milkvetch, *Astragalus miguelensis* (Fig. 98), another member of the pea family that occurs in these Dune habitats, is a pallid endemic with red, inflated pods. This low perennial is common in most of the areas with extensive dunes.

Coast Goldenbush, *Isocoma menziesii,* is a prostrate species of yellow sunflower that lacks the usual circle of ray flowers. This sometimes fleshy species occurs in stabilized, sandy areas on all of the Channel Islands except Santa Barbara. There are two varieties: *Isocoma menziesii* var. *sedoides* occurs on the Northern Channel Islands and *Isocoma menziesii* var. *vernonioides* occurs on the Southern Channel Islands. Either variety may be accompanied by a rare root parasite, the Short-lobed Broom-rape, *Orobanche parishii* ssp. *brachyloba* (Fig. 154). This short, fleshy yellowish plant bears two-lipped pinkish flowers.

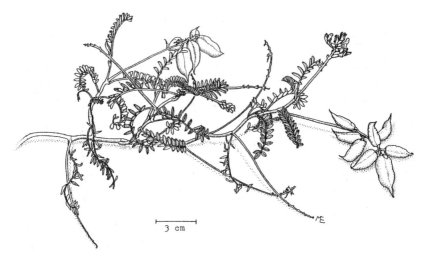

Figure 98. San Miguel Milkvetch, *Astragalus miguelensis.*

Red Buckwheat, *Eriogonum grande* var. *rubescens,* is found in the same areas and in rocky places inland. This low grayish endemic has heart-shaped leaves and round clusters of tiny red flowers in the summer; it resembles a compact version of Island Buckwheat, *Eriogonum grande* var. *grande* (Fig. 72).

The Island Wallflower, *Erysimum insulare* (Fig. 99), is a near-endemic in the mustard family (Brassicaceae). It is common on the north-central part of San Miguel Island but rare elsewhere, and it also occurs sporadically on the mainland coast north of Point Conception. It is a low bush that sprawls with age and has rather pale, narrow leaves; showy, four-petaled yellow flowers; and long, erect seed pods.

Also in the mustard family is Sea Rocket, *Cakile maritima,* a semi-succulent, herbaceous species with deeply lobed leaves and purple to lavender flowers. This species is native to Europe but now is found on beaches all over the world, including those on all of the Channel Islands except Santa Barbara. As is true of most members of the mustard family, the entire plant is edible; older plants are usually eaten after being boiled in water.

Other dune species mentioned elsewhere in this chapter include Dunedelion, *Malacothrix incana* (Fig. 75), and Soft-leaved Indian Paintbrush, *Castilleja mollis,* a federally listed endangered species.

Coastal Grassland

Valley and Southern Coastal Grassland is the technical name for the native grassland community found on the Channel Islands. The most widespread type of vegetation on many of the California islands today, it

Figure 99. Island Wallflower, *Erysimum insulare.*

generally occurs on slopes, marine terraces (Plate 10A), and alluvial plains with fairly deep soils (usually clay), especially where woody plants cannot grow because of wind, seasonal dryness, grazing, or burning. Grassland also forms an understory in the more open Scrub, Woodland, and Chaparral communities.

In their original state, the island grasslands were probably composed mainly of perennial bunchgrasses and herbaceous ephemeral (annual) species. In their present, highly disturbed condition, they consist primarily of introduced ephemeral grasses and weeds.

Among the native perennial bunchgrasses, *Nassella* (=*Stipa*) spp.— including Nodding Needlegrass (*Nassella cernua*), Foothill Needlegrass (*Nassella lepida*), and Purple Needlegrass (*Nassella pulchra*)—occur at widely scattered locations throughout all of the California islands.

Many native herbaceous species characteristic of grasslands have survived the onslaught of nonnative herbivores, but their distribution is spotty. Among these are a number of bulb-producing species, such as Golden Stars (*Bloomeria crocea*), Blue Dicks (*Dichelostemma capitatum*) (Fig. 198), and various mariposa lilies (*Calochortus* spp.) (Plate 10C). Wild parsleys

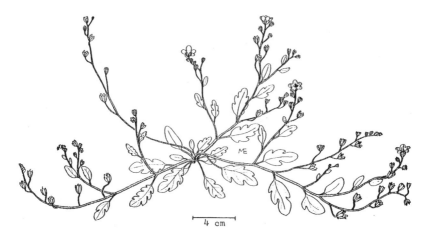

Figure 100. Northern Channel Islands Phacelia, *Phacelia insularis* ssp. *insularis.*

(*Lomatium* spp.) and Blue-eyed Grass, *Sisyrinchium bellum,* return each year from underground stems (rhizomes), a strategy similar to that followed by plants that return from bulbs. Everything above ground dies and the plants remain in a dormant state underground until the rains return. Of the common native ephemeral species, the clovers (*Trifolium* spp.), lupines (*Lupinus* spp.), phacelias (*Phacelia* spp.) (Fig. 100), fiddlenecks (*Amsinckia* spp., *Cryptantha* spp.), and poppies (*Eschscholzia* spp., *Papaver* spp.) return sporadically each year from seeds. Most of the tiny endemics that formerly characterized the island grasslands are now extremely rare and confined to cliffs, where introduced herbivores cannot reach them.

One member of the poppy family (Papaveraceae) that is common in sandy grasslands on north-facing slopes of San Miguel Island and is less abundant in other areas is a dwarf, nearly hairless version of California Cream Cups. Formerly it was described as a distinctive variety under the name *Platystemon californicus* var. *ornithopus* (Fig. 101). It is an attractive spring annual with six-petaled whitish flowers.

With the introduction of domesticated grazing animals such as cattle and sheep, many grasses and weeds were introduced inadvertently. Seeds of these plants arrived from the Mediterranean in the animals' food, fur, and digestive tracts. Many of the weedy species, such as mustards (*Brassica* spp.) were also introduced deliberately as human food species. Unlike the bulk of the native species, which were perennial plants that returned each year from underground structures, the invaders tended to be ephemeral and return each year from seeds. As might be expected, the ephemeral species produced an enormous number of seeds, contrary to the strategy of the native perennial plants, which invested most of their energy in stor-

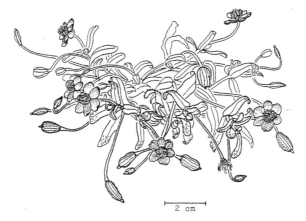

Figure 101. California Cream Cups, *Platystemon californicus* var. *ornithopus*.

ing food in such underground organs as bulbs or rhizomes. Over time, particularly under the onslaught of the hooves and jaws of nonnative herbivores, the nonnative ephemeral species replaced the native species.

Among the nonnative grasses are wild oats (*Avena* spp.) (Fig. 59A), bromes or chesses (*Bromus* spp.) (Fig. 59D), foxtails (*Hordeum* spp.) (Fig. 59B), and ryegrasses (*Lolium* spp.) (Fig. 59C). Other nonnative weeds—such as mustards (*Brassica* spp.), filarees (*Erodium* spp.), burclovers (*Medicago* spp.), and sweet clovers (*Melilotus* spp.)—have also displaced the native grassland species.

At present, grasslands in all of their versions represent the most common plant community on the Northern Channel Islands. Estimates of total coverage vary, but it appears that on Santa Rosa Island about 67 percent of the total area is covered by grassland. On the other northern islands estimates of total coverage vary from 25–33 percent for Anacapa Island to 33–50 percent for San Miguel Island to 58 percent for Santa Cruz Island.

TERRESTRIAL ANIMALS

With fifty-six species of vertebrate animal inhabitants, Santa Cruz Island has the greatest diversity of species of all the Channel Islands. Santa Rosa Island is third, behind Santa Catalina Island (which is discussed in Chapter 5). The animals found on each of the Northern Channel Islands are quite similar, which is to be expected, based on the islands' close proximity to one another and the fact that during periods of lowered sea level the islands were connected to one another (see Chapters 1 and 2).

As might be expected in a depauperate fauna, many of the existing species (both endemic and nonendemic) show signs of *competitive release,* a phenomenon in which individual species in the absence of competition undergo explosive increases in population size. The outcomes of competitive release can include great abundance, utilization of a broad range of habitats, seasonal shifts in life cycle, increased variability, or all of these results. Most of these trends, however, have not been studied sufficiently well to permit us to draw general conclusions.

Invertebrates

Invertebrates of the Northern Channel Islands have not been well studied, with the exception of certain groups, such as the land snails, grasshoppers, butterflies, and moths. In general, the invertebrate fauna is a depauperate mixture of northern and southern species with a few endemics scattered among the various groups. Additional collections and taxonomic revisions will undoubtedly alter our perception of the status and distribution of many endemic invertebrates, including those discussed here. Because invertebrates are often not conspicuous and because they are most often discussed by specialists, most species do not have common names. Therefore the scientific names of certain invertebrates discussed in this chapter are not accompanied by common names.

The land snails of the Northern Channel Islands probably have a greater percentage of endemics than any other major group of invertebrates. Of the eleven species and subspecies of land and freshwater snails and slugs recorded there, three or four are not native, one or two are native but nonendemic, one endemic is now extinct, and five are strictly insular. Therefore, about three-quarters of all the native land snails known to have inhabited the islands are endemic. Of these, the majority are extremely small, rare, localized, and secretive. The only species likely to be found by the casual observer is *Helminthoglypta ayresiana* (Fig. 102), the three subspecies of which are restricted to the Northern Channel Islands. Easily recognized as the only snail on the northern islands with a large, spiral shell, it is a handsome species with a dark brown band on a tan background. This snail is common on San Miguel and West Anacapa Islands and is rare on the other islands; it is most common in Coastal Bluff Scrub vegetation, but it may be found in almost any habitat. Although the species is active during the winter rains, dormant specimens may be found under plants and surface objects during the summer. Interestingly, this genus is absent from the Southern Channel Islands, where it is replaced by several endemic forms of the similar genus *Micrarionta*.

The group of animals that includes insects, spiders, and scorpions is known as the phylum Arthropoda. Among arthropods, some groups appear to be predisposed to evolving island endemics. The only scorpion

Figure 102. Land snail, *Helminthoglypta ayresiana.*

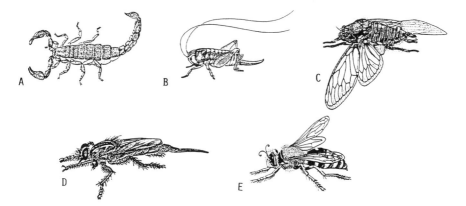

Figure 103. Arthropods of the Northern Channel Islands. (A) Scorpion, *Vejovis minimus thompsoni.* (B) Silk-spinning Sand Cricket, *Cnemotettix caudalus.* (C) Cicada, *Okanagana hirsuta.* (D) Robber fly, *Stenopogon neojubatus.* (E) Digger wasp, *Bembix americana hamata.*

on the Northern Channel Islands is *Vejovis minimus thompsoni* (Fig. 103A). This small, light brown, venomous species is found under surface objects on the three eastern islands, where it is uncommon. Two of the most common darkling ground beetles on the Channel Islands are endemic: *Coniontis lata,* a reddish-black species found under rocks, and *Coelus pacificus,* a black species that burrows in sand dunes. Many other members of this family occur as nonendemics on the islands.

Five of the forty kinds of Orthoptera (crickets and grasshoppers) believed to be native to the Northern Channel Islands are endemic. All of these are flightless species with flightless ancestors, suggesting that the northern islands are not sufficiently isolated to allow highly mobile species to evolve separately there. The most interesting orthopteran endemics are

Silk-spinning Crickets (*Cnemotettix* spp.), which are small, grayish crickets that line their burrows with silk; they are related to Jerusalem Crickets (*Stenopelmatus* spp.). Though generally uncommon, secretive, and inconspicuous, these endemics are of interest because of their pattern of distribution on the northern islands. *Cnemotettix spinulus* occurs on the three eastern islands and San Nicolas Island; it is most common around the lighthouse on East Anacapa Island. *Cnemotettix caudalus* (Fig. 103B) is found only on the three western islands, where it is locally common in the central part of San Miguel Island. Both species are found mainly in sand dunes. The short, egg-laying appendage (ovipositor) of *Cnemotettix caudalus* appears to be specialized for laying eggs in hardened sand, but both species occur marginally in chaparral (the most typical habitat for the two mainland species).

The presence of only one *Cnemotettix* species on each of the two smaller northern islands seems to reflect the history of emergence and submergence of the Northern Channel Islands. Assuming that the islands were originally colonized by a single, common ancestor, the present distribution of these crickets has been explained as the result of evolutionary divergence during periods when the islands were separated by high sea levels, followed by range extension and mingling when the islands merged during glacial periods, and finally the extinction of one of the forms on each of the smaller, ecologically restricted islands as sea levels rose again. Complex though this scenario may seem, it is the simplest explanation that takes into account all the known facts. It is also the best example of *adaptive radiation* (the derivation of multiple species from a common ancestor) in any group of invertebrates or vertebrates on the Northern Channel Islands.

Of the remaining orthopteran endemics, the only one likely to be encountered is the recently described Pygmy Grasshopper, *Morsea californica islandica*. This little insect is common in a variety of habitats on the two larger islands. It may be green, gray, tan, brown, black, or a combination of these colors.

The remaining endemic insects fly well. Their potentially strong dispersal powers suggest an interesting evolutionary problem, although many insects that can fly do so reluctantly or nevertheless remain in a very small area. A cicada, *Okanagana hirsuta* (Fig. 103C), is a dark brown insect with orange spots. It is locally common and noisy in scrub vegetation on the three eastern islands: Anacapa, Santa Cruz, and Santa Rosa. Juvenile cicadas live underground, where they feed on fungi that are associated with the roots of plants. When they are ready to metamorphose into adults they emerge from the ground and crawl up the trunks or stems of nearby plants and shed their skins. Veins in their wings are then filled with fluid, and the new skin and wings harden up. Adult cicadas are robust insects with long, membranous wings. Males make a loud buzzing noise to attract females. After mating, fertilized eggs are deposited on the branches of shrubs and trees; when they hatch, the juveniles fall to the ground and burrow under the soil again, sometimes for years.

A small, brownish robber fly, *Stenopogon neojubatus* (Fig. 103D), is fairly common on the three larger Northern Channel Islands, where it catches flying insects. Two endemic digger wasps share the habit of stocking their nests (dug into the sand) with insects paralyzed by a sting. *Bembix americana hamata* (Fig. 103E) is uncommon on the three western islands, but it is conspicuous because of its fairly large size and distinctive yellowish and black markings. *Palmodes insularis* is a more common black species that feeds on crickets and grasshoppers, including some of the endemic forms; it has been reported from all of the northern islands.

In comparing common moths and butterflies (Lepidoptera) on Santa Cruz Island with those on the adjacent mainland, among five groups of conspicuous, larger forms, 30–62 percent of the species were represented on the island. For example, among common butterflies such as Swallowtails and Skippers, 35 percent of the species were represented. Preliminary analysis of the island species suggests that the northern island fauna is mainly composed of widespread forms, but with a slightly greater affinity to the fauna of the San Francisco Bay area than to that of the nearby Santa Monica Mountains, a pattern that probably reflects the distribution of the insects' host plants. The butterfly fauna in general exhibits the typical island pattern of missing species and overabundant replacements, but there are only a few weakly differentiated endemics in this mobile group.

The moths of the island make up the great majority of lepidopterans, though many groups have scarcely been studied. They range from large night-flying species to tiny forms whose larvae mine the interior of plant leaves. In comparing the distributions of small, leaf-mining moths it was discovered that 71 percent of the species were represented on the islands. In examining those species that use common host plants, such as willows, oaks, and California lilacs, it was discovered that 87 percent of the leaf-miners were also present on the islands. The high number of leaf-miners represented on the islands may be explained by the increased probability of small species' surviving in small patches of host plants. Among the leaf-mining moths are two presumably relict species found only on Island Ironwood. A few other endemic species are scattered among various families, but most are rare, inconspicuous, secretive, and unlikely to be found (or identified) by the nonspecialist. One endemic micromoth

(*Argyrotaenia franciscana insulana*), is readily seen by the observant visitor on all of the northern islands. Though inconspicuously drab in color, this miniature species is commonly flushed by walking through Coastal Sage Scrub at almost any time of the year.

Amphibians and Reptiles (Herpetofauna)

Only three species of amphibians are currently known to inhabit the Northern Channel Islands. The Pacific Treefrog, *Hyla* (=*Pseudacris*) *regilla* (Fig. 63), is common around water holes and streams on Santa Cruz and Santa Rosa Islands; it is also found on Santa Catalina Island. Even though this species has expanded toe tips that act like suction cups, it spends most of its time on the ground. The Red-legged Frog, *Rana aurora,* was apparently collected on the northern slope of Santa Cruz Island in the early 1900s, but the current status of this species on this island is unclear, and its status on the mainland is precarious as well. It was listed as threatened by the federal government in 1996.

The Channel Islands Slender Salamander, *Batrachoseps pacificus pacificus* (Fig. 104), occurs on all four islands and represents the only endemic amphibian on any of the California islands. This secretive creature is found under rocks and logs (mainly near streams) during the winter and spring rainy season. It retreats into cracks in the ground during periods of summer drought. On Santa Cruz Island an additional species, the Black-bellied Slender Salamander, *Batrachoseps nigriventris,* occurs in similar habitats, and it also occurs on the mainland. The nonendemic form is very similar to the endemic, but it may be distinguished by its smaller size and the absence of white flecks on the belly. The endemic is one of the more primitive species in a genus that contains several species in California. The occurrence of two species of *Batrachoseps* in the same place is rather unusual and has formed the basis for a number of studies. Of particular interest is the possibility that the two forms tend to be distributed on either side of the major fault that runs through the island's Central Valley. As explained in Chapters 1 and 2 and discussed later in this chapter, the land masses on each side of the fault were at one time different islands, and it is possible that the salamanders originally inhabited the separate islands and have been inadvertently juxtaposed by right-lateral translocation along the fault.

The reptiles of the Northern Channel Islands consist of three lizards and three snakes, none of which is venomous. The Island Western Fence Lizard, *Sceloporus occidentalis becki* (Fig. 105), is represented by an endemic subspecies restricted to the three larger northern islands. It is about 9 in. (23 cm) in total length, with spiny scales and a blotched, brownish

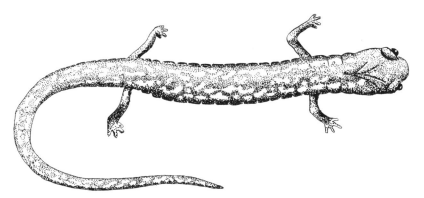

Figure 104. Channel Islands Slender Salamander, *Batrachoseps pacificus pacificus*.

2 cm

Figure 105. Island Western Fence Lizard, *Sceloporus occidentalis becki*.

coloration. The males, often called "blue-bellied lizards," have distinctive blue patches on the underparts and blue spots scattered above. Uncommon in most areas, this lizard achieves its greatest population density in Coastal Sage Scrub along the south side of Santa Cruz Island.

The Side-blotched Lizard, *Uta stansburiana* (Fig. 60A), is a nonendemic found abundantly in sunny areas on Anacapa and Santa Cruz Islands. It is superficially similar to the Island Western Fence Lizard, from which it

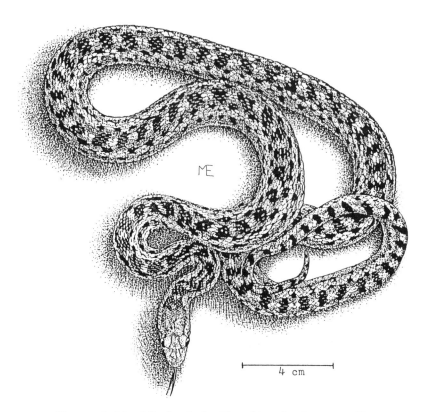

Figure 106. Island Gopher Snake, *Pituophis melanoleucus pumilis.*

may be distinguished by its smaller size, its granular scales, and a dark spot behind each front leg. Where it occurs, this is the most common species on the California islands.

The other lizard found on the Northern Channel Islands is the Southern Alligator Lizard, *Elgaria multicarinatus* (Fig. 60C), a large species with small legs, a long tail, platelike scales, and a lateral fold of skin. This sedentary lizard is found on all of the Channel Islands except San Clemente and Santa Barbara. Although insects probably form the main part of the diet of all of the island lizards, this nonendemic is powerful enough to overcome small vertebrates, including smaller members of its own species.

The only endemic snake on the Northern Channel Islands is the Island Gopher Snake, *Pituophis melanoleucus pumilis* (Fig. 106), which is more common on Santa Cruz than on Santa Rosa Island. This snake reaches a length of about 4 ft (1.25 m) and is tan with darker blotches on the back and sides. It is the smallest of the several races of this widespread species. Mice are its main food item, but lizards and small birds may also be eaten occasionally.

The Racer, *Coluber constrictor mormon* (Fig. 191), occurs on Santa

Figure 107. Spotted Night Snake, *Hypsiglena torquata.*

Cruz Island, where it is rare and elusive in Grassland and Coastal Sage Scrub. The adults are grayish above and yellow below. Averaging about 3 ft (1 m) in length, they feed mainly on small vertebrates and large insects. The only other snake that has been reported from the northern islands is the Spotted Night Snake, *Hypsiglena torquata* (Fig. 107). Three specimens of this snake were collected on one occasion at Prisoners' Harbor on Santa Cruz Island in August 1939. The current status of this species on the island is unclear. The Night Snake is a small, blotched species that is easily confused with the young of the other two snakes on the islands. It differs from them in its pupils, which are vertically oriented, like a cat's. A highly secretive snake, it is usually found in cracks or under rocks and logs.

Land Birds

The land birds of the Northern Channel Islands have long been the object of intense study. A great many species migrate through the islands but do not breed there, and in addition to those that migrate through without breeding, new breeding species could arrive at any time. It is therefore difficult to compile species lists that will remain accurate over time. The exact number of species varies from one island to the next and from year to year, as localized extinctions and natural immigration continue to occur. Of the more than fifty native species that have been known to breed on the islands during this century, about 25 percent are represented by endemic races. For comparison, the Southern Channel Islands support between 18 and 32 percent endemics. In all, eighteen races of endemic birds are currently recognized on the Channel Islands. The nonendemic land birds of the Northern Channel Islands are generally the same ones that are found on the southern islands (see Chapter 5).

The most distinctive endemic bird on the Channel Islands is the Island Scrub Jay, *Aphelocoma insularis* (Plate 1B). Although the island form was formerly described as a subspecies of the mainland scrub jay, recent analysis has revealed that it is quite different. There are now three kinds of scrub jay in the United States. The Florida Scrub Jay has retained the original species name, *Aphelocoma coerulescens,* and the species in the western United States is now known as the Western Scrub Jay, *Aphelocoma californica.* A resident only of Santa Cruz Island, the Island Scrub Jay is the only single-island endemic species of vertebrate on the Channel Islands. There is a more pronounced difference between it and the mainland form, only 20 miles (32 km) away, than between the Western Scrub Jay and the Florida Scrub Jay, which are separated by about 2000 miles (3200 km).

This large, intensely blue bird is often abundant and conspicuous in Chaparral, woodland, and Closed-cone Pine Forests on Santa Cruz Island, where it feeds on a wide variety of plant and animal foods. Island Jays prefer nesting and foraging in oak trees and may be important as "uphill planters" of oak trees, since they feed heavily on acorns in the fall and may bury surplus stores. Jays are curious and will often approach a quiet observer closely. This bird is highly territorial and monogamous, advertising its presence with a variety of calls, many of which are different from those of mainland Scrub Jays. An interesting feature of the social organization of Island Scrub Jays is that young birds are often unable to establish breeding territories during the first two or three years of life, during which time they congregate in flocks that forage in marginal habitats such as Grassland or Coastal Sage Scrub. Island Scrub Jays also live longer than other scrub jays: they are known to live at least 18 years, and probably live longer, whereas the oldest known Florida Scrub Jay lived about 14.5 years. Part of the reason for the extended life span of Island Scrub Jays is that they are relatively free of the predators that capture them on the mainland.

The sparrow and warbler family (Emberizidae) is heavily represented by endemic forms on the Northern Channel Islands. Two subspecies of Song Sparrow occur: *Melospiza melodia micronyx* (Fig. 120) is restricted to San Miguel Island, and *Melospiza melodia clemente* breeds abundantly on Santa Rosa Island and less commonly on Santa Cruz Island, as well as

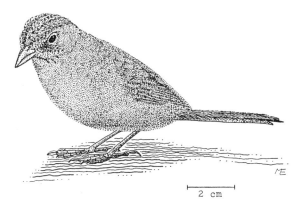

Figure 108. Rufous-crowned Sparrow, *Aimophila ruficeps obscura.*

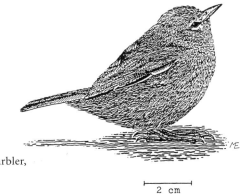

Figure 109. Orange-crowned Warbler, *Vermivora celata sordida.*

on the islands to the south. Both are nondescript grayish sparrows, with heavy streaking on their breasts, that produce elaborate and beautiful songs. Both are fairly common in Coastal Sage Scrub, especially on windswept slopes and in ravines. Similar habitats on Santa Cruz Island usually support equally abundant populations of the endemic Rufous-crowned Sparrow, *Aimophila ruficeps obscura* (Fig. 108), an inconspicuous, ground-dwelling species that also breeds on Anacapa Island. Competitive exclusion between the two species is suggested by the Song Sparrow's relative scarcity on Santa Cruz Island—where it is most common in its typical (for mainland races) habitat along streams—and by the Rufous-crowned Sparrow's absence in its usual habitat on Santa Rosa Island.

The Orange-crowned Warbler, *Vermivora celata sordida* (Fig. 109), is a small, insectivorous bird, olive green above and dirty yellow below with an inconspicuous orange spot on the head. It is fairly common in Coastal

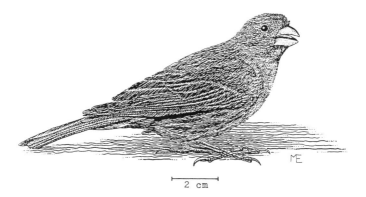

Figure 110. House Finch, *Carpodacus mexicanus.*

Sage Scrub, Chaparral, and woodlands on each of the islands. Although less migratory than mainland races, the endemic form has established limited colonies on the mainland coast to the south during postbreeding wanderings.

Another member of the sparrow and warbler family, the Rufous-sided Towhee, *Pipilo erythrophthalmus* (Fig. 64H), is represented by an endemic race on Santa Rosa Island. This species, with its black head and heavily spotted back, exhibits a color pattern that is well suited for a bird that spends a good part of its time feeding on the ground in filtered light under shrubs.

In the finch family (Fringillidae), one common species has become differentiated on the islands. The House Finch of the Northern Channel Islands is included in the mainland subspecies, *Carpodacus mexicanus frontalis,* but the San Miguel and Santa Rosa Island populations (Fig. 110) share some characteristics with the endemic race of the southern islands, *Carpodacus mexicanus clementis.* This finch resembles a large-billed sparrow, but the males have a scarlet head and breast.

Endemic birds belonging to other families are also commonly observed on the islands. The Horned Lark, *Eremophila alpestris insularis* (Fig. 64E), is one of the few island birds that nests in open grassland. This is a small bird, chestnut brown above and yellow below, with black and white markings on the head and throat. Male Horned Larks have small black "horns" on their heads.

Loggerhead Shrikes, *Lanius ludovicianus anthonyi* (Fig. 111), are common in grassland and open woodlands on Santa Rosa Island and the western end of Santa Cruz Island. They also have been known to breed on the other Northern Channel Islands. These predatory birds are gray with black and white markings, resembling stocky mockingbirds with black masks.

Figure 111. Loggerhead Shrike, *Lanius ludovicianus anthonyi.*

Figure 112. Bewick's Wren, *Thryomanes bewickii nesophilus.*

Close inspection will reveal that they even have small hooks on the ends of their beaks, making them look like miniature versions of raptors. They are also known as "Butcher Birds" because of the male's habitat of hanging its prey on sharp thorns and barbed wire fences; apparently this behavior is intended to impress the female with the male's hunting prowess.

The Northern Channel Islands' form of Bewick's Wren, *Thryomanes bewickii nesophilus* (Fig. 112), is abundant in Chaparral on the three eastern islands. Only weakly differentiated from the mainland subspecies, this tiny, insectivorous brown songster is similar to the larger, nonendemic Rock Wren, *Salpinctes obsoletus* (Fig. 64I), which breeds on all the islands.

Figure 113. Allen's Hummingbird, *Selasphorus sasin sedentarius*.

2 cm

The endemic Allen's Hummingbird, *Selasphorus sasin sedentarius* (Fig. 113), occurs on all of the Northern Channel Islands and Santa Catalina. This tiny bird differs from the nonendemic Anna's Hummingbird, *Calypte anna,* in having rufous-colored sides and a rounded tail. Anna's Hummingbird is larger and greener and has a squarish tail, although the male's tail tends to be slightly forked. The two species occur on Santa Cruz Island and on the mainland, where both hummingbirds compete for the scarce flowers of early fall. On the island, the endemic is more successful in holding optimal territories, a reversal of the mainland pattern.

The Western Flycatcher of the Channel Islands (including Santa Rosa and Santa Cruz Islands) is sometimes considered an endemic subspecies, *Empidonax difficilis insulicola,* but it has not been universally recognized.

Among the raptors, the Red-tailed Hawk, *Buteo jamaicensis,* and the American Kestrel, *Falco sparverius* (Fig. 64B), are common. The Burrowing Owl, *Athene cunicularia* (Fig. 64A), and the Barn Owl, *Tyto alba,* are the nocturnal predatory birds. The Bald Eagle, *Haliaeetus leucocephalus* (Fig. 65), and the Osprey, *Pandion haliaetus* (Fig. 41), are now extirpated from the Northern Channel Islands. The Peregrine Falcon, *Falco peregrinus,* once extirpated from the Northern Channel Islands as a result of DDT-induced eggshell thinning, is now making a comeback through a combination of reintroductions and natural colonization. As of 1998 there were at least fourteen pairs of breeding birds distributed over all five islands in Channel Islands National Park.

Sea Birds

The most important rookeries for sea birds in southern California occur on Anacapa and San Miguel Islands. Those birds are discussed in Chapter 4. The Snowy Plover, *Charadrius alexandrinus,* an endangered species that breeds in coastal dunes, has found a refuge on the outer, windswept islands, nesting on San Miguel, San Nicolas, and Santa Rosa Islands. Technically not a sea bird but a shore bird, it nevertheless depends on the marine intertidal zones for its food.

Mammals

All four of the native, terrestrial mammals on the islands are represented by endemic subspecies. The most abundant and widespread species is the Deer Mouse, *Peromyscus maniculatus* (Fig. 3), which is represented by eight different endemic subspecies, each on a different one of the Channel Islands. Deer Mice are common in habitats where they are sheltered from predation: rocky outcroppings, coastal bluffs, buildings, and the marsh at Prisoners' Harbor, Santa Cruz Island. This fairly large, grayish species feeds on a variety of plants and animals.

The Santa Cruz Island Harvest Mouse, *Reithrodontomys megalotis santacruzae,* is restricted to Santa Cruz Island. It is the smallest of the island mice. It can be differentiated from the Deer Mouse by its smaller head and body size, its much longer tail, and the grooves on the front surface of the upper incisors.

The Island Spotted Skunk, *Spilogale gracilis amphialus* (Fig. 114), fairly common on Santa Rosa Island, is currently scarce on Santa Cruz Island. The size of a small house cat, it is marked with white blotches on a black background. Natural history of the island race is poorly known, but the skunk probably feeds on any available plants and animals. This weakly defined race is nocturnal and rarely observed. It differs from its cousin the Striped Skunk, *Mephitis mephitis,* in being smaller and having white blotches instead of stripes on its back. It also differs in its threat behavior: whereas the Striped Skunk erects its large, conspicuous tail, the Spotted Skunk stands on its hands, elevating its entire back and tail.

The main predator and largest native land mammal on the Channel Islands is the Island Fox, *Urocyon littoralis* (Fig. 4; Plate 1A), of which a different endemic subspecies occurs on each of the three larger islands: San Miguel, Santa Cruz, and Santa Rosa. About the size of a house cat, this engaging creature is a miniature version of the mainland Gray Fox, *Urocyon cinereoargenteus.* Some authorities consider the two foxes to be members of the same species. The Island Fox is gray above with rusty, black, and white markings below. It is active day and night and is frequently observed foraging for the lizards, fruit, and smaller insects that constitute its diet. Sometimes it climbs into trees to prey on the nests of jays and other birds. The Island Fox shows no great fear of humans and will

Figure 114. Island Spotted Skunk, *Spilogale gracilis amphialus.*

sometimes take food from their hands. (Lack of fear in the presence of
humans is not uncommon in animals that have been isolated on islands.)
Lacking predators, Island Foxes usually die of old age. Different subspecies
of the fox have been described for each of the six largest Channel Islands,
but the differences among the races are slight. Some authorities believe
the foxes may originally have been transported to the islands by Native
Americans (see Chapter 1).

Although bats constitute a large proportion of the mammals recorded
from the Northern Channel Islands, their precise distribution is poorly
known and there are no endemic forms. Three species apparently breed
on Santa Cruz Island: the California Bat (*Myotis californicus*), Townsend's
Long-eared Bat (*Plecotus townsendii*), and the Pallid Bat (*Antrozous pallidus*). The island population of the latter species has reportedly developed a distinctive dialect in its communication sounds. The California
Bat has also been collected on Santa Rosa Island and is expected to occur
on San Miguel Island. Five additional species have been recorded from
Santa Cruz Island, probably as migrants and vagrants: the Long-eared Bat
(*Myotis evotis*), Big Brown Bat (*Eptesicus fuscus*), Silver-haired Bat

(*Lasionycteris noctivagans*), Hoary Bat (*Lasiurus cinereus*), and Mexican Free-tailed Bat (*Tadarida brasiliensis*).

Extinct Vertebrates

The most famous extinct vertebrate on the islands is the Exiled Mammoth, *Mammuthus exilis,* which occurred only on the northern islands during the late Pleistocene. This small elephant (about 4–6 ft at the shoulder, compared with 11 ft for existing elephants) may have still been on the island when humans arrived and might have been exterminated by early humans. Fossil evidence from the north shore of Santa Rosa Island also suggests that near the end of the Pleistocene the mainland Imperial Mammoth, *Mammathus columbi,* became established on the islands and the two forms mingled for a time. It is possible that the original elephants on the island were of full size, and that over time natural selection favored smaller and smaller size, resulting in the pygmy Exiled Mammoth.

An extinct, endemic mouse, *Peromyscus nesodytes,* is also known from San Miguel and Santa Rosa Islands. This large species (which was not ancestral to the modern Deer Mouse of the islands) became extinct about 2000 years ago. A related but smaller species, *Peromyscus anyapahensis,* occurred on West Anacapa Island.

Also inhabiting the islands during the Pleistocene and later were the flightless diving geese, *Chendytes* spp., which probably bred only on the islands but foraged along the mainland coast as well.

An interesting nonendemic in the fossil record of the post-Pleistocene is the extinct Vampire Bat, *Desmodus stockii,* which probably fed on the blood of pinnipeds and sea birds on San Miguel Island. Two other species that are questionably native or endemic have also been found in recent deposits on the island: the Spotted Skunk (Fig. 114) and Ornate Shrew, *Sorex ornatus.*

Many of the modern vertebrates of the islands have apparently existed there for several thousand years, including the Island Fox, which has been found in late Pleistocene deposits on Santa Rosa Island. A number of nonendemic native species have become extirpated in this century owing to human disturbance. The most notable recent loss was the disappearance of the large raptors, such as the Bald Eagle, *Haliaeetus leucocephalus* (Fig. 65), and the Osprey, *Pandion haliaetus* (Fig. 41). The decline of these spectacular predatory birds was not unique to the islands. They disappeared all over California, apparently the victims of shooting, pesticides, or both. Bald Eagles have recently been reintroduced to Santa Catalina Island, and the Peregrine Falcon is now nesting on Anacapa, San Miguel, Santa Barbara, Santa Cruz, and Santa Rosa Islands.

Figure 115. Acorn Woodpecker, *Melanerpes formicivorus.*

Introduced Vertebrates

At the opposite end of the spectrum from the extinct species are those that have come to inhabit the islands only recently. Included in this group are the cattle, horses, sheep, goats, and pigs discussed in Chapter 1, as well as the Mule Deer and Wapiti (Roosevelt Elk) of Santa Rosa Island. A recent report of the California Ground Squirrel, *Spermophilus beecheyi,* on Santa Cruz Island is likely unfounded. The species apparently is not established there.

Although most of the recent invaders were brought by humans, a few birds have apparently colonized the islands naturally during this century. The most conspicuous recent immigrants include the Acorn Woodpecker, *Melanerpes formicivorus* (Fig. 115), on Santa Catalina and Santa Cruz Islands. Killdeer, *Charadrius vociferus,* also recently appeared on the same islands as well as Santa Rosa Island.

Introductions of game birds include those of the Santa Catalina Island race of the California Quail, *Callipepla californica catalinensis* (Fig. 64D), as well as Wild Turkeys, *Meleagris gallopavo,* which have been introduced to Santa Cruz and Santa Rosa Islands. Peafowl, *Pavo cristatus,* were once introduced to Santa Cruz Island but are not established there.

The European Starling, *Sturnus vulgaris,* is established on all of the Channel Islands, and the House Sparrow, *Passer domesticus,* formerly bred on

Santa Rosa Island. The failure of the latter species to maintain a population on the islands may be due to competition with the endemic sparrows there. Domestic Pigeons or Rock Doves, *Columba livia,* have been observed on Santa Cruz and Santa Rosa Islands, although they apparently are not breeding there.

Similarly, the cosmopolitan House Mouse, *Mus musculus,* has never established itself on the northern islands, perhaps because Deer Mice (Fig. 3) are already abundant in human habitations on each island. However, the Black Rat, *Rattus rattus,* is established on Anacapa and San Miguel Islands, where it may pose a threat to several endemics, including Deer Mice.

SAN MIGUEL ISLAND

The visitor to San Miguel Island (Fig. 116) is invariably struck by a sense of desolation and mystery. Stripped bare in many places by persistent winds, the land reveals the skeletons of its past: ancient shells, trees, bones, and the remains of Native American and more recent habitations. The rocks and reefs surrounding the island are littered with shipwrecks caused by treacherous currents. The wind, fog, and barren landscape may initially seem uninviting, but there is much to recommend a visit to this island, particularly as it recovers from the devastation wreaked by domestic animals.

The most northern and westerly of the Channel Islands, San Miguel Island lies 26 miles (42 km) south of Point Conception and 3 miles (5 km) west of Santa Rosa Island. It is fairly small, only about 6 miles (10 km) long and 14 square miles (34 km^2) in total area. Most of the land area is a plateau, 400–500 ft (130–160 m) in elevation with two rounded hills over 800 ft (244 m) high. The many deep ravines that dissect the generally even topography are partly the result of recent erosion caused by overgrazing, agriculture, military construction, and test bombing—all of which have been discontinued. Episodes of vegetation stripping have a long history on San Miguel Island, extending back to at least the late Pleistocene, when mammoths grazed the island's vegetation (including various trees and shrubs). The arrival of humans probably increased the incidence of fires, resulting in further vegetation stripping and sand encroachment. It can be assumed that the present biota of San Miguel Island has been greatly influenced by thousands of years of extreme disturbance.

The island receives the full force of the California Current as it sweeps around Point Conception. As D. L. Johnson states, "[The current makes] San Miguel Island one of the windiest, foggiest, most maritime, and wave-pounded areas on the west coast of North America." The island is

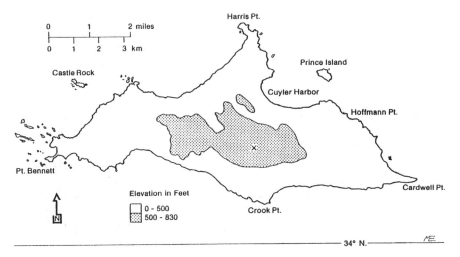

Figure 116. San Miguel Island.

Figure 117. Sand dunes near Cuyler Harbor, San Miguel Island.

surrounded by numerous reefs and rocks, the largest of which is Prince Island. This islet guards the entrance to graceful Cuyler Harbor, a large, semicircular bay on the northeast shore that provides the only sheltered anchorage on the island. Strong northwesterly winds blow almost constantly, driving sand dunes (Fig. 117) before them and pruning the vegetation to a low, scrubby form. Rainwater trapped by the dunes is a source for freshwater springs, making this one of the few Channel Islands

Figure 118. Caliche casts of ancient plants on San Miguel Island.

with drinkable, though poor-tasting, water. Dense fog is frequent and helps keep temperatures cool and even, averaging 59°F (14°C). Annual precipitation averages about 14 in. (356 mm), though great fluctuations are characteristic.

Geology

Structurally San Miguel is the northern flank of a mass of sedimentary rocks that is broken by faults. In general the beds tip northeastward. The ages of the bedrock range from Cretaceous (145 million years B.P.) to Miocene (24 million years B.P.). Sand dunes, running parallel to the direction of the prevailing winds, dominate the landscape. The persistent winds have blown away most of the topsoil, revealing "dune rock": wind-deposited sand that has become cemented by minerals such as calcium salts. Crusts of this calcium material mixed with sand and silt are also known as *caliche*. It is formed by capillary action that draws mineral-rich ground water to the surface, where it evaporates in the wind and sun, leaving the salts.

One of the most interesting features of the island are the caliche forests, calcified casts of ancient vegetation that have been exposed in several areas by the eroding sand (Fig. 118). Although the large, straight trunks of many of these fossils suggest the possibility that they are casts of the pines and possibly cypresses that might have grown on the island at an earlier time, the original plants may have been smaller; the casts' present size may be the result of accumulated deposits of calcium carbonate and sand. Most of the casts appear to date from the late Pleistocene, when sand dunes smothered woody vegetation.

Volcanic rocks of Oligocene age (>24 million years B.P.) are found at various points about the island. Tiny Prince Island (also called Gull Island) is composed of an intrusive volcanic rock known as *dacite*. This island is only 296 ft (95 m) high and 1500 ft (500 m) at its widest point. Yet it is the site of a major sea bird rookery.

Paleontology and Archaeology

San Miguel Island has probably the richest paleontological and archaeological record of all the Channel Islands. There are over 500 Indian sites and a large accumulation of bones of the Exiled Mammoth, *Mammuthus exilis,* at Running Springs, near Dry Lake on the west side of the island. Three miles (4.8 km) west of Cardwell Point on the southeast shore of the island is a site at which pygmy mammoth bones have been discovered. In addition to caliche-covered mammoth bones, there are burned mammoth bones, mammoth tusks and teeth, and cypress charcoal, suggesting that early humans hunted the pygmy mammoth.

Perhaps the most significant paleontological and archaeological locality on the Channel Islands—and perhaps the mainland as well—is Daisy Cave, a cave and rock shelter complex located just above an isolated, rough stretch of shoreline on the northeast coast of San Miguel Island. Today the cave is about 30 ft (10 m) above sea level. It is a narrow fissure about 35 ft (11 m) deep, in which humans could escape from the persistent winds. It is about 4–10 ft (1.5–3 m) wide in the interior, but it also contains an outer rock shelter about 12–15 ft (4–5 m) wide and a stratified shell midden on the slope in front.

Until 1986 the age of the Daisy Cave deposits was thought to be only about 3000 years. Then a team of scientists headed by J. M. Erlandson of the University of Oregon established new carbon-14 dates for marine shells from the midden in association with small quantities of chipped stone artifacts. The new data indicate that human occupation of the cave dates back to at least 11,700 years B.P., making Daisy Cave the oldest shell midden in North America. In addition, a total of five archaeological components have been found in the cave, dating from 12,000 to 700 years B.P. Remains of basketry and cordage made from sea grass have been dated to between 10,000 and 8500 years B.P., a finding that doubles the documented antiquity of perishable woven technologies along the Pacific coast. The available data suggest that Daisy Cave was occupied by humans primarily during five periods: an ephemeral episode about 12,000 years ago; repeated occupations between about 10,000 and 8500 years B.P.; a brief episode about 6700 years B.P.; extensive occupations dating to about 3200 years B.P.; and one or more episodes about 700 years ago.

Of prime significance is the fact that data from Daisy Cave have enabled scientists to discern a great deal about human association with island habitats over time. Of no less significance is the fact that evidence from Daisy Cave has played a key role in recreating the environmental and organismal chronology so important to understanding events along the California coast since the last period of glaciation in North America (the end of the Pleistocene).

Research on the paleontological and archaeological remains found in Daisy Cave has produced at least five important contributions to our knowledge of the California coastline since the Pleistocene:

1. Pollen analysis indicates that pine forest habitats, consisting of Closed-cone Pines and Torrey Pines, were probably widespread in the Santa Barbara Channel area until about 12,000 to 13,000 years ago.

2. Old shell middens reveal that the Northern Channel Islands were settled by humans about 12,000 (at least 11,700) years ago, a colonization that required relatively seaworthy watercraft and a reliance on such marine resources as abalone.

3. Maritime peoples that occupied Daisy Cave made extensive use of such marine resources as shellfish, marine mammals, and fish.

4. Artistic expression on the part of the Chumash is established by the presence of a diversified material culture that included circular shell fishhooks, a wide range of beads and ornaments, a bird-bone pan pipe, a fragment of a redwood plank boat, asphaltum-coated baskets and tarring pebbles, a beadmaker's kit, and a finished stone pestle.

5. From a scientific perspective, close correlation of radiocarbon dates from marine shells and charcoal samples is an important step in verifying the credibility of radiocarbon dating of shell materials.

History

The history of San Miguel Island has been the subject of some controversy. Following the demise of the Native American population, the island was occupied by a succession of otter hunters, seal hunters, and sheep ranchers. Drought and overgrazing turned the island into a desert of shifting sand in the later nineteenth century. At the time the first Europeans viewed San Miguel Island, two Chumash villages with a total population of about 100 inhabitants were present.

San Miguel Island was quite different when Juan Rodríguez Cabrillo visited the island late in 1542. Attempting to round Point Conception in

Figure 119. Cabrillo monument, San Miguel Island.

November 1542, Cabrillo was driven back by northwesterly winds. His small armada apparently took refuge in what is now Cuyler Harbor, so that emergency repairs could be made to one of his ships. Apparently Cabrillo named the island, along with Santa Catalina, Isla de Posesión or La Posesión. It was not until 1792 that Captain George Vancouver, whose mission it was to establish claims for England and investigate Spanish holdings, named it San Miguel. Legend has it that Cabrillo was injured in a fall on this island. Reportedly, gangrene poisoning took his life during the return voyage and he was buried on San Miguel Island. A large granite cross erected in his honor overlooks Cuyler Harbor (Fig. 119).

Lois J. Roberts of Carmel, California, has reinterpreted the history of Cabrillo and San Miguel Island (see Chapter 5). First, it appears that the fall that shattered Cabrillo's shinbone in fact occurred on Santa Catalina Island and that Cabrillo died there sometime during the winter of 1542–43.

If that is really the case, the monument is misplaced—although it will nevertheless afford material for interesting talks by National Park Service guides.

Second, the large ranch house on the island, which has been known as the Lester Ranch House, was actually built by William G. Waters, who proclaimed himself "King of San Miguel Island," probably about 1895, when he became sole owner. Waters and W. I. Nichols had been co-owners of the island from 1888 to 1895. In a complicated lawsuit, in which it was revealed that the island was public land, Waters claimed that the United States had no right to the island because California's islands had not been written into the Treaty of Guadalupe Hidalgo, in which Mexico ceded the Southwest, including California, to the United States. He concluded that the island was his for the taking and declared himself king of a new nation. In 1911 Waters wrote to President Taft, asking that the president revoke a public entitlement for a lighthouse and that he be allowed to remain as king. Taft denied the request and Waters remained a citizen of the United States. Waters died in 1917 after ranching on the island for over thirty years.

The island has a reputation for tragedy. The huge ranch house, which has since burned down, was often attributed to Herbert Lester. In 1928 Lester and his wife became caretakers of the island. They established a small sheep ranch, lived in the large house, and educated their two daughters in the "tiniest school in the world." While chopping wood, Lester lost two fingers. He never fully recovered from the accident, sank into depression, and committed suicide in 1942. The island is the final resting place of Lester, one of several men who have claimed to be king of San Miguel. His grave lies near the Cabrillo monument. The members of the Lester family were the last long-term residents of San Miguel in this century, and the island has been uninhabited ever since, except for National Park Service personnel, who are usually present on the island to protect its fragile ecosystem.

Another accident involved Ralph Hoffmann, director of the Santa Barbara Museum of Natural History and an important botanist during the early period of island study. He fell to his death from what is now Hoffmann Point while collecting plants in 1932.

Then on July 5, 1943, a B-24 crashed on Green Mountain, an 831-ft (261-m) hill on the island, killing all twelve crew members. Ironically the aircraft had been dispatched to search for ten crew members who had bailed out of a similar plane over water before it crashed into the hills near Santa Barbara. Subsequently eight of the ten were rescued. The wreck on San Miguel Island was not discovered until 1944, at which time the remains of the crew were removed. The wreckage was "rediscovered" in 1954 by hikers, who also discovered human bones near the site and therefore assumed that the crash had not been reported. For some reason, a quick check of military records revealed no history of the wreckage, so the Coast Guard dispatched a boat to check on it. The Coast Guard vessel collided with a sailboat, the *Aloha,* which sank; two of its passengers drowned. The whole matter was finally put to rest when the original crash record was uncovered. Nevertheless a tradition of tragedy remains an inescapable part of the history of San Miguel Island.

Terrestrial Vegetation

About 170 species of native plants have been recorded from the island. The island's vegetation reflects its overall aridity and proximity to the ocean. Coastal Sage Scrub vegetation less than 5 ft (1.5 m) high predominates over much of the island (Plate 13C), interspersed with Coastal Grassland on the marine terraces (which may reach the top of the island). Small tidal marshes occur around some of the stream mouths, and patches of Freshwater Marsh occur in association with the springs. Coastal Bluff Scrub vegetation covers north-facing cliffs, providing spectacular floral displays in the spring. Coastal Dune vegetation follows the rivers of sand that streak across the island, occurring relatively far inland. On these sand stripes the Dunedelion, *Malacothrix incana* (Fig. 75), covers vast areas with yellow flowers during the spring. These dunes are currently undergoing stabilization and will presumably become restricted to beach areas in the future.

Most of the plants and animals of San Miguel Island have been discussed elsewhere, and no plants are known to be restricted to San Miguel Island, although a few hybrids have been found there that may not occur elsewhere. A pale, dwarf form of Giant Rye Grass, *Leymus condensatus,* was collected on Prince Island, and specimens with similar color have been collected on adjacent areas of San Miguel Island and the mainland coast. The Deerweed, *Lotus dendroideus* var. *veatchii*—a near-endemic common to the cliffs and dunes, where its abundant yellow flowers are conspicuous in the spring—is also found in northwestern Baja California but is absent from the other Channel Islands, which have different varieties.

Some of the more conspicuous and interesting plants on the island include several endemics (Table 8) and near-endemics, such as milkvetches or locoweeds (*Astragalus* spp.) (Fig. 98), Island Wallflower (Fig. 99), California Cream Cups (Figs. 101 and 162), Greene's Live-forever (Fig. 79B), Island Morning-glory (Fig. 81), Red Buckwheat, Cliff Aster (Fig. 74; Plate 6E), Giant Coreopsis (Plate 9A–C), and the perennial Dunedelion (Fig. 75).

The conspicuous palms that greet visitors who disembark on the island at Cuyler Harbor are native California Fan Palms, *Washingtonia filifera,* but they are not native to the island. The palms were planted in the 1960s

TABLE 8   ENDEMIC VASCULAR PLANTS OF SAN MIGUEL ISLAND

Asteraceae (sunflower family)
   Santa Cruz Island Malacothrix (*Malacothrix indecora*)—Endangered

Cistaceae (rockrose family)
   Island Rush-rose (*Helianthemum greenei*)—Threatened

Convolvulaceae (morning-glory family)
   Island Morning-glory (*Calystegia macrostegia*)

Crassulaceae (stonecrop family)
   Greene's Dudleya (*Dudleya greenei*)

Fabaceae (pea family)
   San Miguel Milkvetch (*Astragalus miguelensis*)

Hydrophyllaceae (waterleaf family)
   Northern Channel Islands Phacelia (*Phacelia insularis* ssp. *insularis*)
      —Endangered

Malvaceae (mallow family)
   Northern Channel Island Malva Rosa (*Lavatera assurgentiflora* ssp.
      assurgentiflora)

Polygonaceae (buckwheat family)
   Red Buckwheat (*Eriogonum grande* var. *rubescens*)

Rubiaceae (madder family)
   Sea-cliff Bedstraw (*Galium buxifolium*)—Endangered
   San Miguel Island Bedstraw (*Galium californicum* ssp. *miguelensis*)

Scrophulariaceae (figwort family)
   Island Paintbrush (*Castilleja lanata* ssp. *hololeuca*)—Rare

at one of the springs near the landing. Some people think that the palms were planted during the filming of the movie *Mutiny on the Bounty,* but that story has become confused with the one regarding the palms on Santa Catalina, which were indeed planted in 1935 during work on that film.

Recovery of the vegetation from the insult of grazing is under way (Plate 13C). Particularly conspicuous are the milkvetches or locoweeds (*Astragalus* spp.), lupines (*Lupinus* spp.), Coyote Bush (*Baccharis pilularis*), and Saw-toothed Goldenbush (*Hazardia squarrosa*). San Miguel Island today is a living laboratory of evolution, and no doubt it will be the subject of considerable scientific research.

Terrestrial Animals

A number of invertebrates are sufficiently common on San Miguel Island to attract the attention of the visiting naturalist. The land snail shells that litter parts of the island belong to the endemic species *Helminthoglypta ayresiana* (Fig. 102). The large, fossilized specimens are of the extinct subspecies, *Helminthoglypta ayresiana lesteri,* which is known only from this island.

TABLE 9   VERTEBRATE ANIMALS OF SAN MIGUEL ISLAND

Amphibians
  Channel Islands Slender Salamander (*Batrachoseps pacificus pacificus*)
    —Northern Channel Islands endemic

Reptiles
  Island Western Fence Lizard (*Sceloporus occidentalis becki*)
  Southern Alligator Lizard (*Elgaria multicarinatus*)

Birds: See Table 10

Native terrestrial mammals
  San Miguel Island Deer Mouse (*Peromyscus maniculatus streatori*)—Endemic
  San Miguel Island Fox (*Urocyon littoralis littoralis*)—Endemic
  California Bat (*Myotis californicus*)

Introduced mammals
  Black Rat (*Rattus rattus*)
  Domestic Sheep (*Ovis aries*)

Marine mammals
  Sea Otter (*Enhydra lutris*)—Occasional
  Harbor Seal (*Phoca vitulina*)
  California Sea Lion (*Zalophus californianus*)
  Northern Sea Lion (*Eumetopias jubatus*)
  Northern Elephant Seal (*Mirounga angustirostris*)
  Northern Fur Seal (*Callorhinus ursinus*)
  Guadalupe Fur Seal (*Arctocephalus townsendi*)

Two species of weevils appear to be restricted to San Miguel Island. *Sitona cockerelli* is a small, beige beetle that has rarely been collected. *Trigonoscuta miguelensis* is larger, silvery, and fairly common in dunes. The latter species is the most distinctive of a series of forms that have been described on the various islands. Some other endemic invertebrates likely to be encountered on San Miguel Island include two darkling ground beetles; the Silk-spinning Sand Cricket, *Cnemotettix caudalus* (Fig. 103B); a robber fly, *Stenopogon neojubatus* (Fig. 103D); two wasps; and a micromoth.

The native terrestrial vertebrates (Table 9) consist of the Channel Islands Slender Salamander (Fig. 104), the Southern Alligator Lizard (Fig. 60C), the Island Western Fence Lizard (Fig. 105), the San Miguel Island Deer Mouse (*Peromyscus maniculatus streatori*), and the Island Fox (Fig. 4; Plate 1A). None of them is especially abundant on the island.

Seventeen species of native land birds (Table 10) have been known to breed on the island, including several endemic races. The San Miguel Island Song Sparrow, *Melospiza melodia micronyx* (Fig. 120), is completely restricted to this island, where it is common in brushy ravines. The House Finch (Fig. 110), Horned Lark (Fig. 64E), and Orange-crowned Warbler

TABLE 10   BREEDING BIRDS OF SAN MIGUEL ISLAND

Land birds
   Endemic to San Miguel
      San Miguel Island Song Sparrow (*Melospiza melodia micronyx*)

   Island endemics
      Loggerhead Shrike (*Lanius ludovicianus anthonyi*)
      House Finch (*Carpodacus mexicanus frontalis*)
      Orange-crowned Warbler (*Vermivora celata sordida*)
      Allen's Hummingbird (*Selasphorus sasin sedentarius*)
      Horned Lark (*Eremophila alpestris insularis*)

   Nonendemics
      Peregrine Falcon (*Falco peregrinus*)
      Red-tailed Hawk (*Buteo jamaicensis*)
      American Kestrel (*Falco sparverius*)
      Burrowing Owl (*Athene cunicularia*)
      White-throated Swift (*Aeronautes saxatalis*)
      Costa's Hummingbird (*Calypte costae*)—Possible
      Barn Swallow (*Hirundo rustica*)
      Western Meadowlark (*Sturnella neglecta*)
      Rock Wren (*Salpinctes obsoletus*)
      Lesser Goldfinch (*Carduelis psaltria*)

   Introduced species
      European Starling (*Sturnus vulgaris*)

Sea birds
      Western Gull (*Larus occidentalis*)
      Black Oystercatcher (*Haematopus bachmani*)
      Snowy Plover (*Charadrius alexandrinus*)
      Brown Pelican (*Pelecanus occidentalis*)
      Brandt's Cormorant (*Phalacrocorax penicillatus*)
      Double-crested Cormorant (*Phalacrocorax auritus*)
      Pelagic Cormorant (*Phalacrocorax pelagicus*)
      Pigeon Guillemot (*Cepphus columba*)
      Cassin's Auklet (*Ptychoramphus aleuticus*)
      Leach's Storm-Petrel (*Oceanodroma leucorhoa*)
      Ashy Storm-Petrel (*Oceanodroma homochroa*)
      Xantus' Murrelet (*Synthliboramphus hypoleucus*)
      Common Murre (*Uria aalge*)—Rare
      Tufted Puffin (*Fratercula cirrhata*)—Rare

(Fig. 109) are well established on the island, but the Loggerhead Shrike (Fig. 111) and Allen's Hummingbird (Fig. 113) are somewhat tenuous breeders there.

Recovery of the Peregrine Falcon, *Falco peregrinus,* on the Northern Channel Islands dates to the early 1980s, when scientists began releasing young birds on San Miguel Island. Peregrine Falcons prey almost exclusively on birds, so San Miguel Island—with its large colonies of sea birds and remoteness from DDT contamination—seemed an ideal location for the experiment. Since then a combination of releases and natural colonization

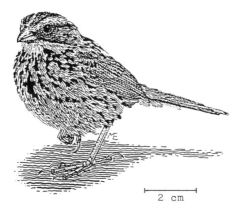

Figure 120. San Miguel Island
Song Sparrow, *Melospiza melodia
micronyx.*

from the mainland has reestablished the species on all five of the islands in Channel Islands National Park. Records kept by Park Service scientists show that nearly seventy birds have fledged on the islands since 1990.

Sea Birds

The most impressive populations of birds and mammals on San Miguel Island are not usually considered endemics, even though many of these species breed only on islands. The most important sea bird rookeries in southern California, in terms of both diversity and abundance, are found on Prince Island and Castle Rock near San Miguel Island. A total of 14,000–15,000 pairs from twelve species breed in these rookeries.

Most abundant are Brandt's Cormorants (*Phalacrocorax penicillatus*), Cassin's Auklets (*Ptychoramphus aleuticus*) (Fig. 171), and Western Gulls (*Larus occidentalis*) (Fig. 192A; Plate 3D). Smaller numbers of Leach's Storm-Petrels (*Oceanodroma leucorhoa*), Ashy Storm-Petrels (*Oceanodroma homochroa*) (Fig. 174), Double-crested Cormorants (*Phalacrocorax auritus*) (Plate 3B), Pelagic Cormorants (*Phalacocrorax pelagicus*), Pigeon Guillemonts (*Cepphus columba*) (Fig. 175), and Xantus' Murrelets *(Synthliboramphus hypoleucus)* (Fig. 164) also nest there. The Common Murre (*Uria aalge*) (Fig. 173), Tufted Puffin (*Fratercula cirrhata*) (Fig. 176), and Brown Pelican (*Pelecanus occidentalis*) (Fig. 192J; Plate 3A) bred in these rookeries until early in this century. The Brown Pelican, which was thought to have been extirpated, appears to have made a recovery. Most of these sea birds are wideranging and northern species. Although small numbers of gulls, cormorants, guillemots, murrelets, and pelicans nest on some of the cliffs and offshore rocks of the other islands, the only other major sea bird rookeries on the Northern Channel Islands occur on Anacapa Island. The largest rookeries of sea birds are found on the Farallon Islands (see Chapter 9).

A complete discussion of sea birds is found in Chapter 4.

Marine Mammals

A walk out to Point Bennett reveals a beautiful seascape that at its optimum may contain some 40,000 marine mammals. The waters around the islands harbor a diverse assemblege of whales, dolphins, and porpoises, as well as an occasional, wandering Sea Otter (*Enhydra lutris*) (Fig. 36). It appears, for example, that about ten Sea Otters, probably from San Nicolas, are now residents of San Miguel Island. San Nicolas is the only other Channel Island with significant breeding populations of so many marine mammals, although Año Nuevo and the Farallon Islands also have breeding colonies of marine mammals. The most conspicuous sea mammals on San Miguel Island are the pinnipeds: seals and sea lions. One of the largest and most diverse pinniped rookeries in the world is on this island, where more than 40,000 animals of six species come ashore, mainly on the sandy beaches along the southern and western sides of the island. California Sea Lions (*Zalophus californianus*) (Fig. 39; Plate 2C) and Northern Elephant Seals (*Mirounga angustirostris*) (Figs. 38 and 167) are the most abundant species. It has been estimated that about 70 percent of the breeding population of Northern Elephant Seals hauls out on San Miguel and San Nicolas Islands. Northern Fur Seals (*Callorhinus ursinus*) are rapidly increasing in number on San Miguel after colonizing the island from Alaska since 1960. Harbor Seals (*Phoca vitulina*) (Fig. 37; Plate 2C) are not uncommon, but the Northern Sea Lion (*Eumetopias jubatus*) (Fig. 40; Plate 2D) has nearly disappeared from the island. Occasional individuals of the rare Guadalupe Fur Seal (*Arctocephalus townsendi*) haul out on San Miguel Island but do not presently breed there, as they did before being nearly exterminated by hunters in the early nineteenth century. Although a few seals and sea lions visit some of the other Northern Channel Islands, they do not breed there in substantial numbers.

The importance of natural environmental factors in regulating populations of marine mammals was never more apparent than during the El Niño episode that warmed the waters during the winter of 1997–98. California Sea Lion and Northern Fur Seal populations that had been gradually increasing since the El Niño of 1982 suffered a near-collapse of the year's reproductive effort on San Miguel Island. Thousands of the year's pups died, perhaps three-fourths of them in all. Emaciated bodies lay rotting on the beaches, their mothers too thin and weak to produce milk. The cause seemed simple: the schools of fish upon which the seals and sea lions feed had been driven out of the local waters by the rise in water temperature.

Like the sea birds, the pinnipeds represent both northern and southern species, many of which are at the extremes of their distributions on the Northern Channel Islands. As some species recover from the near-extinction that accompanied economic exploitation during the last century, the population dynamics of the peripheral colonies appears to be in a state of flux, with some species increasing in number and others diminishing locally. The general trend for pinnipeds as a whole, however, is toward a spectacular increase in population size and distribution. In the case of the Northern Elephant Seal, this expansion has been so rapid that there has been no opportunity for natural selection to raise the level of genetic variability. All of them were recently derived from the same small herd that narrowly escaped extinction on remote Guadalupe Island off central Baja California. Although the huge Elephant Seals will allow close approach by humans, the other species of pinnipeds and sea birds are extremely sensitive to disturbance, and the rookeries are closed to visitors during the breeding season.

For a more thorough discussion of marine mammals, see Chapter 4.

SANTA ROSA ISLAND

Santa Rosa Island (Fig. 121) lies 27 miles (44 km) south of the mainland. Three miles (5 km) separate the island from San Miguel Island to the west, and Santa Cruz Island lies 6 miles (9 km) to the east. Second largest of the Channel Islands, Santa Rosa measures about 10 by 15 miles (16 by 24 km) and is 84 square miles (217 km²) in area. The western part of the island is low and sandy, closely resembling San Miguel Island. The eastern half is topographically more diverse, with gently rolling hills cut by deep canyons, rising in the central part of the island to a group of rounded peaks over 1500 ft (457 m) in elevation.

Santa Rosa Island is a rancher's paradise. Gently rolling hills, densely cloaked with grass, cover much of the island, providing expansive vistas that reveal its large size. No predators, rattlesnakes, or even ground squirrel holes lie in wait for the fat cattle. The headquarters of the Vail and Vickers Cattle Company ranch is located on Beecher's Bay in the northeastern part of the island (Fig. 122) and includes a number of fine old buildings. Despite receiving some protection from nearby hills, the introduced Blue Gums and Monterey Cypress at the ranch grow more horizontally than vertically, mute testimony to the strong northwesterly winds that persist through most of the year on this exposed island.

Geology

Santa Rosa Island is mainly composed of sedimentary rocks overlain by Pleistocene marine terrace deposits, which largely cover the island except where they have been eroded. A major fault, the Santa Rosa fault, trends

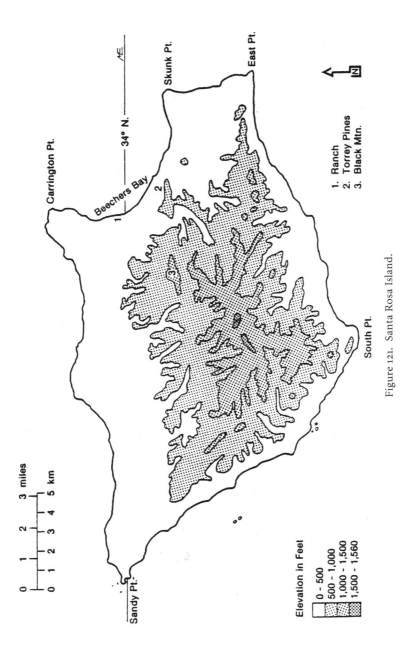

Figure 121. Santa Rosa Island.

Figure 122. Ranch house on Santa Rosa Island. Note the windblown Monterey Cypress, *Cupressus macrocarpa.* Coyote Brush, *Baccharis pilularis,* is in the foreground.

eastward across the island, producing distinct differences in topography between the northern and southern parts of the island. The northern half of the island has broad, flat terraces into which streams have cut steep canyons. The underlying rock material north of the fault is primarily Pleistocene and Pliocene sandstones and shales, similar to that on the mainland coast. Lobos Canyon in the northern part of the island contains some beautifully sculptured sandstone shaped by wind and water. High bluffs drop to the beach on the northern side. White sandy beaches, flanked by sand dunes up to 400 ft (130 m) in height, occur along the northern and western sides. Extensive deposits bearing fossils of the Exiled Mammoth occur in Arlington Canyon in the northwestern section.

South of the Santa Rosa fault, the land is higher and more rugged. The highest point, Soledad Peak, at 1574 ft (508 m), lies on a ridge that follows the trend of the fault. The underlying rock south of the fault is primarily volcanic in origin, produced during the major period of Miocene volcanism that has influenced much of the Channel Island topography.

History

Cabrillo called it San Lucas and Vizcaíno called it San Ambrosio, but Juan Perez of the Portolá expedition gets credit for the name Santa Rosa. Captain George Vancouver made it official with his map in 1792. The Indian name for the island, Wima, meant "driftwood." In 1980, Santa Rosa was included in the new Channel Islands National Park, but the island remained in private hands until 1986, when the National Park Service purchased it from Vail and Vickers. The Beecher's Bay ranch house and the surrounding 7.6 acres (3 ha) remained in private hands as headquarters for the cattle ranch and a commercial hunting operation for introduced Roosevelt Elk and Mule Deer, to be managed under a revocable special use permit until the year 2011.

After 1995, when numerous species from Santa Rosa Island were included on a list of federally proposed endangered species, a controversy erupted among environmentalists, the National Park Service, and the ranchers. Part of the problem resulted from the action of the Central Coast Regional Water Quality Control Board, which handed down a cleanup or abatement order after finding excessive amounts of fecal coliform bacteria from cow manure in the island's streams. The Park Service proposed a series of restrictive management plans that would require fencing to protect sensitive species, a reduction in the number of acres available for grazing animals, and the elimination of the deer herd. Armed with information on the pollution and the subsequently listed endangered species, a watchdog environmental group, claiming that the management plan was too lenient, filed a suit that charged the National Park Service with mismanagement. The settlement that resulted called for a restrictive management plan that required elimination of the cattle in 1998 but allowed continued commercial hunting for the deer and elk, along with periodic monitoring and analysis to ensure that environmental damage did not continue.

When Europeans first arrived on Santa Rosa Island they found eight Native American villages supporting more than 600 inhabitants. The archaeology of this island has been the subject of intense study for many years. Recent investigations suggest that the human occupation of Santa Rosa Island may have begun more than 40,000 years ago. However, others dispute the validity of these findings and give approximately 7000 years B.P. as the earliest reliable date for the arrival of humans on the island, associating the event with charred remains of the dwarf Exiled Mammoth that have been found on Santa Rosa.

By the early nineteenth century the Chumash no longer inhabited Santa Rosa Island, partly because they had been frightened off by a severe earthquake in 1812. The ownership of Santa Rosa was the subject of several claims and counterclaims until it was purchased by Vail and Vickers in 1902.

The subsequent removal of sheep helped slow the erosion that has devastated the native flora of islands such as San Miguel. On the other hand, the cattle herd roamed the entire island until 1998 and seemed to keep it in a desertlike state. The extent of the recovery of the island flora and the future of the herds of Roosevelt Elk and Mule Deer remain open questions.

The U.S. Air Force formerly operated two installations on the island, which are now abandoned. Access to Santa Rosa has been limited, but with the island now under National Park Service stewardship, many aspects of its ecology and biology are currently under study.

Terrestrial Vegetation

The climate of Santa Rosa Island has not been well documented, but it appears to be slightly drier than that of San Miguel Island, at least at lower elevations. The highlands undoubtedly receive greater precipitation. The winds on Santa Rosa Island tend to be somewhat more westerly than those on San Miguel Island, and the greater local relief provides more extensive areas of local shelter where some trees grow. Dense fog is also characteristic of the island and seems to be instrumental in maintaining certain plant communities such as pine groves. In all, approximately 380 species of plants have been collected on Santa Rosa Island.

Santa Rosa probably supports as diverse an assemblage of plant communities as Santa Cruz Island. Except for Coastal Grassland, however, most of these habitats exist in small, scattered patches, and the overall impression of the island is one of low ecological diversity. Coastal Beach and Dune vegetation occurs mainly in sandy areas at the western and eastern ends of the island. Although the dominant, widespread species are probably the same in both sandy areas, the endemics that characterize them are somewhat different. The western dunes support many of the same species found on San Miguel Island, whereas the slightly more sheltered, eastern dunes harbor some of the endemics and near-endemics peculiar to Santa Rosa Island. Coastal Bluff Scrub occupies appropriate habitats but is not extensive. Coastal Sage Scrub and Island Chaparral occur on the steep slopes of many of the canyons and mountains, growing prostrate in areas exposed to the wind and achieving greater stature in sheltered areas (Fig. 88A). Oak Woodland, Island Woodland, and Riparian Woodland are restricted to well-watered canyons and highlands. Bishop Pine forests are poorly represented on the leeward side of Black Mountain, and a substantial grove of Torrey Pine occurs on the hills above Beecher's Bay near the northeastern corner of the island (Plate 13B).

Some authorities consider the Torrey Pine on the island to be an endemic subspecies known as Santa Rosa Island Pine, *Pinus torreyana* ssp. *insularis* (Fig. 94A). As noted previously, these pines, located in a few groves on Santa Rosa Island and on the mainland near Del Mar, may have the smallest range of any pine species in the world. The soil on which the island forms grow is a clay-rich material derived from shales of the Monterey Formation, another example of an "island within an island." The island form is not considered a distinct subspecies by many authorities, but it differs from the mainland form in having smaller stature and larger cones. (The distribution of Torrey Pine on Santa Rosa Island is an interesting biogeographic story that is discussed earlier in this chapter and in Chapter 1.)

At least three plants are restricted to Santa Rosa Island (Table 11), but at least ten were listed as species of special concern and formally proposed by the U.S. Fish and Wildlife Service for listing as endangered species. On September 2, 1997, all but two were officially listed as endangered or threatened. The Santa Rosa Island Dudleya, *Dudleya blochmaniae* ssp. *insularis* (Fig. 79D), a species of special concern, has one of the most limited distributions of any plant, yet it was withdrawn from listing. It is found only on a few small patches of barren ground at the eastern tip of the island. A newly described species of live-forever—known as Dwarf Greene's Live-forever or Munchkin Dudleya, *Dudleya nana*—is a diminutive form of Greene's Dudleya, *Dudleya greenei* (Fig. 79B) that is also known from only one population near East Point.

Slightly more wide-ranging, yet officially listed as endangered, Hoffman's Slender-flowered Gilia, *Gilia tenuiflora* ssp. *hoffmannii* (Fig. 97), is locally abundant in the sandy Grassland near the northeastern corner of the island, where its purple flowers bloom conspicuously in the spring.

One of three manzanitas on Santa Rosa Island, Santa Rosa Island Manzanita, *Arctostaphylos confertiflora* (Fig. 123), is a broad-leafed species that is treelike in sheltered areas and prostrate on windy slopes. It can be distinguished from the other manzanitas on Santa Rosa by the absence of a burl at ground level. Large specimens of this Santa Rosa Island endemic can be found as an understory species in the Torrey Pine grove overlooking Beecher's Bay. It also was listed as endangered by the federal government in 1997, partly because of browsing by Mule Deer. The other two manzanitas on Santa Rosa Island have scattered distribution. Subcordate Manzanita, *Arctostaphylos tomentosa* ssp. *subcordata* (Fig. 82A), and Island Manzanita, *Arctostaphylos tomentosa* ssp. *insulicola* (Fig. 82B), are two island variants of a manzanita that is widespread in the southern Coast Ranges.

Two species that are conspicuous in Coastal Sage Scrub on Santa Rosa Island but are not found on the other northern islands deserve mention. A weakly differentiated island variant of Bladderpod, *Isomeris arborea* (Fig. 124), is a small shrub with pale, trifoliate leaves; yellow flowers; and large, inflated pods. It also occurs on some of the islands to the south.

Closely related to the Black Sage of the adjacent mainland and Santa Cruz Island, Brandegee's Sage, *Salvia brandegei* (Fig. 125), is a low, fragrant bush with narrow, wrinkled leaves and globose heads of small, blue flowers. The

TABLE 11   ENDEMIC VASCULAR PLANTS
OF SANTA ROSA ISLAND

Asteraceae (sunflower family)
    Island Hazardia (*Hazardia detonsa*)
    Santa Cruz Island Malacothrix (*Malacothrix indecora*)—Endangered
    Cliff Malacothrix (*Malacothrix saxatilis* var. *implicata*)
Berberidaceae (barberry family)
    Island Barberry (*Berberis pinnata* ssp. *insularis*)—Endangered
Brassicaceae (mustard family)
    Hoffman's Rock Cress (*Arabis hoffmannii*)—Endangered
Cistaceae (rockrose family)
    Island Rush-rose (*Helianthemum greenei*)—Threatened
Convolvulaceae (morning-glory family)
    Island Morning-glory (*Calystegia macrostegia*)
Crassulaceae (stonecrop family)
    Santa Rosa Island Live-forever (*Dudleya blochmaniae* ssp. *insularis*)—Rare[a]
    Candleholder Dudleya (*Dudleya candelabrum*)—Rare
    Greene's Dudleya (*Dudleya greenei*)
    Munchkin Dudleya (*Dudleya nana?*)—Rare[a]
Ericaceae (heath family)
    Santa Rosa Island Manzanita (*Arctostaphylos confertiflora*)—Endangered[a]
    Island Manzanita (*Arctostaphylos tomentosa* ssp. *insulicola*)
    Subcordate Manzanita (*Arctostaphylos tomentosa* ssp. *subcordata*)
Fabaceae (pea family)
    San Miguel Milkvetch (*Astragalus miguelensis*)
    Island Deerweed (*Lotus dendroideus* var. *dendroideus*)
Fagaceae (oak family)
    MacDonald Oak (*Quercus ×macdonaldii*)
    Island Scrub Oak (*Quercus pacifica*)
    Island Oak (*Quercus tomentella*)
Hydrophyllaceae (waterleaf family)
    Northern Channel Islands Phacelia (*Phacelia insularis* ssp. *insularis*)
      —Endangered
Papaveraceae (poppy family)
    Channel Island Tree Poppy (*Dendromecon harfordii*)
    Island Poppy (*Eschscholzia ramosa*)
Polemoniaceae (phlox family)
    Island Gilia (*Gilia nevinii*)
    Hoffmann's Slender-flowered Gilia (*Gilia tenuiflora* ssp. *hoffmannii*)
      —Endangered[a]
Polygonaceae (buckwheat family)
    Santa Cruz Island Buckwheat (*Eriogonum arborescens*)
    Red Buckwheat (*Eriogonum grande* var. *rubescens*)
Rhamnaceae (buckthorn family)
    Feltleaf Ceanothus (*Ceanothus arboreus*)
    Island Ceanothus (*Ceanothus megacarpus* var. *insularis*)
    Island Redberry (*Rhamnus pirifolia*)
Rosaceae (rose family)
    Prostrate Chamise (*Adenostoma fasciculatum* var. *prostratum?*)
    Island Ironwood (*Lyonothamnus floribundus* ssp. *aspleniifolius*)—Rare
Rubiaceae (madder family)
    Narrow-leaved Bedstraw (*Galium angustifolium* ssp. *foliosum*)
    Sea-cliff Bedstraw (*Galium buxifolium*)—Endangered
    San Miguel Island Bedstraw (*Galium californicum* ssp. *miguelensis*)
    Nuttall's Island Bedstraw (*Galium nuttallii* ssp. *insulare*)

TABLE 11   (*Continued*)

Saxifragaceae (saxifrage family)
    Island Alumroot (*Heuchera maxima*)—Rare
    Island Jepsonia (*Jepsonia malvifolia*)
Scrophulariaceae (figwort family)
    Island Paintbrush (*Castilleja lanata* ssp. *hololeuca*)—Rare
    Soft-leaved Indian Paintbrush (*Castilleja mollis*)—Endangered[a]
    Island Monkeyflower (*Mimulus flemingii*) [=*Mimulus aurantiacus?*])
Solanaceae (nightshade family)
    Island Nightshade (*Solanum clokeyi*)

[a]Single-island endemic.

Figure 123. Santa Rosa Island Manzanita,
Arctostaphylos confertiflora.

only other locality from which it is known is a single colony near Santo Tomas in northwestern Baja California, Mexico.

    Rounding out the recently listed endangered species are Hoffman's Rock-cress (*Arabis hoffmannii*) (Fig. 126), Soft-leaved Indian Paintbrush (*Castilleja mollis*), Island Phacelia (*Phacelia insularis* ssp. *insularis*) (Fig. 100), and Island Barberry (*Berberis pinnata* ssp. *insularis*) (Fig. 96). Island Alumroot (*Heuchera maxima*) (Fig. 91) was withdrawn from official listing. Island Rush-rose (*Helianthemum greenei*) was listed as threatened, but it is believed to have been extirpated from Santa Rosa Island, not having been seen there since the 1930s. An attractive shrub in the rock-rose family (Cystaceae), Island Rush-rose is known from fourteen sites on Santa Cruz Island and one on Santa Catalina Island. In 1994 four fires on

3 cm

Figure 124. Bladderpod, *Isomeris arborea*.

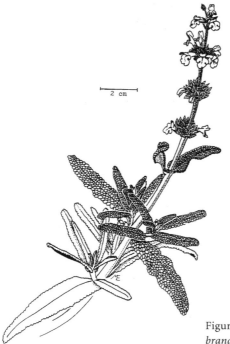

2 cm

Figure 125. Brandegee's Sage, *Salvia brandegei*.

Figure 126. Hoffman's Rock-cress, *Arabis hoffmannii.*

4 cm

Santa Cruz stimulated germination of long-dormant seeds, producing 500–1000 new plants at each site.

Other endemics and near-endemics that are conspicuous on the eastern (more accessible) part of the island include Island Ceanothus (*Ceanothus megacarpus* var. *insularis*) (Fig. 84A), Island Mountain Mahogany (*Cercocarpus betuloides* var. *blanchae*) (Fig. 85), Island Ironwood (*Lyonothamnus floribundus* ssp. *aspleniifolius*) (Fig. 89; Plate 5B), Catalina Cherry (*Prunus ilicifolia* ssp. *lyonii*) (Plate 5C,D), Island Oak (*Quercus tomentella*) (Fig. 92), and Giant Coreopsis (*Coreopsis gigantea)* (Plate 9A–C). The red-flowered Island Monkeyflower—formerly the endemic *Mimulus flemingii* (Plate 6C)—is now lumped under Orange Bush Monkeyflower, *Mimulus aurantiacus* (Fig. 47), as is the yellow- to orange-flowered species, formerly known as *Mimulus longiflorus.* Because all authorities do not recognize these three forms as a single species, the Island Monkeyflower is mentioned here as a possible endemic. It is considered a species of special concern by the National Park Service. This red-flowered form is also found on Anacapa, San Clemente, and Santa Cruz Islands.

Terrestrial Animals

The invertebrate fauna of Santa Rosa Island has been poorly studied. Only one insect is known to be restricted to the island, the Island Checkerspot (*Euphydryas editha insularis*) (Fig. 127), a butterfly that is locally common

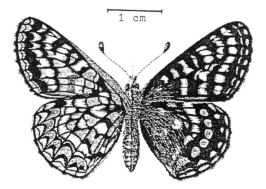

Figure 127. Island Checkerspot, *Euphydryas editha insularis.*

in grasslands during the spring. This is a handsome butterfly with orange and yellow markings on a dark brown background. The other endemic invertebrates likely to be encountered on the island have been discussed previously along with the other invertebrates of the Northern Channel Islands.

Among the mammals only the Santa Rosa Deer Mouse, *Peromyscus maniculatus sanctaerosae* (Fig. 3), and the Santa Rosa Island Fox, *Urocyon littoralis santarosae* (Fig. 4; Plate 1A), are limited in distribution to Santa Rosa Island (Table 12). Other vertebrates native to Santa Rosa include the Pacific Treefrog (*Hyla* [=*Pseudacris*] *regilla*) (Fig. 63), Channel Islands Slender Salamander (*Batrachoseps pacificus pacificus*) (Fig. 104), Island Western Fence Lizard (*Sceloporus occidentalis becki*) (Fig. 105), Southern Alligator Lizard (*Elgaria multicarinatus*) (Fig. 60C), Island Gopher Snake (*Pituophis melanoleucus pumilis*) (Fig. 106), and Island Spotted Skunk (*Spilogale gracilis amphialus*) (Fig. 114). The mouse, skunk, and fox are fairly common. Introduced mammals include cattle, horses, Mule Deer, and Wapiti (Roosevelt Elk). (Management of the latter two species is discussed earlier in this chapter and in Chapter 1.) The introduced population of pigs has since been removed. There is some talk of allowing horses to remain on Santa Rosa and Santa Cruz Islands in a feral state, presumably for historical or perhaps sentimental reasons.

Thirty-one species of land birds have been known to breed on the island (Table 13). The following are island endemic races that are also known from Santa Rosa Island: Song Sparrow (*Melospiza melodia clementae*), Horned Lark (*Eremophila alpestris insularis*) (Fig. 64E), Loggerhead Shrike (*Lanius ludovicianus anthonyi*) (Fig. 111), Bewick's Wren (*Thryomanes bewickii nesophilus*) (Fig. 112), Orange-crowned Warbler (*Vermivora celata sordida*)

TABLE 12 VERTEBRATE ANIMALS OF SANTA ROSA ISLAND

Amphibians
> Pacific Treefrog (*Hyla* [=*Pseudacris*] *regilla*)
> Red-legged frog (*Rana aurora*)—Extirpated(?)
> Channel Islands Slender Salamander (*Batrachoseps pacificus pacificus*)
> —Northern Channel Islands endemic

Reptiles
> Island Western Fence Lizard (*Sceloporus occidentalis becki*)
> Southern Alligator Lizard (*Elgaria multicarinatus*)
> Island Gopher Snake (*Pituophis melanoleucus pumilis*)—Northern Channel
> Islands endemic

Birds: See Table 13

Native terrestrial mammals
> Santa Rosa Island Deer Mouse (*Peromyscus maniculatus sanctaerosae*)
> —Endemic
> Santa Rosa Island Fox (*Urocyon littoralis santarosae*)—Endemic
> Island Spotted Skunk (*Spilogale gracilis amphialus*)—Northern
> Channel Islands endemic
> California Bat (*Myotis californicus*)

Introduced mammals
> Mule Deer (*Odocoileus hemionus*)
> Wapiti (Roosevelt Elk) (*Cervus elaphus*)
> Cattle (*Bos taurus*)
> Horse (*Equus caballus*)
> Domestic Dog (*Canis familiaris*)
> House Cat (*Felis domesticus*)
> Pig (*Sus scrofa*)—Removed

(Fig. 109), and Allen's Hummingbird (*Selasphorus sasin sedentarius*) (Fig. 113). Especially interesting is the San Clemente Rufous-sided Towhee (*Pipilo erythrophthalmus clementae*) (Fig. 64H), which otherwise is found only on the Southern Channel Islands. Nonnative birds include the California Quail (Fig. 64D) and European Starling.

One of the most significant biogeographic patterns evident on Santa Rosa Island is the strong southern affinity exhibited by many of the endemic plants and animals, in direct contrast to the majority of the island's flora and fauna. Those organisms that are otherwise found only on the islands or mainland to the south include the Torrey Pine (Fig. 94A; Plate 13B), Bladderpod, Black Sage, and Rufous-sided Towhee.

SANTA CRUZ ISLAND

The largest of the Channel Islands, Santa Cruz Island (Fig. 128) is sufficiently diverse that an overall impression of it is not easily formed. It does, however, possess one unique and conspicuous feature: the large Central

TABLE 13   BREEDING BIRDS OF SANTA ROSA ISLAND

Land birds
  Island endemics
    Bewick's Wren (*Thryomanes bewickii nesophilus*)
    Loggerhead Shrike (*Lanius ludovicianus anthonyi*)
    Western Flycatcher (*Empidonax difficilis insulicola*)
    San Clemente Rufous-sided Towhee (*Pipilo erythrophthalmus clementae*)
      —Southern Channel Islands endemic
    Song Sparrow (*Melospiza melodia clementae*)
    House Finch (*Carpodacus mexicanus frontalis*)
    Orange-crowned Warbler (*Vermivora celata sordida*)
    Allen's Hummingbird (*Selasphorus sasin sedentarius*)
    Horned Lark (*Eremophila alpestris insularis*)

  Nonendemics
    Peregrine Falcon (*Falco peregrinus*)
    Red-tailed Hawk (*Buteo jamaicensis*)
    American Kestrel (*Falco sparverius*)
    Burrowing Owl (*Athene cunicularia*)
    Killdeer (*Charadrius vociferus*)
    Mourning Dove (*Zenaida aurita*)
    White-throated Swift (*Aeronautes saxatalis*)
    Black Phoebe (*Sayornis nigricans*)
    Barn Swallow (*Hirundo rustica*)
    Common Raven (*Corvus corax*)
    Hutton's Vireo (*Vireo huttoni*)
    Western Meadowlark (*Sturnella neglecta*)
    Northern Mockingbird (*Mimus polyglottos*)
    Rock Wren (*Salpinctes obsoletus*)
    Lesser Goldfinch (*Carduelis psaltria*)
    Chipping Sparrow (*Spizella passerina*)

  Introduced species
    California Quail (*Callipepla californica catalinensis*)
    European Starling (*Sturnus vulgaris*)
Sea birds
    Western Gull (*Larus occidentalis*)
    Black Oystercatcher (*Haematopus bachmani*)
    Snowy Plover (*Charadrius alexandrinus*)
    Brandt's Cormorant (*Phalacrocorax penicillatus*)
    Pigeon Guillemot (*Cepphus columba*)

Valley that effectively isolates the visitor from the immediate influence of the ocean. The valley strongly resembles a smaller version of the upper Santa Ynez Valley north of Santa Barbara, with its steep, brushy slopes enclosing a narrow, grassy plain studded with oak trees and watered by a stream that usually dries up in summer. Impressive groves of Blue Gums are found there, with massive trees reaching more than 250 ft (76 m) in height. The Central Valley (Fig. 129; Plate 12A) shelters the headquar-

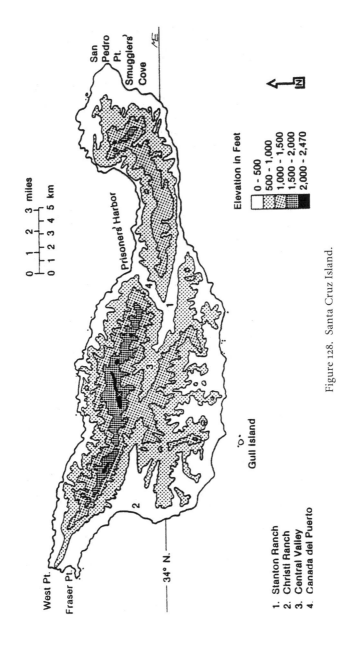

Figure 128. Santa Cruz Island.

Figure 129. View eastward of the Central Valley of Santa Cruz Island. Prostrate Chamise, *Adenostoma fasciculatum* var. *prostratum,* is visible in the foreground.

ters of The Nature Conservancy, and nearby is the headquarters of the Santa Cruz Island Reserve, which is part of the University of California's Natural Reserve System. Summer afternoons there take on an almost magical quality, as the sun lingers at the head of the valley, filling it with golden light and the perfection of stillness and isolation. Some observers have described work on the island as "research in paradise."

Covering 96 square miles (249 km²), Santa Cruz Island is 24 miles (38 km) long and 11 miles (16 km) wide, narrowing to less than 2 miles (3 km) in the eastern part of the island. The eastern tip lies 19 miles (30 km) from the mainland and 5 miles (7 km) from Anacapa Island. The western end is 25 miles (40 km) south of the mainland and 6 miles (9 km) from Santa Rosa Island.

Santa Cruz is topographically diverse, being dominated by two main ridges separated by the Central Valley. The northern ridge is the longer and higher of the two, extending nearly the length of the island and reaching 2450 ft (753 m), the highest point on the Channel Islands, at Picacho Diablo. The northern ridge is rugged. Once severely overgrazed, its north face has many beautiful groves of oak, closed-cone pines, Island Ironwood, and other trees on the lower slopes. The western end of Santa Cruz Island, in the vicinity of the Christy Ranch (Plate 10A), resembles adjacent parts of Santa Rosa, with its grassy hills, sandy beaches, windswept chaparral, and foggy Bishop Pine Forests (Plate 12B). The Sierra

Blanca in the southwestern part of the island is uncannily similar to parts of the Sierra Nevada near timberline, an illusion caused by the presence of stunted Bishop Pines set in scree fields. The illusion, however, is shattered by the barking of sea lions that wafts up from the beaches below!

The bulk of the island is broken into a rugged and complex system of ridges and valleys characterized by steep, rocky slopes covered with arborescent chaparral. The isthmus is a relatively low, rolling saddle in the northern ridge covered mostly with grasses and wind-sculpted shrubs and some Bishop Pine trees. Beyond the overgrazed badlands around High Mount, the eastern end is again grassy and relatively level.

Meteorological records for Santa Cruz Island are relatively complete, especially for the main ranch headquarters. Prevailing westerly winds are strongest at the western end of the island, where fog is most frequent. Rainfall averages about 20 in. (50 cm) at the ranch but probably varies with proximity to the highest peaks. Temperatures on the island are generally mild, closely resembling those in comparable locations on the adjacent mainland. The main ranch lies in the lowest part of the Central Valley, where cold air drainage results in temperatures much lower than those on nearby slopes. Even so, the ranch averages about 60°F (16°C) annually, with January lows around 41°F (5°C) and July highs about 77°F (25°C). Averages for slightly higher elevations may be 5–10°F (3–6°C) greater. Rare extremes of 15°F (−7°C) and 110°F (43°C) have been recorded in the Central Valley and may occur elsewhere on the island in sheltered areas. Humidity is usually high, averaging nearly 70 percent annually, and more than one-third of all days are overcast or partly cloudy in the morning, especially along the immediate coast during the summer.

Geology

The extremely complex geology of Santa Cruz Island is dominated by a major fault, the East Santa Cruz Basin fault or more specifically the Santa Cruz Island fault, running through the Central Valley (Fig. 130). Right-lateral movement along this fault brought two island masses together to form a single island about 20 million years ago. This movement has led one geologist to characterize the two parts of the island as "two ships passing in the night"—an appropriate analogy if one considers that each half of the island carries a cargo of animals and plants that may have evolved in isolation and are now part of a single land mass. This could well be the case for the two species of Slender Salamander (*Batrachoseps*), described elsewhere in this chapter, that inhabit terranes on each side of the fault.

The region north of the fault is composed mostly of Miocene volcanics

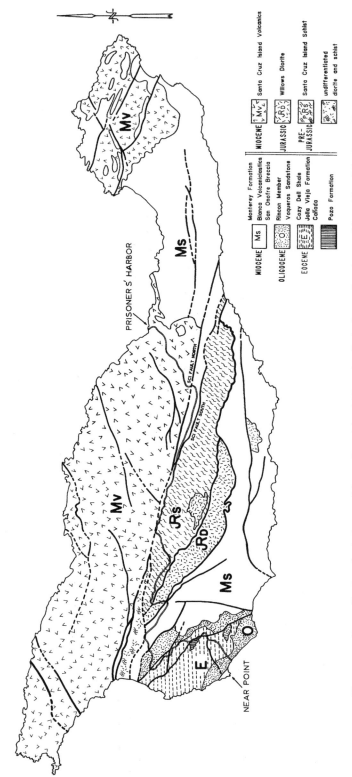

Figure 130. Generalized geological map of Santa Cruz Island. Note the dissimilar rock units on either side of the Santa Cruz Island fault (SCI fault), which have led geologists to conclude that Santa Cruz was formerly two islands that have been joined by right-lateral translocation along the fault. (From Weaver et al. 1969.)

overlain with eroded Pleistocene terrace deposits. In the isthmus area, most of the bedrock material is thinly bedded cherts and diatom-rich shales of the Monterey Formation. This material, which erodes easily, is responsible for the lowered appearance of the isthmus on Santa Cruz Island. In many places it weathers into a reddish, claylike soil that supports mostly Island Grassland.

The southern part of the island consists primarily of older sedimentary and metamorphic rocks (see Chapter 2). Among these is the Santa Cruz Island schist. Correlating this schist to other old schist deposits has been controversial. Some authorities relate it to Catalina schist and others to the Pelona schist near the east end of the Santa Monica Mountains. This schist, presumably the oldest rock material on the Northern Channel Islands, is present south of the fault in a band about 10 miles (16 km) long and 1.5 miles (2.4 km) wide. The oldest plutonic rocks on the Northern Channel Islands are associated with this schist as well. These granitic-type rocks, known as tonolite and diorite, occur in a band south of the schist. This hard material does not erode easily, so it is covered with a thin layer of gritty soil.

Another geological feature of interest is a smoking vent (fumarole) above China Harbor, reportedly the result of a petroleum-bearing deposit that has been smoldering underground for many years. There are also deposits containing plant fossils from the Pleistocene, including logs of Douglas Fir (*Pseudotsuga menziesii*) up to 3 ft (1 m) in diameter.

Different kinds of soils—of varying color, composition, and texture—result from the weathering of the different bedrock materials. In some cases, specific plants are associated with certain soils. For example, the best-developed and most diverse stands of Island Chaparral (Fig. 131) are on soils derived from the schist. Most of the woodlands are found on volcanic soils, which tend to contain water. In contrast, the Monterey shale degrades to a soil that repels water and consequently is covered mostly with Island Grassland. One chaparral dominant, McMinn's Manzanita, *Arctostaphylos viridissima* (Fig. 82D), is found only on Monterey shale. The endemic Santa Cruz Island Live-forever, *Dudleya nesiotica* (Fig. 79A), officially classified as a threatened species, grows only on the western end of the island on terrace gravels derived from volcanic rocks. Sixteen of the rarest plants on the island occur only on the soils derived from igneous and metamorphic rocks.

History

In 1769 Fray Juan Vizcaíno of the Portolá expedition left the island, forgetting his staff with the cross on top. When friendly Indians returned it the Spaniards named the island La Isla de Santa Cruz. The Indian name for the island was Limu, which meant "center" or "in the sea"—

Figure 131. Island Chaparral on Santa Cruz Island.

a reference to the significance the island held within the Chumash culture. The earliest European explorers found eleven Chumash villages on Santa Cruz Island and more than a thousand inhabitants. The provincial capital of the island was located in the Central Valley near the present Nature Conservancy headquarters. According to one legend, the Chumash believed the island to be the site of the creation of the first humans, who had crossed to the mainland over a rainbow bridge. Those who disobeyed divine warnings not to look down fell into the Santa Barbara Channel and became dolphins.

The Chumash were removed to the mainland early in the nineteenth century, and a Mexican land grant initiated the period of private ownership. One of the most important early owners was Justinian Caire, who developed an extensive ranch on the island in the last quarter of the nineteenth century. He planted vineyards in the fertile Central Valley and built, from bricks made of native clay, some of the beautiful old structures that still grace the island. Santa Cruz Island wines were among the finest in early California until Prohibition ended their production. The Stanton family acquired most of the island in 1937. Some of Caire's descendants, the Gherini family, owned the eastern tenth of the island until 1997, running a sheep ranch based at Smugglers' Cove. The entrance to the ranch, which had also been operated as a bed-and-breakfast, is marked by an impressive grove of Blue Gums and an old olive orchard on the hillside. At present, Santa Cruz Island also supports a U.S. Navy communications installation, which relays signals from the missile-tracking facility on San Nicolas Island to the headquarters at the Point Mugu Naval Air Weapons Station.

In 1978, The Nature Conservancy, a private conservation organization, entered into a complex agreement with the Stanton family's Santa Cruz Island Company, which granted the organization a conservation easement on the western 90 percent of the island. With the death of Carey Stanton in 1987, The Nature Conservancy became the sole owner of most of Santa Cruz Island. Although all of the island is officially included in the Channel Islands National Park, The Nature Conservancy's holdings are specifically exempt from being condemned and purchased by the federal government, and the organization's proposed conservation and research programs will not be directly affected by the activities of the National Park Service. As of 1992 the Service had acquired about 75 percent of the Gherini property on the east end of the island, and, using the "legislative taking" provision passed by Congress, took possession of the entire property in 1997. Removal of the 2000 sheep from the eastern end began in earnest during the summer of 1997; the animals were captured alive and transported to the mainland. Total public acquisition of the east end marks the beginning of a new era in resource management on Santa Cruz Island, the most diverse of California's islands.

Terrestrial Vegetation

The diversity of its geology, topography, soil, and microclimate is reflected in the diversity of vegetation types on Santa Cruz Island. Although Island Grassland covers the greatest area on the island, Island Chaparral (Fig. 131) is the most conspicuous plant community in many areas. The Chaparral of south-facing slopes is very open and patchy, but even north-facing slopes have a woodland or parklike aspect, with large, well-spaced trees and shrubs. In windy areas, however, chaparral vegetation may grow prostrate (Fig. 129). Fairly large stands of Coastal Sage Scrub, Southern Oak Woodland, Island Woodland, and Bishop Pine Forest (Plate 12B) are also scattered over the island. Coastal Bluff Scrub (Plate 9A–C) and Riparian Woodland are less extensive. A small, relatively fresh Coastal Marsh is found at Prisoners' Harbor. Southern Beach and Dune vegetation is restricted to the western and southwestern beaches and a few scattered pocket beaches along the otherwise vertical coastline.

As noted earlier in this chapter, the most thorough analysis of plants on all of the Channel Islands is presented by *A Flora of Santa Cruz Island* (1995) by Junak, Ayers, Scott, Wilken, and Young. The total number of native plants recorded from Santa Cruz Island is about 480, making up the

TABLE 14   ENDEMIC VASCULAR PLANTS OF SANTA CRUZ ISLAND

Asteraceae (sunflower family)
    Island Hazardia (*Hazardia detonsa*)
    Santa Cruz Island Malacothrix (*Malacothrix indecora*)—Endangered
    Cliff Malacothrix (*Malacothrix saxatilis* var. *implicata*)
    Island Malacothrix (*Malacothrix squalida*)—Endangered
Berberidaceae (barberry family)
    Island Barberry (*Berberis pinnata* ssp. *insularis*)—Endangered
Brassicaceae (mustard family)
    Hoffman's Rock Cress (*Arabis hoffmannii*)—Endangered
    Santa Cruz Island Rock Cress (*Sibara filifolia*)—Endangered
    Santa Cruz Island Fringepod (*Thysanocarpus conchuliferus*)—Endangered[a]
Cistaceae (rockrose family)
    Island Rush-rose (*Helianthemum greenei*)—Threatened
Convolvulaceae (morning-glory family)
    Island Morning-glory (*Calystegia macrostegia*)
Crassulaceae (stonecrop family)
    Candleholder Dudleya (*Dudleya candelabrum*)—Rare
    Greene's Dudleya (*Dudleya greenei*)
    Santa Cruz Island Live-forever (*Dudleya nesiotica*)—Threatened[a]
Ericaceae (heath family)
    Santa Cruz Island Manzanita (*Arctostaphylos insularis*)[a]
    Island Manzanita (*Arctostaphylos tomentosa* ssp. *insulicola*)
    Subcordate Manzanita (*Arctostaphylos tomentosa* ssp. *subcordata*)
    McMinn's Manzanita (*Arctostaphylos viridissima*)[a]
Fabaceae (pea family)
    San Miguel Milkvetch (*Astragalus miguelensis*)
    Santa Cruz Island Bird's-foot Trefoil (*Lotus argophyllus* var. *niveus*)
        —Endangered[a]
    Island Deerweed (*Lotus dendroideus* var. *dendroideus*)
Fagaceae (oak family)
    MacDonald Oak (*Quercus* ×*macdonaldii*)
    Island Scrub Oak (*Quercus pacifica*)
    Island Oak (*Quercus tomentella*)
Grossulariaceae (gooseberry family)
    Santa Cruz Island Gooseberry (*Ribes thacherianum*)—Rare[a]
Malvaceae (mallow family)
    Santa Cruz Island Bush Mallow (*Malacothamnus fasciculatus* spp.
        nesioticus)—Endangered[a]
Papaveraceae (poppy family)
    Channel Island Tree Poppy (*Dendromecon harfordii*)
Polemoniaceae (phlox family)
    Island Gilia (*Gilia nevinii*)
Polygonaceae (buckwheat family)
    Santa Cruz Island Buckwheat (*Eriogonum arborescens*)
    Island Buckwheat (*Eriogonum grande* var. *grande*)
    Red Buckwheat (*Eriogonum grande* var. *rubescens*)
Rhamnaceae (buckthorn family)
    Feltleaf Ceanothus (*Ceanothus arboreus*)
    Island Ceanothus (*Ceanothus megacarpus* var. *insularis*)
    Big-pod Ceanothus (*Ceanothus megacarpus* var. *megacarpus*)
    Island Redberry (*Rhamnus pirifolia*)
Rosaceae (rose family)
    Prostrate Chamise (*Adenostoma fasciculatum* var. *prostratum*?)
    Island Ironwood (*Lyonothamnus floribundus* ssp. *aspleniifolius*)—Rare

TABLE 14   (*Continued*)

Rubiaceae (madder family)
    Narrow-leaved Bedstraw (*Galium angustifolium* ssp. *foliosum*)
    Sea-cliff Bedstraw (*Galium buxifolium*)—Endangered
    Nuttall's Island Bedstraw (*Galium nuttallii* ssp. *insulare*)
Saxifragaceae (saxifrage family)
    Island Alumroot (*Heuchera maxima*)—Rare
    Island Jepsonia (*Jepsonia malvifolia*)
Scrophulariaceae (figwort family)
    Island Paintbrush (*Castilleja lanata* ssp. *hololeuca*)—Rare
    Santa Cruz Island Monkeyflower (*Mimulus brandegei*)—Rare[a]
    Island Monkeyflower (*Mimulus flemingii*) (=*Mimulus aurantiacus?*)
Solanaceae (nightshade family)
    Island Nightshade (*Solanum clokeyi*)

[a]Single-island endemic.

richest flora of all of the Channel Islands. The three families with the most
representatives on the island are the Sunflower family (Asteraceae), the
Grass family (Poaceae), and the Pea family (Fabaceae). About forty-five
of the island's native plants (species, subspecies, or varieties) are island
endemics (Table 14), and at least eight of these are completely restricted
to Santa Cruz Island.

Among the Santa Cruz Island endemics is Santa Cruz Island Live-
forever, *Dudleya nesiotica* (Fig. 79A), which has been officially classified
as a threatened species. This small succulent, known only from the vicinity of Fraser Point and Forney's Cove, is apparently a tetraploid hybrid (one
carrying four times the basic chromosome number) between the ancestor
of the Santa Rosa Island Dudleya, *Dudleya blochmaniae* ssp. *insularis*
(Fig. 79D), and another diploid form, perhaps Candleholder Dudleya, *Dudleya candelabrum* (Fig. 79C). Unlike most members of this genus, *Dudleya nesiotica* produces a basal rosette of leaves in the winter, followed by
a relatively large flower stalk with white blossoms in late spring, after which
the plant dies back to a bulblike base.

The endemic member of the currant family (Grossulariaceae) is the
Santa Cruz Island Gooseberry, *Ribes thacherianum* (Fig. 132). It can be found
with some regularity in a few canyons on the southwestern part of the
island, including floodplains, in communities such as Southern Oak Woodland, Riparian Woodland, and Bishop Pine Forest. It has long, drooping
stems, adorned with pink flowers in winter and spring. The spiny purple fruits, which appear in the summer, are edible.

Two manzanitas are restricted to Santa Cruz Island. Santa Cruz Island
Manzanita, *Arctostaphylos insularis* (Fig. 82C), grows up to 25 ft (5 m) in
height. It has relatively hairless twigs and is characterized by not having

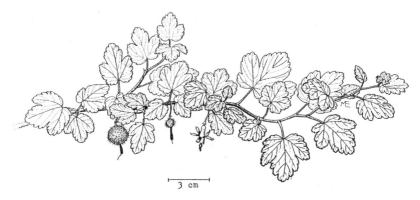

Figure 132. Santa Cruz Island Gooseberry, *Ribes thacherianum.*

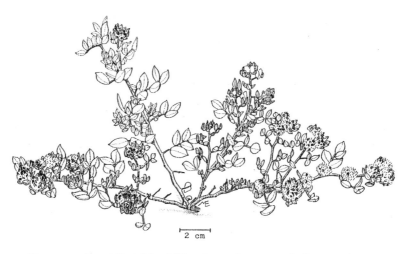

Figure 133. Santa Cruz Island Silver Lotus, *Lotus argophyllus* var. *niveus.*

a ground-level burl from which new stems arise. Its leaves are elliptical to oval and about 0.75–1.75 in. (2–4.5 cm) long. McMinn's Manzanita, *Arctostaphylos viridissima* (Fig. 82D), is abundant on rocky slopes and ridges. It has whitish, hairy twigs and its leaves are crowded and overlapping on the stem. It also has no ground-level burl. The other manzanitas of Santa Cruz Island have a ground-level burl, an adaptation that enables the shrubs to resprout after a fire. The manzanitas endemic to the island must return after a fire from seeds, which presumably require the heat of a fire, the presence of leachate, or both in order to germinate.

An endemic legume is Santa Cruz Island Silver Lotus, *Lotus argophyllus* var. *niveus* (Fig. 133). This variety, of special environmental concern, appears to be common on rocky slopes, exposed ridgetops, gravel floodplains, and

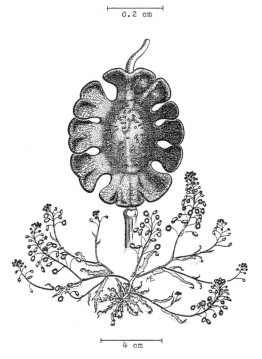

0.2 cm

4 cm

Figure 134. Santa Cruz Island Fringepod,
Thysanocarpus conchuliferus.

sandy flats and in washes (mostly on igneous and metamorphic soils). This perennial herbaceous shrub, up to 1.5 ft (0.5 m) in height, has branches that may lie flat on the ground. Its silvery, hairy foliage is composed of compound leaves broken into three to six leaflets. Because many of the leaves have only three leaflets, like a bird's foot, the plant is sometimes called a Trefoil. In the spring, blooming shrubs (which may occur locally in great abundance) turn some ridgetops a bright yellow color.

The Santa Cruz Island Bush Mallow, *Malacothamnus fasciculatus* ssp. *nesioticus* (Fig. 77), is a spindly shrub up to 6 ft (2 m) in height. It is rare and officially classified as endangered, occurring on south-facing slopes in the Central Valley. In spring, rose-pink flowers occur in great profusion all along its branches.

Santa Cruz Island Fringepod, *Thysanocarpus conchuliferus* (Fig. 134), is a member of the mustard family (Brassicaceae). It is called Lacepod or Fringepod because the flattened, oval, cup-shaped fruits (silicles) have lobed margins, giving them the appearance of miniature flowers. These low ephemerals grow primarily on north-facing slopes on the north side of the island. The four-petaled flowers are pink to purple. Another member of the mustard family, Santa Cruz Island Rockcress, *Sibara filifolia* (Fig. 149), has pink to purplish flowers. Its fruit is long and narrow, like that of many mustards. It was formerly recorded on San Clemente and Santa Catalina Islands, too, but it has not been seen on Santa Cruz Island since 1936 or on Santa Catalina since 1973. It has been relocated on San Clemente, and it was officially listed as endangered in 1997.

Santa Cruz Island Monkeyflower, *Mimulus brandegei,* is probably extinct. This tiny, purple-flowered ephemeral was known only from open, rocky slopes at about 200 ft (60 m) in elevation. It has not been collected since 1932, at which time there were only three specimens. As mentioned previously as part of the discussion of Santa Rosa Island, there is also a possible island endemic species, the red-flowered Island Monkeyflower, formerly known as *Mimulus flemingii* (Plate 6C), which occurs on coastal bluffs and rocky north-facing slopes. It is mentioned here because it is still considered a species of special concern by the National Park Service.

Besides the manzanitas listed previously, some of the more conspicuous endemic and near-endemic plants of Santa Cruz Island include Giant Coreopsis (Plate 9A–C), the "Giant" Buckwheats (Figs. 71 and 72), Island Deerweed (Fig. 73), the California lilacs (Fig. 84), Toyon (Fig. 54), Island Mountain Mahogany (Fig. 85), Channel Island Tree Poppy (Fig. 86), Orange Bush Monkeyflower (Fig. 47), Island Ironwood (Fig. 89; Plate 5B), Catalina Cherry (Plate 5C,D), and Bishop Pine (Figs. 94B and 95; Plate 12B).

The presence of two possible forms of Bishop Pine on Santa Cruz Island may be another example of island endemism. Bishop Pine, *Pinus muricata,* is a species recognized by most authorities, one of the closed-cone pines that occurs sporadically along coastal California and Baja California. It also occurs on Santa Rosa Island and, according to some authorities, on Cedros Island off Baja California. These pines have rather specific ecological requirements: they usually occur in areas with significant fog and impoverished soil. They are also associated with areas that experience relatively frequent fires, and hence they are known as one of the "fire pines." The heat from a fire opens the cones, and the seeds drop to the ground, where they germinate after the next rainstorm. Other closed-cone pines include Monterey Pine, *Pinus radiata,* and Knob-cone Pine, *Pinus attenuata.* Bishop Pine differs from these species in having its needles arranged in clumps of two rather than three, and in having smaller cones. The cones of these fire pines tend to be arranged along the stems, rather than at the tips of the branches, and they are curled backward and downward (reflexed) toward the stem (Fig. 95A). Another version of Bishop Pine has been called by some authorities Santa Cruz Island Pine, *Pinus remorata.* It differs from the standard Bishop Pine in having its cones extending straight out from the stem, that is, not reflexed (Fig. 95B).

The story of pines on islands is discussed further in Chapter 1 and earlier in this chapter.

Terrestrial Animals

Santa Cruz Island is the only one of the Northern Channel Islands on which extensive collections of many groups of invertebrates have been made. Consequently a number of insects have been found there that may in fact not be completely restricted to the island. These include two undescribed scale insects, two crane flies, and two micromoths. Two subspecies are more definitely restricted to the island. One is the flightless katydid, *Neduba morsei santacruzae,* which is replaced on Anacapa and Santa Rosa Islands by another endemic subspecies. This is a small brown insect with a prominent thoracic shield. Although the males are commonly heard singing on summer nights throughout the island in Chaparral and Oak Woodlands, the species is rarely seen because of its secretive habits. The other endemic is a subspecies of the common Woodland Skipper, *Ochlodes sylvanoides santacruza,* a small, mothlike yellow butterfly with club-shaped antennae.

Some other endemic insects likely to be encountered on this island in the appropriate season and habitat include two beetles, a cicada (Fig. 103C), a robber fly (Fig. 103D), a digger wasp (Fig. 103E), and a micromoth.

The vertebrate fauna of Santa Cruz Island is the most diverse of the Northern Channel Islands, supporting essentially all of the species found on each of the other islands and several more (Table 15). Native amphibians consist of the Pacific Treefrog, *Hyla* (=*Pseudacris*) *regilla* (Fig. 63), and the two Slender Salamanders, *Batrachoseps pacificus pacificus* (Fig. 104) and *Batrachoseps nigriventris,* mentioned earlier.

The three lizards include the Side-blotched Lizard (*Uta stansburiana*) (Fig. 60A), the Island Western Fence Lizard (*Sceloporus occidentalis becki*) (Fig. 105), and the Southern Alligator Lizard (*Elgaria multicarinatus*) (Fig. 60C). Three snakes occur on Santa Cruz Island. The only reptile endemic to the Northern Channel Islands, the Island Gopher Snake, *Pituophis melanoleucus pumilis* (Fig. 106), is also found on Santa Rosa Island. The Racer, *Coluber constrictor mormon* (Fig. 191), is rare in grasslands, and the rare Spotted Night Snake, *Hypsiglena torquata* (Fig. 107), may have been extirpated on the island.

Among the mammals, there are three endemic subspecies: the Santa Cruz Island Deer Mouse (*Peromyscus maniculatus santacruzae*) (Fig. 3), the Santa Cruz Island Harvest Mouse (*Reithrodontomys megalotis santacruzae*),

TABLE 15   VERTEBRATE ANIMALS OF SANTA CRUZ ISLAND

Amphibians
    Pacific Treefrog (*Hyla* [=*Pseudacris*] *regilla*)
    Red-legged frog (*Rana aurora*)—Extirpated(?)
    Channel Islands Slender Salamander (*Batrachoseps pacificus pacificus*)
        —Northern Channel Islands endemic
    Black-bellied Slender Salamander (*Batrachoseps nigriventris*)

Reptiles
    Island Western Fence Lizard (*Sceloporus occidentalis becki*)
    Side-blotched Lizard (*Uta stansburiana*)
    Southern Alligator Lizard (*Elgaria multicarinatus*)
    Island Gopher Snake (*Pituophis melanoleucus pumilis*)—Northern Channel
        Islands endemic
    Racer (*Coluber constrictor*)
    Spotted Night Snake (*Hypsiglena torquata*)—Extirpated(?)

Birds: See Table 16

Native terrestrial mammals
    Santa Cruz Island Harvest Mouse (*Reithrodontomys megalotis santacruzae*)
        —Endemic
    Santa Cruz Island Deer Mouse (*Peromyscus maniculatus santacruzae*)
        —Endemic
    Santa Cruz Island Fox (*Urocyon littoralis santacruzae*)—Endemic
    Island Spotted Skunk (*Spilogale gracilis amphialus*)—Northern
        Channel Islands endemic
    California Bat (*Myotis californicus*)
    Long-eared Bat (*Myotis evotis*)—Occasional
    Pallid Bat (*Antrozous pallidus*)
    Townsend's Long-eared Bat (*Plecotus townsendii*)
    Big Brown Bat (*Eptesicus fuscus*)—Occasional
    Silver-haired Bat (*Lasionycteris noctivagans*)—Occasional
    Hoary Bat (*Lasiurus cinereus*)—Occasional
    Mexican Free-tailed Bat (*Tadarida brasiliensis*)—Occasional

Introduced mammals
    Domestic Sheep (*Ovis aries*)
    Cattle (*Bos taurus*)
    Horse (*Equus caballus*)
    Domestic Dog (*Canis familiaris*)
    Pig (*Sus scrofa*)

and the Island Fox (*Urocyon littoralis santacruzae*) (Fig. 4; Plate 1A). The Island Spotted Skunk, *Spilogale gracilis amphialus* (Fig. 114), is also found on Santa Rosa Island. The mammal fauna includes several bats as well.

The Santa Cruz Island Harvest Mouse is found only on this island, where it has mainly been collected in the marsh at Prisoners' Harbor. The species is extremely rare and has been increasingly hard to find in recent years, perhaps because of the competition it faces from the Deer Mouse. Although mainland subspecies of the Western Harvest Mouse are typically found in marshes and Deer Mice are not, genetic studies on the island indicate that the Deer Mice of the marsh have undergone localized adaptation to their new environment. The two species are similar, but the Harvest Mouse is smaller and more delicate, with a long tail and small eyes; it probably builds spherical, grassy nests among the cattails and rushes of the marsh.

About forty-five species of land birds have been recorded nesting on Santa Cruz Island (Table 16). The avifauna of the island is generally similar to that of Santa Rosa Island, but there are a number of differences in the distribution of several endemics, especially members of the sparrow

TABLE 16   BREEDING BIRDS OF SANTA CRUZ ISLAND

Land birds
  Endemic to Santa Cruz
    Island Scrub Jay (*Aphelocoma insularis*)

  Island endemics
    Bewick's Wren (*Thryomanes bewickii nesophilus*)
    Loggerhead Shrike (*Lanius ludovicianus anthonyi*)
    Western Flycatcher (*Empidonax difficilis insulicola*)
    Rufous-crowned Sparrow (*Aimophila ruficeps obscura*)
    Song Sparrow (*Melospiza melodia clementae*)
    House Finch (*Carpodacus mexicanus frontalis*)
    Orange-crowned Warbler (*Vermivora celata sordida*)
    Allen's Hummingbird (*Selasphorus sasin sedentarius*)
    Horned Lark (*Eremophila alpestris insularis*)

  Nonendemics
    Peregrine Falcon (*Falco peregrinus*)
    Red-tailed Hawk (*Buteo jamaicensis*)
    American Kestrel (*Falco sparverius*)
    Barn Owl (*Tyto alba*)
    Burrowing Owl (*Athene cunicularia*)
    Northern Saw-whet Owl (*Aegolius acadicus*)
    Killdeer (*Charadrius vociferus*)
    Mourning Dove (*Zenaida aurita*)
    White-throated Swift (*Aeronautes saxatalis*)
    Anna's Hummingbird (*Calypte anna*)
    Northern Flicker (*Colaptes auratus*)
    Acorn Woodpecker (*Melanerpes formicivorus*)
    Ash-throated Flycatcher (*Myiarchus cinerascens*)
    Black Phoebe (*Sayornis nigricans*)
    Barn Swallow (*Hirundo rustica*)
    Common Raven (*Corvus corax*)
    Bushtit (*Psaltriparus minimus*)
    Red-breasted Nuthatch (*Sitta canadensis*)
    American Robin (*Turdus migratorius*)
    Blue-gray Gnatcatcher (*Polioptila caerulea*)
    Hutton's Vireo (*Vireo huttoni*)
    Western Meadowlark (*Sturnella neglecta*)

(Continued)

TABLE 16   (*Continued*)

Land birds (*Continued*)
    Red-winged Blackbird (*Agelaius phoeniceus*)
    Northern Mockingbird (*Mimus polyglottos*)
    Rock Wren (*Salpinctes obsoletus*)
    Black-headed Grosbeak (*Pheucticus melanocephalus*)
    Lesser Goldfinch (*Carduelis psaltria*)
    Rufous-sided Towhee (*Pipilo erythrophthalmus*)
    Chipping Sparrow (*Spizella passerina*)

  Introduced species
    California Quail (*Callipepla californica catalinensis*)
    Wild Turkey (*Meleagris gallopavo*)
    European Starling (*Sturnus vulgaris*)

Sea birds
    Western Gull (*Larus occidentalis*)
    American Oystercatcher (*Haematopus palliatus*)
    Black Oystercatcher (*Haematopus bachmani*)
    Snowy Plover (*Charadrius alexandrinus*)—Possibly established
    Brandt's Cormorant (*Phalacrocorax penicillatus*)
    Ashy Storm-Petrel (*Oceanodroma homochroa*)
    Cassin's Auklet (*Ptychoramphus aleuticus*)
    Pigeon Guillemot (*Cepphus columba*)

---

and finch families. The Song Sparrow, *Melospiza melodia clementae,* is much less common on this island and occurs in more limited habitats, apparently because of competition from the endemic Rufous-crowned Sparrow, *Aimophila ruficeps obscura* (Fig. 108), which is absent on Santa Rosa Island. In both the House Finch (Fig. 110) and the Rufous-sided Towhee (Fig. 64H), the Santa Cruz Island populations resemble the mainland form, but the Santa Rosa Island populations are more closely related to endemics of the southern islands.

The other endemic birds on Santa Cruz Island are the Horned Lark (Fig. 64E), Loggerhead Shrike (Fig. 111), Bewick's Wren (Fig. 64J), Orange-crowned Warbler (Fig. 109), and Allen's Hummingbird (Fig. 113).

California Quail (Fig. 64D), turkeys, peafowl, chickens, pigs, sheep, cattle, horses, ground squirrels, and dogs have been introduced to the island by humans.

For a thorough discussion of terrestrial animals, see the general discussion in this chapter and that in Chapter 1.

ANACAPA ISLAND

Considered by many who sail by her rugged shores to be little more than a string of three dry, lifeless rocks (cover illustration; Plate 13A), Anacapa Island

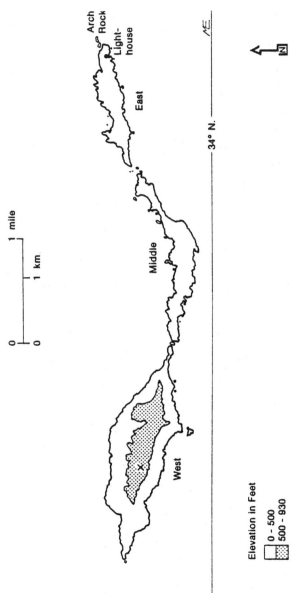

Figure 135. Anacapa Island.

(Fig. 135) is a surprisingly beautiful place on closer inspection. Although Anacapa is often considered a single island, it is composed of three parts, separated by narrow channels that are usually filled with water. During the lowest of low tides the connections may be revealed.

In spring, sea birds nest among a rich tapestry of red, yellow, and blue wildflowers set on a tableland, while herds of sea lions bark and swim in the waves at the bottom of precipitous cliffs. Across the narrow gaps the three segments of the island stretch away in a graceful, rocky arc (cover illustration; Plate 13A).

Anacapa Island is the second smallest of the Channel Islands and the smallest of the northern group. The island covers 1.1 square miles (1.8 km²), about half of which is West Anacapa Island. The island is also the closest to shore of the Channel Islands, lying only 12 miles (19 km) off the coast of Ventura County, of which it is a part (the other northern islands are in Santa Barbara County). Of the three islets, West Anacapa Island is by far the highest, reaching 936 ft (285 m) at Summit Peak; Middle Anacapa Island is 325 ft (99 m) high, and East Anacapa Island reaches only 250 ft (80 m) in elevation. The two smaller islets are flat topped, but West Anacapa Island rises steeply to a sharp ridge. All three islets are almost completely surrounded by unscalable cliffs (Fig. 70), which form a chain about 5 miles (8 km) long. Frequently, only high West Anacapa Island is visible from the mainland coast.

Meteorological records for Anacapa Island are rather incomplete, but annual rainfall probably averages less than 12 in. (305 mm) on East and Middle Anacapa Islands, and somewhat more on West Anacapa Island. Winds are mostly out of the west, but are not as strong or persistent as they are farther west. Temperatures probably are slightly warmer than those in coastal areas of the other Northern Channel Islands. There is a complete lack of surface water except for a few springs near the base of the sea cliffs, and no Chumash villages are known from Anacapa Island, though it was visited occasionally by early seafarers.

Geology

Anacapa Island is the exposed top of a Miocene volcanic ridge composed mainly of basalt and sculpted Pleistocene marine terraces and overlain with thin, clay soils. A large vein of chalcedony, a waxy silicate mineral, is exposed near Frenchy's Cove on West Anacapa Island. Cobbles and pebbles of this material are scattered all over the beach there. Due to the volcanic nature of the island, one of the characteristic features of the Anacapas is black sand beaches.

One of Anacapa's most distinctive features is the presence of pic-

Figure 136. Wave-erosional landforms, arch and stacks, on the eastern end of Anacapa Island.

turesque wave-erosional landforms (Fig. 136) such as arches, stacks, sea caves, surge channels, and blowholes. A well-developed surge channel and blowhole is near Cat Rock on the south side of West Anacapa Island. When conditions are correct, water rushing into the channel is forced through the fissures in the rock and is sprayed onto the surrounding area. The south side of the island has been extensively eroded by wave action, and the cliffs are highest offshore.

History

The island's name is apparently a corruption of the Chumash word *Anya-pah,* which means "ever-changing," or perhaps "deception" or "mirage." It may be a reference to distortions of the island's shape when it is viewed from the mainland, an effect caused by the atmospheric marine layer. In 1792, at the time that explorer George Vancouver produced the first map of the area, he retained the Indian name for Anacapa Island. It is ironic that the word for "ever-changing" should itself be so frequently changed, but Vancouver used the word *Eneeapah* in his log while writing *Enecapa* on his chart. A map produced by the U.S. Coast and Geodetic Survey in 1852 used the word *Anacape,* and finally in 1854 the present spelling *Anacapa* appeared on a map prepared by Parke-Custer.

One of the most famous early visitors to Anacapa Island was the painter James McNeill Whistler, who in 1854 made a beautiful engraving of East Anacapa Island and Arch Rock. Not yet famous, Whistler was at the time employed as an engraver for the U.S. Boundary Survey. He took artistic license with his drawing of Arch Rock and added a flock of gulls— an offense for which he was discharged.

During heavy fog in December 1853, the *Winfield B. Scott,* a 225-ft (69-m) side-wheeler on its way from San Francisco to Panama, ran aground and became wedged near the eastern end of Middle Anacapa Island. Having apparently survived on rations salvaged from the steamer, the 250 passengers were saved eight days later by the steamer *California.* The downside of this event is that Black Rats, *Rattus rattus rattus,* escaped from the ship and colonized the island. The rats are still there, as are the remains of the ship.

For the next 85 years a series of individuals attempted to use Anacapa Island as an outpost for fishing boats and for raising sheep. The sheep were actually able to survive without potable water. One theory is that the fog condensed on their thick wool and that they survived by licking it off, all the while devastating the native plants.

Recognizing the navigational hazard posed by Anacapa's rocky shores, in 1912 the National Lighthouse Service erected the first lighthouse. The lighthouse, located on the east end of the island, contained a small acetylene lamp. A much larger lighthouse, the one currently in use, was installed in 1932 (Fig. 70). The light and its bellowing foghorn were automated in 1966. Present plans for the lighthouse include the possibility that the Coast Guard will transfer ownership of it and twelve others across the state to private hands. This cost-cutting move could ultimately open these lighthouses to public access, and perhaps even the establishment of a bed-and-breakfast, such as the one in the old lighthouse on East Brother Island in San Francisco Bay (see Chapter 10).

In 1938 Anacapa and Santa Barbara Islands were established as the original Channel Islands National Monument by President Franklin Delano Roosevelt. In 1980, Congress included Anacapa in the present Channel Islands National Park. The island is currently occupied by a few National Park Service personnel on East Anacapa Island, where they live in a small, villagelike compound. Visitors to the new Channel Islands National Park usually land there, climbing a metal staircase attached to the side of a cliff. An attractive building high on the hill in this area at first appears to be a church, although it is actually merely a structure that covers the island's water supply.

Terrestrial Vegetation

The vegetation of Anacapa Island reflects its dry and exposed nature. Yet despite its small size and aridity, the total number of native plant species

TABLE 17   ENDEMIC VASCULAR PLANTS OF ANACAPA ISLAND

Asteraceae (sunflower family)
    Island Hazardia (*Hazardia detonsa*)
    Island Tarweed (*Hemizonia clementina*)
    Leafy Malacothrix (*Malacothrix foliosa crispifolia*)
    Junak's Malacothrix (*Malacothrix junakii*)
    Cliff Malacothrix (*Malacothrix saxatilis* var. *implicata*)
    Island Malacothrix (*Malacothrix squalida*)—Endangered
Berberidaceae (barberry family)
    Island Barberry (*Berberis pinnata* ssp. *insularis*)—Endangered
Convolvulaceae (morning-glory family)
    Island Morning-glory (*Calystegia macrostegia*)
Crassulaceae (stonecrop family)
    Greene's Dudleya (*Dudleya greenei*)
Fabaceae (pea family)
    San Miguel Milkvetch (*Astragalus miguelensis*)
    Island Deerweed (*Lotus dendroideus* var. *dendroideus*)
Fagaceae (oak family)
    Island Oak (*Quercus tomentella*)
Malvaceae (mallow family)
    Northern Channel Island Malva Rosa (*Lavatera assurgentiflora* ssp.
        assurgentiflora)
Polemoniaceae (phlox family)
    Island Gilia (*Gilia nevinii*)
Polygonaceae (buckwheat family)
    Santa Cruz Island Buckwheat (*Eriogonum arborescens*)
    Island Buckwheat (*Eriogonum grande* var. *grande*)
    Red Buckwheat (*Eriogonum grande* var. *rubescens*)
Rhamnaceae (buckthorn family)
    Island Ceanothus (*Ceanothus megacarpus* var. *insularis*)
Rubiaceae (madder family)
    Narrow-leaved Bedstraw (*Galium angustifolium* ssp. *foliosum*)
Saxifragaceae (saxifrage family)
    Island Alumroot (*Heuchera maxima*)—Rare
Scrophulariaceae (figwort family)
    Island Paintbrush (*Castilleja lanata* ssp. *hololeuca*)—Rare
    Island Monkeyflower (*Mimulus flemingii*) (=*Mimulus aurantiacus?*)

recorded from the island (about 170) is relatively high. The endemic vascular plants are listed in Table 17. Coastal Sage Scrub predominates, especially on south-facing slopes, grading into Coastal Bluff Scrub vegetation on northern slopes. Island Grassland apparently was more prevalent on the terraces during the period of grazing; it is now being replaced by scrub. On the northern slope of West Anacapa Island two gullies support a few groves of trees and shrubs associated with the Island Chaparral or Woodland communities. A single pocket beach on the north side of West Anacapa Island supports some Beach and Dune vegetation. A few stunted Eucalyptus trees grow on Middle Anacapa Island.

Just as the Island Ironwood is a classic example of relict endemism, the

3 cm

Figure 137. Leafy Malacothrix, *Malacothrix foliosa.*

chicory genus *Malacothrix* offers some striking examples of rapid, autochthonous evolution on Anacapa Island and other islands. Recent analysis places three closely related species on Anacapa Island. Leafy Malacothrix, *Malacothrix foliosa* (Fig. 137), has been divided into four subspecies. One of these, *Malacothrix foliosa crispifolia,* is found on East and West Anacapa Islands. It is a small spring annual resembling a Dandelion. Its yellow flowers can be found only rarely in a few grassy locations such as near the lighthouse. Middle Anacapa Island lacks this form but has another newly described species, *Malacothrix junakii,* which at one time was described as *Malacothrix insularis.* Another species, known as Island Malacothrix, *Malacothrix squalida,* occurs on Middle Anacapa and Santa Cruz Islands. The other three subspecies of Leafy Malacothrix are found on the outer Southern Channel Islands and will be discussed in Chapter 7.

Also found on the Northern Channel Islands is Santa Cruz Island Malacothrix, *Malacothrix indecora,* which was formerly found on San Miguel, Santa Cruz, and Santa Rosa Islands. It is now known only locally on Santa Cruz Island. Additional species are near-endemic and nonendemic; some are large perennials, such as the Cliff Aster, *Malacothrix saxatilis* var. *implicata* (Fig. 74; Plate 6E). The bewildering range of characteristics and distributions is further confused by hybridization and self-pollination.

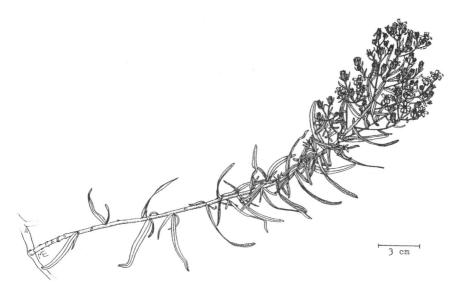

Figure 138. Island Tarweed, *Hemizonia clementina.*

Although this complex is still under study, it appears that these seemingly uninteresting plants may provide examples of ongoing speciation by plants on the islands. A more thorough discussion of the genus is offered in the section dealing with Coastal Sage Scrub earlier in this chapter.

A similar but less complex pattern is exhibited by another member of the sunflower family, the Island Tarweed, *Hemizonia clementina* (Fig. 138). This tarweed is an island endemic found on all of the Channel Islands except San Miguel and Santa Rosa. The tarweed is an unattractive (to some people), sprawling shrub with a woody base, thick leaves, and small yellow flowers. It forms thick mats scattered in Coastal Sage Scrub on East and Middle Anacapa Islands, where its acid-green foliage is conspicuous from a distance. The Anacapa Island population is subtly different from the populations on the Southern Channel Islands, suggesting the early stages of evolutionary divergence.

Another tarweed found at scattered localities on many of the Channel Islands as well as the mainland is an ephemeral species known as Common Tarweed, *Hemizonia fasciculata.* One unusual feature is that it tends to flower late in the season, into the autumn. In this way it does not compete with spring-blooming flowers for pollinators. It has been documented that the Cahuilla Indians boiled and ate this plant for sustenance in emergency situations. It has also been reported that Native Americans ate the roots of another species, *Hemizonia fitchii,* found along the mainland coast and on Santa Cruz Island.

Figure 139. Gumplant, *Grindelia stricta* var. *platyphylla.*

The tarweeds have evolved additional species on the mainland and on the islands off Baja California. A closely related group has undergone spectacular adaptive radiation on the Hawaiian islands, which has produced such distinctive forms as the giant Ahinahina Silversword, *Argyroxiphium sandwicense.* In common with the annual chicories of Anacapa Island, the tarweed demonstrates a strong biogeographic link with the Southern Channel Islands, especially Santa Barbara Island.

Gumplant, *Grindelia stricta* var. *platyphylla* (Fig. 139), another yellow sunflower that blooms conspicuously in the fall, is an important component of the windswept vegetation on Anacapa Island. Recognized by its gummy, resinous leaves, it is also found on San Miguel and Santa Rosa Islands. Related species occur on San Nicolas, Santa Catalina, and Santa Cruz Islands. Native Americans used the plants medicinally, preparing them either dried or raw.

A population of Island Wallflower, *Erysimum insulare* (Fig. 99), on West Anacapa Island may prove to represent a single-island endemic. At present the species in general is known only from fragmentary collections on all of the Northern Channel Islands. This member of the mustard family is a perennial herb with four-petaled, bright yellow flowers. Another member of the mustard family, this one with white flowers, is known as Hoffman's Rock-cress, *Arabis hoffmannii* (Fig. 126). This endangered species, believed to have been a victim of grazing by nonnative animals, has been located once more on Santa Rosa Island, and the three small populations on Santa Cruz Island are doing well. The species has not been located on Anacapa Island.

Visitors to East Anacapa Island are likely to encounter the following endemic and near-endemic plants: Giant Coreopsis (Plate 9B,C), Island Morning-glory (Fig. 81), the "Giant" Buckwheats (Figs. 71 and 72), and Island Deerweed (Fig. 73). The flora of Middle Anacapa Island is generally similar to that of East Anacapa Island, but West Anacapa Island supports a number of woody plants not found on the other two islets, including Island Ceanothus, *Ceanothus megacarpus* var. *insularis* (Fig. 84A); Toyon (Fig. 54); Island Monkeyflower (Fig. 47); Catalina Cherry (Plate 5C,D); Island Oak (Fig. 92); and Island Barberry (Fig. 96).

Terrestrial Animals

No endemic invertebrates are known to be restricted to Anacapa Island at this time, although some species exhibit slight local differences. A small gray tick, *Ixodes peromysci,* parasitizes mainly the endemic Deer Mice (Fig. 3) of Anacapa, San Clemente, and Santa Barbara Islands but does not occur on the other northern islands. Some common, endemic invertebrates on Anacapa Island include the land snail, *Helminthoglypta ayresiana* (Fig. 102), which is abundant only on the western islet; two beetles; the Silk-spinning Sand Cricket, *Cnemotettix spinulus,* which is common near the lighthouse on East Anacapa Island; a cicada (Fig. 103C); a digger wasp (Fig. 103E); and a micromoth.

As might be expected for such a small and ecologically restricted island, Anacapa Island supports few native land vertebrates (Table 18). Among them are the Channel Islands Slender Salamander, *Batrachoceps pacificus pacificus* (Fig. 104), and two lizards, the Southern Alligator Lizard, *Elgaria multicarinatus* (Fig. 60C), and the Side-blotched Lizard, *Uta stansburiana* (Fig. 60A). The Anacapa Island Deer Mouse, *Peromyscus maniculatus anacapae,* is the only vertebrate that is endemic to Anacapa Island. Unfortunately, nonnative Black Rats, *Rattus rattus,* are established on the island. The European Hare, *Lepus europaeus,* formerly established on East Anacapa Island, is no longer present.

Twenty-six species of land birds have been known to breed on the island (Table 19), including the following endemic races: the Rufous-crowned Sparrow (Fig. 108), Horned Lark (Fig. 64E), Loggerhead Shrike (Fig. 111),

TABLE 18   VERTEBRATE ANIMALS OF ANACAPA ISLAND

Amphibians
  Channel Islands Slender Salamander (*Batrachoseps pacificus pacificus*)
    —Northern Channel Islands endemic

Reptiles
  Side-blotched Lizard (*Uta stansburiana*)
  Southern Alligator Lizard (*Elgaria multicarinatus*)

Birds: See Table 19

Native terrestrial mammals
  Anacapa Island Deer Mouse (*Peromyscus maniculatus anacapae*)—Endemic
  California Bat (*Myotis californicus*)—Possible

Introduced mammals
  Domestic Sheep (*Ovis aries*)—Removed
  Black Rat (*Rattus rattus*)
  European Hare (*Lepus europaeus*)—Removed

TABLE 19   BREEDING BIRDS OF ANACAPA ISLAND

Land birds
  Island endemics
    Bewick's Wren (*Thryomanes bewickii nesophilus*)
    Loggerhead Shrike (*Lanius ludovicianus anthonyi*)
    Western Flycatcher (*Empidonax difficilis insulicola*)
    House Finch (*Carpodacus mexicanus frontalis*)
    Orange-crowned Warbler (*Vermivora celata sordida*)
    Allen's Hummingbird (*Selasphorus sasin sedentarius*)
    Horned Lark (*Eremophila alpestris insularis*)
    Rufous-crowned Sparrow (*Aimophila ruficeps obscura*)

  Nonendemics
    Peregrine Falcon (*Falco peregrinus*)
    Red-tailed Hawk (*Buteo jamaicensis*)
    American Kestrel (*Falco sparverius*)
    Barn Owl (*Tyto alba*)
    Burrowing Owl (*Athene cunicularia*)—Possible
    Mourning Dove (*Zenaida aurita*)
    White-throated Swift (*Aeronautes saxatalis*)
    Black Phoebe (*Sayornis nigricans*)
    Barn Swallow (*Hirundo rustica*)
    Common Raven (*Corvus corax*)
    Hutton's Vireo (*Vireo huttoni*)
    Western Meadowlark (*Sturnella neglecta*)
    Northern Mockingbird (*Mimus polyglottos*)
    Rock Wren (*Salpinctes obsoletus*)
    Chipping Sparrow (*Spizella passerina*)

  Introduced species
  European Starling (*Sturnus vulgaris*)
Sea birds
    Western Gull (*Larus occidentalis*)
    Black Oystercatcher (*Haematopus bachmani*)
    Brandt's Cormorant (*Phalacrocorax penicillatus*)
    Double-crested Cormorant (*Phalacrocorax auritus*)
    Brown Pelican (*Pelecanus occidentalis*)
    Xantus' Murrelet (*Synthliboramphus hypoleucus*)—Extirpated

Bewick's Wren (Fig. 52), Orange-crowned Warbler (Fig. 109), and Allen's Hummingbird (Fig. 113). The avifauna of Anacapa Island appears to be changing as vegetation becomes more dense following the overgrazing of years past.

Marine Life

Although the island itself supports relatively few organisms, the waters surrounding it are full of life. The largest colonies of Western Gulls, *Larus occidentalis* (Fig. 192A; Plate 3D), and Brown Pelicans, *Pelecanus occidentalis* (Fig. 192J; Plate 3A), on the Channel Islands occur on the island, as do small numbers of several other sea birds. The pelican colony on West Anacapa Island is the only major nesting site of this species left on the Pacific coast of the United States, and access to the site is restricted to protect these impressive birds. For a more thorough discussion of the rise and fall of the Brown Pelican, see Chapter 4.

California Sea Lions and Harbor Seals (Plate 2C) commonly bask on the rocky shores of the island, and the Gray Whale (Plate 2A) and other cetaceans can be seen from its cliffs. The tide pools at Anacapa Island are a popular focus of study because they are legally protected from collecting, and therefore species diversity is high. A number of subtidal algae have been described from around the island.

CHAPTER SEVEN

THE OUTER SOUTHERN CHANNEL ISLANDS: SAN CLEMENTE, SAN NICOLAS, AND SANTA BARBARA

In general the more distant islands are from the mainland and the smaller they are, the more depauperate will be their fauna and flora; this relationship holds true for the three outer Southern Channel Islands. San Clemente, the largest of the three, has the most diverse wildlife. San Nicolas is the farthest from the mainland, and Santa Barbara is the smallest of the Channel Islands. As would be expected, their fauna and flora are indeed limited in diversity.

There are currently U.S. Navy installations on both San Clemente and San Nicolas Islands, including small airfields, and each island is occupied by several hundred personnel. No public landing facilities are present on either island, and camping and picnicking are not allowed. A journey to San Nicolas Island is a long trip, even in the largest sportfishing or sportdiving boats. High winds as well as rough seas make this most remote California island difficult to reach even today. The fact that the first human inhabitants of California became established there well over a thousand years ago is a credit to their navigation and survival abilities, traveling as they did in small canoes through a potentially very treacherous open-water environment.

The Southern Channel Islands also include Santa Catalina, and a significant portion of the faunal and floral relationships among these outer islands is necessarily related to Santa Catalina. The reader should therefore refer to Chapter 5 for an overall discussion of the history, geology, and natural history of the plant communities and animal inhabitants of the Southern Channel Islands.

SAN CLEMENTE ISLAND

San Clemente Island (Fig. 140) is the southernmost of the eight Channel Islands located off the southern California coast. It is a relatively large

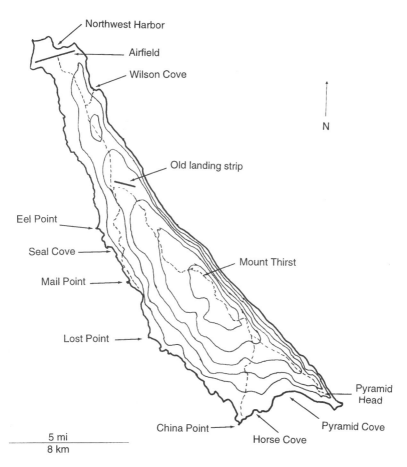

Figure 140. San Clemente Island (contour interval 100 m).

island, having an area of 56 square miles (148 km²), making it the fourth largest of the Channel Islands. It lies 21 miles (34 km) south of Santa Catalina, about 63 miles (102 km) west-northwest of San Diego, and 49 miles (79 km) from the mainland at the Palos Verdes Peninsula. The island is about 21 miles (34 km) in length, and its width varies from 1.5 to 4.0 miles (2.4–6.4 km).

When approached from the sea the island appears to be a long, relatively flat bench that gradually rises to an elevation of about 1965 ft (600 m). The eastern face of the island drops from that elevation directly into the sea. The northern end of the island is low and flat, and to the south the land rises slowly to the high point known as Mount Thirst at about midisland. (San Clemente Island has many peculiar place names, many of which are doubtless associated with military occupation, but their origins

Figure 141. Fog pouring like a waterfall over the eastern escarpment of San Clemente Island. (Photo by William Mautz.)

are otherwise unknown.) The southern end of the island is dominated by a series of marine terraces that drop down to small salt marshes at Pyramid and Horse Coves. The eastern face of the island is a steep cliff that drops into the sea, but on the western side the series of marine terraces is perhaps the most spectacular on the California coastline (Fig. 11; Plate 14A).

San Clemente Island's topography appears more arid than that of the other larger, more northern Channel Islands. In part, this appearance is due to the extensive defoliation inflicted upon the island by goats and pigs. Rainfall normally occurs between December and April, and the annual average is about 6 in. (15 cm) at the northern end. The central highlands receive twice that amount. The mean summer temperature is 65°F (18°C) and the mean winter temperature is 55°F (13°C). Weather patterns for the island are similar to those for the mainland coast, but the island gets significantly more fog. In spring the whole island is often shrouded in fog, whereas in summer the upper slopes often emerge from the fog and may be 12–24°F (7–14°C) warmer than the lowlands. A spectacular weather phenomenon can often be seen on a summer afternoon from a position above the inversion layer: fog moving eastward over the island pours over the huge eastern escarpment like an immense waterfall (Fig. 141).

Geology

San Clemente is composed mostly of volcanic rocks of Miocene age. It is a tilted fault block with its eastern edge uplifted nearly 2000 ft (645 m) above sea level along the San Clemente fault. Above the volcanic basement rocks are the usual sedimentary layers indicating various periods of submergence during the Pleistocene ice ages. The wave-cut terraces, so visible on the western side, reach an elevation of 900 ft (290 m), indicating that sea level probably was never high enough to cover the highest point on the island, although some evidence indicates that, at its maximum, the Pleistocene inundation may have reached as high as 1500 ft (500 m) on the island. Sedimentary rocks on the island contain fossils of marine mammals. Certain iron-rich soils also imply that pines may have occurred on the island in the past, although there is no direct evidence in the form of fossils. A small area of sand dunes is located on the northwestern portion of the island (Fig. 148).

History

San Clemente Island has been occupied by humans for thousands of years. As they did on Santa Catalina, the Gabrielino people used the area extensively, even though sites for permanent water seem not to exist. Numerous archaeological sites, particularly shell middens, occur on the island, and various Native American artifacts, such as metates and tools for harvesting marine mammals, have been discovered. There is even evidence of burials having taken place on the island.

Perhaps because of its size and distance from the mainland, it appears that early mariners stopped on the island and probably introduced goats sometime during the early to mid-1800s. There is some evidence that goats were introduced to San Clemente along with sheep when ranchers were granted leases in 1848. In 1877 the U.S. Department of Commerce leased the island to the San Clemente Sheep and Wool Company, and it was used for cattle and sheep ranching until 1934, when the U.S. Navy took over the island. Pigs probably were introduced for food and sport hunting. Mule Deer, *Odocoileus hemionus,* were also introduced, but the population died off as a result of natural causes during the 1970s.

At the present time, the U.S. Navy owns San Clemente Island and uses it as part of the naval defense system. Concrete platforms that formerly held artillery for possible use during World War II are still in evidence. A large runway lies diagonally across the northern end, and it is still used by the planes that ferry naval personnel to and from the island. Flights from San Diego run back and forth nearly every day, carrying personnel—including a full-time firefighter—who are stationed at Wilson Cove on the east side of the island. The southern end of the island has been used extensively for target practice by naval vessels at sea. On the flat top of the island, part of a missile target range, is a mock airfield, complete with a nonfunctional jet fighter and dummy missiles. This area is in fact an old airfield; it has been used for various military exercises, including as a test target for cruise missiles.

On any given day warships may gather offshore to hammer their targets on the island with missiles. Navy SEALs use the cover of darkness to practice climbing steep slopes and planting explosives; apparently San Clemente Island is the only location associated with the entire Pacific fleet where they can test weapons that actually explode. Generations of troops have been trained there, and no doubt many more will be.

Terrestrial Vegetation

The first thorough plant collections on San Clemente Island were made by Blanche Trask, who moved to Santa Catalina Island in 1895. For twelve years she worked tirelessly to document the flora of the Southern Channel Islands. However, it was not until 1963 that Peter Raven published the first comprehensive account of the flora of San Clemente Island. Robert Thorne added to it in 1969 at the same time that he updated his Santa Catalina Island flora. Finally in 1985 Gary Wallace summarized and updated the flora of San Clemente Island in his compilation of the vascular plants of the Channel Islands.

As of now 382 different plants have been recorded from San Clemente Island, 272 of which are considered to be natives. With seventeen species, the island harbors the greatest number of single-island endemic plants of any of the California islands (Table 20). Six of these species are federally listed as endangered; indeed four of these were the first plant species added to the federal list after the Endangered Species Act was passed. In all, more island-endemic plants are found on this island than on any other California island.

Although San Clemente can be considered to be rich floristically, the native flora has been seriously altered, primarily by more than a hundred years of grazing by a feral goat population. Most of the trees and large shrubs now occur only in canyons. As a result of this heavy grazing the island appears quite barren, especially during the fall and summer months. Several of the island's endemic plants are now probably extinct, and twenty-nine species previously reported to be present have not been observed in recent years.

No one knows what San Clemente Island looked like 100 or 200 years ago. There are vague references in old literature to forests of Malva Rosa, *Lavatera assurgentiflora* (Plate 6B), on the northern uplands. Remnant populations of species inaccessible to goats leave clues to what must have been a verdant landscape. Woodlands of Island Oak, *Quercus tomentella* (Fig. 92), localized stands of Canyon Live Oak, *Quercus chrysolepis,* and Catalina Cherry, *Prunus ilicifolia* ssp. *lyonii* (Plate 5C,D), occurred in the canyons and on the eastern scarp. Groves of Island Ironwood, *Lyonothamnus*

TABLE 20   ENDEMIC VASCULAR PLANTS OF SAN CLEMENTE ISLAND

Dicots
  Apiaceae (celery family)
    San Nicolas Island Lomatium (*Lomatium insulare*)—Extinct(?)
  Asteraceae (sunflower family)
    Island Sagebrush (*Artemisia nesiotica*)
    Nevin's Eriophyllum (*Eriophyllum nevinii*)—Rare
    San Clemente Island Hazardia (*Hazardia cana*)—Rare[a]
    Island Tarweed (*Hemizonia clementina*)
    Leafy Malacothrix (*Malacothrix foliosa* ssp. *foliosa*)
    Blair's Munzothamnus (*Stephanomeria blairii*)—Rare[a]
  Boraginaceae (borage family)
    Trask's Cryptantha (*Cryptantha traskiae*)
  Brassicaceae (mustard family)
    Santa Cruz Island Rock Cress (*Sibara filifolia*)—Endangered
  Convolvulaceae (morning-glory family)
    Island Morning-glory (*Calystegia macrostegia*)
  Crassulaceae (stonecrop family)
    Bright Green Dudleya (*Dudleya virens* ssp. *virens*)
  Crossosomataceae (crossosoma family)
    Catalina Crossosoma (*Crossosoma californicum*)
  Fabaceae (pea family)
    San Miguel Milkvetch (*Astragalus miguelensis*)
    San Clemente Island Milkvetch (*Astragalus nevinii*)—Rare[a]
    San Clemente Island Bird's-foot Trefoil (*Lotus argophyllus* var. *adsurgens*)
      —Endangered[a]
    Island Bird's-foot Trefoil (*Lotus argophyllus* var. *argenteus*)
    Trask's Island Lotus (*Lotus dendroideus* var. *traskiae*)—Endangered[a]
    Island Pinpoint Clover (*Trifolium gracilentum* var. *palmeri*)
  Fagaceae (oak family)
    Island Oak (*Quercus tomentella*)
  Hydrophyllaceae (waterleaf family)
    San Clemente Island Phacelia (*Phacelia floribunda*)—Rare[a]
    Lyon's Phacelia (*Phacelia lyoni*)
  Malvaceae (mallow family)
    Southern Channel Island Malva Rosa (*Lavatera assurgentiflora* ssp. *glabra*)
    San Clemente Island Bush Mallow (*Malacothamnus clementinus*)
      —Endangered[a]
  Onagraceae (evening primrose family)
    San Clemente Island Evening Primrose (*Camissonia guadalupensis* ssp.
      clementina)—Rare[a]
  Papaveraceae (poppy family)
    Channel Island Tree Poppy (*Dendromecon harfordii*)
    Island Poppy (*Eschscholzia ramosa*)
  Polemoniaceae (phlox family)
    Island Gilia (*Gilia nevinii*)
    Pygmy Linanthus (*Linanthus pygmaeus* ssp. *pygmaeus*)[a]
  Polygonaceae (buckwheat family)
    San Clemente Island Buckwheat (*Eriogonum giganteum* var. *formosum*)[a]
    Island Buckwheat (*Eriogonum grande* var. *grande*)
  Ranunculaceae (buttercup family)
    San Clemente Island Larkspur (*Delphinium variegatum* ssp. *kinkiense*)—Rare[a]
    Thorne's Royal Larkspur (*Delphinium variegatum* ssp. *thornei*)—Rare[a]

TABLE 20   (*Continued*)

Dicots (*Continued*)
    Rhamnaceae (buckthorn family)
        Island Ceanothus (*Ceanothus megacarpus* var. *insularis*)
        Big-pod Ceanothus (*Ceanothus megacarpus* var. *megacarpus*)
        Island Redberry (*Rhamnus pirifolia*)
    Rosaceae (rose family)
        Island Ironwood (*Lyonothamnus floribundus* ssp. *aspleniifolius*)—Rare
    Rubiaceae (madder family)
        San Clemente Island Bedstraw (*Galium catalinense* ssp. *acrispum*)
            —Endangered[a]
    Saxifragaceae (saxifrage family)
        Island Jepsonia (*Jepsonia malvifolia*)
        San Clemente Island Woodland Star (*Lithophragma maximum*)—Endangered[a]
    Scrophulariaceae (figwort family)
        San Clemente Island Indian Paintbrush (*Castilleja grisea*)—Rare[a]
        Island Monkeyflower (*Mimulus flemingii*) (=*Mimulus aurantiacus?*)
        Santa Catalina Figwort (*Scrophularia villosa*)—Rare
    Solanaceae (nightshade family)
        Santa Catalina Island Desert-thorn (*Lycium brevipes* var. *hassei*)—Extinct(?)
Monocots
    Liliaceae (lily family)
        San Clemente Island Brodiaea (*Brodiaea kinkiensis*)—Rare[a]
        San Clemente Island Triteleia (*Triteleia clementina*)—Rare[a]
    Poaceae (grass family)
        California Dissanthelium (*Dissanthelium californicum*)—Extinct(?)

[a]Single-island endemic.

floribundus ssp. *aspleniifolius* (Fig. 89; Plate 5B), occurred at the upper ends of the canyons. The appearance of these canyons today is grim evidence of the devastation caused by introduced goats and pigs (Fig. 142).

Prior to the defoliation of the island, the two most common plant communities were Coastal Sage Scrub and Island Chaparral, as described in Chapter 5. Remnants of Coastal Sage Scrub—including Toyon, *Heteromeles arbutifolia* (Fig. 54); Lemonade Berry, *Rhus integrifolia* (Fig. 53A; Plate 7C); and Coyote Brush, *Baccharis pilularis* (Fig. 45B)—remained in inaccessible areas. Some of the truly attractive island endemics, such as the Hibiscus-like Malva Rosa and scarlet-flowered Showy Island Galvezia, *Galvezia speciosa,* seemed to hang on in protected sites. The island endemic Island Tarweed, *Hemizonia clementina* (Fig. 138), hung on in spite of the grazing pressure. The two prickly-pears, *Opuntia littoralis* (Fig. 51A; Plate 8C) and *Opuntia oricola* (Fig. 52), became dominant species on the landscape after all the other perennial vegetation was eaten. Chaparral species such as Chamise, *Adenostoma fasciculatum* (Fig. 88; Plate 11C), and Island Ceanothus, *Ceanothus megacarpus* var. *insularis* (Fig. 84A), as well as common Coastal Sage Scrub species such as California Buckwheat,

Figure 142. Island Ironwood, *Lyonothamnus floribundus*
ssp. *aspleniifolius,* a victim of grazing by goats.

Eriogonum fasciculatum, and Coastal Sagebrush, *Artemisia californica*
(Fig. 45A), were nearly nonexistent on San Clemente Island. A fleshy,
ephemeral grass known as California Dissanthelium, *Dissanthelium californicum,* was formerly an understory component of Coastal Sage Scrub on
San Clemente and Santa Catalina Islands. It has not been seen since 1912 and
is presumed extinct. The endemic San Clemente Island Bedstraw, *Galium
catalinense* ssp. *acrispum,* is a rare cliff-dwelling shrub with squarish stems
and its leaves in whorls. It has been listed by the state as an endangered species.
The significance of bedstraws as endemic species is discussed in Chapter 6.

Most of San Clemente became covered with Island Grassland, as discussed
in Chapter 6. The landscape was dominated by introduced ephemerals
(Fig. 59), such as oats (*Avena fatua* and *Avena barbata*), brome grasses or
chesses (*Bromus diandrus* and *Bromus madritensis* ssp. *rubens*), and Storks-
bill, a filaree (*Erodium cicutarium*). A few native bunchgrasses, such as Purple Needlegrass (*Nassella pulchra*) and Fescue (*Festuca megalura*), were also

present. The grassland habitat was best developed at the northern end of the island and along the higher eastern terraces. The southern end of the island has been subject to such heavy grazing that most of this area and the terraces to the west were barren, showing signs of severe erosion.

An experiment begun on San Clemente Island may yield a technique that could be used to eliminate Wild Oats. A virulent strain of a rust fungus that attacks Wild Oats and no other grasses is being cultivated in the laboratory. If, when released, this parasite succeeds in eliminating its host on San Clemente, it may prove useful elsewhere.

The bulb-bearing species such as Blue Dicks, *Dichelostemma capitatum* (Fig. 197), are particularly hard hit by the rooting of pigs. There are no Mariposa Lilies (*Calochortus* spp.) recorded from San Clemente Island, but there are two endemic members of the lily family (Liliaceae) that have barely escaped the pigs. San Clemente Island Brodiaea, *Brodiaea kinkiensis,* a grassland species, and San Clemente Island Triteleia, *Triteleia clementina*, a tall light-blue lily of moist places on rocky walls, are now considered rare on San Clemente Island.

The San Clemente Island version of Leafy Malacothrix, *Malacothrix foliosa* ssp. *foliosa* (Fig. 137), is found scattered about in the grassland. This newly described subspecies was formerly also found on the Los Coronados Islands. However, it has not been seen there since 1926; if it is indeed extirpated there, then the San Clemente Island subspecies would become a single-island endemic.

The most distinctive community of San Clemente Island is the succulent version of Coastal Sage Scrub known as Maritime Desert Scrub (Fig. 143). It is also present on Santa Catalina Island, but it reaches its greatest development on San Clemente, where it covers most of the lower slopes, particularly on the western side of the island. Because of the thorny nature of this community, it is better at resisting the "hoofed locusts." The dominant shrubs in this area are California Box Thorn, *Lycium californicum* (Fig. 144), and Cliff Spurge, *Euphorbia misera* (Fig. 145). The Santa Catalina Island Desert-thorn, *Lycium brevipes* var. *hassei,* a similar species with small succulent leaves also formerly occurred in this community and on Santa Catalina Island. It is now believed extinct. These drought-deciduous species are leafless most of the year. Native Americans ate the fruit and roots of Box Thorn, but Cliff Spurge is poisonous. The succulent members of this community include the prickly-pears (Figs. 51A and 52; Plate 8C); Coastal Cholla, *Opuntia prolifera* (Fig. 51B; Plate 8A,B); and Golden Cereus or Button Cactus, *Bergerocactus emoryi* (Fig. 146; Plate 8D).

The lichen flora on the coastal rocks and shrubs of this community is also impressive (Fig. 147; Plate 1C); it is particularly well represented at

Figure 143. Maritime Desert Scrub dominated by Button Cactus, *Bergerocactus emoryi.*

Figure 144. California Box Thorn, *Lycium californicum.*

Eel Point on the western side of the island. Lichens on San Clemente Island show most of their affinity to northwestern Baja California. In spite of the removal by goats of the trunks and stems of trees and shrubs that served as substrates for the lichens, 138 species of lichens have been reported on San Clemente Island. This abundance of lichens is due to the foggy,

Figure 145. Cliff Spurge, *Euphorbia misera.*

Figure 146. Button Cactus, *Bergerocactus emoryi.*

maritime climate of the island, as well as the absence of air pollution, a known killer of lichens. One particular species, the Lace Lichen, *Ramalina menziesii,* hangs on in small groves of oaks on the island, having formerly been abundant on the mainland in the Santa Monica Mountains. Its absence there is attributed to air pollution.

Figure 147. Abundant lichens in Maritime Desert Scrub, west side of San Clemente Island.

Coastal Bluff Scrub, the community of coastal cliffs typical of the other Channel Islands, has always been a bit different on San Clemente Island, if for no other reason than that this is the only island from which Giant Coreopsis, *Coreopsis gigantea,* is absent. In addition, whereas other islands may have two or more species of Live-forever, there is only one on San Clemente. Bright Green Dudleya or Green Live-forever, *Dudleya virens* (Fig. 55B), is a component of this community on the Southern Channel Islands, including San Clemente. The San Clemente Island Green Live-forever was recently described as a unique subspecies, *Dudleya virens* ssp. *virens.* Coastal Bluff Scrub is also the preferred habitat of Showy Island Galvezia, the lovely red-flowered shrub in the snapdragon family (Scrophulariaceae).

The dune field on the northwestern part of the island contains good examples of Coastal Strand or Southern Beach and Dune vegetation (Fig. 148), a community that is thoroughly described in Chapter 6. On San Clemente Island, typical plants on the dunes include Silver Beachbur (*Ambrosia chamissonis*); two woolly insular locoweeds, San Miguel Milkvetch (*Astragalus miguelensis*) (Fig. 98) and the endemic San Clemente Island Milkvetch (*Astragalus nevinii*); and two yellow-flowered evening primroses, Beach Evening Primrose (*Camissonia cheiranthifolia*), and the endemic San Clemente Island Evening Primrose (*Camissonia guadalupensis* ssp. *clementina*).

With the advent of the Endangered Species Act, the U.S. Navy began

Figure 148. Dune field on northwestern end of San Clemente Island. Silver Beach-bur, *Ambrosia chamissonis,* is visible in the foreground.

a program to restore San Clemente Island from the ravages of introduced plants and animals. Removal of the *Eucalyptus* grove, the "San Clemente Island National Forest," was part of that program (see Chapter 1).

Of extreme importance to the survival of native plants was elimination of the feral pigs and goats. Removal of the pigs was an easier job; removal of the goats took 20 years (see Chapter 1). At the outset, it was estimated that there were about 12,500 goats on the island. The process began in 1973, using techniques such as herding, water trapping, and sport hunting. By 1978 about 16,000 goats had been removed, but 1500 still remained. They were still reproducing, and they were becoming more difficult to catch. In 1979 the Navy and the U.S. Fish and Wildlife Service decided to shoot them from helicopters—a proposal that ran into instant opposition. The Fund for Animals filed suit and stopped the process, after which the Fund (for a fee) began a removal program involving nets dropped from helicopters. The trapped goats were put up for adoption. Over the course of two years all but an estimated 750 goats were removed, but the final holdouts proved too difficult to trap because of the rugged terrain. The Navy took over the operation again, and by 1989 a total of nearly 29,000 goats had been removed. Yet the remaining animals were still reproducing! Between 1989 and 1991 the goat-capture process was completed using "Judas goats," tame female goats whose pregnancies had been terminated just prior to release. These females in heat act like magnets for wild male goats. The

Judas females are lured to food, and entire groups are then captured. During the three years of the program over 200 goats, the remainder of the population, were captured. Now the process of vegetational recovery is under way.

Biologists who have visited the island since 1991 have been impressed with the extent of the recovery. The total process will take many years, but Coastal Sage Scrub species such as California Sagebrush, *Artemisia californica* (Fig. 45A), and Coast Brittlebush, *Encelia californica* (Fig. 46; Plate 7B), are now moving into areas that were previously bare. In the center of the island, Coyote Brush, *Baccharis pilularis* (Fig. 45B), is spreading out. Extensive stands of native grassland, dominated by needlegrasses (*Nassella* spp.), are notable in the absence of grazers. In the grasslands, herbaceous native plants—such as Goldfields (*Lasthenia californica*) (Plate 10B), Island Gilia (*Gilia nevinii*), Guadalupe Island Lupine (*Lupinus guadalupensis*), and Pygmy Linanthus (*Linanthus pygmaeus*)—are also making a comeback. Two endemic subspecies of Royal Larkspur, formerly considered rare in the grassland, also may be recovering. These plants, white-flowered San Clemente Island Larkspur, *Delphinium variegatum* ssp. *kinkiense,* and violet-colored Thorne's Royal Larkspur, *Delphinium variegatum* ssp. *thornei,* are poisonous to livestock, so they probably suffered mostly from trampling. The woodland trees are also making a striking comeback, sprouting from their bases.

A number of plants that were known from only a few locations have spread to new areas. For example, a federally listed endangered endemic, San Clemente Island Bush Mallow, *Malacothamnus clementinus,* which was known only from a landfill site, is now growing in some southern canyons. Another San Clemente Island endemic, Blair's Munzothamnus, *Stephanomeria* (=*Munzothamnus*) *blairii,* was formerly found only on a few cliff faces. Now this fleshy shrub with chicorylike purple flowers is becoming a vegetative cover on some of the lower slopes. San Clemente Island Woodland Star, *Lithophragma maximum,* is an endemic state- and federally listed endangered species. This member of the saxifrage family, found normally in rock crevices within Coastal Bluff Scrub, was thought to be extinct, but now it is returning from rhizomes and bulblets in moist places on north-facing slopes. The San Clemente Island Silver Lotus, *Lotus argophyllus* var. *adsurgens,* which is listed by the state as endangered and is closely related to the endangered Silver Lotus of Santa Cruz Island, was once known only from a small population at the southern tip of the island. Now it has moved up the slopes at the southern end, where it can be found with rejuvenated Coastal Sage Scrub. In the same area, the once rare San Clemente Island Indian Paintbrush, *Castilleja grisea,* is also making a comeback. This

Figure 149. Santa Cruz Island Rockcress, *Sibara filifolia.*

$\vdash$———$\dashv$
2 cm

yellow-flowered paintbrush with ash-gray foliage is a hemiparasite in Coastal Sage Scrub. It too is federally listed as endangered. Also endemic to San Clemente Island is one of the "Giant" Buckwheats that has diversified on several of the Channel Islands. San Clemente Island Buckwheat, *Eriogonum giganteum* var. *formosum,* which used to be rare, now forms bands of silvery vegetation on many of the canyon slopes. Similarly, the hairy silvery sunflower known as Nevin's Eriophyllum, *Eriophyllum nevinii,* which is also found on Santa Barbara and Santa Catalina Islands, has been rare on the cliffs of San Clemente Island. It too is forming bands of silvery vegetation.

One of the biggest surprises was that the Santa Cruz Island Rockcress, *Sibara filifolia* (Fig. 149), a white-flowered ephemeral in the mustard family (Brassicaceae) that was thought to have been extirpated on Santa Catalina and Santa Cruz Islands, was not formerly known on San Clemente Island. This rare plant, formerly found on talus slopes in Coastal Sage Scrub, has since been discovered on San Clemente in an area that was heavily grazed by goats. The species was added to the federal list of endangered species in September 1997.

A downside to the recovery of vegetation on San Clemente Island, particularly that of the nonnative grasses, is that the island is now more likely to burn. This is particularly a problem because of the Navy's use of the

TABLE 21   VERTEBRATE ANIMALS OF SAN CLEMENTE ISLAND

Reptiles
  Side-blotched Lizard (*Uta stansburiana*)
  Island Night Lizard (*Xantusia riversiana*)—Outer Southern Channel Islands
    endemic

Birds: See Table 22

Native terrestrial mammals
  San Clemente Island Deer Mouse (*Peromyscus maniculatus clementis*)
    —Endemic
  San Clemente Island Fox (*Urocyon littoralis clementae*)—Endemic
  Fringed Bat (*Myotis thysanodes*)
  California Bat (*Myotis californicus*)
  Townsend's Long-eared Bat (*Plecotus townsendii*)
  Guano Bat or Free-tailed Bat (*Tadarida brasiliensis*)

Introduced mammals
  Domestic Sheep (*Ovis aries*)—Removed
  Domestic Goat (*Capra hircus*)—Removed
  Cattle (*Bos taurus*)—Removed
  Pig (*Sus scrofa*)—Removed
  Mule Deer (*Odocoileus hemionus*)—Extirpated
  House Cat (*Felis domesticus*)
  Domestic Dog (*Canis familiaris*)
  Black Rat (*Rattus rattus*)
  House Mouse (*Mus musculus*)
  Meadow Mouse (*Microtus californicus*)
  Harvest Mouse (*Reithrodontomys megalotis*)

Marine mammals
  Harbor Seal (*Phoca vitulina*)
  California Sea Lion (*Zalophus californianus*)

island for target practice. Fires caused by bombs were not a problem when the goats kept the island denuded. Although periodic fires are a natural component of scrub ecosystems, frequent fires tend to eliminate native species in favor of nonnative grasses.

Terrestrial Animals

The remoteness of San Clemente makes it equally interesting as a location for the study of endemic animal life (Table 21). Unfortunately a number of introduced species have greatly altered the island and caused some native species to become extinct. In addition to the goats, sheep, deer, and pigs already mentioned, San Clemente is home to Black Rats (*Rattus rattus rattus*), House Mice (*Mus musculus*), and Feral Cats (*Felis domesticus*) (which ironically may help to control the introduced rats and mice). The California Vole or Meadow Mouse, *Microtus californicus* (Fig. 150), and the Harvest Mouse, *Reithrodontomys megalotis,* are also introduced species, having arrived along with a load of baled hay that was used to feed

Figure 150. California Vole or Meadow Mouse, *Microtus californicus.*

the horse of a U.S. Marshal who was stationed on the island in the 1930s. Nonnative birds include Chukar (*Alectoris chukar*), Gambel's Quail (*Callipepla gambelii*), California Quail (*Callipepla californica*) (Fig. 64D), and Cattle Egret (*Bubulcus ibis*).

There are ten species or subspecies of land snails on San Clemente Island, and most of these are endemics. The dead shells of these terrestrial invertebrates are quite commonly observed.

Only two lizards are present, the Side-blotched Lizard, *Uta stansburiana* (Fig. 60A), and the Island Night Lizard, *Xantusia riversiana* (Fig. 151; Plate 1C). No other reptiles or amphibians have apparently been able to cross the ocean to reach this island. The Island Night Lizard is also found on San Nicolas and Santa Barbara Islands but not on the mainland, and thus it is an island endemic. Because of habitat destruction, limited range, and the presence of introduced predators, this lizard has been listed as a threatened species by the federal government (although at this writing there has been a proposal to delist it). For a more detailed description of the interesting biogeographic story of the Island Night Lizard, see Chapter 1. Of particular interest is the fact that this species is larger than other members of the genus and therefore is an example of island gigantism. Its incredibly high population density on the island, maintained by a lack of predators and competitors, is also remarkable. There are apparently over 3500 lizards per acre (1450/ha), amounting to a biomass of 55–85 lb/acre (10–16 kg/ha). The Side-blotched Lizards on this island are also typically larger than their mainland counterparts.

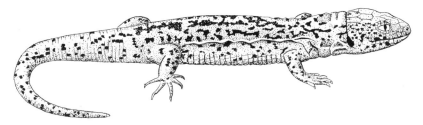

Figure 151. Island Night Lizard, *Xantusia riversiana.*

About 200 species of land birds have been observed on San Clemente Island, and of these 19 are known to breed there (Table 22). There are two endemic birds on the island. The San Clemente Sage Sparrow, *Amphispiza belli clementeae,* prefers dense brush as its habitat. It has been a victim of habitat destruction and competition from other seed-eaters. The population was down to fewer than 100 birds by 1989, causing this subspecies to be listed as threatened by the federal government.

The other endemic bird is the San Clemente Loggerhead Shrike, *Lanius ludovicianus mearnsi.* This, the "Butcher Bird" of San Clemente Island, like its cousins, catches lizards and insects, which it hangs on thorns and barbed wire. Obviously there is no shortage of lizards or thorns on a cactus-covered island, so this species ought to be doing well. On the contrary: by 1989 there were only a few nesting birds left, so the subspecies was given endangered status by the federal government. The problem, it seems, is that shrikes hunt from a perch, and with defoliation in such an advanced stage on the island, there was a shortage of perches. No doubt the feral cats also raided a number of nests, particularly given the shortage of nesting sites. Competition and harassment from predatory Common Ravens, *Corvus corax,* also took their toll. Of particular concern is the fact that one of the other predators, the San Clemente Island Fox, is also listed as an endangered species.

Some authorities consider the San Clemente Loggerhead Shrike to be the most seriously endangered bird in North America because, as of 1997, there were fewer than twenty birds left in the wild. An additional thirteen kept in captivity were being used as part of a captive breeding program. Unfortunately this program has not been successful so far: of the forty captive-reared birds released on the island to date, not one is known to have survived. All appear to have been victims of the same sorts of dangers that befell the native population. There is reason for optimism, however, because programs to restore San Clemente Island vegetation and remove feral cats are beginning to show results.

TABLE 22 BREEDING BIRDS OF SAN CLEMENTE ISLAND

Land birds

Endemic to San Clemente
San Clemente Sage Sparrow (*Amphispiza belli clementeae*)
San Clemente Loggerhead Shrike (*Lanius ludovicianus mearnsi*)

Island endemics
Loggerhead Shrike (*Lanius ludovicianus anthonyi*)
Western Flycatcher (*Empidonax difficilis insulicola*)
House Finch (*Carpodacus mexicanus clementis*)
Orange-crowned Warbler (*Vermivora celata sordida*)
Allen's Hummingbird (*Selasphorus sasin sedentarius*)
Horned Lark (*Eremophila alpestris insularis*)

Nonendemics
Red-tailed Hawk (*Buteo jamaicensis*)
American Kestrel (*Falco sparverius*)
Barn Owl (*Tyto alba*)
Burrowing Owl (*Athene cunicularia*)
Mourning Dove (*Zenaida aurita*)
White-throated Swift (*Aeronautes saxatalis*)
Anna's Hummingbird (*Calypte anna*)
Black Phoebe (*Sayornis nigricans*)
Barn Swallow (*Hirundo rustica*)
Common Raven (*Corvus corax*)
Western Meadowlark (*Sturnella neglecta*)
Northern Mockingbird (*Mimus polyglottos*)
Rock Wren (*Salpinctes obsoletus*)
Hooded Oriole (*Icterus cucullatus*)
Chipping Sparrow (*Spizella passerina*)

Introduced species
House Sparrow (*Passer domesticus*)
European Starling (*Sturnus vulgaris*)
Cattle Egret (*Bubulcus ibis*)
Chukar (*Alectoris chukar*)
Gambel's Quail (*Callipepla gambelii*)
California Quail (*Callipepla californica*)

Sea birds
Western Gull (*Larus occidentalis*)
Black Oystercatcher (*Haematopus bachmani*)
Brandt's Cormorant (*Phalacrocorax penicillatus*)

Common resident birds include the Horned Lark (Fig. 64E), Common Raven, Rock Wren (Fig. 64I), Northern Mockingbird (Fig. 64G), Orange-crowned Warbler (Fig. 109), House Sparrow, House Finch (Fig. 110), and Western Meadowlark (Fig. 64F). Raptors include the American Kestrel (Fig. 64B), Barn Owl, and Burrowing Owl (Fig. 64A).

At least six kinds of birds (two of them endemic) have been extirpated in recent years owing to extreme habitat destruction. The Bald Eagle, *Haliaeetus leucocephalus* (Fig. 65); Osprey, *Pandion haliaetus* (Fig. 41); and Peregrine Falcon, *Falco peregrinus,* are raptors that formerly lived on San Clemente Island. Among the songbirds, the following endemics are now gone from San Clemente Island: Bewick's Wren (*Thryomanus bewickii leucophrys*), San Clemente Island Song Sparrow (*Melospiza melodia clementae*), and San Clemente Island Rufous-sided Towhee (*Pipilo erythrophthalmus clementae*).

Among mammals there are two endemics. The San Clemente Island Fox, *Urocyon littoralis clementae* (Fig. 4; Plate 1A), is the star of the show. This version of the Island Fox seems especially tame and abundant. Even though it is an endangered species, this diminutive carnivore may actually have been helped by the defoliation of San Clemente Island. It is believed that this animal was carried to San Clemente from San Nicolas Island by Native Americans. For a more thorough discussion of the biogeography and taxonomic relationships of this species, see Chapter 1. The other endemic is the San Clemente Island Deer Mouse, *Peromyscus maniculatus clementis* (Fig. 3) , which may be threatened by competition from the three species of introduced mice and predation by feral cats.

Four species of bats are known to occur on the island, and all are known from both the mainland and the other Channel Islands. These include the Guano Bat or Free-tailed Bat (*Tadarida brasiliensis*), Townsend's Long-eared Bat (*Plecotus townsendii*), the California Bat (*Myotis californicus*), and the Fringed Bat (*Myotis thysanodes*).

SAN NICOLAS ISLAND

San Nicolas Island (Fig. 152), located in Ventura County, is the most distant of the California islands, lying approximately 61 miles (98 km) from the mainland. The island is 9.7 miles (13 km) in length and about 3 miles (5 km) in width, and it has a maximum elevation of 910 ft (277 m) at Jackson Hill. Much of the island is very sparsely vegetated and extremely eroded. Grassy slopes and a terraced plateau dominate the appearance of the island. Dune sands are present in several areas, and the island's general appearance is quite arid; in fact the annual rainfall is only 6.61 in. (16.8 cm). The weather is characterized by low clouds and fog most of the year, with prevailing westerly winds that regularly reach velocities of 35–50 mph (55–80 km/hr).

U.S. Navy–owned San Nicolas Island accommodates a $30 million installation for testing guided missiles. On test days, missiles may be fired at supersonic targets while a series of instruments on the island, as well as on ships and aircraft, gather data, which are ultimately relayed to the Point Mugu Naval Air Weapons Station for evaluation.

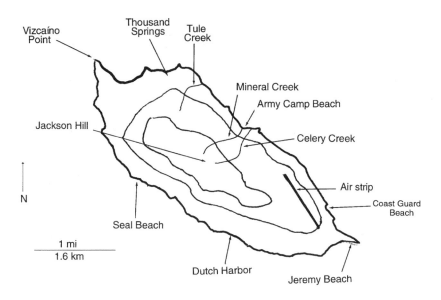

Figure 152. San Nicolas Island.

Geology

San Nicolas Island lies west of the San Clemente fault and has been displaced
northward along with San Clemente Island. The basement rock of San
Nicolas Island, similar to that of San Clemente Island, is composed of
Miocene volcanic materials. Sedimentary rocks, eroded into terraces, are
found around the perimeter of the island. Sands that accumulate on the
island are blown by the persistent winds into a series of dunes (Plate 14B).

History

In December 1602, Sebastián Vizcaíno spotted San Nicolas Island from his
launch, the *Tres Reyes*. Cabrillo's log from 1542 does not mention San Nicolas or its Native American inhabitants. No actual descriptions exist of these
early Americans, but an abundance of archaeological remains give us a
clue as to what it must have been like for those living on this remote outpost.

Sixty-eight archaeological sites have been identified on San Nicolas
Island. It has been estimated that 1500 Native Americans, known as
Nicoleños, must have inhabited the island at one time. They survived on
abundant marine resources such as fish and abalone. Water was obtained
from freshwater springs. A lack of Spanish-American artifacts on the island
leads to the conclusion that the natives had little or no trade with the Spanish settlements.

One of the most interesting archaeological sites on all of the Channel Islands is the Cave of the Whales at sea level on the south side of San Nicolas. This is a sea cave that extends narrowly to a depth of about 150 ft (50 m), although the main chamber extends back about 35 ft (7 m). The oblong entrance is 19 ft (6 m) wide and 9 ft (3 m) high and seems to be guarded by a grooved petroglyph of what appears to be a shark. A large boulder protects the entrance from the full force of the surf during the highest tides, but erosion is nevertheless taking its toll on about forty examples of rock art, mostly petroglyphs chiseled into the sandstone surface. The pictographs, created using a black pigment painted on the rocks, can by now barely be distinguished from the algae and lichens on the rock surface. The images on the rocks are of sea creatures, such as sharks, whales, killer whales, and dolphins. Two panels that fell off the walls have been transported to the mainland, where they are on display at the Southwest Indian Museum in Highland Park.

Native Americans probably lived on the island for thousands of years before the Aleut Sea Otter hunters arrived. The hunters had firearms and apparently killed nearly all of the men in disagreements over property rights and Native American women. In addition, the Aleuts, as well as recruiters for the missions, carried diseases that were lethal to the Nicoleños. In 1812 a tremendous earthquake, with an epicenter near Santa Cruz Island, rocked the California coast; apparently it was responsible in part for convincing the natives that they should leave their homes and accompany the mission fathers to the mainland. In 1835 the last dozen survivors of the original population were transported to the mainland.

The Lone Woman of San Nicolas Island One of the most dramatic episodes in the history of the California islands tells of a native woman who was somehow stranded by herself on remote San Nicolas Island. In 1835, as the remaining Nicoleños were being transferred to the mainland, a single woman was left behind. She would survive alone on the island for eighteen years. Her story of solitude and survival was the inspiration for a work of children's fiction entitled *Island of the Blue Dolphin*.

One account of the stranding states that the woman was "away in the mountains" when the others were removed. Another, unpublished, account was compiled by former National Park Service ranger Harold D. Casey; he described the events in a more romantic manner. In Casey's version, the dozen or so Nicoleños were evacuated during a storm. They were being hurriedly boarded onto a schooner named the *Peor es Nada* (Spanish for "Worse Than Nothing") when it was discovered that the woman's child had inadvertently been left ashore. As Captain Hubbard set out for the open sea into the storm, the woman leaped overboard in what everyone assumed would be a futile attempt to swim back to the island.

Hubbard apparently intended to return to San Nicolas; however, the schooner had orders to sail directly to Santa Barbara to take George Nidever and a party of otter hunters to Santa Rosa Island. Subsequent orders further precluded a quick return, and less than a month after the woman had been abandoned the *Peor es Nada* foundered at the entrance to San Francisco Bay. The schooner drifted out to sea and was lost, but the crew was rescued.

Although it was common knowledge that a Nicoleño woman and her child had been left on San Nicolas Island, no attempt was made to rescue them or at least to learn their fate. Apparently there were no available seaworthy vessels that could make the dangerous crossing. Besides, nearly everyone believed it was impossible for the woman and child to have survived, even if she had been successful in swimming back to the island in the storm.

It was not until 1850 that the first attempt was made to find her. Father Gonzales Rubio of the Santa Barbara Mission offered Thomas Jeffries $200 to find and return with the woman and child. Jeffries returned from San Nicolas to report that the island was inhabited by numerous birds, foxes, wild dogs, and marine mammals, and that he had found the remains of a curious hut, made of whale ribs planted in a circle. This, he surmised, was the former residence of a Nicoleño chief, or perhaps a place of worship. He also returned with several ollas or stone vessels, including one made of clouded green serpentine.

Although his return to the mainland sparked some local interest in the fate of the woman, it was not until 1852 that Jeffries, accompanied by George Nidever, returned to San Nicolas Island. In April of that year, while gathering gull eggs, they discovered small human footprints embedded in the dry clay a short distance from the beach. They also found three circular, roofless enclosures made of woven sagebrush, and pieces of seal blubber drying atop several upright poles. Dried fish and seal blubber were also found wedged into rock fissures adjacent to a spring. Upon their return to the mainland, they told several people about having seen the footprints, and the story soon spread.

Father Gonzales Rubio, ever hopeful of finding the woman, asked Nidever to return to the island to search for her. The following winter, on a trip to hunt for Sea Otters, Nidever and his men discovered more footprints and artifacts, but after spending the winter on the island, they found no further trace of the woman.

In July 1853 the otter hunters, led by Nidever, made a third trip to San

Nicolas Island. This time they discovered a fresh footprint in the wet sand. A thorough search of the island by six crew members rediscovered the whalebone hut, and a man named Carl Detman, commonly called Charlie Brown, found the woman, accompanied by a pack of dogs, busily cleaning a seal skin.

The woman was taken back to Santa Barbara, where she apparently was taken in by Nidever and his wife. Father Gonzales Rubio visited her regularly and made attempts to converse with her, but her language was unknown. Attempts were made to locate Nicoleño survivors in the local missions, but by then none could be found.

The woman apparently became quite attached to the Nidevers' children and would play with them by the hour. As the story goes, she was able to explain to Mrs. Nidever, using sign language, that when she had swum back to shore her baby was gone, and she believed the dogs had eaten it.

The sad ending to the story is that the woman who had survived in isolation for eighteen years died after but five weeks on the mainland. One account says that she became ill from eating too much fruit! Christened Juana Maria by a local priest, she was buried on October 19, 1853, in the graveyard of Mission Santa Barbara. A plaque placed in 1928 is inscribed as follows:

Juana Maria
Indian Woman Abandoned on
San Nicolas Island Eighteen Years
Found and Brought to Santa Barbara
By Captain George Nidever in 1853

Recently a bound leather notebook was discovered in a personal library in Santa Barbara. Most of it had been used as a business ledger in the latter part of the nineteenth century. However, it also contained a number of pages of handwritten notes by Emma Hardacre, a woman who had moved to Santa Barbara in 1873 and become interested in the story of the lone woman of San Nicolas Island. She published the results of her research in 1880, and her account is similar to the one just presented.

The notes in the journal were apparently written afterwards. They suggest that the woman was not Native American but rather an Aleut brought to the island sometime between 1805 and 1820. Otter hunters often brought along the more aggressive northern Aleuts to assist with the hunting. The evidence in Hardacre's journal that suggests that Juana Maria was an Aleut is as follows:

1. No local natives could be found who could understand her. Yet we know that J. P. Harrington, an early anthropologist who worked

extensively in California, interviewed several Native Americans who were descendants of islanders as late as 1915.

2. Hardacre "doubted she was an island Indian because she behaved like a woman who had a knowledge of the amenities of life." Had she been an islander, she would no doubt have been shocked at the sight of horses, wagons, and people. Yet by all accounts she delighted in every aspect of nineteenth-century life in Santa Barbara, especially in fruit and rich foods.

3. Hardacre noted that the dogs that were on the island with her "were black and white, of Alaskan breed." This information was obtained from Captain Nidever's sons, who were sent to San Nicolas Island soon after the rescue to kill off all of the wild dogs so that the island could be used for sheep grazing.

A photograph of a woman, found with one of Mrs. George Nidever and now in the Southwest Indian Museum, may be of the lone woman of San Nicolas Island. A cursory look at the woman's face does not reveal a resemblance to photographs of Aleuts, but her appearance is very similar to that of such southwestern tribes as the Apache and Shoshone. Whatever her origin, this latest Aleut twist continues to lend an air of intrigue and romance to a great part of California history, the saga of the first California islanders.

Incidentally, the wild dogs left on the island survived until the first sheep ranchers arrived in 1857. Captain Martin Kimberly began the first sheep ranch at Corral Harbor on the north shore, and by 1890 San Nicolas was supporting more than 30,000 sheep. Operations were moved to Brooks Landing in 1920, and a pier was constructed. Overgrazing continued, and by 1930 only 4000 of the original 10,000 acres remained vegetated.

The Military Presence on San Nicolas Island The U.S. Navy acquired San Nicolas Island in 1933 and built a weather station there at Brooks Landing. Along with San Clemente, the island was used as a gunnery range. The last sheep rancher, Roy Agee, left the island in 1941 when his lease was revoked. During World War II the U.S. Army assumed control, setting up air surveillance facilities at Brooks Landing. In 1946 jurisdiction was transferred back to the Naval Air Station at Point Mugu.

In 1995 the Navy began a massive cleanup of toxic waste on San Nicolas Island. Over the years thousands of drums of hydraulic fluids, fuel oil, solvents, lubricants, pesticides, and old batteries were tossed down more than three dozen ravines spread across the island. Environmental contractors have also unearthed mounds of debris from a fire-training pit,

Figure 153. Flat-topped surface of San Nicolas Island showing disturbed grassland. (Photo by William Mautz.)

where old planes and other materials were torched so that runway crews could practice their firefighting techniques.

Terrestrial Vegetation

The island's vegetation is generally limited to grasses and a few shrubs (Fig. 153); no trees occur except in a ravine where a freshwater spring (Thousand Springs) is located. The trees there are introduced California Fan Palms, *Washingtonia filifera*. Prior to 1850 and the introduction of sheep, San Nicolas Island was very different in appearance. Captain George Nidever, the rescuer of the lost woman, reported that a part of the island was covered by trees and brush. The only remnants of these now-extinct plants are the white calcareous casts of the roots. After the sheep were removed, the Navy, in an attempt to control erosion, spread fertilizers and grass seed by airplane; thus today grass-covered slopes cover most of the island. Erosion on the island's windward side has created a badlands topography of hundreds of ravines. The island has been so altered by grazing and erosion that it is impossible to know what the original vegetation was like. Indeed it was not until 1897 that the first botanist examined the island— long after the sheep had been introduced.

The total flora is composed of about 270 species, subspecies, and varieties but half of them are nonnative, representing the largest proportion of introduced species on the Channel Islands. San Nicolas is the least diverse of the California islands, ecologically as well as biotically. Its small size, distance from the mainland, and lack of diverse habitats are all factors that probably contribute to the low number of plant species present.

Coastal Bluff Scrub is the dominant native community. The largest and most obvious plants on the island are Coyote Bush, *Baccharis pilularis* (Fig. 45B), and Giant Coreopsis, *Coreopsis gigantea* (Plate 9B,C). Common plants that have survived on the sea bluff areas include California Box Thorn (*Lycium californicum*) (Fig. 144), Coastal Prickly-pear (*Opuntia littoralis*) (Fig. 51A; Plate 8C) and Coastal Cholla (*Opuntia prolifera*) (Fig. 51B; Plate 8A,B), California Saltbush (*Atriplex californica*), and Yarrow (*Achillea millefolium*). Bright Green Dudleya or Green Live-forever, *Dudleya virens* (Fig. 55B), also found on other Southern Channel Islands and the mainland at Palos Verdes, is a distinctive member of this community.

Among the island endemics (Table 23) are the Island Bird's-foot Trefoil (*Lotus argophyllus* var. *argenteus*) and two plant species that occur in the sandy soils on the wind-exposed side of the island. Trask's Milkvetch, *Astragalus traskiae,* is a hairy grayish locoweed with cream-colored flowers. It is found only on San Nicolas and Santa Barbara Islands. A rare endemic to San Nicolas Island (although it has been reported from San Clemente and Guadalupe Islands as well) is the San Nicolas Island Lomatium, *Lomatium insulare.* This member of the celery family (Apiaceae) looks a bit like parsley. When it occurs, it is found in sandy soil among rocks. Another rare plant found in the sandy areas is the strange, fleshy yellowish root-parasite, the Short-lobed Broomrape, *Orobanche parishii* ssp. *brachyloba* (Fig. 154). This peculiar plant seems always to parasitize the Coast Goldenbush, *Isocoma menziesii.* It is also found on San Miguel, Santa Catalina, Santa Cruz, and Santa Rosa Islands, but it is rare on all of them.

A popcorn flower known as Trask's Cryptantha, *Cryptantha traskiae,* is a small white-flowered ephemeral in the borage or fiddleneck family (Boraginaceae). The name "Fiddleneck" refers to the way in which the flower clusters (inflorescences) form a coil at the end of the stems, like the carved end of a violin neck. This species also occurs on San Clemente Island. Another member of this family, also found in the dunes, is a yellow-flowered fiddleneck, *Amsinckia spectabilis* var. *spectabilis* (Fig. 155). This variety, also found on other Channel Islands and the mainland, now includes what used to be considered an island endemic, *Amsinckia spectabilis* var. *nicolai,* which was believed to occur only on San Clemente, San Nicolas, and San Miguel Islands.

Only two plants are known to be specifically endemic to san Nicolas

TABLE 23   ENDEMIC VASCULAR PLANTS OF SAN NICOLAS ISLAND

Apiaceae (celery family)
    San Nicolas Island Lomatium (*Lomatium insulare*)—Rare
Asteraceae (sunflower family)
    Island Sagebrush (*Artemisia nesiotica*)
    San Nicolas Island Leafy Malacothrix (*Malacothrix foliosa* ssp. *polycephala*)[a]
    Cliff Malacothrix (*Malacothrix saxatilis* var. *implicata*)
Boraginaceae (borage family)
    Trask's Cryptantha (*Cryptantha traskiae*)
Convolvulaceae (morning-glory family)
    Island Morning-glory (*Calystegia macrostegia*)
Crassulaceae (stonecrop family)
    Bright Green Dudleya (*Dudleya virens*)
Fabaceae (pea family)
    Trask's Milkvetch (*Astragalus traskiae*)—Rare
    Island Bird's-foot Trefoil (*Lotus argophyllus* var. *argenteus*)
    Island Pinpoint Clover (*Trifolium gracilentum* var. *palmeri*)
Papaveraceae (poppy family)
    Island Poppy (*Eschscholzia ramosa*)
    Cream cups (*Platystemon californicus* var. *ciliatus*)[a]
Polemoniacea (phlox family)
    Island Gilia (*Gilia nevinii*)
Polygonaceae (Buckwheat Family)
    San Nicolas Island Buckwheat (*Eriogonum grande* var. *timorum*)
       —Endangered[a]
Saxifragaceae (saxifrage family)
    Island Jepsonia (*Jepsonia malvifolia*)
Solanaceae (nightshade family)
    San Nicolas Island Desert-thorn (*Lycium verrucosum*)—Extinct(?)[a]

[a]Single-island endemic.

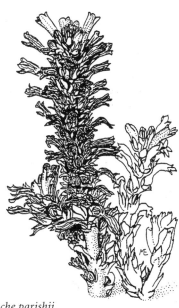

Figure 154. Short-lobed Broom-rape, *Orobanche parishii*
ssp. *brachyloba*.

2 cm

Figure 155. Fiddleneck, *Amsinckia spectabilis.*

Island. The "giant" buckwheat known as the San Nicolas Island Buckwheat, *Eriogonum grande* var. *timorum,* is a state-listed endangered species found at scattered locations on the sea cliffs. The newly described San Nicolas Island Leafy Malacothrix, *Malacothrix foliosa* ssp. *polycephala,* is a pale yellow Dandelion-like annual that occurs on clay slopes near the west end of the island at about 200 ft (65 m) elevation.

Terrestrial Animals

The only invertebrate peculiar to San Nicolas Island is *Eleodopsis subvestitus,* a beetle that resembles the stink beetles (*Eleodes* spp.) of the mainland.

Table 24 lists the vertebrate animals known from San Nicolas Island. Three lizards are known from the island. Distribution of the Island Night Lizard, *Xantusia riversiana* (Fig. 151; Plate 1C), is patchy; it is found only in small areas with high densities of cactus and Boxthorn. The Side-blotched Lizard, *Uta stansburiana* (Fig. 60A), is found on the lower slopes of the east side of the island in Coastal Bluff Scrub. The Southern Alligator Lizard, *Elgaria multicarinatus* (Fig. 60C), seems primarily to inhabit the upland portion of the island near Jackson Hill, where it is associated with debris.

In early publications, most notably that by Jay Savage in 1967, the Southern Alligator Lizard was not mentioned as inhabiting San Nicolas Island. This absence could lead to the tentative conclusion that the lizard is a recent introduction. This concept seems to have been verified by Duncan Parks of the University of California at Berkeley, who, using mitochondrial DNA analysis, concluded that both the Side-blotched Lizard and the Alligator Lizard were recent introductions and that the source populations appear

TABLE 24   VERTEBRATE ANIMALS OF SAN NICOLAS ISLAND

Reptiles
  Island Night Lizard (*Xantusia riversiana*)—Outer Southern Channel Islands
    endemic
  Side-blotched Lizard (*Uta stansburiana*)
  Southern Alligator Lizard (*Elgaria multicarinatus*)

Breeding land birds
  Island endemics
    Horned Lark (*Eremophila alpestris insularis*)
    Orange-crowned Warbler (*Vermivora celata sordida*)
    House Finch (*Carpodacus mexicanus clementis*)—Southern
      Channel Islands endemic
    Bewick's Wren (*Thryomanes bewickii nesophilus*)—Northern
      Channel Islands endemic
  Nonendemics
    American Kestrel (*Falco sparverius*)
    Burrowing Owl (*Athene cunicularia*)
    Barn Swallow (*Hirundo rustica*)
    Common Raven (*Corvus corax*)
    Northern Mockingbird (*Mimus polyglottos*)
    Rock Wren (*Salpinctes obsoletus*)
    Western Meadowlark (*Sturnella neglecta*)
    White-crowned Sparrow (*Zonotrichia leucophrys*)
    Brewer's Blackbird (*Euphagus cyanocephalus*)
  Introduced species
    House Sparrow (*Passer domesticus*)
    European Starling (*Sturnus vulgaris*)

Sea birds
    Western Gull (*Larus occidentalis*)
    Black Oystercatcher (*Haematopus bachmani*)
    Brandt's Cormorant (*Phalacrocorax penicillatus*)
    Brown Pelican (*Pelecanus occidentalis*)
    Snowy Plover (*Charadrius alexandrinus*)

Terrestrial mammals
    San Nicolas Island Deer Mouse (*Peromyscus maniculatus exterus*)—Endemic
    San Nicolas Island Fox (*Urocyon littoralis dickeyi*)—Endemic

Introduced mammals
    Domestic Sheep (*Ovis aries*)—Removed
    House Cat (*Felis domesticus*)
    Domestic Dog (*Canis familiaris*)—Removed

Marine mammals
    Sea Otter (*Enhydra lutris*)
    Elephant Seal (*Mirounga angustirostris*)
    Harbor Seal (*Phoca vitulina*)
    California Sea Lion (*Zalophus californianus*)
    Northern Sea Lion (*Eumetopias jubatus*)—Occasional

Figure 156. White-crowned Sparrow, *Zonotrichia leucophrys.*

to be Point Mugu and Port Hueneme, respectively. Because both of these areas have military bases and because the Navy operates the radar station where both lizards are known to occur, it could be that the lizards were introduced in recent times in shipments of construction materials.

Among the land birds, only nine species are resident. The House Finch, *Carpodacus mexicanus clementis* (Fig. 110), is endemic to the Southern Channel Islands. In contrast, Bewick's Wren, *Thryomanes bewickii nesophilus* (Fig. 112), is endemic to the Northern Channel Islands. The now-extinct Bewick's Wren of San Clemente Island is a different subspecies. Surprisingly, two birds common on the mainland have been known to breed on San Nicolas Island but on none of the other islands: the White-crowned Sparrow, *Zonotrichia leucophrys* (Fig. 156), and Brewer's Blackbird, *Euphagus cyanocephalus.* Common resident land birds include Common Raven, Mourning Dove, Horned Lark (Fig. 64E), and Rock Wren (Fig. 64I).

Among raptors, a small population of Burrowing Owls, *Athene cunicularia* (Fig. 64A), is found on the island, as on all of the islands except Anacapa. Occasionally a Red-tailed Hawk, *Buteo jamaicensis,* is spotted. The American Kestrel, *Falco sparverius* (Fig. 64B), is known to breed there as well.

Large numbers of shore birds and other aquatic bird species are also present. Of particular interest is the presence of the Snowy Plover,

Charadrius alexandrinus, which nests in the dunes. This species, also found on San Miguel and Santa Rosa Islands, has experienced a serious decline in numbers throughout its range, particularly because of the loss of undisturbed dune habitat on the mainland.

Only two resident land mammals are endemic to San Nicolas island: the San Nicolas Island Deer Mouse, *Peromyscus maniculatus exterus* (Fig. 3), and the San Nicolas Island Fox, *Urocyon littoralis dickeyi* (Fig. 4; Plate 1A). Although this fox appears to have come from San Clemente Island, it differs from those on the other islands in being slightly larger and having a reddish-black color instead of the more usual silvery-gray. The remoteness of San Nicolas, as well as its lack of ecological diversity, is probably responsible for its small vertebrate fauna.

Marine Life

As on San Miguel Island, marine mammals find the distant shores of San Nicolas Island an ideal environment. Large herds of California Sea Lions, *Zalophus californianus* (Fig. 39; Plate 2C), inhabit the southwest shore between Vizcaíno Point and Seal Beach. Elephant Seals, *Mirounga angustirostris* (Figs. 38 and 168); Harbor Seals, *Phoca vitulina* (Fig. 37; Plate 2C); and (although they are no longer common) Northern Sea Lions, *Eumetopias jubatus* (Fig. 40; Plate 2D), also can be observed here from time to time. For a more thorough discussion of the significance of these islands to marine life, see Chapters 4 and 6.

The story of the reintroduction of the Sea Otter, *Enhydra lutris* (Fig. 36), to San Nicolas Island is worth recounting. In the mid-1980s the U.S. Fish and Wildlife Service decided that, to safeguard the population in the event of a disaster such as an oil spill along the coast, a backup population of Sea Otters should be established. Because of its abundance of shellfish and because it was within the former range of the species, San Nicolas Island was chosen as the site for the program. Beginning in 1987 and for three years thereafter, a total of 139 Sea Otters were translocated from the mainland to the island. But San Nicolas represented a major source of abalone and lobster for commercial fishermen, and howls of outrage were soon heard. In order to compensate for the loss of fishing grounds, a law was passed to forbid reintroduction of the Sea Otter from Point Conception southward except at San Nicolas Island. The major unforeseen problem with the reintroduction was that most of the Sea Otters attempted to return to the waters in which they had been trapped. As of 1995, only ten to fifteen Sea Otters remained on the island, but they were reproducing, and it is hoped that they will become the progenitors of a new, healthy population.

As does San Miguel Island, San Nicolas has a large population of nesting sea birds. In particular, there are large numbers of Western Gulls, Brandt's Cormorants, and Brown Pelicans. Shore birds—including the endangered Snowy Plover, *Charadrius alexandrinus,* and the Black Oystercatcher, *Haematopus bachmani*—are also present at the water's edge.

SANTA BARBARA ISLAND

Santa Barbara Island is the smallest of the Channel Islands, with a total area of about 1 square mile or 639 acres (259 ha) (Fig. 157). Given that it is a little over a mile across, its coastline is a little over 3.1416 miles in distance. It is located 38 miles (61 km) southwest of the mainland at Point Dume near Malibu, and it is 24 miles (39 km) northwest of Santa Catalina Island, about midway between Santa Catalina and San Nicolas. The island is technically the northernmost of the Southern Channel Islands, but it is included in the Channel Islands National Park, most of which is composed of the Northern Channel Islands. It is discussed in this chapter as one of the outer Southern Channel Islands because of its biological affinities with San Clemente and San Nicolas Islands. Another peculiarity is that Santa Barbara Island is a part of Santa Barbara County, whereas Santa Catalina is in Los Angeles County and San Nicolas and Anacapa are in Ventura County!

The island appears as a high, rounded dome when approached by boat (Fig. 158). The shoreline consists of steep cliffs, from 200 to 600 ft (65–195 m) high, with only a few narrow, rocky beaches. Near Webster Point, at the northwest corner of the island, the land forms a gentle ramp that descends to near sea level. The best landing point is at Landing Cove on the eastern shore, where there is shelter from the persistent wind. Once one climbs the steep trail from Landing Cove to the visitor center, the island's topography is seen as one of undulating slopes. The trail to the southwest leads to Signal Peak, which is the highest point on the island, 635 ft (194 m) above sea level. A north-south ridge connects Signal Peak to North Peak, at 562 feet (171 m), near the northern end of the island. The view northward overlooks Elephant Seal Cove and Shag Rock, a tiny islet. Sutil Island, a small islet covering only a few acres, lies off the island's southern shore. Marine terraces up to 250 ft (81 m) in elevation are present both to the east and to the west of the north-south ridge, and these give the island its somewhat flattened appearance.

The island's climate is mild but strongly influenced by prevailing winds from the west-northwest, which average 17 mph (27 km/hr). The soil varies from thin and coarse at windy locations to deep and relatively fertile on the terraces. An annual rainfall of about 9 in. (22.5 cm) between

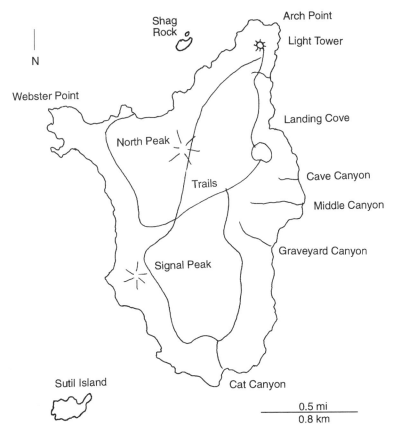

Figure 157. Santa Barbara Island.

Figure 158. Santa Barbara Island as it appears from the sea.

October and April is supplemented by frequent wet fogs during the summer and fall months.

History

Santa Barbara Island was named by Sebastián Vizcaíno, who arrived there on Saint Barbara's Day, December 4, 1602. Although there is no evidence of Native American villages on this island (there is no surface water), there are numerous shell middens, indicating that the island was used as a stopover by seafaring natives.

The earliest record of modern humans for the island indicates that a large feral goat population was present by 1846. In 1887 a visitor noted that there were an old lobsterman's hut and a few scattered bones of sheep. Feral house cats were extremely abundant by 1896 and persisted on the island until the mid-1950s.

About 1915 the Alvin Hyder family moved to the island. A total of eleven structures were built, including a series of catch basins and reservoirs to store water. The family, which numbered as many as seventeen people at times, also brought two mules and two horses along. At first barley was raised in a large field on the east slope, just east of Signal Peak. Later corn and other crops were planted.

Large parts of the island were burned prior to plowing and planting. Sheep were brought in, as well as rabbits (Belgian Hares), geese, ducks, chickens, turkeys, pigs, and goats. By 1926 the Hyder group had moved off the island, and only the cats, rabbits, and a few *Eucalyptus* trees remained. Without additional water, the trees ultimately died out.

In 1938 Santa Barbara and Anacapa Islands were proclaimed by President Franklin Delano Roosevelt as the Channel Islands National Monument, and then in 1980 an act of Congress added them to Channel Islands National Park. From 1942 through 1946 the island was used as a military station. Barracks and various other buildings were erected, and motor vehicles were brought over. At this time more rabbits (New Zealand Red Rabbits) were introduced, and the rabbit population slowly began to increase. By 1954 hundreds of rabbits were observed and a great decrease in native vegetation was evident. After a rabbit extermination program was begun, the island's plants and animals suffered another setback in the summer of 1959, when an accidental fire burned two-thirds of the island from the east shore to the crest of the ridge. As a result of the fire and predation by house cats, the Santa Barbara Song Sparrow, an endemic bird found only on the island, became extinct.

Visitors to the island will not see military buildings that remained from the World War II period. The only buildings now are a ranger station and visitor center built in 1993. However, little remains to indicate the destructive effect that humans and domestic animals had upon tiny Santa Barbara Island. It is hoped that the flora will slowly recover; however, the Song Sparrow is gone forever.

Geology

Santa Barbara Island is related to Anacapa Island, as both islands are composed primarily of Miocene volcanic rocks, mostly basalts that were deposited under water. There are no vents on the island, and the source of the basalts is unknown. Sedimentary marine beds and six distinct marine terraces lie upon the bedrock, indicating periods of inundation by seawater. At various times during the Pleistocene the island was completely covered. Terraces at 30 ft (10 m) and 130 ft (42 m) contain fossils of marine organisms, such as molluscs, corals, and microscopic foraminifera and ostracods (Crustacea). Fossils of a Bald Eagle and a sea lion have also been found there.

The shoreline of Santa Barbara Island shows the typical features of marine erosion, including coves, inlets, sea caves, and an arch. On the northeast corner of the island, known as Arch Point, there is a tall, narrow arch topped by a 130-ft (42-m) fossiliferous terrace. The arch itself is the product of marine erosion's cutting into a fault that offset the headland.

Terrestrial Vegetation

In early spring Santa Barbara Island appears totally green, covered with a dense growth of grasses and herbaceous plants. However during the dry summer and fall months the island takes on a grayish-brown color and appears barren. No trees are present on the island, and shrubby vegetation occurs in only a few scattered patches. Attempts to plant *Eucalyptus,* to give the landscape a bit of shade, have failed on this island.

The major plant communities are Island Grassland, Coastal Sage Scrub, Maritime Desert Scrub, and Coastal Bluff Scrub, all of which appear in a highly disturbed state. The revised flora of this island has been catalogued by Steve Junak, Ralph Philbrick, and Charles Drost and published by the Santa Barbara Botanic Garden. Santa Barbara Island has the fewest native species of all the Channel Islands. Some of the most conspicuous plants on the island are the introduced species, which make up about a third of the island's approximately 135 kinds of plants.

The history of abusive land use is similar to that of the other Channel Islands. In the early 1900s native vegetation was disturbed by the introduction of nonnative grasses and numerous large herbivores, including

Figure 159. European Rabbit, *Oryctolagus cuniculus.*

horses, mules, goats, and sheep. Perhaps the greatest insult to native plants were the two introductions of European Rabbits, *Oryctolagus cuniculus* (Fig. 159) mentioned previously. The first took place in 1915, when Alvin Hyder introduced about 2000 Belgian Hares. The second introduction occurred in 1942, when U.S. Navy personnel stationed on the island introduced the New Zealand Red Rabbit as a source of food. In 1954 National Park Service and U.S. Fish and Wildlife Service personnel began a thirty-year program of extermination. In 1955 the rabbit population reached a peak estimated at 2621 individuals, and strychnine poisoning was added to the shooting control program. In 1979 a daily program of rabbit hunting began, which finally succeeded in removing all the rabbits; however, by then the island's animal and plant populations had suffered catastrophic damage.

Much of the island's terraced areas and slopes are covered with grasses intermixed with Crystalline Ice Plant, *Mesembryanthemum crystallinum* (Fig. 160), and Sea Blite, *Suaeda californica.* The Crystalline Ice Plant and Sea Blite form dark patches that can easily be seen from the sea (Plate 14C). Ten species of introduced grasses (Fig. 59) occur mainly on the upper terraced portion of the island. The most common of these are Wild Oats, *Avena fatua,* and several bromes or chesses, *Bromus* spp.

The sea bluffs remain one of the best refuges for native plants (Table 25). One of the most spectacular native plants is the Giant Coreopsis, *Coreopsis gigantea* (Fig. 161; Plate 9B,C), which spreads great, candelabralike branches covered with a green, carrotlike foliage and large yellow flowers in the spring months. Coastal Bluff Scrub also includes such island endemics as Island Tarweed, *Hemizonia clementina* (Fig. 138), and Nevin's Eriophyllum, *Eriophyllum nevinii.*

Three (possibly four) plants are endemic to Santa Barbara Island.

Figure 160. Crystalline Ice Plant, *Mesembryanthemum crystallinum.*

TABLE 25   ENDEMIC VASCULAR PLANTS
OF SANTA BARBARA ISLAND

Asteraceae (sunflower family)
　　Island Sagebrush (*Artemisia nesiotica*)
　　Nevin's Eriophyllum (*Eriophyllum nevinii*)—Rare
　　Island Tarweed (*Hemizonia clementina*)
　　Philbrick's Leafy Malacothrix (*Malacothrix foliosa* ssp. *philbrickii*)[a]

Convolvulaceae (morning-glory family)
　　Island Morning-glory (*Calystegia macrostegia*)

Crassulaceae (stonecrop family)
　　Santa Barbara Island Live-forever (*Dudleya traskiae*)—Endangered[a]

Fabaceae (pea family)
　　Trask's Milkvetch (*Astragalus traskiae*)—Rare
　　Island Bird's-foot Trefoil (*Lotus argophyllus* var. *argenteus*)
　　Island Pinpoint Clover (*Trifolium gracilentum* var. *palmeri*)

Papaveraceae (poppy family)
　　Island Poppy (*Eschscholzia ramosa*)
　　Santa Barbara Island Cream Cups (*Platystemon Californicus* var. *ciliatus?*)[a]

Polygonaceae (buckwheat family)
　　Santa Barbara Island Buckwheat (*Erigonum giganteum* var. *compactum*)[a]

[a]Single-island endemic.

Among those that were protected on the cliffs is the Santa Barbara Island Live-forever, *Dudleya traskiae.* This small, perennial succulent, listed as endangered by the federal and state governments, was thought to be extinct in 1970. Following the successful removal of rabbits, the species made a recovery and is now appearing in a variety of habitats, although no specimens have been found on the northern side of the island.

Figure 161. Vegetation of Santa Barbara Island showing Giant Coreopsis, *Coreopsis gigantea,* surrounded by grasses.

The Santa Barbara Island Buckwheat, *Eriogonum giganteum* var. *compactum,* is another endemic cliff dweller. This is a variety of the "Giant" Buckwheat (Fig. 50) that also has endemic varieties on San Clemente and Santa Catalina Islands. All of these cliff-dwelling endemics are visible from the trail that leads from Landing Cove to the visitor center.

Two plants with limited distribution on Santa Barbara Island have from time to time been described as unique to the island. A variety of Cream Cups, *Platystemon californicus* var. *ciliatus* (Fig. 162), is a member of the poppy family (Papaveraceae) that is not recognized as distinct by botanists in general. It is presently known only from the northeast portion of the island. This small annual is characterized by small white to yellowish flowers.

The other endemic is a recently recognized subspecies of Leafy Malacothrix (Fig. 137), *Malacothrix foliosa philbrickii.* This Dandelion-like member of the sunflower family (Asteraceae) also has subspecies on Anacapa, San Clemente, and San Nicolas Islands. A thorough discussion of this group of plants is presented in Chapters 1 and 6.

Two members of the pea family (Fabaceae) are island endemics that are localized on the cliffs. Trask's Milkvetch, *Astragalus traskiae,* found on sandy bluffs on Santa Barbara Island, is also found on San Nicolas Island. Bird's-foot Trefoil, *Lotus argophyllus* var. *argenteus,* is found on the other Southern Channel Islands.

Figure 162. Cream Cups, *Platystemon californicus,* is found on all Channel Islands except San Clemente. Some authorities recognize the variety *ciliatus* as the endemic Santa Barbara Island Cream Cups.

A remnant of Coastal Sage Scrub vegetation is represented by Island Sagebrush, *Artemisia nesiotica.* This island endemic occurs in several localities scattered among the grasses, and it is also present on San Clemente and San Nicolas Islands.

Plants representative of the Maritime Desert Scrub community of the California islands also occur here. California Box Thorn, *Lycium californicum* (Fig. 144), is scattered over much of Santa Barbara Island. Two species of prickly-pear cactus are also present. Coastal Prickly-pear, *Opuntia littoralis* (Fig. 51A; Plate 8C), occurs below elevations of 300 ft (100 m) from Landing Cove to Graveyard Canyon and in Cat Canyon. The other prickly-pear is *Opuntia oricola* (Fig. 52), which is distinguished from the more prostrate form by being taller and having more circular stem joints. Surprisingly more common than Coastal Prickly-pear, it is present

Figure 163. Island Poppy,
Eschscholzia ramosa.

from Cliff Canyon to Cat Canyon and on Sutil Island. The Coastal Cholla,
Opuntia prolifera (Fig. 51B; Plate 8A,B)—recognized by its erect, jointed
structure—is also common on Santa Barbara Island.

Typical of Island Grassland, during the late winter and spring months,
numerous ephemeral wildflowers can also be seen. Some of the more common include Blue Dicks (*Dichelostemma capitatum*) (Fig. 197), Island Poppy
(*Eschscholzia ramosa*) (Fig. 163), Maritime Popcorn Flower (*Cryptantha
maritima*), Fiddleneck (*Amsinckia spectabilis*) (Fig. 155), Rock Daisy (*Per-
ityle emoryi*), and an introduced bedstraw known as Goose Grass (*Galium
aparine*).

Terrestrial Animals

The native terrestrial vertebrates on the island are few (Table 26). Included
is the insular endemic Island Night Lizard, *Xantusia riversiana* (Fig. 151;
Plate 1C), which also occurs on San Clemente and San Nicolas Islands.
Because it is difficult to imagine rafting as a form of interisland transport, and vicariant transport seems impossible because Santa Barbara Island
was totally inundated by seawater from time to time, some biologists speculate that this lizard may have been brought to the island by Native
Americans (see Chapter 1).

TABLE 26   VERTEBRATE ANIMALS OF SANTA BARBARA ISLAND

Reptiles
    Island Night Lizard (*Xantusia riversiana*)—Outer Southern Channel Islands
      endemic

Breeding land birds
    Endemic to Santa Barbara
      Song sparrow (*Melospiza melodia graminea*)—Extirpated
    Island endemics
      Horned Lark (*Eremophila alpestris insularis*)
      Orange-crowned Warbler (*Vermivora celata sordida*)
      House Finch (*Carpodacus mexicanus clementis*)—Southern
        Channel Islands endemic
      Loggerhead Shrike (*Lanius ludovicianus anthonyi*)—Occasional
    Nonendemics
      Peregrine falcon (*Falco peregrinus*)
      Osprey (*Pandion haliaetus*)—Occasional
      American Kestrel (*Falco sparverius*)
      Barn Owl (*Tyto alba*)
      Burrowing Owl (*Athene cunicularia*)
      Costa's Hummingbird (*Calypte costae*)
      Barn Swallow (*Hirundo rustica*)
      Common Raven (*Corvus corax*)
      Northern Mockingbird (*Mimus polyglottos*)
      Rock Wren (*Salpinctes obsoletus*)
      Western Meadowlark (*Sturnella neglecta*)
    Introduced species
      European Starling (*Sturnus vulgaris*)

Sea birds
    Western Gull (*Larus occidentalis*)
    Black Oystercatcher (*Haematopus bachmani*)

Terrestrial mammals
    Santa Barbara Island Deer Mouse (*Peromyscus maniculatus elusus*)—Endemic
    California Bat (*Myotis californicus*)

Introduced mammals
    Domestic Sheep (*Ovis aries*)—Removed
    Domestic Goat (*Capra hircus*)—Removed
    Horse (*Equus caballus*)—Removed
    House Cat (*Felis domesticus*)—Removed
    European Rabbit (*Oryctolagus cuniculus*)—Removed

Marine mammals
    Northern Elephant Seal (*Mirounga angustirostris*)
    Harbor Seal (*Phoca vitulina*)
    California Sea Lion (*Zalophus californianus*)

At least seventy different species of birds have been reported from tiny Santa Barbara Island, but only six appear to be permanent residents: Western Meadow Lark (Fig. 64F), Horned Lark (Fig. 64E), European Starling, Rock Wren (Fig. 64I), Burrowing Owl (Fig. 64A), and Black Oystercatcher (Plate 3C). An endemic race of Song Sparrow, *Melospiza melodia graminea,*

Figure 164. Xantus' Murrelet, *Synthliboramphus hypoleucus*. More of these birds nest on Santa Barbara Island than anywhere else in the world. (Drawing by Gene Christman, from Cogswell 1977.)

is now extinct, as described earlier in this chapter, as a consequence of predation by house cats and a major fire that ravaged the island in 1959. The House Finch (Fig. 110), Bald Eagle (Fig. 65), and Osprey (Fig. 41), all former inhabitants, also appear to have been extirpated. The Peregrine Falcon has apparently reestablished itself on the island recently, along with the Northern Channel Islands. Santa Barbara is the only island on which Costa's Hummingbird, *Calypte costae,* a desert species, has been reported to breed.

At least eleven species of sea birds nest on Santa Barbara Island, making it second in importance only to the islets of San Miguel as a nesting site in the Channel Islands. Thousands of Western Gulls, *Larus occidentalis* (Fig. 192A; Plate 3D), make their open nests in the grasses on the upper terraces (Plate 14C), and the cliffs provide habitat for the nests of Brown Pelicans, *Pelecanus occidentalis* (Fig. 192J; Plate 3A), and what is billed as the world's largest colony of Xantus' Murrelets, *Synthliboramphus hypoleucus* (Fig. 164). About 1500 pairs of these small members of the auk family (Alcidae) nest here.

Among the mammals, the Santa Barbara Island Deer Mouse, *Peromyscus maniculatus elusus* (Fig. 3), is the only endemic. Unfortunately for this small rodent and the nesting land birds previously mentioned, Domestic Cats, *Felis domesticus,* were among the introduced mammals. They first appeared in the late 1800s and by the early 1900s had taken quite a toll. An extermination program was initiated, and by 1978 the last cat had been removed. A small bat, the California Myotis, *Myotis californicus,* is the only other native land mammal reported.

Marine Life

Marine mammals are frequently seen in the waters around the island and on some of the narrow rocky beaches and large rocks. California Sea Lions and Harbor Seals (Figs. 37 and 39; Plate 2C) are present year round. During the months of May and June, Sea Lions use the small, rocky shelf and beaches south of Landing Cove for pupping and mating. Northern Elephant Seals (Figs. 38 and 167) also breed on the island, particularly in the cove that bears their name.

CHAPTER EIGHT

AÑO NUEVO ISLAND

Año Nuevo is located about 20 miles (33 km) north of Santa Cruz in central California. The island is small and rocky, lying about 2600 ft (800 m) offshore. It is separated by a shallow channel from Point Año Nuevo—a low, flat headland that juts 1.2 miles (2 km) out into the Pacific Ocean (Fig. 165). The small, low island is approximately 1300 ft (396 m) long and 850 ft (259 m) wide. There are two sandy beaches, one on each side of the island. Many of the higher parts of the island are also covered with sand and contain the remains of Foghorn House, the former home of the lighthouse keepers.

HISTORY

When the area was first explored by Sebastián Vizcaíno in early 1603, the coastline was much different than it is today. He named Punta de Año Nuevo as he passed it on his way to Point Reyes. No mention was made of the island, and it is believed that the point or cape extended out into the ocean as far as the present island. However, a map of Monterey Bay drawn in 1793 by a Spanish Captain, either Francisco Eliza or Juan Martinez y Zayas, shows an island off Punta Año Nuevo. Apparently erosion of the shoreline formed a channel in the late 1700s. By 1850 the new island was about 1300 ft (400 m) from shore.

Typical erosional processes have continued to alter the coastline in this area. Wind has moved sand dunes across the point, and wave action has caused considerable cliff erosion.

The Native Americans who inhabited the area were Costanoans (Ohlones). We know little about these groups other than that they depended on the sea for their sustenance: they hunted marine mammals in addi-

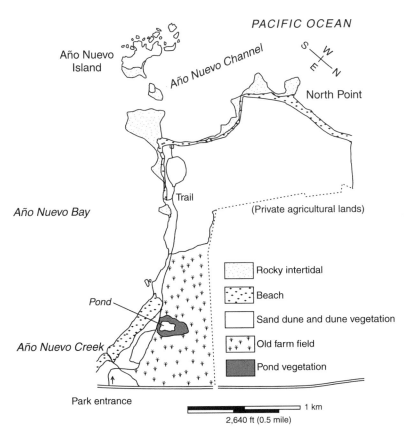

PACIFIC OCEAN

Año Nuevo Island

Año Nuevo Channel

North Point

Trail

Año Nuevo Bay

(Private agricultural lands)

Pond

Año Nuevo Creek

Park entrance

	Rocky intertidal
	Beach
	Sand dune and dune vegetation
	Old farm field
	Pond vegetation

1 km
2,640 ft (0.5 mile)

Figure 165. Año Nuevo State Park.

tion to harvesting intertidal invertebrates. The cherts of the region served as important raw materials for the manufacture of tools, and tool fragments have been found in the sands there. In 1791, with the establishment of the Santa Cruz Mission, alteration of the native life-style and suppression of its culture had begun.

Private ownership of the point and its island began in 1840 when José Simeon de Nepomuceno Castro of Monterey constructed a house and introduced 400 head of cattle, thus establishing occupancy of the new rancho, some 17,753 acres (7187 ha) between the point and Butano Creek. After the Mexican War, in 1851 the land was purchased from Castro's heirs by well-known "mountain man" Isaac Graham, who gained title for $18,000 at a sheriff's sale. Graham took advantage of the fur trade and the gold rush, but his luck eventually ran out and in 1862 the rancho was sold at public auction. Thereafter ownership of the rancho was transferred several

Figure 166. Año Nuevo Island as seen from the mainland.

times. Finally, in response to numerous shipwrecks, in 1870 the federal government purchased the island and nearby Pigeon Point for $10,000 as locations on which to build lighthouses.

The deteriorating lighthouse buildings are still evident on the island (Fig. 166). The first light, on Pigeon Point, was mounted on a 130-ft (42-m) tower atop a 40-ft (33-m) bluff. This light was eventually complemented by a light on the island itself that was on a 68-ft (22-m) tower. As a result one light would shine above the fog and the other below. The first lighthouse keepers and their families shared a small, one-story building on the island. In 1904 a substantial two-story house with fifteen rooms and two baths (now known as Foghorn House) was constructed. It was renovated in 1911. In order to provide fresh water, a catchment basin and a large cistern for rainwater were constructed.

Meanwhile, the sea air, shifting sand, and the presence of numerous sea lions made constant maintenance a problem for the lighthouse keepers, and after World War II the island light station was deemed more trouble than it was worth. The U.S. Coast Guard ordered the station closed in 1948. It was replaced with an automated light on a marker buoy that is anchored just under a mile (1485 m) south of the island.

After the island was abandoned the structures deteriorated rapidly. Vandals destroyed the buildings, sea lions moved in, and the relentless weathering caused the concrete to crack. The metal tower eventually fell over. In 1955 the federal government finally decided to sell the island to the state for $18,094—half its market value. However, the state apparently could not come up with the money, and the sale went into limbo until 1958, when the island was set to pass into private hands for $100,000 at a public auction. But this action merely forced the state to exercise its preexisting option to buy the land, and it did so, paying $52,000, representing half of the market value (as determined by the auction price) plus costs. The state then began buying up portions of the old rancho on the mainland, and by 1979 it owned a large part of the coastline in the area.

Today Año Nuevo Point is a beautiful state park, and the island is classified as a scientific reserve managed by the University of California, Santa Cruz.

GEOLOGY

Año Nuevo Point is a low headland extending from the foot of the Santa Cruz Mountains to the ocean. The point is actually a wave-cut platform or marine terrace known as the Santa Cruz Terrace; it was formed by wave action during an interglacial period that began about 135,000 years ago. At that time sea level was about 25 ft (8 m) higher that it is today.

Remnants of this inundation and subsequent exposure can be seen as a layer of fossil marine organisms in the terrace edge. Molluscs such as rock-boring clams and a few Pliocene corals are present on a bedrock platform that was formed 3.5–5 million years ago.

During the cooler Pleistocene weather and as another glacial period returned, the sea level dropped and beach sands covered the marine deposits. Heavy rainfall in the Santa Cruz Mountains brought large amounts of sand, silt, and gravel out onto the terrace, creating layers of coastal stream deposits on top of the marine material. A small amount of this terrace material still remains on the island, although most has been eroded away over the past several hundred years.

The marine terrace at Año Nuevo Point lies upon bedrock known as the Monterey Formation. This distinctive, light-colored mudstone is the hard, layered rock seen at Año Nuevo Point, and it also forms most of the island. These siliceous mudstones were formed on the ocean floor as clay and silts mixed with the skeletal remains of planktonic organisms, such as radiolarians, diatoms, and certain flagellates. As these organisms died and fell to the ocean floor they were buried within the sediments, resulting in the formation of hard mudstone.

Año Nuevo Island is thus composed of a small remnant portion of the old sea terrace overlying bedrock that is mudstone. The marine terrace material remains along the highest portion of the island. A small area on the northeast or channel side of the island is also covered with beach sand.

Figure 167. Male Northern Elephant Seal, *Mirounga angustirostris.*

TERRESTRIAL VEGETATION

The vegetation of Año Nuevo Island must withstand a variety of abuses. Winds of up to 60 mph (95 km/hr) along with sand and salt spray buffet the low-lying island. On days when the fog evaporates, the island and the peninsula are exposed to intense solar radiation. During the winter months marine mammals haul out on the island and crush the vegetation. Northern Elephant Seals, *Mirounga angustirostris* (Fig. 167), often cover every available beach and lowland area on the island. Two kinds of sea lions use higher areas on the island, creating an additional burden for plants. Their urine increases the nitrogen content of the soil to levels that are toxic to most plants.

The plant communities of nearby Año Nuevo Peninsula are presumably representative of those that formerly occurred on the island itself. Several researchers from the University of California at Santa Cruz have published a compilation of the natural history of the Año Nuevo area with an emphasis on the mainland. Their information, found in *The Natural History of Año Nuevo* by Burney LeBoeuf and Stephanie Kaza, indicates that the plant communities of Año Nuevo include Closed-Cone Pine Forest (the northernmost grove of native Monterey Pines, *Pinus radiata*), Riparian, Freshwater Pond, Coastal Bluff Scrub, and Coastal Strand. In the spring and early summer numerous showy annuals—such as fiddlenecks, *Amsinckia* spp., and paintbrushes, *Castilleja* spp.—as well as beautiful perennials—including the Yellow Bush Lupine, *Lupinus arboreus* (Fig. 168), and Seaside Woolly Sunflower, *Eriophyllum staechadifolium* (Fig. 80)—cover large areas of Año Nuevo.

Figure 168. Yellow Bush Lupine, *Lupinus arboreus.*

ANIMALS

Although Año Nuevo Island is not open to the public except for scientific purposes, the point or peninsula provides an excellent area from which to view both marine and terrestrial life.

On the island, the abundance of terrestrial animals is limited by the absence of vegetation and the impact of marine mammals. However, on the nearby peninsula an assemblage of species typical of the central Coast Ranges is observable.

The rocky intertidal community at the end of Año Nuevo Point supports a large assemblage of marine plants and animals. Numerous species of red, brown, and green algae can be observed at low tide, along with numerous intertidal invertebrates. In several areas along the south shore isolated rocks rise out of sandy substratum and present perfect examples of the intertidal zonation that is so characteristic of the Pacific coast of

North America. For a more extensive discussion of this marine life, see Chapter 4.

Many visitors come to Año Nuevo Island each week to look at water birds. The rocky shores of the point and the sandy beaches of Año Nuevo Bay provide a diverse habitat for many shore birds. Brown Pelicans, gulls, terns, and cormorants can also often be observed in the bay. Each autumn large numbers of Brown Pelicans, *Pelecanus occidentalis* (Fig. 192J; Plate 3A), and Heerman's gulls, *Larus heermanni,* travel north from Mexico to the central California coast to feed on anchovies and other small fish in the rich waters of Año Nuevo Bay.

The most spectacular inhabitants of Año Nuevo Island are the marine mammals that find in the protection of the island an ideal environment for their rookeries. Tiny Año Nuevo Island is the most important pinniped rookery and resting area in central California. At present the island is used by four mammal species: the Northern Elephant Seal (*Mirounga angustirostis*) (Fig. 167), Harbor Seal (*Phoca vitulina*) (Fig. 37; Plate 2C), Northern Sea Lion (*Eumetopias jubatus*) (Fig. 40; Plate 2D), and California Sea Lion (*Zalophus californianus*) (Fig. 39; Plate 2C). Of these, only the California Sea Lion does not breed on the island. All four species of pinnipeds can be observed at any time of the year, although the greatest concentrations of them occur in the winter.

By far the most obvious resident on Año Nuevo Island is the Northern Elephant Seal, a species that came very close to becoming extinct in the late nineteenth century but has made a remarkable recovery in this century. In 1961 the first pups were born on Año Nuevo Island and by 1980 annual pup births on this tiny island exceeded 1200. In fact, beach space became so limited that in the mid-1970s Elephant Seals began using the mainland beaches on Año Nuevo Point. Scientists have taken advantage of this convenient situation. Using small transmitters that can be attached to the animals, as well as satellite tracking technology, investigators have been able to determine that Northern Elephant Seals spend about 90 percent of their time under water when they are at sea, and that males and females feed in different parts of the north Pacific (see Chapter 4).

On the Año Nuevo Peninsula during January and February, visitors can observe Northern Elephant Seal reproductive behavior from a trail leading from the parking area. Before Northern Elephant Seals returned to Año Nuevo, observation of their remarkable breeding behavior was only possible on such remote islands as San Miguel Island, San Nicolas Island, or the islands of Baja California, such as Guadalupe and San Benitos Islands.

The Año Nuevo area is an excellent place to study both plants and animals at any time of the year. In the spring and summer months beautiful flowers can be observed. Low tides during the spring and fall allow the rich intertidal fauna to be exposed for brief periods, and water birds are also numerous at this time. In the winter months marine mammals use the beaches to haul out, and observations of these spectacular animals are experiences never to be forgotten. (Winter visitation at the point and its marine mammal rookeries is by guided tour only; advance registration and purchase of tickets is required.)

CHAPTER NINE

THE FARALLON ISLANDS

The Farallon Islands, also known as the Farallones, are a small group of five islands situated 32 miles (51 km) west of San Francisco. The closest point on the mainland is Point Reyes, 20 miles (32 km) to the northeast. On a rare clear day, they can just be seen from the mainland. The islands are projections of a granitic ridge, about a half mile (800 m) wide and 12 miles (19 km) long, that rises from a seafloor depth of 500 ft (150 m). The total land acreage is 211 acres (83 ha). The South Farallon Islands (Fig. 169), made up of two islands known as West End and Southeast Farallon Island, cover a little over 90 acres (44 ha). West End and Southeast Farallon Island are separated by a narrow gap known as Jordan Channel. Southeast Farallon Island, the largest of the Farallons, is the subject of most of the reports about the group and is the only island in the collection that has been occupied by humans. The highest point of land in the group, at 343 ft (105 m), occurs on this island. Wave-cut terraces at 27 ft (8 m) and 50 ft (15 m) give the island a steplike appearance in profile. Middle Farallon Island is about 2.5 miles (4 km) to the northwest, and the North Farallon Islands are a group of five rocks located 5 miles (8 km) farther to the northwest.

The temperature on the islands is cool throughout the year, with average maximums of 58°F (14°C) in the summer and 54°F (12°C) in the winter, and the warmest temperatures during late summer and early autumn. Yearly precipitation, most of which falls during the winter months, averages about 25 in. (63 cm). Dense fog prevails during summer.

The Farallons are the only major offshore islands in central California, strategically located at the edge of the continental shelf and at the southern margin of the largest upwelling center along the California coast. This combination of factors promotes a nutrient-rich region of high

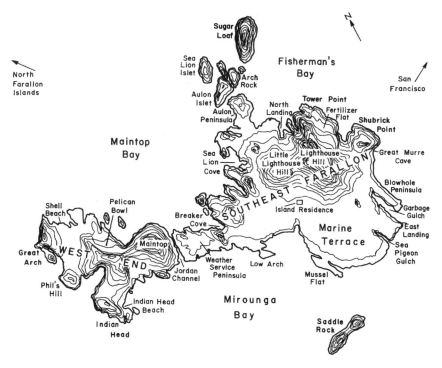

Figure 169. South Farallon Islands (contour interval 6 m). (From Ainley and Boekelheide 1990.)

productivity that encourages large populations of oceanic fishes, sea birds, and marine mammals in a region where there are limited breeding sites for nesting birds and marine mammals. Thus these islands support the greatest breeding sea bird colony in the lower forty-eight states as well as important rookeries for marine mammals.

Rough seas prevent most access to the northern islands, and Southeast Farallon Island can be reached only by means of a somewhat precarious lift by a crane and a conical ring-net known as "Billy Pugh." The inaccessibility of these islands to humans adds to their desirability as nesting sites for sea birds. Because disturbance is a major threat to these birds, human visitation is restricted to authorized research and official inspection.

HISTORY

The Spanish named the Farallon Islands in the 1600s. The word *farallon* is a Spanish nautical term meaning "cliff" or "small island in the sea."

The history of the Farallon Islands is primarily a story of exploitation of marine life. The islands were first visited by Europeans in 1579 when Sir Frances Drake stopped there to kill seals for meat. In the early 1800s hunters took thousands of Northern Fur Seals and Northern Elephant Seals from the islands. During the 1850s the islands were a regular stop for egg collectors, who gathered millions of murre eggs for the booming mining town of San Francisco. Apparently there were few domestic hens in San Francisco, and commercial egg collecting from tiny Southeast Farallon Island continued until the turn of the century, when the California Academy of Sciences and the American Ornithological Union succeeded in halting commercial egg collecting. Of course, poachers continued to collect eggs illegally on the island for many years thereafter.

One of the first lighthouses on the west coast was established on Southeast Farallon Island in 1855 by the U.S. Coast Guard. Two frame houses, along with a narrow-gauge rail system, were later built to service the light. Several keepers and their families, along with domestic animals (including cats, dogs, pigs, and a mule) lived there until 1965. In 1972 the facility was automated and all Coast Guard personnel were withdrawn.

The North Farallon Islands were designated a national wildlife refuge in 1909, but the South Farallon Islands were not included until 1969. The refuge is administered by the Sacramento National Wildlife Refuge under the U.S. Fish and Wildlife Service. Since 1968 biologists from the Point Reyes Bird Observatory have been monitoring bird populations on East Farallon Island. With headquarters on Bolinas Lagoon near Stinson Beach, the observatory was begun in 1965 by bird enthusiasts of the San Francisco Bay area. The observatory is now funded by contracts and grants from the U.S. Fish and Wildlife Service, the National Science Foundation, and several private companies and foundations.

GEOLOGY

The rocks that make up the Farallons are largely granitic. The quartz diorite is coarsely crystalline, much fissured, easily decomposed, and similar to that exposed at Point Reyes, on the mainland to the northeast. Sugarloaf Rock, a small islet to the north, is composed of a conglomerate of huge, rounded boulders and sandstone, similar to that found at the Point Reyes Light.

Point Reyes and the Farallon Islands lie west of the San Andreas fault on a geological terrane known as the Salinian Block (Fig. 7). They form the northernmost portions of this granitic terrane. Northern translocation of this block has brought much of the southern Coast Ranges (including the Farallon Islands and Point Reyes) northward from a former position south of the Sierra Nevada range. The granitics of the Farallon Islands, therefore, were formerly located at about the latitude of present-day Los Angeles.

There seems to be no evidence of possible connections to the main-

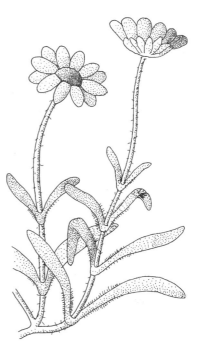

Figure 170. Maritime Goldfields, *Lasthenia maritima.*

land, although the maximum water depth between the island and the mainland is 180 ft (60 m); this implies that at its lowest point, a lowered sea level about 20,000 years ago would have been sufficient to permit connection of South Farallon Island to the mainland. A rising sea level could have created the island group about 11,000 years ago.

TERRESTRIAL VEGETATION

Only a portion of Southeast Farallon Island near the lighthouse provides suitable habitat for terrestrial plants. One group of past visitors, perhaps Russian fur hunters, introduced the European Rabbit, *Oryctolagus cuniculus* (Fig. 159), to Southeast Farallon Island, and the population has fluctuated between forty and several hundred individuals over the years. These rabbits probably had considerable impact on the sparse vegetation of the island and contributed to the extirpation of the Rhinoceros Auklet, *Cerorhinca monocerata.* The rabbbits and the last cats were removed in 1974, but House Mice, *Mus musculus,* which were introduced in the 1800s, are still present.

The island with all its rocky cliffs offers little foothold for plants. Most of the vegetation is on the 50-ft (15-m) terrace. The most common species is Maritime Goldfields, *Lasthenia maritima* (Fig. 170). Known locally as "Farallon Weed," this is a low-growing, yellow-flowered composite that forms a mat over some of the eastern portion of the island, where it can actually reach a thickness of about 1.5 ft (40 cm). Approximately twenty-three species of introduced plants, mostly grasses, occur on the island, mainly in the southeast corner. An additional thirteen species of native plants have been found, many of which are spring-blooming wildflowers. A few introduced Monterey Cypress, *Cupressus macrocarpa,* used to occur near the lighthouse, and two of these trees, about 25 ft (8 m) tall, still remain.

TERRESTRIAL ANIMALS

No systematic surveys of the terrestrial or marine invertebrates of the Farallon Islands have been carried out. Apparently various insects, such as carabid beetles and several species of Orthoptera, have been found. Two large banana slugs (*Ariolimax* spp.) and other mollusc species have also been identified on the islands.

There is a population of Arboreal Salamanders, *Aneides lugubris* (Fig. 62), on the Farallon Islands. These salamanders are frequently associated with oak trees, although there are no native oaks on the Farallons. Throughout most of its range the salamander is characterized by small yellow spots. Of interest here is that on the islands the salamanders show a pattern of large spots that is also typical of the forms in the Gabilan Range east of Monterey. The Farallon Islands and the Gabilan Range are both west of the San Andreas fault. The Farallons are pure weathered granite and the Gabilans also contain much granite. It is apparent that the Gabilan Range was also once an island. Thus it has been postulated that the Gabilans and Farallons were once part of a single long peninsula. Whether or not the Farallons were ever large enough to have remained continuously above sea level is subject to some conjecture. It is possible that the salamanders were carried to the island on a log raft, or it may be that these wave-lashed outcrops are all that remain of a former large land mass, perhaps connected to the mainland as recently as 11,000 years ago. Small spotted members of this species are also found on Santa Catalina Island, but they have not been studied thoroughly enough to determine how different they are from the mainland forms.

No native reptiles or mammals are present on the islands.

As for vertebrates, the Farallons are known primarily for their birds. As a result of the activities of the Point Reyes Bird Observatory, hundreds of scientists have conducted studies on the Farallon Islands since 1965. A continuous monitoring program has identified 337 bird species on or near the islands. In addition to the sea birds, hundreds of vagrant land birds land on Southeast Farallon Island, especially during May and June. Many of these birds are banded and released; their subsequent recovery provides information on the species' life history and migration patterns. Although most research on the islands centers on birds, marine mammals are also being studied.

The only resident land bird appears to be the Rock Wren, *Salpinctes obsoletus* (Fig. 64I). Winter residents include the American Kestrel (*Falco sparverius*) (Fig. 64B), European Starling (*Sturnus vulgaris*), Western Meadowlark (*Sturnella neglecta*), and White-crowned Sparrow (*Zonotrichia leucophrys*) (Fig. 156). In total, however, the migrant bird tally including sea birds numbers 380 species.

SEA BIRDS

Sea birds are extremely abundant on the Farallons. At the peak of the breeding season in May, as many as 150,000 nesting adult birds are present. They make up two-thirds of the marine bird species that reproduce on the Pacific Coast north of Mexico, the largest sea bird rookery south of Alaska. For a complete discussion of sea birds see Chapter 4.

Twelve species of sea birds are known to nest on the Farallons. One of the most numerous species, some 40,000 to 50,000 strong, is the burrow-nesting Cassin's Auklet, *Ptychoramphus aleuticus* (Fig. 171), which nests on the marine terraces and talus slopes. These pelagic birds flock to small islands along the coast of California to breed during the winter months. Although they were formerly the most common bird on the Farallons, their population has been cut in half in the last twenty years, perhaps because of an increase in water temperature or competition for nest sites with Western Gulls and cormorants. These krill-feeding birds nest in burrows, where it takes about 40 days for chicks to fledge. On East Farallon Island the burrows were once so common that the area was dubbed the "auklet minefield."

The world's largest nesting population of Western Gulls, *Larus occidentalis* (Figs. 172 and 192A; Plate 3D), is found on East Farallon Island. Western Gulls nest mainly on the lower slopes and flat areas of the island. For a number of years biologists from the Point Reyes Bird Observatory have fitted more than 2000 Western Gull chicks with color-coded leg bands each spring for future identification. It is believed that the Western Gulls increased their nesting on Southeast Farallon Island when Common Murre colonies were decimated by egg hunters in the last part of the nineteenth century. It is also believed that the gulls fly to the mainland to feed in the dumps, and that that abundant food source has enabled their numbers to increase while populations of other bird species were in decline.

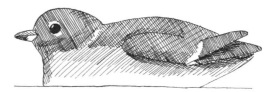

Figure 171. Cassin's Auklet, *Ptychoramphus aleuticus*.

Figure 172. The world's largest nesting population of Western Gulls, *Larus occidentalis,* occurs on Southeast Farallon Island. (Photograph by Ian C. Tait.)

Common Murres, *Uria aalge* (Fig. 173), nest on inaccessible cliffs and ledges. Egg collectors often climbed down these steep cliffs with ropes and placed the eggs in baskets. The Common Murre population of Southeast Farallon Island has recovered so that about 75,000 of these birds now breed there, making them the most common birds on the island.

Many thousands of Brandt's Cormorants, *Phalacrocorax penicillatus*—the large, crestless species—also nest on the island in closely aggregated colonies on relatively flat areas. Several thousand of the smaller Pelagic Cormorants, *Phalacrocorax pelagicus,* also nest, chiefly on cliff areas and rocky ledges of the island. The Double-crested Cormorant, *Phalacrocorax auritus* (Plate 3B), is represented by only one nesting colony.

Two species of storm-petrels nest on Southeast Farallon Island: the Ashy Storm-Petrel, *Oceanodroma homochroa* (Fig. 174), and Leach's Storm-Petrel, *Oceanodroma leucorhoa.* These small birds feed on tiny fish and planktonic animals and, like the auklets, only come ashore to nest.

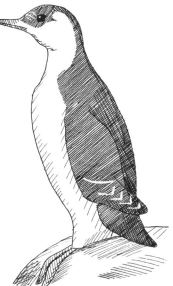

Figure 173. Common Murre, *Uria aalge.*

Figure 174. Ashy Storm-Petrel,
Oceanodroma homochroa.

Another bird that nests on the island and is closely related to the murres is the Pigeon Guillemot, *Cepphus columba* (Fig. 175). This medium-sized dark bird with white wing bands and red feet feeds on small fish and is common on Southeast Farallon Island. Other nesting birds include a few pairs of Black Oystercatchers, *Haematopus bachmani* (Plate 3C), and Tufted Puffins, *Fratercula cirrhata* (Fig. 176).

Figure 175. Pigeon Guillemot, *Cepphus columba.*

Figure 176. Tufted Puffin, *Fratercula cirrhata.* The southernmost breeding colony of these colorful sea birds is on the Farallon Islands.

The effect of all of these nesting birds on the other biota is of concern to some biologists. It has been reported, for example, that the tremendous number of cormorants has collapsed the burrows of some of the petrels and auklets. Western Gulls prey on the other species, particularly the storm-petrels. In addition, biologists have found the seeds of Maritime Gold-fields stuck in the feathers of some of the birds, indicating that birds are an important dispersal mechanism for the plant. Seeds of the nonnative Ice Plant, along with gelatinous ooze from the plants, have been found on the feet of certain sea birds. In other cases, droppings from numerous birds affect the flora by altering the chemical composition of the soil. The influence of nesting herons on the flora of the Marin Islands in San Francisco Bay is discussed in Chapter 10. Now that most of the California islands are administered by public agencies, the influence of humans has been reduced to a minimum. In the absence of human interference, the size of bird populations on many islands will increase, and the impact of this trend will no doubt be the subject of considerable controversy.

MARINE MAMMALS

Northern Fur Seals, *Callorhinus ursinus,* probably first attracted the attention of hunters in the 1800s. A small Russian fishing and sealing colony was established on Southeast Farallon Island at the beginning of the nineteenth century. The Russians brought in Aleuts from Alaska to hunt the seals, and by 1825 they had killed off all Northern Fur Seals and begun to hunt the other pinnipeds, namely Northern Elephant Seals, *Mirounga angustirostris* (Figs. 38 and 167), Northern Sea Lions, *Eumetopias jubatus* (Fig. 40; Plate 2D) and California Sea Lions, *Zalophus californianus* (Fig. 39; Plate 2C).

The Northern or Steller's Sea Lion continues to be present on the island, but the population of Northern Fur Seals appears not to have recovered. It is interesting to note, however, that in 1996 a Northern Fur Seal bull, three females, and a pup were found on West End Island. This record, along with increasing numbers on San Miguel Island, may signify that the species is returning to southern waters.

One of the most significant aspects of Farallon Island natural history involves the recent reestablishment of Northern Elephant Seals on Southeast Farallon Island. In 1959 the first one was sighted, and by 1971 over 100 juveniles had been counted during the winter-to-spring breeding season, when most adults come ashore. California Sea Lions and Harbor Seals, *Phoca vitulina* (Fig. 37; Plate 2C), are now also breeding on the Farallon Islands. For a complete discussion of marine mammals see Chapter 4.

A large number of attacks by Great White Sharks, *Carcharodon carcharias,* occur on various species of seals and sea lions in the vicinity of the Farallons. Since 1969 scientists from the Point Reyes Bird Observatory have observed such attacks, mainly in the late summer and early fall months, while conducting censuses of bird and marine mammal populations. In 1987 a continuous watch during daylight hours was established each fall by observers stationed at the peak of Lighthouse Hill on

Southeast Farallon Island, and videotape records were kept from 1988 to 1992. The sharks visit the Farallon Islands during the fall, their arrival corresponding to the arrival of juvenile Northern Elephant Seals, their apparent favorite prey.

From direct observations and analysis of the videotapes, a fairly clear picture of white shark predatory behavior has emerged. Around the Farallon Islands, Great White Sharks attack pinnipeds relatively close to shore, with most attacks occurring within a zone extending from 80 to 1500 ft (25–450 m) from shore. Most attacks occur during the morning hours, apparently at times when high tides have displaced basking seals from their beaches. Great White Sharks tend to attack by biting the animals first, apparently in order to induce bleeding and cause death by blood loss. The dead animals are typically observed some time later floating motionless on the surface; the sharks then return to the prey and begin feeding.

The Farallon Islands are the setting for some of the most intense and powerful predator-prey interactions on earth. They are a great location for viewing natural history firsthand, but because of their fragile bird populations, access must be restricted. Furthermore, with such a large population of Great White Sharks, the islands are not a suitable area for diving or other water sports.

CHAPTER TEN

THE ISLANDS OF SAN FRANCISCO BAY

San Francisco Bay (Fig. 177) is a drowned river mouth occurring at the confluence of two great rivers, the Sacramento and the San Joaquin, which together drain the 430-mile (690-km)–long Great Central Valley of California. The bay—with its single entrance, the Golden Gate, and its elongate shape—was formed by the downcutting of the two rivers during a Pleistocene glacial interval when sea level was much lower. Now, with warmer temperatures, sea level has risen, flooding the old river mouths and isolating hilltops as islands. On a clear day many of the islands—including Alcatraz Island, Angel Island, Brooks Island, the Brothers, Red Rock, the Sisters, the Marin Islands, and Yerba Buena/Treasure Island—are visible from each other.

The point at which the two river systems converge is a large delta, the Sacramento–San Joaquin Delta, which today has been developed mostly for agricultural purposes. Within this delta are many natural and man-made islands caused by the braiding of preexisting and artificial waterways. With the exception of Browns Island, these islands will not be considered here, nor will other largely disturbed land masses, such as Mare Island Naval Shipyard.

The climate in the San Francisco Bay area is typically maritime, and it is heavily influenced by cold sea waters. During the winter the water temperature averages a chilly 52°F (11°C). In summer it is scarcely warmer, averaging only 60°F (16°C). Fog is frequent, particularly in the spring, and the sky is overcast more than half the time year round. The average daily maximum air temperature is 69°F (21°C) and the average daily minimum is 46°F (8°C). Average yearly precipitation is 21 in. (533 mm), most of which falls during the winter, as is typical of California's Mediterranean climate.

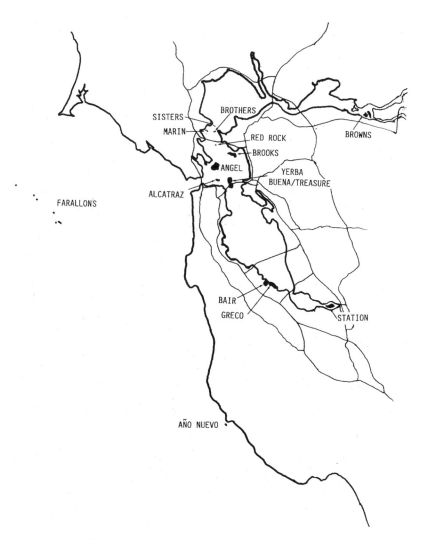

Figure 177. Location of islands in San Francisco Bay.

HISTORY

Shell middens, indicative of habitation by Native Americans, are found on Angel Island, Brooks Island, East Marin Island, and Yerba Buena Island. No doubt several tribal groups—such as the Costanoan (Ohlone), Miwok, and Wintun (Patwin)—traveled the waters of San Francisco Bay over the years, but the tribe most often identified with the islands is the Coast Miwoks. These Native Americans called themselves the *Mewah,* which means "the people." The Spanish called them the *Mewan,* which later became *Miwok.* The Miwoks consisted of at least three linguistic groups:

the Coast Miwoks, Lake Miwoks, and Sierra Miwoks. For the most part, the Coast Miwoks inhabited the area to the north and west of San Francisco Bay.

Native Americans traveled about the area in simple boats made of tules or bulrushes (*Scirpus* spp.), the marsh plants that bordered the bay. These boats, called *balsas* by the Spanish, were about 10 ft (3 m) long and were constructed with rolls of the marsh plants lashed together.

The first sighting of San Francisco Bay and its islands by Europeans took place in 1769 when Gaspar de Portolá's men climbed to the top of Sweeney Ridge west of the bay. Padre Crespi, the priest accompanying the expedition, recorded sighting two large islands in the bay, which are known today as Angel Island and Yerba Buena Island. In August 1775 Juan Manuel de Ayala sailed through the Golden Gate in a Spanish packet ship, the *San Carlos,* and made the first nautical survey of the bay. Ayala named Angel Island "Nuestra Señora de Los Angeles" and first called Yerba Buena Island "Isla de Los Alcatraces" after the pelicans or cormorants he observed there. In 1826 the name "Alcatraz" was erroneously transferred to the small sandstone island that bears that title today.

In 1821 Mexico declared its independence from Spain and took control of California. In 1835, under Mexican rule, the pueblo of San Francisco was founded as the commercial center for the ranches around San Francisco Bay. The pueblo was first known as Yerba Buena, after an aromatic plant that grew in the area, and that was later to become the name of the island that lay to the east. In July 1846, two months after war broke out with Mexico, Captain John B. Montgomery landed at the pueblo of Yerba Buena in his sloop-of-war, the USS *Portsmouth,* and raised the American flag, claiming the territory for the United States. The Treaty of Guadalupe Hidalgo, officially ending the Mexican War, was signed on February 2, 1848, just a few days after gold was discovered at Sutter's Mill. Thus began the period of American control that led to the building of military facilities on Alcatraz, Angel, and Yerba Buena Islands.

Today Angel Island is a state park, Alcatraz Island and its former prison are managed by the National Park Service as part of the Golden Gate National Recreation Area, and Yerba Buena Island (along with its connected, artificial Treasure Island) at this writing is being vacated by the U.S. Navy as recommended by the 1993 Base Realignment and Closure Commission. Brooks Island and Browns Island are managed by the East Bay Regional Park District. The Marin Islands are currently managed by the U.S. Fish and Wildlife Service as the Marin Islands National Wildlife Refuge and Ecological Reserve.

The islands have not always appeared as they do today. Before all of the human activity on the islands, Angel Island supported a substantial forest. Alcatraz and Yerba Buena Islands were essentially bird rookeries. According to Edwin Bryant, who published his descriptions of San Francisco Bay in *What I Saw in California,* on October 13, 1846, "Yerba Buena and several other small islands in the bay . . . [were] white, as if covered with snow, from the deposits upon them of bird-manure. Tens of thousands of wild geese, ducks, gulls, and other water-fowls were perched upon them, or sporting in the waters of the bay, making a prodigious cackling and clatter with their voices and wings."

Political boundaries do not always reflect geographic boundaries. One peculiar case is illustrated by the official boundary between Marin and San Francisco Counties. In 1860 the official county line was established as running from the northwest corner of Red Rock Island (west of Point Richmond, just south of the Richmond Bridge) southward to the southeastern point of Angel Island. In this process, the western 731 acres (287 ha) of Angel Island became a part of Marin County, and are now within the city limits of Tiburon. The eastern 31 acres lie in the combined city and county of San Francisco. Thus it is possible to take a boat from San Francisco to Tiburon and within a few steps walk back into San Francisco! Even more unlikely is the situation on the small island of Red Rock, only 9 acres (3.5 ha) in size. County lines converge there in such a way that it is technically possible to stand simultaneously in three counties: Contra Costa, Marin, and San Francisco.

GEOLOGY

In general the islands of San Francisco Bay are the products of faulting, downwarping, and flooding (Fig. 178). The Franciscan Formation makes up the basement rock of all the islands in the bay (Fig. 7). These rocks, dating to the Jurassic period, are about 150 million years old. They are associated with the offshore trench that was formed during subduction of the ocean floor under the North American plate, and they were named for deposits near the city of San Francisco. Franciscan rocks are dominated by sandstones and shales that were formed by rapid erosion of a volcanic highland and deposited in deep marine basins. About 90 percent of Franciscan rocks are gray-green in color and are known as graywackes. Graywackes are sandstones, interbedded with lesser amounts of dark-colored shale, occasional limestone, and reddish, silica-rich cherts. (It is

Figure 178 (*opposite*). General geology of the San Francisco Bay region. (After *Geologic Map of California,* compiled by the U.S. Geologic Survey in cooperation with the California Division of Mines and Geology, 1965.)

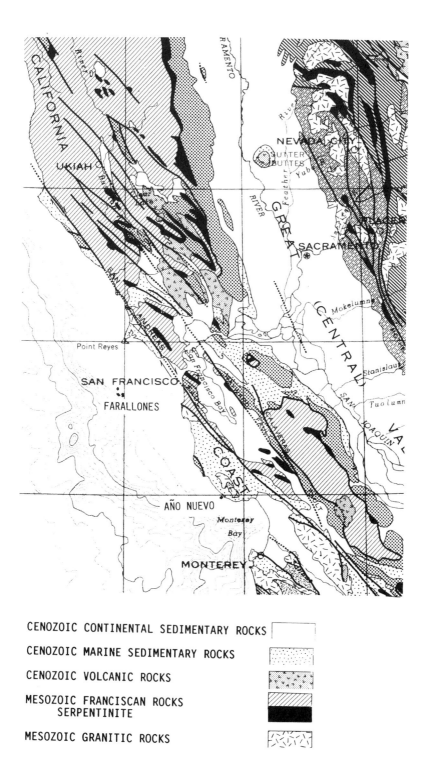

CENOZOIC CONTINENTAL SEDIMENTARY ROCKS

CENOZOIC MARINE SEDIMENTARY ROCKS

CENOZOIC VOLCANIC ROCKS

MESOZOIC FRANCISCAN ROCKS
    SERPENTINITE

MESOZOIC GRANITIC ROCKS

the presence of these cherts that gives Red Rock Island it name.) Franciscan sedimentary rocks have become intruded by volcanic rocks that have become metamorphosed, probably by heated seawater, to become the waxy green rock known as serpentine or serpentinite. This attractive, hydrothermally altered rock has been designated the state rock of California.

The gap that lies between Angel Island and the Tiburon Peninsula, known as Raccoon Strait, is 234 ft (78 m) deep. Except for the main channel of the Golden Gate, this is the deepest part of San Francisco Bay. It is a trough formed by the ancestral Sacramento River during a glacial episode when most of the bay area was above sea level. At that time Angel Island was connected by dry land southward to present-day Alcatraz Island, Yerba Buena Island, and the mainland, most likely in the vicinity of Rincon Hill on the San Francisco peninsula. Borings on each side of Yerba Buena Island to determine the depth of bedrock in the bay indicate that the main prebay channel from the south lay to the east of the island and not to the west, as is currently the case.

Most authorities agree that sea level has continued to rise for the last 16,000–18,000 years and that it reached levels similar to those today about 5000 years ago. It may be inferred, therefore, that most of the islands in the bay have been islands for at least that length of time.

The shape of the modern islands has been altered by the activities of humans. For example, sandstone was quarried from Angel Island, Brooks Island, and East Marin Island. Earth was added to Alcatraz Island to make it flatter and bigger, and the entire mass of Treasure Island is a landfill, now connected to the natural, but smaller, Yerba Buena Island. Since the 1800s military occupation of Alcatraz Island, Angel Island, and Yerba Buena Island has altered not only the terrestrial vegetation but also the topography.

TERRESTRIAL VEGETATION

Most of the native plant communities that once occurred on the San Francisco Bay islands have been so disturbed that we can only guess what they looked like in the 1800s. Several of the islands in the bay were so heavily used by sea birds that significant stands of terrestrial plants were unable to become established. Alcatraz Island, East and West Brothers, the Marin Islands, and Red Rock have been inhabited by sea birds for centuries. Yerba Buena Island, formerly called Bird Island, also had significant bird populations, although it is large enough that terrestrial plant communities were once firmly established there. Angel Island, Brooks Island, the Marin Islands, and Yerba Buena Island were the only islands of sufficient size and topography to support several different plant communities. The native

Figure 179. Pacific Madrone, *Arbutus menziesii.*

communities, which are still present, have been highly altered, but sufficient numbers of native plants remain that it is still possible to get at least
a cursory picture of what the first Europeans must have seen.

More thorough descriptions of plant communities are found in Chapters 5 and 6 on the Channel Islands.

Mixed Evergreen Forest

The only California islands on which this community—a mixture of
broad-leaved evergreen species and conifers (Plate 16B)—is found are in
San Francisco Bay. In the northern Coast Ranges this is a moist forest characterized by Douglas Fir, *Pseudotsuga menziesii.* Farther south, and at lower
elevations, broad-leaved evergreens—such as Pacific Madrone, *Arbutus
menziesii* (Fig. 179; Plate 16C), and California Laurel, *Umbellularia californica* (Fig. 180)—become more common. Although Tanoak or Tanbark
Oak, *Lithocarpus densiflorus,* is also a component of this forest on the mainland, it is apparently not found on the islands today. In canyon bottoms
on Angel Island, a deciduous species, Big-leaf Maple, *Acer macrophyllum*
(Fig. 181), also becomes a significant component of this forest.

Tanoak is an evergreen species of the beech-oak family (Fagaceae) that
is more closely allied to the oaks of southeast Asia. The tree is called Tanoak
because it was once a major commercial source of tannin, the substance

Figure 180. California Laurel, *Umbellularia californica.*

Figure 181. Big-leaf Maple, *Acer macrophyllum*, showing distinctive winged fruits (samaras).

used to preserve or tan leather. Unless the acorns were visible, a person would not guess that this is an oak. The leaves are large, oblong, and leathery, up to 5 in. (13 cm) in length. They have a wavy, toothed margin, and their undersides are hairy. This is a relict species that is distributed in moist locations from southern Oregon to southern California. Along with

Pacific Madrone, California Laurel, and Coast Redwood, it is a remnant of a forest that enjoyed a much larger distribution in the past. The acorns of Tanoak are fairly large; Native Americans found them particularly palatable after the tannins had been leached out.

Pacific Madrone looks like a large manzanita. It is an evergreen tree with large, oblong leaves similar in shape to those of Tanoak. However, the leaves differ from those of Tanoak in lacking a hairy underside and usually lacking a toothed margin. Pacific Madrone grows northward as far as Canada; as such it is the most northerly occurring evergreen hardwood tree. In California its distribution is similar to that of Tanoak, and the two species usually occur together. There should be no mistaking the two species, however: Tanoak has brown, deeply furrowed bark, whereas Pacific Madrone has smooth, red bark that peels off in papery sheets on the branches. The flowers on Pacific Madrone are similar to manzanita flowers: they are white and urn shaped, and they occur in clusters. The flowers are typical of the heath family (Ericaceae), to which both manzanitas and Pacific Madrone belong. Also similar to manzanita, Pacific Madrone produces bright orange to red berries in autumn. Pacific Madrone is a handsome tree that does well in residential landscapes when it receives adequate amounts of water. It is particularly attractive where it occurs among Coast Redwoods: the towering redwoods create so much shade that the Pacific Madrone, in its quest for light, may develop a tortuously twisted trunk, which may be cloaked with bright green lichens.

California Laurel is an evergreen tree with dark green, lance-shaped leaves, up to 5 in. (13 cm) in length. The most distinctive feature of the leaves is their peppery, aromatic odor. They are shaped like bay leaves, and they may be used in cooking; therefore, this tree is sometimes referred to as California Bay or Bay Laurel. The leaves' odor is quite pungent when they are broken and very pleasant in small doses; however, it is not wise to sniff the odor for too long because it is known to cause headaches. Of the three evergreen species mentioned here, this is the one that occurs most commonly in southern California, where it is a frequent component of riparian communities. This tropical relict belongs to the laurel family (Lauraceae), which includes several trees of economic importance, such as avocado, camphor, and cinnamon. California Laurel is the only member of this tropical family to occur in California. The wood of this tree is very beautiful, and it is commonly used in the manufacture of carved figurines, gun stocks, trays, and bowls. Along the southern coast of Oregon the tree is called Oregon Myrtle, and carvings made of so-called myrtlewood are popular among tourists in Oregon. Many myrtlewood objects carry a sticker with the erroneous information that this tree is unique to the Oregon coast or the "Holy Land." How strange that one would make such a claim, when the scientific name of the tree refers to the state of California!

In the northern Coast Ranges, California Laurel is commonly called Pepperwood. In areas associated with serpentine-derived soils, particularly where springs keep the soil wet, California Laurel may form shrubby thickets. In the northern Coast Ranges alone, there are at least ten localities called Pepperwood.

Historically, only Angel Island probably had significant stands of Mixed Evergreen Forest, although the Marin Islands and Yerba Buena may have had some members of the community growing on them. But the wood-cutting activities of early visitors took care of that. Richard Henry Dana, author of *Two Years Before the Mast,* referred to Angel Island as Wood Island in 1835. Upon his return, 24 years later, he noted that the island was nearly denuded. Photographs from the late 1800s show the hillsides of Angel Island to be quite barren, perhaps like the south-facing slope appears today, as a result of the removal of the nonnative forest of Blue Gums. Since Dana's time, however, native trees have reappeared, and a disturbed version of Mixed Evergreen Forest can be seen in the canyons and on the slopes of the north side of the island. In the wooded canyons near Ayala Cove there are mature specimens of Big-leaf Maple, California Laurel, and Pacific Madrone. Mixed in with these species are components of Oak Woodland, described in the following section.

Oak Woodland

Communities dominated by various oak species occur throughout California. On the Channel Islands there are Island Woodland and Southern Oak Woodland; in the foothills of the western Sierra Nevada there is Foothill Woodland; and in the northern Coast Ranges at higher elevations there is a community called Northern Oak Woodland.

Oak woodlands in their various forms are mixtures of trees and grasses. Many authorities refer to this type of community as a savannah, although in canyon bottoms and on north-facing slopes the trees may form more of a forest. In general, the distance between the trees is a function of precipitation, evaporation, or both.

In the Coast Ranges in the vicinity of San Francisco Bay, the dominant tree species include Blue Oak, *Quercus douglasii* (Fig. 93A), and Gray Pine or Digger Pine, *Pinus sabiniana,* although these species do not seem to occur on the islands in San Francisco Bay today. At slightly higher elevations and on north-facing slopes, particularly in the northern Coast Ranges, California Buckeye, *Aesculus californica* (Fig. 182), becomes locally com-

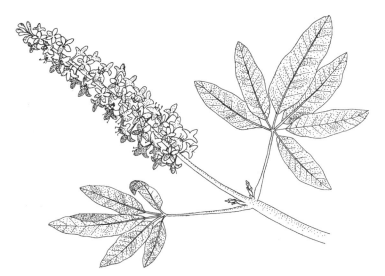

Figure 182. California Buckeye, *Aesculus californica.*

Figure 183. Oaks of the San Francisco Bay islands. (A) Coast Live Oak, *Quercus agrifolia.* (B) Interior Live Oak, *Quercus wislizenii* var. *frutescens.*

mon, and it is found on the islands. Redbud, *Cercis occidentalis,* may be locally common in the northern Coast Ranges as well.

Other oaks of the Coast Ranges include Coast Live Oak, *Quercus agrifolia* (Fig. 183A); Interior Live Oak, *Quercus wislizenii* (Fig. 183B); and Valley Oak, *Quercus lobata* (Fig. 93B). The latter is also absent from the islands today.

To the south of the Coast Ranges, Blue Oak is ultimately replaced by Coast Live Oak. Where the two species occur together, in the southern Coast Ranges, Blue Oak tends to grow on south-facing slopes and Coast Live Oak grows on north-facing slopes. On Angel Island, Coast Live Oak may be the most common tree species. Interior Live Oak and Valley Oak are more common toward the interior of the Coast Ranges, where Oak Woodland grades into Valley Grassland. Valley Oak dominates in valleys and on gentle, upper slopes with deep soils. The shrub version of Interior Live Oak, *Quercus wislizenii* var. *frutescens* (Fig. 183B), is found on some of the islands in San Francisco Bay.

In canyons throughout California, particularly on north-facing slopes, Canyon Live Oak or Golden-cup Oak, *Quercus chrysolepis,* is found. Canyon Live Oak is the most widely distributed oak in California, although today it appears to be absent from the islands in San Francisco Bay. Although Canyon Live Oak resembles Coast Live Oak in size and shape, the leaves of Canyon Live Oak have small whitish hairs on their undersides. The leaf margins of Canyon Live Oak are also highly variable, ranging from smooth to spiny. It may therefore be identified at a glance by noting the white undersides of the leaves and the variety of leaf shapes on a single tree.

North of San Francisco the ranges of Coast Live Oak and Interior Live Oak overlap. Where this occurs, differences in microclimatic preferences between the two species become apparent. Coast Live Oak tends to occur more commonly on the coastal-facing slopes where there is more soil moisture. Interior Live Oak is more common on the slopes that face away from the coast, and it becomes more common toward the interior of the Coast Ranges. Where the two species occur together, they may hybridize, indicating that they have not been separate species for a long time. Identification of the two species where their ranges overlap is complicated by this hybridization, but in their pure forms they can be identified by the color of their leaves. The leaves of Interior Live Oak are bright green and shiny on both surfaces, whereas those of Coast Live Oak are a darker green and shiny only on the top surface. Coast Live Oak also has small tufts of hairs where leaf veins intersect on the lower surfaces of the leaves.

On Angel Island, Coast Live Oak and California Buckeye co-occur with the Mixed Evergreen species to produce a hybrid version of Mixed Evergreen Forest. Vestiges of that mixture still occur on the north side of the Marin Islands as well (Fig. 203). A similar community probably occurred formerly on north-facing slopes of Yerba Buena Island, but that island today contains a forest of introduced tree species (plate 15A).

Northern Coastal Scrub

Northern Coastal Scrub is the northern version of Coastal Sage Scrub. It lacks the succulent species of Coastal Sage Scrub, but it still includes California Sagebrush, *Artemisia californica* (Fig. 45A). Where it occurs on the islands in San Francisco Bay, it is often dominated by Coyote Brush, *Baccharis pilularis* (Fig. 45B; Plate 16A). Also often present is Toyon, *Het-*

Figure 184. Eastwood Manzanita, *Arctostaphylos glandulosa*.

eromeles arbutifolia (Fig. 54), a large-leaved evergreen shrub that grows in canyons and on north-facing slopes. It often becomes mixed with Chaparral or Oak Woodland species as well. More scattered in distribution, but spectacular in bloom, are Yellow Bush Lupine, *Lupinus arboreus* (Fig. 168), and Pitcher Sage, *Lepechinia calycina*.

Island Chaparral

Evergreen sclerophyllous shrubs such as those described for the Channel Islands form a community on the ridges and dry slopes of Angel Island. Although some authors refer to chaparral as occurring on Yerba Buena and West Marin Islands, they are in fact referring to the presence of Toyon, *Heteromeles arbutifolia* (Fig. 54), and Coyote Brush, *Baccharis pilularis* (Fig. 45B), which are more appropriately considered to be components of Northern Coastal Scrub. Indicator species for Island Chaparral on Angel Island include Eastwood Manzanita, *Arctostaphylos glandulosa* (Fig. 184); Chamise, *Adenostoma fasciculatum* (Fig. 88); California Lilac or Blue Blossom, *Ceanothus thyrsiflorus* (Fig. 185); and the shrub version of Interior Live Oak, *Quercus wislizenii* var. *frutescens* (Fig. 183B). Conspicuous in the spring by virtue of its abundant golden-colored pea flowers is the introduced Scotch Broom, *Cytisus scoparius* (Plate 16B). Unfortunately, this attractive shrub is an invasive weed that gradually replaces native vegetation, particularly in disturbed areas.

Coastal Grassland

Some authorities refer to Coastal Grassland as Coastal Prairie. As is the case with grasslands throughout the state, the Coastal Grassland on the

Figure 185. Blue Blossom, *Ceanothus thyrsiflorus.*

islands in San Francisco Bay is composed primarily of nonnative Mediterranean grasses, such as Wild Oats (*Avena* spp.) (Fig. 59A), bromes or chesses (*Bromus* spp.) (Fig. 59D), barleys (*Hordeum* spp.) (Fig. 59B), and ryegrasses (*Lolium* spp.) (Fig. 59C). In the grassland and open spaces of other communities, various native wildflowers—such as Goldfields, *Lasthenia californica* (Plate 10B); Yarrow Milfoil, *Achillea millefolium;* California Buttercup, *Ranunculus californicus;* and Checker Mallow, *Sidalcea malviflora* (Fig. 206)—put on a spectacular show in the spring. Also included here are geophytes, such as Blue Dicks, *Dichelostemma capitatum* (Fig. 198); Death Camas, *Zigadenus fremontii* (Fig. 197); Blue-eyed Grass, *Sisyrinchium bellum;* and Wild Iris, *Iris longipetala* (Fig. 199). Nonnative herbs such as filarees (*Erodium* spp.) and mustards (*Brassica* spp.) are also abundant. On some islands the introduced Pride of Madeira, *Echium candicans,* with its pale blue "Forget-me-not" flowers, may be especially abundant. This species from the Canary Islands may be the most spectacular wildflower on Angel Island.

Grassland is a common plant community on the exposed parts of all the islands in the bay. It dominates the upper slopes of Angel Island and the plateaus of the flat-topped islands such as Brooks, the Marin Islands, and Yerba Buena. The mixture of species on Brooks Island may represent a habitat much more like pristine grassland than that in any other location in the bay area.

Freshwater Marsh

The San Francisco Bay and Delta ecosystem is the largest estuary in North America. Unfortunately it is also one of the most disturbed. Its input of fresh water is intercepted by the largest aqueduct system in the world, the California Aqueduct. In addition its role as one of the world's most important seaports subjects it to a variety of insults, including pollution and the introduction of nonnative species. In fact a 1997 report cited 164 introduced species of microorganisms, plants, and animals in salt and brackish water alone. An additional 84 nonnative species were documented for the freshwater habitats. This total of 248 species suggests that San Francisco Bay is the most invaded estuary in the world.

Freshwater Marshes occur in areas of perpetual standing fresh water. As such they occur only sporadically on California islands and are usually limited to small areas associated with permanent springs. Around San Francisco Bay there is extensive Freshwater Marsh vegetation in the Sacramento–San Joaquin Delta, and there are many islands in the area. Browns Island (Fig. 207) at the east end of Suisun Bay is more nearly pristine than any other part of the delta. There are no levees in the area, and thus no unnatural impoundment of fresh water or seawater.

Marsh vegetation is distributed in distinct bands. The ecological requirements for each of the plant types are precise enough that they occur in single-species clumps or zones that appear as bands on the edge of the water mass. Farthest out in the water are floating plants called *macrophytes,* a term that means "large plants." Floating macrophytes give way to rooted macrophytes in the shallow water. Some of these remain submerged. A distinct progression of rooted plants then occurs from the shallow water to drier land.

Freshwater marshes are dominated by reedlike plants that grow in water-saturated soil. Various species occur throughout different parts of the state, but they fall essentially into four groups. Most common are rushes (*Juncus* spp.) and bulrushes (*Scirpus* spp.). Locally common are sedges (*Cyperus* spp.) and cattails (*Typha* spp.) (Fig. 186). It is not always easy to tell these plants apart because they all have a similar grasslike appearance. Cattails are the easiest to identify: they are the tallest, growing up to 10 ft (3 m) in height, and they have long, bladelike leaves and dense flower spikes that look like long brown sausages. They cannot tolerate deeper water; therefore, they occur at the outer fringes of the marsh. Sedges and rushes are shorter, about 3 ft (1 m) tall. The leaves, if present, are usually located at the base of the plant, and extending above them is a solid stem. Sedges have triangular stems and most rushes have round stems. (Sedges have edges, and rushes are round!) Bulrushes are the forms that are commonly called tules. They are related to sedges, and as such many of them have triangular stems, but others have round stems. They grow up to 6 ft (2 m) in height. Their flowers are borne atop leafless stems in starburstlike clusters known as *umbels.*

Figure 186. Freshwater Marsh dominated by cattails, *Typha* spp.

On higher ground in the marshes are various water-loving trees such as willows (*Salix* spp.). Among the most common are Black Willow, *Salix gooddingii,* and Arroyo Willow, *Salix lasiolepis.* Some of these trees may branch close to the ground, resembling large shrubs. They have elongate, lance-shaped leaves. The plumed seeds of willows are easily carried by the wind, a characteristic that aids dispersal. Yellow-colored branchlets of Black Willow snap off easily and may float to a location where the water is shallow enough for them to root, a further aid in dispersal.

Also on higher ground is a group of shrubs that superficially resemble willows; they typically occur where the water is more alkaline. One common form is known as Mule Fat, *Baccharis salicifolia* (Fig. 187). These willowlike plants, sometimes called Seep-willows, are members of the sunflower family (Asteraceae). They do not possess brightly colored ray flowers, only disc flowers, which are small and white. As in willows, their plumed seeds are wind disseminated.

A plant known as Buttonbush or Button-willow, *Cephalanthus occidentalis,* is a large shrub associated with these marshes. Its lance-shaped leaves have smooth margins, and they are opposite or whorled on the stem. The flowers occur in a spherical head up to an inch (25 mm) in diameter. This is another example of a plant left over from a more tropical period. It belongs to the madder family (Rubiaceae), which is widespread in the tropics today. The family includes the bedstraws, *Galium* spp., as well as many plants of economic importance, such as coffee; cinchona,

Figure 187. Mule Fat, *Baccharis salicifolia*.

the plant from which quinine is derived; and ornamental plants such as gardenias.

Browns Island (Fig. 207) is the only island in San Francisco Bay that has a relatively undisturbed Freshwater Marsh. It lies at the confluence of the Sacramento and San Joaquin Rivers and is far enough upstream that, until recently, it was relatively free of saltwater intrusion. However, with the development of the Central Valley Project and the California Aqueduct, the volume of water contributed by the Sacramento River has been considerably reduced. Thus Salt Marsh species are becoming more common and freshwater species are showing signs of saltwater intrusion.

Salt Marsh

Coastal Salt Marshes are found at sporadic locations on nearly all of the islands in the bay. On the whole, San Francisco Bay contains the largest remaining expanses of Salt Marsh in the state. These areas, characterized by the rise and fall of the tides, occur wherever salty muds accumulate.

Islands in the Salt Marsh of San Francisco Bay, some of which are named, are patches of vegetation that are separated from the mainland by a combination of natural and artificial channels. Many of these channels are waterless during low tide, and thus there are true islands only during high tide.

At the southern end of San Francisco Bay some 19,000 acres (9500 ha) of Salt Marsh, most of which is reclaimed land, have been set aside as the

Figure 188. Greco Island as seen from Bayfront Park. This reclaimed Salt Marsh includes a methane recovery plant.

San Francisco Bay National Wildlife Refuge. This refuge, an important habitat for water birds and the endangered Salt Marsh Harvest Mouse, *Reithrodontomys raviventris,* includes Bair, Greco, and Station Islands.

Bair Island and Greco Island (Fig. 188) are located on the west side of the bay between Redwood City and Dumbarton Bridge. Bayfront Park, overlooking Greco Island, lies on a former garbage dump. Ponds from a decommissioned sewage-treatment plant are now part of the wildlife refuge. At the edge of the marsh a methane recovery plant extracts gas produced underground by the former dump and uses it to generate electricity.

Station Island, at the southeast corner of San Francisco Bay, lies near the mouth of the Coyote River north of Milpitas. Its name refers to the now-abandoned railroad station that formerly lay on the site. The tracks of the Southern Pacific Railroad still cross the island.

As in a Freshwater Marsh, the vegetation in a Salt Marsh is grouped into bands based on the amount of submergence tolerated by the plants (Fig. 189). Among the rooted macrophytes, the plant that occurs farthest into seawater is Eel-Grass, *Zostera marina.* Eel-Grass, which grows from the low-tide level to depths of about 20 ft (6 m), is the same species that grows with surf-grasses in the rocky intertidal zone. Eel-Grass in estuaries tends to be more filamentous in appearance.

The emergent plant that grows farthest into seawater is California Cord Grass, *Spartina foliosa.* This is a plant, up to 3 ft (1 m) in height, that may be half submerged. It spreads through the salty mud by means of

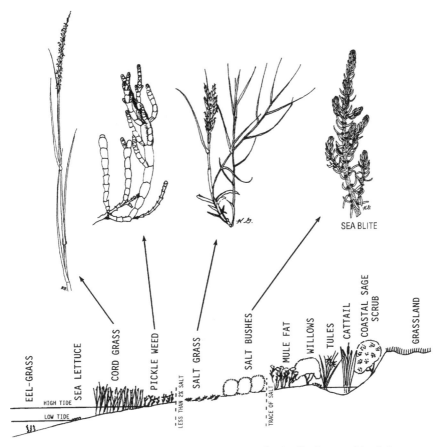

Figure 189. Salt Marsh zonation. (Drawings by Karlin Grunau Marsh.)

buried runners (rhizomes), growing like rice in a paddy. Cord Grass is able to tolerate its harsh habitat by means of several important adaptations. Its stems are hollow and air filled, a feature that enables oxygen to reach submerged roots. Similar to many salt-tolerant plants (halophytes), Cord Grass is equipped with salt glands to excrete excess salts. In addition Cord Grass is one of the very few plants of cool climates that practices C-4 photosynthesis. This type of high-efficiency photosynthesis occurs principally in desert halophytes, such as salt bushes, that must photosynthesize and excrete salts in a hot, dry climate. In order to cope with drought stress, it is probably important for Cord Grass to be able to photosynthesize with its stomates partly closed, and this process is enhanced by high-energy C-4 photosynthesis. Cord Grass is also equipped with nitrogen-fixing bacteria in its roots; therefore, its foliage is an important source of protein for the marsh ecosystem.

Cord Grass is the greatest contributor to the high productivity of the estuarine ecosystem, although it does not make its contribution in the expected way. Since very few organisms are equipped to eat the salty foliage, the contribution of Cord Grass to the ecosystem is made through detritus. Root systems trap sediment and detritus. Microorganisms consume the detritus and contribute to the dissolved organic matter that enters the water. Snails and worms feed directly on the detritus, and nutrients enter the estuarine food web. Fishes and birds feed on the snails and worms. The nitrogenous wastes of those animals return to the system, to complete the cycle. When the tide goes out, soluble nutrients are carried out to sea. It is this outwelling that contributes nutrients to sandy beaches and the rocky intertidal region.

In recent years several nonnative species of Cord Grass have begun to invade the Salt Marsh of San Francisco Bay. Although their full significance is as yet unknown, these species, native to South America and the eastern United States, are believed by many botanists to pose a threat to the native ecosystem. Of particular concern is an eastern native, Salt-water Cord Grass, *Spartina alterniflora,* that is especially invasive.

Inland from the Cord Grass there is a belt of succulent plants. Of these, the pickleweeds (*Salicornia* spp.) are the most common. The roots of pickleweeds are covered by seawater only during the highest tides. Pickleweed absorbs water and salt; by storing the water in its tissues, the plant ensures a favorable flow of water into itself even though it is rooted in salty soil. The plant is leafless, and its stem resembles a series of small green pickles. As the sections at the tips of the stems become filled with salt, they drop off, recycling the salt back into the ecosystem.

Associated with the pickleweeds may be other salt-tolerant plants such as Salt Grass, *Distichlis spicata,* and salt-tolerant shrubs such as Sea Blite, *Suaeda californica.* These shrubs excrete salt upon their leaves through salt glands.

Diversity in the Salt Marsh is maintained by environmental perturbations such as freshwater flooding and tidal flushing. Plant productivity is high and growth of new plants is rapid. Detritus that is recycled into the system enriches the muds. Dense root systems trap the detritus and mud, allowing more nutrients to accumulate. A natural catastrophe such as a flood may scour an area, and the cycle of regeneration then repeats itself. Some call the Salt Marsh a "build-and-tear" ecosystem.

TERRESTRIAL ANIMALS

Very little research has been carried out on the invertebrates of the islands in San Francisco Bay, but the islands are close enough to the mainland that the invertebrate fauna probably is typical of that on the nearby mainland. Of particular interest is the fact that the introduced *Eucalyptus* groves on Angel Island have become "butterfly trees"—winter roost sites for migrating Monarch Butterflies, *Danaus plexippus.*

The terrestrial vertebrates of the islands in San Francisco Bay are summarized in Table 27.

Amphibians

In the 1960s Paul Anderson of the University of California studied the salamanders of the islands in San Francisco Bay. His work, published in 1960, remains the only comparative study of island vertebrates. Salamanders occur on most of the islands in the bay. Of the two documented salamanders, the California Slender Salamander, *Batrachoseps attenuatus* (Fig. 190), is the most common, being found on Alcatraz Island, Angel Island, Brooks Island, Red Rock Island, the Marin Islands, and Yerba Buena Island. The Arboreal Salamander, *Aneides lugubris* (Fig. 62), is found on Angel, Brooks, and Red Rock Islands. There also is an unverified report of the Monterey Salamander, *Ensatina eschscholtzii,* on Angel Island, which is a likely situation.

The only frog species found on the islands is the Pacific Treefrog, *Hyla* (=*Pseudacris*) *regilla* (Fig. 63), and it is only found on Brooks Island. It probably occurs on Browns Island as well.

How did these animals get to the islands? The most logical answer is that they are relicts and have inhabited the islands since a time of lowered sea level when the islands were connected to the mainland. The sedentary nature of salamanders is well known, and therefore it is not unlikely that they have inhabited the present land masses for thousands of years. It is believed that the slender salamander on Alcatraz may have been introduced along with the earth that was used to level the island.

Reptiles

The reptile fauna of the islands consists of three lizards and four snakes. The Western Fence Lizard, *Sceloporus occidentalis* (Fig. 105), is a common lizard on Angel and East Marin Islands. The Northern Alligator Lizard, *Elgaria coeruleus,* is found on Angel, Brooks, and Yerba Buena Islands, and the Southern Alligator Lizard, *Elgaria multicarinatus* (Fig. 60C), has been recorded from Angel Island. Four snakes have been recorded from Angel Island: the Gopher Snake, *Pituophis melanoleucus;* the Racer, *Coluber constrictor* (Fig. 191); the Rubber Boa, *Charina bottae;* and the Western Terrestrial Garter Snake, *Thamnophis elegans.* The only other island that has a snake on it is Brooks Island, on which the Western Terrestrial

TABLE 27 TERRESTRIAL VERTEBRATES OF ISLANDS IN SAN FRANCISCO BAY

	ALCATRAZ	ANGEL	BROOKS	BROWNS	EAST MARIN	RED ROCK	WEST MARIN	YERBA BUENA
Amphibians								
California Slender Salamander (*Batrachoseps attenuatus*)	X	X	X		X	X	X	X
Arboreal Salamander (*Aneides lugubris*)		X			X	X		X
Pacific Treefrog (*Hyla* [=*Pseudacris*] *regilla*)			X					
Reptiles								
Western Fence Lizard (*Sceloporus occidentalis*)		X			X			
Northern Alligator Lizard (*Elgaria coeruleus*)		X	X					
Southern Alligator Lizard (*Elgaria multicarinatus*)		X						
Gopher Snake (*Pituophis melanoleucus*)		X						
Racer (*Coluber constrictor*)		X						
Rubber Boa (*Charina bottae*)		X						
Western Terrestrial Garter Snake (*Thamnophis elegans*)		X	X					
Western Pond Turtle (*Clemmys marmorata*)				X				
Native mammals								
Angel Island Mole (*Scapanus latimanus insularis*) —Endemic		X						
Deer Mouse (*Peromyscus maniculatus*)	X	X						
California Vole (*Microtus californicus*)		X	X					
Raccoon (*Procyon lotor*)		X		X				
Muskrat (*Ondatra zibethicus*)				?				
Mule Deer (*Odocoileus hemionus*)		X						

Introduced mammals

Introduced mammals					
House Mouse (*Mus musculus*)			?		
Norway Rat (*Rattus norvegicus*)	X		X		X
Horse (*Equus caballus*)—Removed	X		X	X	X
Cattle (*Bos taurus*)—Removed	X		X	X	X
Pig (*Sus scrofa*)					
House Cat (*Felis domesticus*)—Removed	X	X			X
Domestic Dog (*Canis familiaris*)—Removed	X	X	X		X
Domestic Sheep (*Ovis aries*)—Removed			X		
Barbary Sheep (*Ammotragus lervia*)—Removed				X	
Domestic Goat (*Capra hircus*)—Removed			X		X

Figure 190. California Slender Salamander, *Batrachoseps attenuatus*. (From Stebbins 1951.)

Figure 191. Racer, *Coluber constrictor* (juvenile).

Garter Snake is found. Brooks Island is also the site for a single recorded specimen of the Western Pond Turtle, *Clemmys marmorata*. Although this specimen may be a waif, it is representative of the constantly changing nature of island faunas.

Land Birds

As might be expected, the number of birds recorded from the islands in the bay is substantial, owing to their close proximity to the mainland. The exact number recorded for each island is unknown, but over 125 species have been recorded for Angel Island and 100 species for Brooks Island. Similar numbers should occur on most of the other islands.

Water Birds

Figure 192 illustrates some of the water birds that may be encountered around the bay.

Browns Island is predominantly a marsh, and therefore any number of water birds—marine, freshwater, or both—could be found there. Similarly, the bird fauna of Bair, Greco, and Station Islands, of the San Francisco Bay National Wildlife Refuge, is dominated by water birds.

Sea birds such as Brown Pelicans, *Pelecanus occidentalis* (Fig. 192J; Plate 3A), and Western Gulls, *Larus occidentalis* (Fig. 192A; Plate 3D), have been documented on all of the islands. Similarly, Brandt's Cormorants (*Phalacrocorax penicillatus*), Double-crested Cormorants (*Phalacrocorax auritus*) (Plate 3B), and occasionally Pelagic Cormorants (*Phalacrocorax pelagicus*) are found breeding on all of the islands. In winter months large American White Pelicans, *Pelecanus erythrorhynchos,* are conspicuous all over the bay. With wings spanning more than 8 ft (2.8 m), these graceful birds are second in size only to the California Condor, *Gymnogyps californianus.*

Among the birds associated with marshes or fresh water, the most commonly mentioned species are Great Blue Herons (*Ardea herodias*) (Fig. 192D), Black-crowned Night-herons (*Nycticorax nycticorax*) (Fig. 204), Great Egrets (*Casmerodius albus*) and Snowy Egrets (*Egretta thula*) (Fig. 193), and Canada Geese (*Branta canadensis*).

The heron rookeries on Brooks Island and West Marin Island are particularly notable. West Marin is apparently the only heronry where all four species of herons and egrets nest together, and from February to July, when the herons breed, there may be as many as 2000 birds on the island. This rookery may be the largest and most important heronry in northern California. The herons and egrets seem particularly to enjoy nesting and perching in the California Buckeyes, making some trees look like Christmas trees heavy with ornaments.

In fact it has now been well documented that the presence of birds in great abundance can have a profound effect on the native vegetation. With more of these islands coming into public hands and reserves being established, the birds on some islands are becoming so numerous that some naturalists consider them a nuisance. The vegetational and floristic differences between the two Marin Islands have been attributed to physical perturbations caused by birds and alterations in soil chemistry caused by an accumulation of bird guano. West Marin Island has large nesting populations of gulls, herons, egrets, and Canada Geese, whereas East Marin has until recently been inhabited and therefore had very few nesting birds.

The introduction of new species and the loss of others can be attributed to birds. Michael Vasey of San Francisco State University reports that on West Brother Island, Double-crested Cormorants and Western Gulls have established rookeries on the northern part of the island. Between the birds' nests, Maritime Goldfields (Farallon Weed), *Lasthenia maritima* (Fig. 170), has become established after apparently being introduced by the birds. Seeds of this plant (so common on the Farallon Islands) have been observed stuck between the feathers of the birds and on the feet of sea birds, along with the gelatinous ooze from the Ice Plant, *Carpobrotus chilensis* (common on many islands). In other cases, nesting of one bird

Figure 192 (*above and opposite*). Some water birds of San Francisco Bay.
(A) Western Gull, *Larus occidentalis*. (B) Marbled Godwit, *Limosa fedoa*.
(C) Willet, *Catoptrophorus semipalmatus*. (D) Great Blue Heron, *Ardea herodias*.
(E) Black Turnstone, *Arenaria interpres*. (F) Sanderling, *Calidris alba*. (G) Heer-
man's Gull, *Larus heermanni*. (H) Wandering Tatler, *Heteroscelus incanus*.
(I) Long-billed Curlew, *Numenius americanus*. (J) Brown Pelican, *Pelecanus
occidentalis*. (K) Western Grebe, *Aechmophorus occidentalis*.

Figure 193. Great Egret, *Casmerodius albus,* and smaller Snowy Egret, *Egretta thula,* in Salt Marsh.

species in great abundance has displaced other birds. For example, excessive numbers of cormorants have been known to collapse the burrows of nesting petrels and auklets on the Farallon Islands.

Terrestrial Mammals

Most of the terrestrial mammals on the islands have been introduced, even the native California species. The Angel Island Mole, *Scapanus latimanus insularis* (Fig. 194), is the only endemic vertebrate on the islands of San Francisco Bay. Evidence of the presence of this species is provided by the humped tunnels that twist and turn in the grassy areas. Transporting a subterranean mammal to an island at first seems problematic, but the fact that it has evolved sufficiently to be a distinctive subspecies implies that it may be a relict, dating back to a time when the island was connected to the mainland.

The Deer Mouse, *Peromyscus maniculatus* (Fig. 3), the most common native mammal on California's islands, is found only on Alcatraz Island in San Francisco Bay. Considering the years of disturbance to which this island has been subjected, it is difficult to believe that this species is actually native to the island. It is more likely that the Deer Mouse was accidentally introduced, perhaps when soil was brought to the island during construction of the prison.

The California Vole, *Microtus californicus* (Fig. 150), is found on Angel and Brooks Islands. There is speculation that this mouse was introduced to Angel Island along with bales of hay, similar to its introduction on San Clemente Island. Before arriving on Brooks Island, the species was first introduced to Bird Island, a small islet to the west. It managed to cross to the main island and subsequently eliminated a population of House Mice, *Mus musculus.*

Figure 194. The Angel Island Mole, *Scapanus latimanus insularis,* is a subspecies of the Broad-footed Mole found on the mainland. (From Storer and Usinger 1963.)

The most widely distributed mammal on the bay islands is the introduced Norway Rat, *Rattus norvegicus.* Populations of this rodent are found on Angel, Brooks, and the two Marin Islands. On Brooks Island, in an attempt to preserve food for game birds, a poisoning program has recently been started to reduce the numbers of rats.

The Raccoon, *Procyon lotor,* is known to inhabit Angel Island and Browns Island. Its presence, along with that of the Muskrat (*Ondatra zibethicus*), would be expected in the marshes of Browns Island, but the occurrence of a predator, such as a Raccoon, would not be expected in a food-limited situation such as that on a small island like Angel Island. Being omnivores, however, Raccoons have the ability to survive on a wide variety of foods, including that which is found in trashcans. It is reported that Raccoons on Angel Island feed on nonnative rats and mice, and in so doing help to keep those potential pests in check.

The Mule Deer, *Odocoileus hemionus,* of Angel Island are, depending on one's point of view, either hated or loved. Without natural predators, the deer population could multiply uncontrollably and do serious damage to the island vegetation, after which the animals would starve. In an attempt to keep the population under control, periodic thinning of the population is a necessity. As might be expected, both policies—thinning the population and permitting uncontrolled growth—have their supporters and their critics. The original source of the deer is unknown. Deer are good swimmers, and waifs occasionally appear on the other islands; it is therefore entirely possible that the deer swam over from the Tiburon Peninsula. They might also have been introduced for food during the early days of military occupancy.

Figure 195. Angel Island (contour interval 50 ft). (Courtesy Angel Island docents.)

Marine Mammals

Harbor Seals, *Phoca vitulina* (Fig. 37; Plate 2C), and California Sea Lions, *Zalophus californianus* (Fig. 39), are the most common visitors to the island beaches, although they tend to avoid the areas frequented by humans. In the old days, Sea Otters, *Enhydra lutris,* no doubt also occurred in the waters around the islands. Russian fur hunters reported that they were abundant in the northern part of San Francisco Bay in the late eighteenth century.

ANGEL ISLAND

Angel Island (Fig. 195) is approximately 3.5 miles (5.6 km) north of San Francisco and separated from the nearest mainland, at Tiburon Peninsula, by a distance of a half mile (0.8 km). This is the largest island in San Francisco Bay. Its area of 760 acres (300 ha) is slightly more than 1 square mile. The water gap known as Raccoon Strait, at 234 ft (78 m), is the deepest part of San Francisco Bay.

The island resembles a triangle, with sides that measure about 1.25 miles

(2 km) in length. The highest point, Mount Livermore, at 781 ft (252 m), forms a central peak with several ridges radiating out from it. The original name for the mountain, Mount Ida, was changed in 1958 to honor Caroline Livermore, a Marin conservationist who led the fight to save Angel Island from private developers. On a clear day, Mount Livermore provides a perfect vantage point from which to view the other islands of San Francisco Bay.

The canyons on the island are densely covered with trees, components of Mixed Evergreen Forest and Oak Woodland (Plate 16A,B). The ridges and more exposed slopes support Coastal Grassland and Northern Coastal Scrub. Chaparral also occurs on certain ridges directly to the east and northeast of Ayala Cove, along the ridge extending from Mount Livermore to Campbell Point (Fig. 200).

History

Evidence from shell middens suggests that there were four Coastal Miwok villages on Angel Island, and that the Miwoks probably inhabited the area at least 3000 years ago.

Angel Island takes its name from a corruption of the original name, Nuestra Señora de Los Angeles, bestowed upon it by Juan Manuel de Ayala in 1775. The island provided a good anchorage, firewood, and water, so Ayala remained encamped there for 40 days while he made extensive nautical surveys of the San Francisco Bay area. The small bay on the northwest side of Angel Island where Ayala anchored his boat was named Ayala Cove in his honor in 1969.

In the 1700s Russian fur hunters used the island as a base for their activities while they hunted Sea Otters. Moving back and forth between Angel Island and the Farallons, they hunted the otters nearly to extinction. Apparently the northern end of San Francisco Bay once held a sizable population of the valuable fur-bearing mammals.

During the nineteenth century, Russian, British, American, and Spanish sailing vessels, many of which were whalers, continued to visit the bay and utilized Angel Island as a source of firewood and water. Richard Henry Dana described visiting Angel Island, known at the time as Wood Island, in December 1835 to cut wood. It did not take long for the Europeans to remove most of the trees from the island, and by 1850, when the Army arrived, they began planting nonnative trees such as *Eucalyptus* to provide shade.

In 1839 the Mexican governor of Alta California granted the island to Antonio Mario Osio. Osio used the island for raising horses and cattle, constructed a dam for the conservation of water, and cultivated crops on a portion of the island.

In 1850, the year California became a state, the U.S. government set aside the island for use as a military camp and quarantine station. The government also built an immigration station at Point Simpton for the isolation and treatment of Asian immigrants suffering from various communicable diseases. From the time it opened in 1909 until this facility was closed in 1940, thousands of Japanese and Chinese immigrants passed through the station before being allowed to settle on the mainland. A larger army post on the island, Fort McDowell, was used during both world wars but was finally closed in 1947.

Quarrying operations began on Angel Island in the early 1850s. High-quality sandstone was taken from a location on the east shore known as Smith's Point. Its name was later changed to Quarry Point. Here a sandstone mountain, 100 ft (30 m) high, came right down to the water's edge. By 1922, when the quarry was closed, the mountain had been leveled to its present condition. Many buildings in the San Francisco area were constructed of Angel Island sandstone, including fortifications on Alcatraz Island. The original Bank of California building, one of San Francisco's grandest edifices, which was completed in 1867, was constructed of blue sandstone from Angel Island.

These various settlements on Angel Island caused the destruction of considerable amounts of natural habitat and resulted in the introduction of cultivated plants, many of which persist today on the abandoned grounds and in the gardens of these old installations. Others, such as *Eucalyptus,* became naturalized. The paved roads, now used by cyclists, hikers, and joggers, and the many old, decaying buildings are remnants of this period in the island's history.

In 1955 the federal government granted a portion of the island to the California State Parks and Recreation Department, which established Angel Island State Park in the Ayala Cove area. In 1962, following the abandonment of an Army Nike missile site on the southern portion of the island, the entire island came under the jurisdiction of the parks department. In 1996, in an attempt to restore the island's native vegetation, parks department employees began a program to strip the island of its nonnative Tasmanian Blue Gums, *Eucalyptus globulus.* In all, more than 12,000 trees covering about 90 acres (35 ha) were "clear-cut," creating the temporary appearance of devastation on the north side of the island, as it starts on its way to restoration.

Geology

The rocks of Angel Island are all associated with the Franciscan Formation (Fig. 7) and were formed during the Jurassic period approximately 150 million years ago. The structure of the island is essentially a synclinal trough with its axis plunging to the northwest, toward Raccoon Strait.

Layers of sandstone, shaped like a trough, dip toward the ocean from the summit of Mount Livermore. Ayala Cove is located where the bottom of the trough passes under water.

Most of the rock is sedimentary and metamorphic, and the major rock groups occurring on the island are Franciscan graywackes, conglomerates, and radiolarian cherts. Metamorphic rocks include jadeite-bearing metagraywackes, glaucophane-schists, and serpentinite. Pillow lavas at Blunt Point indicate a submarine eruption typical of seafloor deposition in the offshore subduction trench. Serpentinite and pyroxenite occur in a vertical, dikelike body near the west end of the island, which is probably the most conspicuous geological feature of the area. Most of the trough, dipping toward Ayala Cove, and the summit of Mount Livermore are composed of the graywacke. The sandstone quarry mentioned previously extracted the graywacke in huge chunks.

The "greenstone" rock exposed on Point Stewart is a good example of altered volcanic rock. Apparently it was formed by a squeezing action that altered the original basalt to wavy layers including black, green, and red rocks. It also extends in an east-west band across the island below the summit of Mount Livermore.

Of these major rock groups, the serpentinite (serpentine) outcrop that extends across the western end of the island is the most prominent geological feature of the island. As explained earlier, the waxy green material is hydrothermally altered basalt. This rock material was crushed to form the roadway around the island. Soils derived from serpentine contain high concentrations of such minerals as magnesium and iron, but they are deficient in calcium and potassium. Therefore only specialized plants can grow on serpentine-derived soils.

Strata of more recent age include the Colma Formation, found on the southern part of the island at about 200-ft (65-m) elevation. This young sandstone is an old marine terrace that is only a few million years old. Clay loams derived from unconsolidated sedimentary rock are also widespread. In addition a fairly large portion of the island is covered with fine- to medium-grained sand, which occurs on the steep cliffs and canyon sides facing the bay.

Terrestrial Vegetation

Although Angel Island has been considerably disturbed by woodcutting and later by military use, considerable amounts of natural habitat remain. Because of its size and elevation, the greatest diversity of natural communities of all the islands in the bay occurs here. According to the floristic analysis carried out by John Ripley in the late 1960s, the following plant communities (with approximate percentage of coverage) were found to be present: Mixed Evergreen Forest (33 percent), Grassland (28 percent), Northern Coastal Scrub (19 percent), Chaparral (4 percent), Coastal Strand (4 percent), and Freshwater Pond (1 percent).

Mixed Evergreen Forest Of all the islands in San Francisco Bay, the Mixed Evergreen Forest community is best developed on Angel Island (Plate 16A,B). As the ferry pulls into Ayala Cove the conspicuous and attractive green trees and shrubs of the northern slopes and ravines are very apparent. In most island and mainland plant communities of California, north-facing slopes hold more moisture and experience less drying than do the more exposed, south-facing slopes. As a result north-facing slopes generally have a more lush vegetative cover. In these areas and several sheltered canyons where moisture also remains, large California Laurel, *Umbellularia californica* (Fig. 180) and Pacific Madrone, *Arbutus menziesii* (Fig. 179; Plate 16C), are present. Farther to the east, excellent specimens of Big-leaf Maple, *Acer macrophyllum* (Fig. 181), occur in the canyons above Fort McDowell. Also present in these densely wooded areas are California Buckeye, *Aesculus californica* (Fig. 182); Toyon, *Heteromeles arbutifolia* (Fig. 54); Hazelnut, *Corylus cornuta;* and Blue Elderberry, *Sambucus mexicana.*

In the shade created by these trees grow woody shrubs and a number of herbaceous species. Among the shade-loving shrubs are Hillside Gooseberry, *Ribes californicum,* and Poison Oak, *Toxicodendron diversilobum* (Fig. 58). During the autumn, the red and yellow provided by these deciduous shrubs is added to that of the Big-leaf Maples, lending splashes of fall color to the groves of trees. In the spring, California Saxifrage, *Saxifraga californica;* Miner's Lettuce, *Claytonia perfoliata;* and Hound's Tongue, *Cynoglossum grande,* add floral beauty to these shaded canyons. Most of the island's ferns are in the community as well. The Western Sword Fern, *Polystichum munitum* (Fig. 196), is most abundant, but Maiden Hair Fern, *Adiantum jordanii;* Coastal Wood Fern, *Dryopteris arguta;* and Goldback Fern, *Pentagramma triangularis,* are also present.

Northern Coastal Scrub The Northern Coastal Scrub community, consisting of low-growing stands of shrubs, dominates the south- and east-facing slopes of the island. The dominant woody species in this community are Coyote Brush, *Baccharis pilularis* (Fig. 45B; Plate 16A), and California Sagebrush, *Artemisia californica* (Fig. 45A), which frequently forms dense thickets. The Spiny Redberry (*Rhamnus crocea*) is also a component of this community. Northern Coastal Scrub also contains a herbaceous flora with a number of attractive wildflower species, such as Death Camas, *Zigadenus fremontii* (Fig. 197); Blue Dicks, *Dichelostemma capitatum* (Fig. 198); and Yarrow Milfoil, *Achillea millefolium.*

Figure 196. Western Sword Fern, *Polystichum munitum*.

Figure 197. Death Camas, *Zigadenus fremontii*.

Figure 198. Blue Dicks, *Dichelostemma capitatum.*

Grassland Community Grassland is common on the island. It occurs mainly on the southern slopes but also extends into the northern half of the island, where it occupies open areas between Chaparral and Coastal Scrub vegetation.

The grass species are mostly of Mediterranean origin (Fig. 59) and include Wild Oats (*Avena barbata* and *Avena fatua*), Bromes (*Bromus* spp.), Annual Bluegrass (*Poa annua*), and Foxtail Barley (*Hordeum jubatum*). Showy wildflower species common in the spring are Goldfields, *Lasthenia californica* (Plate 10B); California Buttercup, *Ranunculus californicus;* and California Poppy, *Eschscholzia californica.* Wild iris, *Iris longipetala* (Fig. 199), often fills meadow areas with a blaze of blue color. One of the distinctive shrubs in the sunflower family (Asteraceae), California Matchweed, *Gutierrezia californica,* occurs primarily on the serpentine outcrop along the margin of the Grassland and Coastal Scrub on the western side of the island.

Figure 199. Wild Iris, *Iris longipetala.*

Chaparral Chaparral is found on the steep ridges directly to the east and northeast of Ayala Cove and along the ridge extending from Mount Livermore to Campbell Point (Fig. 200). As described previously, typical chaparral species include Eastwood Manzanita, *Arctostaphylos glandulosa* (Fig. 184); Chamise, *Adenostoma fasciculatum* (Fig. 88); and California Lilac or Blue Blossom, *Ceanothus thyrsiflorus* (Fig. 185). The invasive but colorful Scotch Broom, *Cytisus scoparius,* is also conspicuous along this ridge (Plate 16B).

Coastal Strand The sandy beaches support many maritime species common to the bay area. In the springtime, masses of both yellow and pink Sand Verbenas (*Abronia latifolia* and *Abronia umbellata*) cover many dunes at Swimmer's Beach. Also present is European Beachgrass, *Ammophila arenaria,* which is a native of Europe and probably was planted by the Army as a sand binder during their occupancy of Fort McDowell.

Figure 200. Chaparral east of Ayala Cove.

Freshwater Ponds Numerous freshwater seepages occur in the canyons of Angel Island, and two ponds, in the drainage that extends from the summit of Mount Livermore to Pearl's Beach, have been formed by damming small springs. The lower pond serves as a water reservoir. The upper pond is relatively undisturbed and is often totally encroached upon by Narrow-leaved Cattail, *Typha angustifolia;* Water Cress, *Rorippa nasturtium-aquaticum;* and other aquatic plant species.

Terrestrial Animals

Surprisingly, there are no up-to-date published lists of vertebrate animals for Angel Island, yet from most anecdotal evidence there are more vertebrates there than on any of the other islands in the bay. Lists of terrestrial and aquatic birds are kept up to date, but references to amphibians, reptiles, and mammals are confusing, if not actually conflicting.

Angel Island is very close to the Tiburon Peninsula (Plate 16A), and yet the channel separating them, although only half a mile (0.8 km) in width, appears to have prevented most terrestrial vertebrates (except of course for birds) from reaching the island. The absence of ground squirrels and rabbits—species that do not cross barriers of water and reach islands very often—seems logical. The list of birds includes many species that are typical for the nearby mainland.

Herpetofauna Two salamanders—the California Slender Salamander, *Batrachoseps attenuatus* (Fig. 190), and the Arboreal Salamander, *Aneides lugubris* (Fig. 62)—are documented inhabitants of the Mixed Evergreen Forest on Angel Island. Anecdotal evidence seems to indicate that the Monterey Salamander, *Ensatina eschscholtzii,* is also present, and this would not be surprising, for abundant habitat is available. The presence of these salamanders indicates probable relict distribution, remaining from a time when Angel Island was connected to the mainland.

Of the reptiles, three common lizards have been reported. The Western Fence Lizard, *Sceloporus occidentalis* (Fig. 105), is the most common lizard on the islands, and it may be seen sunning in nearly any open space. The Northern Alligator Lizard, *Elgaria coeruleus,* is also present, but more secretive. Surprisingly, the Southern Alligator Lizard, *Elgaria multicarinatus* (Fig. 60C), has also been reported from Angel Island.

Four snakes have been documented on Angel Island. Snakes are carnivores, feeding from the top of the food chain. They are, therefore, not common, and it is surprising to find four species on such a small island. The Gopher Snake, *Pituophis melanoleucus* (Fig. 106), is apparently the most common; its preferred prey, burrowing rodents, is evidently abundant enough to support this population. The Western Terrestrial Garter Snake, *Thamnophis elegans,* usually feeds near freshwater habitats, on frogs, salamanders, and freshwater fish. Although some freshwater habitat is available on Angel Island, these snakes must maintain themselves by feeding on lizards and small rodents as well. Garter snakes are known to be carried on rafts and they are good swimmers; it is therefore not unlikely for them to be on an island this close to the mainland. The presence of the Rubber Boa, *Charina bottae,* is interesting because of the sedentary nature of this snake. It may be a relict or a waif. Rubber Boas usually feed on baby mice, entering burrows to obtain them. Their preferred food is apparently available, but it appears that this is the only California island on which the species appears.

The Racer, *Coluber constrictor* (Fig. 191), is not a common snake anywhere, but it is associated with Grasslands and Oak Woodlands, and thus should be at home, feeding on lizards and mice, in appropriate habitat on Angel Island. This is the only California snake in which the juvenile is distinctly different in appearance from the adult. The adult is plain brown, olive, or bluish above and whitish to yellow on the underside. The juvenile, however, has brown saddles on its back, similar to the Gopher Snake. It requires close inspection to determine that the scales of a Racer are smooth, unlike the keeled scales of a Gopher Snake. Its presence on Santa Cruz Island also indicates that it is known to colonize islands.

Mammals The Angel Island Mole, *Scapanus latimanus insularis* (Fig. 194), is the only endemic vertebrate on the islands in San Francisco Bay. This mole is the island version of the Broad-footed Mole, a widely distributed species in California. The moles prefer sandy areas with high soil moisture and a good supply of herbaceous plants. They make humplike tunnels in grassland areas and clearings near the forests on Angel Island and feed underground on various invertebrates, particularly earthworms. Moles are strange little animals with silky grayish fur and greatly broadened front feet, specialized for digging. Unlike gophers, moles remain subterranean. They have no visible eyes or external ears, relying on their other senses to locate food.

The largest animal on Angel Island is the Mule Deer, *Odocoileus hemionus*. This is the only island in the bay that has a permanent breeding population of large mammals. Because there are no natural predators for the deer on the island, the population has to be thinned periodically or it would grow to a size that would cause severe damage to native vegetation. Also conspicuous are the Raccoons, *Procyon lotor*. Interestingly, the name Raccoon Strait, given to the deep-water channel between Angel Island and the Tiburon Peninsula, has nothing to do with the Raccoons on the island. The channel was named for a British warship, HMS *Raccoon,* which was repaired in Ayala Cove in 1814.

Raccoons and Mule Deer are good swimmers and could probably have crossed the strait between Angel Island and the point of the peninsula. Deer have been observed to cross considerable distances by swimming, and hence explaining their presence on the island does not require a land bridge. Either of these species also could have been carried to the island by humans who introduced them for food.

YERBA BUENA/TREASURE ISLAND

Yerba Buena Island is located near the center of San Francisco Bay, midway between San Francisco and Oakland. Its natural size is about 152 acres (60 ha) in area and about 400 ft (130 m) in height. Today the island is essentially a residential area in a forest of Blue Gums and Monterey Pines (Plate 15A). It is connected to the 403-acre (159-ha) artificial island known as Treasure Island (Plate 15B), and the combined islands have housed a naval facility since 1896.

Perhaps the most distinctive feature of Yerba Buena Island is that one of the main support towers for the Oakland Bay Bridge is located just east of the island, and there is a tunnel through the island that connects two sections of the bridge. This means that about 130,000 people per day visit the island and each visit lasts about a minute!

Figure 201. Yerba Buena, *Satureja douglasii,* the plant for which Yerba Buena Island was named.

History

The island has had several names over the years. Its first name, Isla de los Alcatraces, was conferred by explorer Juan Manuel de Ayala in 1775, apparently because of all the Brown Pelicans or Cormorants he observed there. In 1826 the name was erroneously transferred to Alcatraz Island, former home of the famous prison. Yerba Buena has also been known as Sea Bird Island, Wood Island, and then Goat Island, each name a clue to past habitat conditions or uses. It was not until 1931 that historian Nellis Van De Grift Sanchez capped a 15-year effort to have the designation *Yerba Buena* officially applied to the island. The present name, Spanish for "good herb," is derived from an aromatic, trailing, vinelike plant of the mint family (Lamiaceae) that once covered the slopes of the island. Yerba Buena, *Satureja douglasii* (Fig. 201), is a coastal species common in shaded woods.

The island's earlier name, Wood Island, is a reference to the stands of trees that were cut for fuel by early expeditions to the San Francisco Bay area.

In 1836 Captain Graham Nye introduced goats to the island for later sale to trading vessels as a source of meat, hence the name Goat Island. In 1848 Thomas Dowling developed a sand-mining operation on the southeast side of the island. It is said that he turned loose a "bad-tempered bull" to patrol the island and discourage visitors. When the bull turned on the Dowling family, it was killed. In 1849 Edward Everett and William Bernard found the remains of an extensive aboriginal village on the eastern shore. Ruins of old houses and a large collection of bones and shells are believed to have been left by a tribe called the Tuchayunes, members of the Costanoan group. The village was probably a seasonal fishing station.

A lighthouse was constructed in 1875. Various modern settlements were also built, beginning about the middle of the nineteenth century. An old cemetery on the west end of the island has graves with markers that date back to 1852.

The history of military occupancy on Yerba Buena Island began with a presidential proclamation in 1866, setting aside the island for "military purposes." Congress authorized a Navy training station in 1896, and it housed up to 13,000 sailors at a time during its peak years throughout World War I.

Treasure Island (Plate 15B) was built in 1937 on the Yerba Buena shoals, a former navigation hazard. It was built to an elevation of 12 ft (4 m) in 14 months by covering the shoals with tons of rock and silt dredged from the bay. The name Treasure Island, borrowed from Robert Louis Stevenson's book of the same title, was an allusion to the real possibility that the muds dredged from the bay could contain gold that had been washed from the Sierra Nevada by the Sacramento River.

Treasure Island was originally constructed as the site for the Golden Gate International Exposition (San Francisco World's Fair), and it was planned as the future site for the San Francisco International Airport. In 1941, with another world war looming, Treasure Island was leased to the Navy, and naval activities spread out from Yerba Buena to cover both islands. After World War II, Treasure Island was no longer considered a suitable location for an international airport, so San Francisco traded the island for the naval airfield that is now the airport. Naval activities continued until 1993, when the Base Realignment and Closure Commission decided to close the base. Today the Navy operates the Treasure Island Museum, which is open to the public. The museum is devoted to the history of sea service in the Pacific and has a section on the origin of Treasure Island. Recently the naval station has been working with the city of San Francisco to convert the property to a more community-oriented purpose after the planned closure date of September 30, 1997. Proposals include a luxury hotel, a casino, a women's prison, a sports complex, affordable housing, an amusement park, and a restored wetland. All of these are complicated by a recent report that portions of the island have subsided 5–9 ft (1.5–3 m) since its construction.

Geology

The bedrock of Yerba Buena Island is primarily graywacke sandstone, similar in composition to that of Alcatraz Island. Originally the island was a low, flat-topped hump about 400 ft (130 m) high, with a peninsula extending toward the northeast.

Borings in the bedrock of San Franciso Bay indicate that the main channel for prebay drainage lies to the east of Yerba Buena Island. Water in the bay today is deeper to the west of the island. Thus at the height of glaciation, 16,000–18,000 years ago, it appears that Yerba Buena Island was connected to the mainland near Rincon Hill on the San Francico Peninsula. Borings to the southwest show the bedrock to be less than 200 ft (65 m) deep southwest of Yerba Buena Island. The fact that at the height of glaciation sea level could have been as much as 395 ft (120 m) lower establishes that Yerba Buena was connected to the mainland.

Terrestrial Vegetation

Yerba Buena has been completely urbanized by Navy and Coast Guard installations, including homes for military personnel. Vestiges of natural plant communities such as Mixed Evergreen Forest, Chaparral, Coastal Scrub, and Grassland occur at various locations around the island, mixed in with nonnative species.

In preparation for the Golden Gate International Exposition some 4000 trees and 2 million flowering plants were planted. Many of them—including palms, Blue Gums, and Monterey Pines—are still alive. Yerba Buena Island originally had Mixed Evergreen Forest on its northern and eastern slopes. The southern and western slopes had Chaparral, and the flattened top was covered with Grassland.

As noted earlier, the Yerba Buena (*Satureja douglasii*) (Fig. 201), for which the island is named, is an aromatic, vinelike, mat-forming member of the mint family (Lamiaceae). Its slightly hairy oval leaves are about an inch (25 mm) wide and have slightly notched margins, and it has small, two-lipped, white to lavender flowers. Its normal distribution is in shaded woods in the Coast Ranges, and it also occurs on Santa Catalina Island

and in one location on Santa Cruz Island. The dried leaves are used to make a flavorful tea, which was used by Native Americans to treat fevers and stomach ailments.

Terrestrial Animals

There are no streams or ponds on Yerba Buena Island, but irrigation of lawns and other landscaping provides moisture that supports a population of the California Slender Salamander, *Batrachoseps attenuatus* (Fig. 190), and the Northern Alligator Lizard, *Elgaria coeruleus*. Otherwise there is little information available on native species of plants or animals.

ALCATRAZ ISLAND

Alcatraz may be the most famous island in California. As the former site of an infamous federal penitentiary, it certainly has worldwide name recognition. Originally it was little more than a rounded rock island about 22 acres (9 ha) in size. The first recorded description of the island, that of an American army officer, indicated that it was "entirely without resources within itself and the soil is scarcely perceptible, being rocky and precipitous on all sides." The first surveyor, another Army officer, commented that "The island has no beach, and but two or three points where small boats can land." The survey indicated that the island was 1705 ft (550 m) long and 580 ft (187 m) wide. Its two rounded peaks were 135 and 138 ft (43 and 44 m) high.

The strategic location of Alcatraz Island, with its grand view of the Golden Gate, made it an ideal location for a fortress to defend San Francisco Bay, one of the great natural harbors of the world. So, shortly after America took possession of the island in 1846, studies began in preparation for construction of America's first fortress on the Pacific Coast—a project that would forever alter the appearance of Alcatraz Island.

History

Although there are no shell middens to indicate early settlements of Native Americans, no doubt the Coast Miwoks and Ohlones visited Alcatraz, if for no other reason than to gather sea bird eggs. Early descriptions of the island mention its coating of bird guano and numerous nesting birds. One of the island's early names was White Island, in reference to the coating of guano. Darryl Babe Wilson, a member of the Pit River tribe, relates a tale told to him by his grandfather, in which an almost mystical significance is given to the island. His name for the island was *Allisti Ti-tanin-miji,* which translates as "Rock Rainbow" or "Diamond Island." According to the Native American legend, the island possessed a treasure that could heal the troubles of the people.

As mentioned previously, the name "Alcatraz," in reference to abundant Brown Pelicans or Cormorants, was originally applied to Yerba Buena Island. The name was transferred to the present site in 1827 by a British navy surveyor, perhaps because he wanted the island with such a strategic location for the defense of San Francisco Bay to have a name.

Studies and surveys preparatory to construction of the fortress began in 1853 when an officer with the unlikely name of Zealous Bates Tower arrived on Alcatraz Island. The first guns were set into place in 1854, and by 1859 the fort was fully garrisoned. Alcatraz was in a sense a prison from the very beginning in that various military crimes merited imprisonment, but in 1861 it was designated the official military prison for the Department of the Pacific. Through the Civil War and western Indian Wars, the fort was used as a place of internment. In 1907 the "Post on Alcatraz Island" officially became the "United States Military Prison." The fort had outlived its usefulness as a defense post, and with the advent of more powerful guns it appeared to have become vulnerable. The military operated the prison until 1933, when it became the notorious U.S. penitentiary that made the island famous. It remained a prison until 1963, at which time U.S. Attorney General Robert F. Kennedy removed the prisoners and closed the prison.

After the prison was closed the federal government offered it to the state and various local governments, but there were no takers; the island remained uninhabited except for a caretaker. Over time various proposals for new uses surfaced, including converting it into an amusement park. In 1964 a group of Native Americans attempted to occupy the island, invoking an 1868 treaty in which members of the Sioux tribe were granted the right to homestead on surplus federal property. They only stayed a few hours, but in 1969 they occupied the island again and stayed for three years. Eventually the occupation lost its inertia (aided by a fire that gutted a number of buildings and by the government's cutting off electric power and the water barge to the island), and the occupiers left. Finally, in 1972 the Golden Gate National Recreation Area was authorized and management of Alcatraz Island was turned over to the National Park Service.

Another historic first for Alcatraz Island was the establishment in 1854 of the first automated lighthouse on the Pacific coast. Using the light of an oil flame, a Fresnel lens of crystal prisms sent light beaming out 19 miles to warn navigators of the hazard. On foggy nights a huge bell was struck with an automated hammer. The light continued to guide ships for 125 years.

Geology

The bedrock of Alcatraz Island is principally graywacke sandstone. The first surveyor described it as follows: "This island is chiefly composed of irregularly stratified sandstone covered with a thin layer of guano. The stone is full of seams in all directions which render it unfit for any building purposes and probably difficult to quarry."

As soon as construction of the original fort began, reshaping of the island was under way. Material was scraped and blasted from the slopes, the southern end of the island was beveled away, and topsoil was barged over from Marin County, most of it from Angel Island. By 1890 the island had taken on the steep-sided, flat-topped appearance that characterizes it today.

Terrestrial Vegetation

Originally there was very little in the way of vegetation on Alcatraz Island, but with the importation of soil came the seeds of native plants that are now common on Alcatraz. Furthermore, in 1983 an attempt was made to introduce endangered California plants to the island. Of the thirty-one species introduced, apparently only four survived. As of 1992 only twelve native species were considered established on the island, including Coyote Brush, *Baccharis pilularis* (Fig. 45B); California Coffeeberry, *Rhamnus californica;* Checker Mallow, *Sidalcea malviflora* (Fig. 206); Yellow Bush Lupine, *Lupinus arboreus* (Fig. 168); and Monterey Cypress, *Cupressus macrocarpa.* Among the herbaceous species are several ferns and California Poppy, *Eschscholzia californica.* These native plants are scattered among a plethora of ornamental plants that were introduced to Alcatraz Island over the course of more than 100 years of habitation. Elizabeth McClintock, a local botanist, has kept a catalogue of plant species for Alcatraz Island. John Hart, Russell Beatty, and Michael Boland, in their volume *Gardens of Alcatraz,* have documented the history of Alcatraz and its gardens.

Terrestrial Animals

The original inhabitants of Alcatraz Island were the sea birds and marine mammals that still occur in the bay. Numerous accounts mention the guano that covered the island. Blasting of the cliffs actually added to the steep cliff habitat favored by nesting birds, so that the species that occur today on the island are probably similar to those of presettlement times. Sea birds that nest on the island today include the Brown Pelican, *Pelecanus occidentalis* (Fig. 192J; Plate 3A); Brandt's Cormorant, *Phalacrocorax penicillatus;* Double-crested Cormorant, *Phalacrocorax auritus* (Fig. 3B); Pelagic Cormorant, *Phalacrocorax pelagicus;* Pigeon Guillemot, *Cepphus columba* (Fig. 175); Western Gull, *Larus occidentalis* (Fig. 192A; Plate 3D); and Black Oystercatcher, *Haematopus bachmani* (Plate 3C). Among the herons and egrets of San Francisco Bay, fully 15 percent of the Black-

Figure 202. Red Rock Island as seen from the south. The Richmond Bridge and East Brother Island are visible in the background.

crowned Night-herons, *Nycticorax nycticorax* (Fig. 204), nest on Alcatraz Island.

The only native amphibian on the island is the California Slender Salamander, *Batrachoseps attenuatus* (Fig. 190). Genetic analysis of this salamander indicates that it is closely related to those on Angel Island, a finding that implies that the salamander was introduced along with the imported soil.

The Deer Mouse, *Peromyscus maniculatus* (Fig. 3), is particularly common in a fragment of Grassland that occurs on the east side of the island between the powerhouse and the old officer's club. Here the mice have created a network of burrows, where they feed on the seeds produced by the grasses. This is the only island in the bay that contains this native mouse. Although the mice have not differentiated to the subspecies level, as have the Deer Mice on the Channel Islands, they are a lighter buff color than those on the nearby mainland. It is not certain how the Deer Mouse got to the island: Deer Mice are good colonizers, as indicated by their presence on all of the eight Channel Islands, but some think they may have been introduced to Alcatraz Island in a load of lumber.

RED ROCK ISLAND

Red Rock Island is a brick-red island located just south of the Richmond Bridge (Fig. 202). The Spanish called it Moleta (from *moler,* "to grind") in reference to its shape, which suggests a large grinding stone. On the eastern side there is a break in the cliffs that allows a visitor to ascend a steep trail to a cirque-like bowl, and from the bowl the path leads to the summit of the island along a steep shoulder.

Very little has been written about the natural history of Red Rock Island. It is a round-topped island with very steep sides. Although the island is not large, it is surprisingly high, reaching an elevation of 169 ft (54.5 m). This small island of 9 acres (3.5 ha) lies about a mile and a half (2 km) west of Point Richmond, and nearly 3 miles (5 km) east of Point San Quentin. As described previously, it marks the confluence of county lines in such a way that it lies in three counties: Contra Costa, Marin, and San Francisco.

Geology

The name of this island refers to the reddish color produced by the silica-carbonate cherts that make up the bulk of the island. These cherts, typical of the Franciscan Formation, are found at various localities around the bay area. They are formed by replacement of serpentine as hot, alkaline water rises through sheared and crushed serpentine in fault zones, and they are called "mercury rock" by miners because a mercury ore, cinnabar, and liquid mercury frequently occur in them. Of particular interest on this island is the presence of tunnels and trenches on the western side of the island, remnants of attempts to mine cinnabar.

Terrestrial Vegetation

Soil on this island is poorly developed, characterized by large amounts of gravel and talus. Where there is enough soil to grow plants, vegetation seems to be dominated by Coyote Brush, *Baccharis pilularis* (Fig. 45B), particularly on the northern and eastern slopes. Reports of vegetation on the island from the 1950s indicated that the dominant plant was Yellow Bush Lupine, *Lupinus arboreus* (Fig. 168), yet by 1958 these plants were no longer important components of the vegetation.

Terrestrial Animals

It is surprising that the island is home to two species of salamander, the California Slender Salamander, *Batrachoseps attenuatus* (Fig. 190), and— even though there are no oak trees—the Arboreal Salamander, *Aneides lugubris* (Fig. 62). Other than birds, the only other terrestrial vertebrate mentioned as having occupied Red Rock Island was the Norway Rat, *Rattus norvegicus*. Museum records indicate Norway Rats were abundant in 1934, but apparently there are no mammals living on the island today.

Among the birds, the Song Sparrow, *Melospiza melodia,* is the only

Figure 203. The Marin Islands as seen from the northwest, near Point San Pedro.

reported breeding land bird. In recent years, however, the number of water birds using the island has gradually increased. Recent reports indicate nesting colonies of Black-crowned Night-herons, *Nycticorax nycticorax* (Fig. 204), and Snowy Egrets, *Egretta thula* (Fig. 193) (even though there are no trees). Western Gulls, *Larus occidentalis* (Fig. 192A; Plate 3D), and Black Oystercatchers, *Haematopus bachmani* (Plate 3C), also have been reported nesting on the island. It remains to be seen whether the introduction of Maritime Goldfields or Farallon Weed, *Lasthenia maritima* (Fig. 170), will follow the arrival of these birds.

MARIN ISLANDS

The two Marin Islands are located in San Rafael Bay, an arm of San Francisco Bay north of the Golden Gate (Fig. 203). They lie about a half mile (0.8 km) offshore, approximately midway between Point San Pedro and Point San Quentin in Marin County. West Marin is a small, oval island about 3 acres (1.1 ha) in size. It is about an eighth of a mile (200 m) long and 70 ft (23 m) high. East Marin Island is roughly L-shaped and about 11 acres (4.2 ha) in area. It is about the same height as West Marin, but about a quarter of a mile (400 m) long. The two islands are about 190 yards (170 m) apart. These are flat-topped, steep-sided land masses with conspicuous trees on their upper surfaces.

History

West Marin Island has three shell middens, one of them more than 4 ft (1.1 m) deep, indicating that Native Americans, probably Coast Miwoks, used the island for many years. The Mexican government took over the islands in the 1820s and probably drove off the Native Americans. The U.S. government took possession in 1848, after the war with Mexico, and held the islands until 1926, when they were purchased by shipping magnate Tom Crowley. Two houses were built on larger East Marin Island, and Crowley's son used it as a retreat. In 1990 Crowley Maritime Corporation decided to sell the islands, and they were purchased for $3.4 million by a coalition of environmentalists, regional agencies, and private groups. In 1992 the islands came under the management of the U.S. Fish and Wildlife Service and are now known as the Marin Islands National Wildlife Refuge and Ecological Reserve.

Geology

Bedrock on the Marin Islands is of a typical Franciscan assemblage, mostly graywacke sandstone. On the south side of East Marin Island a former quarry is now the site of a small freshwater pond. The islands are so close to the mainland and the channel separating them from it is so shallow that the islands were connected to the mainland for much of their history.

Terrestrial Vegetation

After the islands passed into public hands, a floristic survey of native plants was undertaken by Robert Ornduff of the University of California at Berkeley and Michael Vasey of San Francisco State University. Even though the islands are quite small, and in spite of habitation on East Marin, a significant amount of natural vegetation is still present.

The native plants of the Marin Islands are associated with Mixed Evergreen Woodland, Oak Woodland, Northern Coastal Scrub, Coastal Grassland, and limited amounts of Salt Marsh.

East Marin Island In association with the Crowley family houses on East Marin Island, several species of trees were introduced, the most common of which is Monterey Pine, *Pinus radiata.* These trees are conspicuous on the plateau region of East Island. In the 1980s a small flock of Barbary Sheep, *Ammotragus lervia,* was introduced to East Island, ostensibly to reduce the fire hazard by keeping the herbaceous plants in check. These domestic animals almost certainly had an impact on the native vegetation, but the extent of the impact has never been assessed.

Native trees on the moister, northern side of the island form a sort of forest. Components of Oak Woodland such as Coast Live Oak, *Quercus agrifolia* (Fig. 183A), and California Buckeye, *Aesculus californica* (Fig. 182), are joined here by California Laurel, *Umbellularia californica* (Fig. 180), which is more often associated with Mixed Evergreen Forest. Understory shrubs in this area include Poison Oak, *Toxicodendron diversilobum* (Fig. 58); Blue Elderberry, *Sambucus mexicana;* Toyon, *Heteromeles arbu-*

tifolia (Fig. 54); Snowberry, *Symphorocarpus alba* var. *laevigatus;* and Oceanspray, *Holodiscus discolor.* The foliage of the latter two shrubs is superficially similar, both having serrated to lobed leaf margins. The Snowberry, however, is a member of the honeysuckle family (Caprifoliaceae), as is the Elderberry (unlike that of the Elderberry, the snow-white fruit of the Snowberry is usually poisonous to humans). Snowberry flowers are pinkish and bell-shaped. On the other hand, Oceanspray is characterized by white flowers and serrated leaves, and it is a member of the rose family (Rosaceae).

Northern Coastal Scrub is well developed on East Marin Island, occurring on the tops and faces of cliffs. The dominant shrubs are California Sagebrush, *Artemisia californica* (Fig. 45A); Orange Bush Monkeyflower, *Mimulus aurantiacus* (Fig. 47); and Seaside Woolly Sunflower, *Eriophyllum staechadifolium* (Fig. 80). Coyote Brush, *Baccharis pilularis* (Fig. 45B), which is common on West Marin Island, is, strangely, nearly absent on East Marin. Only one living plant was observed in 1993. On the south side of the island, on the cliff faces, there are also scattered individuals of Deerweed, *Lotus scoparius;* Nude Buckwheat, *Eriogonum nudum;* and the Paniculate Live-forever, *Dudleya cymosa* ssp. *paniculata.*

In the Grassland community on the plateau, the native perennial bunchgrass known as Foothill Needlegrass, *Nassella lepida,* is abundant. Mixed in with the grasses are common native wildflowers such as California Poppy, *Eschscholzia californica;* Yarrow Milfoil, *Achillea millefolium;* Everlasting, *Gnaphalium stramineum;* and Miner's Lettuce, *Claytonia perfoliata.*

The pond associated with the former quarry on the south side of East Island has along its margin a depauperate Coastal Salt Marsh (Fig. 189) characterized mostly by Salt Grass, *Distichlis spicata.* Pickleweed, *Salicornia virginica,* also occurs along the rocky south shore.

West Marin Island Even though West Marin Island has been uninhabited, the forest is not well developed. As would be expected, the largest trees occur on the central and northern slopes. The dominant tree in this area is the California Buckeye, many specimens of which are obviously quite old. On the western part of the island, shrubby Coast Live Oaks and Toyons occur with Wood Rose, *Rosa gymnocarpa.* An understory of introduced ephemeral grasses occurs in this area. On the east side of the island, Coast Live Oaks and Toyons of larger stature are mixed in with Blue Elderberry.

The Northern Coastal Scrub of West Marin Island is somewhat different in composition from that of East Marin Island. On the south and east sides of the island, California Sagebrush dominates and Orange Bush Monkeyflower is less abundant. On the cliffs in the area can be found the

Figure 204. Immature Black-crowned Night-heron, *Nycticorax nycticorax,* in nesting tree. In San Francisco Bay these birds nest on Alcatraz, Brooks, Red Rock, and West Marin Islands. The streaked breast of young birds enables them to remain nearly invisible as they stand motionless in marsh vegetation.

Paniculate Live-forever and Nude Buckwheat. On the western and northern margins of the island Coyote Brush and Everlasting are the common species and the plants on the cliffs are joined by a maroon-flowered snapdragon known as California Figwort, *Scrophularia californica,* and a fern, *Polypodium californicum.*

Along the base of the cliffs at a few localities are vestiges of Coastal Salt Marsh vegetation. Pickleweed occurs in this habitat, and a small patch of Alkali Heath, *Frankenia salina,* occurs at the easern tip of the island.

Terrestrial Animals

The only native amphibian found on the Marin Islands is the California Slender Salamander, *Batrachoseps attenuatus* (Fig. 190), and it is fairly common. The only reptile is the Western Fence Lizard, *Sceloporus occidentalis,* and it is found only on the larger East Marin Island. The only conspicuous mammal on the islands is the introduced Norway Rat, *Rattus norvegicus.* The periodic setting out of poison by the residents of East Marin Island may have eliminated native mice.

The conspicuous vertebrates of the Marin Islands are the birds. It was mentioned previously that the heronry on West Marin Island is probably the largest in northern California. Favored trees for the nests are the huge California Buckeyes that occur on the north-facing slopes. Four species have established twiggy nests in the area: the Black-crowned Night-heron, *Nycticorax nycticorax* (*Fig.* 204); Great Blue Heron, *Ardea herodias* (Fig. 192D); and Snowy Egret, *Egretta thula,* and Great Egret, *Casmerodius albus* (Fig. 193). These birds are so common during the spring breeding season that the clamoring voices of thousands of them drown out all other sounds. They produce so much guano that there is virtually no under-story vegetation. The birds also clip twigs from the trees to make their nests, although no long-term effect of this pruning has been documented.

Other birds that have been documented on the island include Western Gull, *Larus occidentalis* (Fig. 192A; Plate 3D); Black Oystercatcher, *Haemato-pus bachmani* (Plate 3C); Canada Goose, *Branta canadensis;* Red-tailed Hawk, *Buteo jamaicensis;* and Common Raven, *Corvus corax.* Canada Geese and Western Gulls nest on the ground on West Marin Island, but not on East Marin, probably because of the former habitations. Canada Geese congregate there but apparently do not make nests.

BROOKS ISLAND

Brooks Island is located in Contra Costa County, on the eastern edge of San Francisco Bay north of Berkeley (Fig. 205). It lies about half a mile (800 m) south of the Richmond Peninsula and about a mile and a half (2.5 km) from the mainland to the east. The island covers about 45 acres (18 ha) and rises gently to an elevation of 160 ft (52 m). The island is shaped roughly like a right triangle, with the 90° corner to the southwest. Just to the west of that corner is a small islet known as Bird Island or Bird Rock. It is only a half acre (2020 m^2) in size. From the north end of the island, a rock breakwater extends westward about 2 miles (3.2 km), parallel to the shoreline of the Richmond Peninsula. The breakwater protects the Har-bor Canal entrance to Richmond Harbor from waves and siltation, although sediment that has accumulated on the south side of the barrier has had the effect of extending the Brooks Island shoreline westward to an elevation of 10 ft (3 m) above sea level. Water in the channel to the east is only 3–4 ft (1 m) deep during low tide, and the channel appears to be filling slowly with sediment. The house on the northern part of the island, visible from the mainland, is occupied by a full-time caretaker.

History

Costanoan Native Americans, probably of the Huchiam or perhaps Chocheyno tribe, inhabited Brooks Island for thousands of years, and two areas of shell middens found on the island have revealed much about them. More than 9000 cubic feet (1000 m^3) of the middens were excavated,

Figure 205. Brooks Island as seen from the Richmond Peninsula.

yielding projectile points, knives, net sinkers, bone tools, cordage, charm-stones, and some artifacts of European manufacture. Food remains indicate reliance more on aquatic birds than fish, but remnants of such shellfish as Bay Mussels (*Mytilis edulis*) were also abundant. A decrease in the size of the mussel shells toward the top of the middens indicates that the natives may have been overharvesting them. The presence of apparent Spanish and Russian trade items in the topmost portions of the middens suggests that Native Americans may have continued to occupy the site into the 1840s.

The first name for the island was Isla de Carmen, as indicated on the map drawn in 1775 by Jose de Cañizares as part of the Juan Manuel de Ayala survey of San Francisco Bay. The origin of the present name is unknown. As early as 1850, after the U.S. government took possession, charts of the area showed the name *Brooks* on this island. The official map of California adopted by the state legislature in 1853 carried the name *Brooks Island*.

There are also historical references to the island as Rocky, Bird, and Sheep Island. Apparently sheep and cattle were raised on the island until the 1930s. Other agricultural uses for the island included the planting of fruit and grape orchards, although today there is no remaining evidence of cultivation. The Morgan Oyster Company ran a cultured oyster operation from the island for nearly 25 years, from 1886 to 1909. The most visible commercial operation, however, was the quarrying of sandstone on the south end by the Healy-Tibbets Construction Company, which went on for about 50 years, ending in 1938 when the island was sold to Mrs. Mabel

Horton, widow of one of the owners of the company. In the 1920s and 1930s the Army Corps of Engineers also quarried rock to build the breakwater from a site on the west side, near the breakwater. Over the years many commercial uses for the island were proposed, including a naval base, a freight terminal, a heliport, and a marina, but the high asking price for the land apparently discouraged development. Finally, in 1968 the land was acquired by the East Bay Regional Park District for the sum of $625,000, half of which was refunded by the U.S. Department of Housing and Urban Development. Since 1965 the island has been leased to the Sheep Island Gun Club, pending eventual development as a park. As of 1996 the decision had been made to maintain the island as a reserve. Today a caretaker lives on the island and public access is by permit only.

Geology

Brooks Island contains rocks of the Franciscan Formation, similar to the Potrero Hills on the Richmond Peninsula to the north and Marin County on the other side of the bay. The San Pablo fault lies just to the east of the island and the Potrero Hills, forming a partial boundary to the Franciscan rock unit. To the east, on the mainland, bedrock is covered by sediments of Pleistocene age, with Franciscan rocks emerging in the Berkeley Hills, but bounded on the east by the Hayward fault. Franciscan rocks do not crop up again to the east until the foothills of the Sierra Nevada.

The rocks of Brooks Island are mostly graywacke sandstone and greenstone, with some interbedded chert and shale. Because of the impermeable nature of the bedrock, water that percolates into the ground emerges as springs at two localities, one on the northeast side of the island and one on the west side. The western spring has permanent flow, issuing from unsheared graywacke sandstone. At the southern end of the island, the quarrying operation cut into the bedrock, resulting in a region of seeps and two ponds.

Terrestrial Vegetation

Brooks Island supports a mosaic of natural plant communities, but the two most common are Coastal Grassland and Northern Coastal Scrub. The area is a showcase for Coastal Grassland, which occurs on the island in a relatively undisturbed state. Coastal Grassland occupies about 18 acres (7 ha) of terrain, particularly the flat areas. The dominant species include native bunchgrasses such as needlegrasses (*Nassella* spp.), ryegrasses (*Lolium* spp.), and fescues (*Festuca* spp.), mixed in with native wildflowers such as Blue Dicks, *Dichelostemma capitatum* (Fig. 198); Soap Plant, *Chlorogalum parviflorum;* and Checker Mallow, *Sidalcea malviflora*

Figure 206. Checker Mallow, *Sidalcea malviflora*. This bright pink wildflower is common in undisturbed native grassland.

(Fig. 206). This grassland was grazed until the 1930s, but since then, with the exception of a fire in 1956, it has been allowed to exist in an undisturbed state. An additional 8 acres (3 ha) of grassland, characterized by non-native European grasses, has become established on the fill to the west.

The Northern Coastal Scrub occurs on the steeper slopes, particularly to the north and east sides of the island. In all about 24 acres (9 ha) are occupied by this community. Here the dominant species are Coyote Brush, *Baccharis pilularis* (Fig. 45B); Orange Bush Monkeyflower, *Mimulus aurantiacus* (Fig. 47); Poison Oak, *Toxicodendron diversilobum* (Fig. 58); California Wild Rose, *Rosa californica* (Fig. 57A); and California Black-berry, *Rosa ursinus* (Fig. 57B). California Sagebrush, *Artemisia californica* (Fig. 45A), occurs on drier, south-facing slopes such as those near the abandoned quarry on the southwest corner of the island. Seaside Woolly Sunflower, *Eriophyllum staechadifolium* (Fig. 80), is also common in rocky areas above the shoreline. It appears, that in the absence of disturbance, particularly fires, that shrubs, particularly Coyote Brush, are invading and replacing the native grassland. Preservation of the grassland, through a program of prescribed burning has been proposed.

A mixture of Salt Marsh and Coastal Strand species occupies about 25 acres (10 ha) on the sand spit. Closer to the water are Salt Grass, *Distichlis spicata;* Alkali Heath, *Frankenia salina;* Sea Lavender or Western Marsh-rosemary, *Limonium californicum;* and Pickleweeds (*Salicornia* spp.). On higher ground, the sandy areas have typical dune plants such as Beachbur, *Ambrosia chamissonis* (Fig. 148); Beach Evening Primrose, *Camissonia cheiranthifolia;* and Sea Rocket, *Cakile maritima.*

There is a small region of Freshwater Marsh vegetation around the two small ponds in the abandoned quarry at the south end of the island. The dominant plant is Narrow-leaved Cattail, *Typha angustifolia.* Arroyo Willow, *Salix lasiolepis,* has also colonized these ponds.

There are a few native trees on the island, but not enough to characterize a community. Along with the Arroyo Willow there is one specimen of Red Willow, *Salix laevigata,* on the northeast side of the island. The most common trees are large old California Buckeyes, *Aesculus californica* (Fig. 182): about a dozen of them occur in two groups on the northeast side of the island near the shell middens. It may be that these were planted by Native Americans, who ate the fruit. Blue Elderberry, *Sambucus mexicana,* also occurs in the area. Among the landscaping plants that occur near the caretaker's residence are two introduced native species, Monterey Pine, *Pinus radiata,* and Monterey Cypress, *Cupressus macrocarpa.*

Terrestrial Animals

After Angel Island, Brooks Island holds the largest assemblage of terrestrial vertebrates in San Francisco Bay. Among amphibians, two salamanders and a treefrog have been reported on the island. The California Slender Salamander, *Batrachoseps attenuatus* (Fig. 190), occupies the northern and eastern parts of the island, where moisture remains in the soil for most of the year. A small population of the Arboreal Salamander, *Aneides lugubris* (Fig. 62), occurs in the pond area of the abandoned quarry on the south end of the island. The Pacific Treefrog, *Hyla* (=*Pseudacris*) *regilla* (Fig. 63), has been reported from the island, but it may not have established a breeding population.

The Western Terrestrial Garter Snake, *Thamnophis elegans,* occurs on Brooks Island in two color phases, one with a red background and the other with a green background. These snakes probably feed on the resident lizards, although they do eat treefrogs, and they may feed on the Mosquitofish, *Gambusia affinis,* that have been introduced to the ponds. The only lizard on the island is the Northern Alligator Lizard, *Elgaria coeruleus,* which tends to remain in the vicinity of the ponds. The Western Pond Turtle, *Clemmys marmorata,* is known from only one specimen.

Over a hundred species of land birds are known to visit Brooks Island,

and at least eighteen species are known to nest there. The variety of aquatic birds (Fig. 192) that use the island as a refuge is particularly significant. Cormorants, Brown Pelicans, ducks, and other water birds rest on the island. The Black-crowned Night-heron, *Nycticorax nycticorax* (Fig. 204), occurs here in greater concentrations than anywhere else in the bay area except West Marin Island. In the spring and summer about fifty of these birds nest in the California Buckeyes. The Canada Goose, *Branta canadensis,* also nests on the island. Bird Island also has a nesting population of Canada Geese, as well as Black Oystercatchers, *Haemotopus bachmani* (Plate 3C), and Western Gulls, *Larus occidentalis* (Fig. 192A; Plate 3D). In recent years, the Caspian Tern, *Sterna caspia,* has started breeding in the area as well.

The gun club, which leased the island in 1965, introduced a variety of game birds, including Ring-necked Pheasant, *Phasianus colchicus;* Northern Bobwhite, *Colinus virginianus;* and Guineafowl, *Guttera* spp.

All of the mammals on Brooks Island have been introduced. Over the years, introduced domestic mammals have included cattle, sheep, goats, horses, and dogs. The most common mammal today is the California Vole, *Microtus californicus* (Fig. 150); it is most abundant in the grassland habitat, where the ground is perforated by many burrows. A secondary influence of the mice seems to be an infestation of Black Mustard, *Brassica nigra,* that has become established in the region where the mice are most common.

The population of voles on Brooks Island descended from four males and three females that in 1957 were experimentally placed on Bird Island to the west. Apparently the idea was to observe the growth rate of the population on an unoccupied land mass: no one expected the animals to cross 230 yards (209 m) of water and colonize the main island. A consequence of the introduction was the extermination, within two years, of an introduced population of House Mice, *Mus musculus.* The mechanism of the replacement is not completely understood, but William Lidicker of the University of California at Berkeley thinks that it was a function of annoyance, in which the stress imposed by the interaction of the two species caused reproductive failure in the House Mice.

A single gene mutation, responsible for a buffy fur color in these voles, became well established on the island. This is probably an example of *founder effect* or a genetic bottleneck, in which a small group of founders gives rise to a large population that exhibits a unique trait. Research on the inheritance of this color morph was also conducted at the University of California at Berkeley.

A small population of Norway Rats, *Rattus norvegicus,* has been on the

Figure 207. Browns Island as seen across New York Slough from Pittsburg.

island for many years. The rats have tended to live along the shoreline, where they can feed on carrion and certain marine organisms such as Bay Mussels. The rotting bodies of birds that hunters failed to locate provide additional sources of food for the rats. On occasion, particularly during the dry season, they have been known to prey on the voles. However, systematic poisoning by the caretaker tends to keep their numbers low.

BROWNS ISLAND

Browns Island (Fig. 207) is located in the easternmost part of Suisun Bay, just west of the confluence of the Sacramento and San Joaquin Rivers. The Contra Costa County line runs eastward along the bay, but it arches northward and around the island in such a way that it is located entirely within Contra Costa County. Just east of the island, at the Sacramento County line, Suisun Bay becomes the Sacramento River. To the south, Browns Island is separated from Pittsburg, on the mainland, by New York Slough, which joins the San Joaquin River upstream. East of Browns Island is Middle Slough, a narrow channel that separates it from Winter Island; on the east side of Winter Island is the San Joaquin River.

Browns Island is a low-lying island about 4 ft (1.5 m) high and just about a square mile (275 ha) in area. It has about 4.5 miles (7 km) of shoreline. A natural waterway called Crooked Slough, running eastward from Suisun Bay, nearly cuts the island in half. At the eastern end of Crooked Slough is a shallow, 8-acre (3-ha) lake. Because most of the island is barely above water level, it is essentially a wetland lying at the interface of salt water and fresh water. As such, having no levees and minimal disturbance, Browns Island is probably one of the most pristine examples of the Freshwater Marsh that once abounded on the shoreline of San Francisco Bay.

History

No one seems to know how the island got its name, but the name is not a recent one, and Browns Island seems to be the only name of record. Over the years, the island has escaped severe disturbance in spite of its use as a pasture for horses. In the early 1900s, horses that had pulled San Francisco fire wagons and police mounts were sent to the island to recover from injuries. At the turn of the century a bordello, known as the Coney Island Club, was located at the western end of the island. It was accessed by a pier and a boardwalk that crossed the marsh to higher land. The site is marked by two California Fan Palms, *Washingtonia filifera,* and other ornamental plants that apparently were planted by the women during their off hours. The palms, now about 20 ft (6 m) tall, are visible landmarks from the water (Fig. 207). The lake at the end of Crooked Slough has been managed, off and on over the years, by a private duck-hunting club.

In 1978 the East Bay Regional Park District took control of 595 acres (234 ha) of the island. The remaining land, approximately 100 acres (40 ha), forming a rectangle in the center of the island, is owned by the Port of Stockton, which also owns a 3-acre (1.2 ha) plot on the western end near Point Emmet.

Geology

Soil on the island is composed of sediments and detritus typical of a wetland. Beneath the island lie about 30 ft (9 m) of peaty sediments that contain a botanical record reflecting about 4000–6000 years of continuous marsh vegetation. Working for the U.S. Geologic Service in the late 1970s, Brian Atwater analyzed a series of cores taken from the muds of the Sacramento–San Joaquin Delta. His record shows that for most of its existence, Browns Island was a Freshwater Marsh dominated by Common Reed, *Phragmites australis.* However, in the upper 20 ft (6 m) of the sediments there is a gradual decrease in the abundance of underground stems (rhizomes) of the Common Reed. The top 1.5 ft (0.5 m) of sediment contains no Common Reed at all. This disappearance of Common Reed from the island during the last thousand years or so apparently reflects a gradual change away from a predominantly freshwater habitat to one with significant saltwater intrusion. Common Reed cannot tolerate salt water. Its virtual disappearance, accompanied by the arrival of Salt Marsh species, could reflect reduced river discharge or an increase in the elevation of the island. Reduced river discharge would be associated with a drying trend in the climate over the last thousand years.

In recent years, increased salinity of the soil has been associated with reduced flow of the Sacramento River owing to diversions into the California Aqueduct. During drought years, such as 1977–78, the salinity of the water in the area is even more significantly affected, and it must be inferred that increased saltwater intrusion will continue to alter the soil salinity of Brown's Island.

Terrestrial Vegetation

If Brooks Island is a showcase of undisturbed Coastal Grassland, then Browns Island is a showcase for Freshwater Marsh. Walter Knight, a botanist for the East Bay Regional Park District, has documented the flora of Browns Island, identifying 133 plant species, including nonnatives.

The Freshwater Marsh species that are showcased here include three species each of cattail (*Typha*) (Fig. 186), rushes (*Juncus*), and nutsedges (*Cyperus*). Five kinds of bulrushes, *Scirpus* spp., are also found along the watercourses. Two species of floating pondweed (*Potamogeton*) are found in quiet water.

On higher ground, where there is more soil but where the roots may be flooded at high tide, are a number of other conspicuous species. Along the shoreline Tufted Hairgrass, *Deschampsia caespitosa,* grows to about 30 (75 cm) in. in height. In can be recognized in bloom by the abundant drooping flowerheads that turn the top half of each plant a whitish color. One of the "marsh-loving" species of the morning glory family (Convolvulaceae) is Hedge Bindweed, *Calystegia sepium* ssp. *limnophila.* This viney plant grows over other plants all around the island.

Several plants listed by the California Native Plant Society as rare or endangered are also found on the island. The Delta Tule Pea, *Lathyrus jepsonii* var. *jepsonii,* is an abundant vine that can be seen growing through and over other plants along waterways and at Botany Cove. This member of the pea family (Fabaceae) is a vine with lovely pink to pink-purple flowers. The Suisun Marsh Aster, *Aster lentus,* is a rare sunflower with violet petals. It can be seen around Botany Cove, where the plants reach 7 ft (2 m) in height. Another rare member of the sunflower family (Asteraceae) is Marsh Gumplant, *Grindelia stricta* var. *angustifolia,* a small shrub with abundant bright yellow flowers that is common between Point Emmet and Botany Cove. Delta Lilaeopsis or Mason's Lilaeopsis, *Lilaeopsis masonii,* is a low-growing, mat-forming plant in the parsley family (Apiaceae). It is classified as rare, but it is common on the island, where it forms a lawnlike turf anywhere the ground is flat and wet. A species known as California Loosetrife, *Lythrum californicum,* has also been proposed for listing as rare or endangered. It grows in with the rushes in the area between Botany Cove and Sandy Knoll.

On the high parts of the island, large woody plants associated with marshes may be found. Arroyo Willow, *Salix lasiolepis;* Black Willow, *Salix gooddingii;* and White Alder, *Alnus rhombifolia,* are trees found here, along with large shrubs such as Mule Fat, *Baccharis salicifolia* (Fig. 187), and Button-willow, *Cephalanthus occidentalis.*

At the highest part of the island near South Landing, salt-tolerant plants are becoming more common. Although the area is not yet a true Salt Marsh habitat, Alkali Weed, *Cressa truxilensis;* Pickleweed, *Salicornia virginica;* and a salt-tolerant, purple-flowered sunflower known as Jaumea, *Jaumea carnosa,* are common. In this area the trees mentioned earlier are showing signs of salt stress.

At the west end of the island, along with the California Fan Palms, are some other introduced trees that were probably also planted by the residents of the bordello. These include another California native, Fremont Cottonwood, *Populus fremontii,* and the Australian native known as Blackwood Acacia or Black Wattle, *Acacia melanoxylon.* Also conspicuous in the area are huge clumps of the invasive Pampas Grass, *Cortaderia selloana.*

Terrestrial Animals

Apparently there has been no scientific study of the animal population of Browns Island. Its close proximity to the mainland, however, implies that any sort of terrestrial animals that inhabit marshes could be expected there. Raccoons, *Procyon lotor,* are known to occur there, and the presence of the Muskrat, *Ondatra zibethicus,* is not unlikely. Among the small rodents, it should not be a surprise if the House Mouse, *Mus musculus,* and the Norway Rat, *Rattus norvegicus,* occur there. It would be extremely significant if a healthy population of the endangered, federally listed Salt Marsh Harvest Mouse, *Reithrodontomys raviventris,* were to be discovered. This little mouse builds a nest similar to that of a bird in the vegetation and comes out at night to feed on seeds. Salt Marsh Harvest Mice are truly unique in their ability to survive on seawater.

Birds of the area are typical marsh species. The Northern Harrier, *Circus cyaneus,* can often be seen flying low over the island in search of prey. Similarly, the White-tailed Kite, *Elanus caeruleus,* resembling a gull, can be seen hovering over the marsh on nearly every visit. The Marsh Wren, *Cistothorus palustris,* moves about incessantly, feeding on insects it gleans from the vegetation. Even though the bird is seldom seen, its call—

a series of loud, rapid notes and rattles—can be heard day and night during the breeding season. Large numbers of water birds, all typical residents of marsh habitats, are also common inhabitants of the island, particularly during the winter.

THE BROTHERS AND THE SISTERS

It is an old international custom to assign the name "brothers" or "sisters" to geographic features that lie near each other and have a similar appearance. Two rock outcrops located at the northern end of San Francisco Bay near Point San Pablo in Contra Costa County are known as the Brothers (Plate 15C). East Brother Island is known for its elegant ginger and white Victorian house and square light station, which was staffed from 1874 to 1969. In 1973 it was placed on the National Register of Historic Places, and by 1979 it was being managed as a bed-and-breakfast by a nonprofit corporation that uses the revenue to maintain the light station. The island also contains the ruins of what may have been the last whaling station in the United States.

To the west of East Brother Island is what appears to be a barren, bleached boulder. It is known as West Brother Island. Farther to the northwest, near the opposite shore in Marin County, are two more bits of pale rock, known as the Sisters. Like many of the apparently barren islands of San Francisco Bay, West Brother and the Sisters are homes to a variety of sea birds (Fig. 192), such as the Western Gull, Brown Pelican, and Double-crested Cormorant. The islands are covered with bird guano and also have been known to support distinctive populations of Maritime Goldfields or Farallon Weed, *Lasthenia maritima*, which were probably introduced by the birds. The ebb and flow of these populations, as the numbers of birds fluctuate, is the subject of ongoing research.

EPILOGUE

California's islands are marvelous evolutionary laboratories on which, by virtue of their long isolation, many unique plants and animals can be found. In addition, because development often has not replaced the native biota, the plants and animals that greeted the discoverers of the islands can usually be seen by visitors today. Grazing, agriculture, and introduced species did significant damage to many of the islands over the years, but every island is now in public hands, and various organizations and conservancies are dedicated to helping the islands return to their original conditions. Californians are truly fortunate to have these world-famous islands at their doorstep. Natives and visitors alike should not miss the opportunity to explore them whenever possible.

SELECTED REFERENCES

General

Abbott, I. A., and G. L. Hollenberg. 1976. *Marine Algae of California*. Stanford University Press, Stanford, Calif. 827 pp.

Bakker, E. 1984. *An Island Called California*. University of California Press, Berkeley. 484 pp.

Barbour, M. G., and J. Major (eds.). 1988. *Terrestrial Vegetation of California*. Special Publication 9. California Native Plant Society, Sacramento. 1022 pp.

Brandegee, T. S. 1890. Flora of the Californian Islands. *Zoe* 1:129–48.

Brown, P. E. 1980. Distribution of bats of the California Channel Islands. In D. M. Power (ed.), *The California Islands: Proceedings of a Multidisciplinary Symposium*, pp. 751–58. Santa Barbara Museum of Natural History, Santa Barbara, Calif.

Carlquist, S. C. 1965. *Island Life: A Natural History of the Islands of the World*. Natural History Press, Garden City, N.Y. 451 pp.

———. 1974. *Island Biology*. Columbia University Press, New York. 650 pp.

Carrol, M. C., L. L. Laughrin, and A. C. Bromfield. 1993. Fire on the California islands: Does it play a role in Chaparral and Closed Cone Pine Forest habitats? In F. G. Hochberg (ed.), *Third California Islands Symposium: Recent Advances in Research on the California Islands*, pp. 73–88. Santa Barbara Museum of Natural History, Santa Barbara, Calif.

Collins, P. W. 1993. Taxonomic and biogeographic relationships of the Island Fox (*Urocyon littoralis*) and Gray Fox (*U. cinereoargentus*) from Western North America. In F. G. Hochberg (ed.), *Third California Islands Symposium: Recent Advances in Research on the California Islands*, pp. 351–90. Santa Barbara Museum of Natural History, Santa Barbara, Calif.

Crooks, K. R., and D. V. Vuren. 1994. Conservation of the Island Spotted Skunk and Island Fox in a recovering island ecosystem. In W. L. Halvorson and G. J. Maender (eds.), *The Fourth California Islands Symposium: Update on the Status of Resources*, pp. 379–86. Santa Barbara Museum of Natural History, Santa Barbara, Calif.

Daily, M. 1987. *California's Channel Islands: 1001 Questions Answered*. McNally and Loften, Santa Barbara, Calif. 284 pp.

Davis, W. S. 1980. Distribution of *Malacothrix* (Asteraceae) on the California islands and the origin of endemic insular species. In D. M. Power (ed.), *The California Islands:*

Proceedings of a Multidisciplinary Symposium, pp. 227–36. Santa Barbara Museum of Natural History, Santa Barbara, Calif.

———. 1997. The systematics of the annual species of *Malacothrix* (Asteraceae: Lactuaceae) endemic to the California islands. *Madroño* 44(3):223–44.

Diamond, J. M. 1969. Avifaunal equilibrium and species turnover rates of the Channel Islands of California. *Proceedings of the National Academy of Sciences of the USA* 64:57–62.

Diamond, J. M., and H. L. Jones. 1980. Breeding land birds of the Channel Islands. In D. M. Power (ed.), *The California Islands: Proceedings of a Multidisciplinary Symposium,* pp. 597–612. Santa Barbara Museum of Natural History, Santa Barbara, Calif.

Doran, A. L. 1980. *Pieces of Eight Channel Islands: A Bibliographical Guide and Source Book.* Arthur H. Clark, Glendale, Calif. 340 pp.

Dowty, K. J. 1984. *A Visitor's Guide to the California Channel Islands.* Seaquit, Ventura, Calif. 200 pp.

Dunkle, M. B. 1950. Plant ecology of the Channel Islands. In *Allan Hancock Pacific Expeditions,* vol. 13, pp. 247–86. University of Southern California Press, Los Angeles.

George, S. B., and R. K. Wayne. 1991. Island foxes: A model for conservation genetics. *Terra* 30(1):18–24.

Gill, A. E. 1980. Evolutionary genetics of California islands: *Peromyscus.* In D. M. Power (ed.), *The California Islands: Proceedings of a Multidisciplinary Symposium,* pp. 719–44. Santa Barbara Museum of Natural History, Santa Barbara, Calif.

Grant, P. R. 1965. Plumage and the evolution of birds on islands. *Systematic Zoology* 14:47–52.

———. 1968. Bill size, body size, and the ecological adaptations of bird species to competitive situations in islands. *Systematic Zoology* 17:319–33.

Grinnell, J., and A. H. Miller. 1944. The distribution of the birds of California. *Pacific Coast Avifauna* 27.

Halvorson, W. L. 1994. Ecosystem restoration on the California Channel Islands. In W. L. Halvorson and G. J. Maender (eds.), *The Fourth California Islands Symposium: Update on the Status of Resources,* pp. 485–90. Santa Barbara Museum of Natural History, Santa Barbara, Calif.

Halvorson, W. L., and G. J. Maender (eds.). 1994. *The Fourth California Islands Symposium: Update on the Status of Resources.* Santa Barbara Museum of Natural History, Santa Barbara, Calif. 530 pp.

Hickman, J. C. (ed.). 1993. *The Jepson Manual: Higher Plants of California.* University of California Press, Berkeley. 1400 pp.

Hillinger, C. 1958. *The California Islands.* Academy, Los Angeles. 165 pp.

Hitchcock, A. S. 1950. *Manual of the Grasses of the United States.* U.S. Department of Agriculture Miscellaneous Publication 200. U.S. Government Printing Office, Washington, D.C. 1051 pp.

Hochberg, F. G. (ed.). 1993. *Third California Islands Symposium: Recent Advances in Research on the California Islands.* Santa Barbara Museum of Natural History, Santa Barbara, Calif. 661 pp.

Hochberg, M. C. 1980. Factors affecting leaf size of Chaparral shrubs on the California islands. In D. M. Power (ed.), *The California Islands: Proceedings of a Multidisciplinary Symposium,* pp. 189–206. Santa Barbara Museum of Natural History, Santa Barbara, Calif.

Holder, C. 1910. *The Channel Islands of California.* A. C. McClung, Chicago, 397 pp.

Holland, V. L., and D. J. Keil. 1995. *California Vegetation.* Kendall/Hunt, Dubuque, Ia. 516 pp.

Howell, A. B. 1917. Birds of the islands off the coast of Southern California. *Pacific Coast Avifauna* 12. 127 pp.

Howorth, P. C. 1986. *Channel Islands: The Story Behind the Scenery.* KC Publications, Las Vegas, Nev. 48 pp.

Johnson, N. K. 1972. Origin and differentiation of the avifauna of the Channel Islands, California. *Condor* 74:295–315.

Laughrin, L. L. 1980. Populations and status of the Island Fox. In D. M. Power (ed.), *The California Islands: Proceedings of a Multidisciplinary Symposium,* pp. 745–49. Santa Barbara Museum of Natural History, Santa Barbara, Calif.

MacArthur, R. H., and E. O. Wilson. 1967. *The Theory of Island Biogeography.* Princeton University Press, Princeton, N.J. 203 pp.

Miller, S. E. 1985. Butterflies of the California Channel Islands. *Journal of Research on Lepidoptera* 23:282–96.

———. 1993. Entomological bibliography of the California Islands. Supplement 2. In F. G. Hochberg (ed.), *Third California Islands Symposium: Recent Advances in Research on the California Islands,* pp. 171–88. Santa Barbara Museum of Natural History, Santa Barbara, Calif.

Minnich, R. A. 1980. The vegetation of Santa Cruz and Santa Catalina Islands. In D. M. Power (ed.), *The California Islands: Proceedings of a Multidisciplinary Symposium,* pp. 123–37. Santa Barbara Museum of Natural History, Santa Barbara, Calif.

Munz, P. A. 1974. *A Flora of Southern California.* University of California Press, Berkeley. 1086 pp.

Philbrick, R. N. (ed.) 1967. *Proceedings of the Symposium on the Biology of the California Islands.* Santa Barbara Botanic Garden, Santa Barbara, Calif. 363 pp.

———. 1980. Distribution and evolution of endemic plants of the California Islands. In D. M. Power (ed.), *The California Islands: Proceedings of a Multidisciplinary Symposium,* pp. 173–87. Santa Barbara Museum of Natural History, Santa Barbara, Calif.

Philbrick, R. N., and J. R. Haller. 1988. The Southern California Islands. In M. G. Barbour and J. Major (eds.), *Terrestrial Vegetation of California,* pp. 893–906. Special Publication 9. California Native Plant Society, Sacramento.

Powell, J. A. 1994. Biogeography of Lepidoptera on the California Channel Islands. In W. L. Halvorson and G. J. Maender (eds.), *The Fourth California Islands Symposium: Update on the Status of Resources,* pp. 449–64. Santa Barbara Museum of Natural History, Santa Barbara, Calif.

Power, D. M. 1972. Numbers of bird species on the California Islands. *Evolution* 26:451–63.

———. 1976. Avifauna richness on the California Channel Islands. *Condor* 78:394–98.

———. 1980a. Evolution of land birds on the California Islands. In D. M. Power (ed.), *The California Islands: Proceedings of a Multidisciplinary Symposium,* pp. 613–50. Santa Barbara Museum of Natural History, Santa Barbara, Calif.

——— (ed.). 1980b. *The California Islands: Proceedings of a Multidisciplinary Symposium.* Santa Barbara Museum of Natural History, Santa Barbara, Calif. 787 pp.

Raven, P. H. 1967. The floristics of the California Islands. In R. N. Philbrick (ed.), *Proceedings of the Symposium on the Biology of the California Islands,* pp. 57–67. Santa Barbara Botanic Garden, Santa Barbara, Calif.

Remington, C. L. 1971. Natural history and evolutionary genetics on the California Channel Islands. *Discovery* 7(1):2–18.

Roberts, F. M. 1995. *The Oaks of the Southern Californian Floristic Province.* F. M. Roberts Publications, Encinitas, Calif. 112 pp.

Robins, W. W., M. K. Bellue, and W. S. Ball. 1970. *Weeds of California*. State of California Documents and Publications. State Printing Office, Sacramento, Calif. 547 pp.

Savage, J. M. 1960. Evolution of a peninsular herpetofauna. *Systematic Zoology* 9(3):184–212.

———. 1967. Evolution of the insular herpetofauna. In R. N. Philbrick (ed.), *Proceedings of the Symposium on the Biology of the California Islands*, pp. 219–28. Santa Barbara Botanic Gardens, Santa Barbara, Calif.

Sawyer, J. O., and T. Keeler-Wolf. 1995. *A Manual of California Vegetation*. California Native Plant Society, Sacramento. 471 pp.

Schoenherr, A. A. 1976. *The Herpetofauna of the San Gabriel Mountains*. Special Publication. Southwestern Herpetologists Society, Van Nuys, Calif. 88 pp.

———. 1992. *A Natural History of California*. University of California Press, Berkeley. 772 pp.

Simberloff, D. S. 1974. Equilibrium theory of island biogeography and ecology. *American Review of Ecology and Systematics* 5:161–82.

Skinner, M. W., and B. Pavlik. 1994. *Inventory of Rare and Endangered Vascular Plants of California*. Special Publication 1. California Native Plant Society, Sacramento. 168 pp.

Stebbins, R. C. 1951. *Amphibians of Western North America*. University of California Press, Berkeley. 539 pp.

Steinhart, P. 1990. *California's Wild Heritage: Threatened and Endangered Animals in the Golden State*. California Department of Fish and Game, California Academy of Sciences, and Sierra Club Books, Sacramento. 108 pp.

Storer, T. I., and R. L. Usinger. 1963. *Sierra Nevada Natural History*. University of California Press, Berkeley.

Thorne, R. F. 1969. The California Islands. *Annals of the Missouri Botanical Garden* 56:391–40.

Van Balgooy, M. M. J. 1969. A study on the diversity of island floras. *Blumea* 17:139–78.

Von Bloeker, J. C. 1967. The land mammals of the Southern California islands. In R. N. Philbrick (ed.), *Proceedings of the Symposium on the Biology of the California Islands*, pp. 245–64. Santa Barbara Botanic Garden, Santa Barbara, Calif.

Wallace, G. D. 1985. *Vascular Plants of the Channel Islands of Southern California and Guadalupe Island, Baja California, Mexico*. Contributions in Science 365. Natural History Museum of Los Angeles County, Los Angeles. 136 pp.

Wenner, A. M., and D. L. Johnson. 1980. Land vertebrates on the islands. In D. M. Power (ed.), *The California Islands: Proceedings of a Multidisciplinary Symposium*, pp. 497–530. Santa Barbara Museum of Natural History, Santa Barbara, Calif.

Wilcox, B. A. 1980. Species number, stability, and equilibrium status of reptile faunas on the California islands. In D. M. Power (ed.), *The California Islands: Proceedings of a Multidisciplinary Symposium*, pp. 551–64. Santa Barbara Museum of Natural History, Santa Barbara, Calif.

Yanev, K. P. 1980. Biogeography and distribution of three parapatric salamander species in coastal and borderland California. In D. M. Power (ed.), *The California Islands: Proceedings of a Multidisciplinary Symposium*, pp. 531–50. Santa Barbara Museum of Natural History, Santa Barbara, Calif.

Geology

Bailey, E. H., W. P. Irwin, and D. L. Jones. 1964. *Franciscan and Related Rocks and Their Significance in the Geology of Western California*. Bulletin 183. California Division of Mines and Geology, Sacramento.

Boles, J. R., and W. Landry. 1997. *Santa Cruz Island: Geology Field Trip Guide.* San Diego Association of Geologists, San Diego. 124 pp.

Boundy-Sanders, S. Q., J. G. Vedder, C. O. Sanders, and D. G. Howell. 1993. Miocene geologic history of eastern Santa Catalina Island, California. In F. G. Hochberg (ed.), *Third California Islands Symposium: Recent Advances in Research on the California Islands,* pp. 3–14. Santa Barbara Museum of Natural History, Santa Barbara, Calif.

Bremner, C. S. 1932. *Geology of Santa Cruz Island, Santa Barbara County, California.* Occasional Papers 1. Santa Barbara Museum of Natural History, Santa Barbara, Calif. 33 pp.

Davidson, G. 1897. The submerged valleys of the coast of California, USA, and of Lower California, Mexico. *California Academy of Sciences Proceedings,* 3rd Series: Geology 1(1):74–102.

Diblee, T. 1982. Geology of the Channel Islands, Southern California. In D. Fife and J. Minch (eds.), *Geology and Mineral Wealth of the California Transverse Ranges,* pp. 27–39. Annual Symposium and Guidebook 10. South Coast Geological Society, Santa Ana, Calif.

Howell, D. G., C. J. Stuart, J. P. Platt, and D. J. Hill. 1974. Possible strike-slip faulting in the southern California borderland. *Geology* 2:93–98.

Junger, A., and D. L. Johnson. 1993. Was there a Quaternary land bridge to the Northern Channel Islands? In D. M. Power (ed.), *The California Islands: Proceedings of a Multidisciplinary Symposium,* pp. 33–40. Santa Barbara Museum of Natural History, Santa Barbara, Calif.

Legg, M. L. 1991. Developments in understanding the tectonic evolution of the California continental borderland. In R. H. Osborne (ed.), *Shoreline to Abyss,* pp. 291–312. Special Publication 46. Society of Economic Paleontologists and Mineralogists, Tulsa, Oklahoma.

Lipps, J. H. 1964. Late Pleistocene history of West Anacapa Island, California. *Geological Society of America Bulletin* 75:1169–76.

Lipps, J. H., J. W. Valentine, and E. Mitchell. 1968. Pleistocene paleoecology and biostratigraphy, Santa Barbara Island, California. *Journal of Paleontology* 42(2):291–307.

Norris, R. M. 1991. A visit to Santa Barbara Island. *California Geology* 44(4):147–51.

———. 1995. Little Anacapa Island. *California Geology* 48(1):3–9.

Rowland, S. M. 1984. Geology of Santa Catalina Island. *California Geology* 37(11): 239–51.

Simila, G. W. 1993. A review of seismicity of the California Islands. In F. G. Hochberg (Ed.). *Third California Islands Symposium: Recent Advances in Research on the California Islands,* pp. 15–20. Santa Barbara Museum of Natural History, Santa Barbara, Calif.

Smith, W. S. T. 1897. The geology of Santa Catalina Island. *California Academy of Sciences Proceedings,* 3rd Series: Geology 1(1):1–71.

———. 1898. A geological sketch of San Clemente Island, California. *U.S. Geological Survey 18th Annual Report* 2:459–96.

———. 1900. A topographic study of the islands of southern California. *University of California Publications in Geology* 2(7):179–230.

Sorlien, C. C. 1994. Faulting and uplift of the Northern Channel Islands, California. In W. L. Halvorson and G. J. Maender (eds.), *The Fourth California Islands Symposium: Update on the Status of Resources,* pp. 281–96. Santa Barbara Museum of Natural History, Santa Barbara, Calif.

Vedder, J. G., L. A. Beyer, A. Junger, G. W. Moore, A. E. Roberts, J. C. Taylor, and H. C. Wagner. 1974. *Preliminary Report on the Geology of the Continental Borderland of*

Southern California. United States Geologic Survey Miscellaneous Field Investigations Map MF-624. 34 pp.

Vedder, J. G., and R. M. Norris. 1963. Geology of San Nicolas Island, California. *U.S. Geological Survey Professional Papers* 369:1–65.

Weaver, D. W., D. P. Doerner, and B. Nolf. 1969. *Geology of the Northern Channel Islands, Southern California Borderland.* American Association of Petroleum Geologists, Los Angeles. 200 pp.

Weigand, P. 1994. Petrology and geochemistry of Miocene volcanic rocks from Santa Catalina and San Clemente Islands, California. In W. L. Halvorson and G. J. Maender (eds.), *The Fourth California Islands Symposium: Update on the Status of Resources,* pp. 267–80. Santa Barbara Museum of Natural History, Santa Barbara, Calif.

Early Humans

Berger, R. 1980. Early man on Santa Rosa Island. In D. M. Power (ed.), *The California Islands: Proceedings of a Multidisciplinary Symposium,* pp. 73–78. Santa Barbara Museum of Natural History, Santa Barbara, Calif.

Colten, R. H. 1994. Prehistoric animal exploitation, environmental change, and emergent complexity on Santa Cruz Island, California. In W. L. Halvorson and G. J. Maender (eds.), *The Fourth California Islands Symposium: Update on the Status of Resources,* pp. 201–14. Santa Barbara Museum of Natural History, Santa Barbara, Calif.

Cushing, J. E. 1993. The carbonization of vegetation associated with "fire areas," mammoth remains and hypothesized activities of early man on the Channel Islands. In F. G. Hochberg (ed.), *Third California Islands Symposium: Recent Advances in Research on the California Islands,* pp. 551–56. Santa Barbara Museum of Natural History, Santa Barbara, Calif.

Edgar, B. 1990. First Californians. *Pacific Discovery* 43(4):26–33.

Erlandson, J. M., D. J. Kennett, B. L. Ingram, D. A. Guthrie, D. P. Morris, M. A. Tveskov, G. J. West, and P. L. Walker. 1996. An archeological and paleontological chronology for Daisy Cave (CA-SMI-261), San Miguel Island, California. *Radiocarbon* 38:355–73.

Guthrie, D. A. 1993. New information on the prehistoric fauna of San Miguel Island, California. In F. G. Hochberg (ed.), *Third California Islands Symposium: Recent Advances in Research on the California Islands,* pp. 391–404. Santa Barbara Museum of Natural History, Santa Barbara, Calif.

Heizer, R. F., and A. E. Elsasser. 1980. *The Natural World of the California Indians.* California Natural History Guides, no. 46. University of California Press, Berkeley. 271 pp.

Holland, F. R., Jr. 1962. Santa Rosa Island, an archaeological and historical study. *Journal of the West* 1:45–62.

———. 1963. San Miguel Island: Its history and archaeology. *Journal of the West* 2:145–55.

Johnson, D. L. 1980. Episodic vegetation stripping, soil erosion, and landscape modification in prehistoric time, San Miguel Island, California. In D. M. Power (ed.), *The California Islands: Proceedings of a Multidisciplinary Symposium,* pp. 103–21. Santa Barbara Museum of Natural History, Santa Barbara, Calif.

Orr, P. C. 1968. *Prehistory of Santa Rosa Island.* Santa Barbara Museum of Natural History, Santa Barbara, Calif. 253 pp.

Marine Life

Bartholomew, G. A. 1967. Seal and sea lion populations of the California islands. In E. N. Philbrick (ed.), *Proceedings of the Symposium on the Biology of the California Islands,* pp. 229–43. Santa Barbara Botanic Garden, Santa Barbara, Calif.

Bleitz, D. E. 1993. The prehistoric exploitation of marine mammals and birds at San Nicolas Island, California. In F. G. Hochberg (Ed.), *Third California Islands Symposium: Recent Advances in Research on the California Islands*, pp. 519–36. Santa Barbara Museum of Natural History, Santa Barbara, Calif.

Browne, D. R. 1994. Understanding the oceanic circulation in and around the Santa Barbara Channel. In W. L. Halvorson and G. J. Maender (eds.), *The Fourth California Islands Symposium: Update on the Status of Resources*, pp. 27–34. Santa Barbara Museum of Natural History, Santa Barbara, Calif.

Bushing, W. W. 1994. Biogeographic and ecological implications of kelp rafting as a dispersal vector for marine invertebrates. In W. L. Halvorson and G. J. Maender (eds.), *The Fourth California Islands Symposium: Update on the Status of Resources*, pp. 103–10. Santa Barbara Museum of Natural History, Santa Barbara, Calif.

Cogswell, H. L. 1977. *Water Birds of California*. California Natural History Guides, no. 40. University of California Press, Berkeley. 399 pp.

Daily, M. (ed.). 1989. *Northern Channel Islands Anthology*. Occasional Paper 2. Santa Cruz Island Foundation, Santa Barbara. 177 pp.

Dailey, M. D., B. Hill, and N. Lansing (eds.). 1974. *A Summary of Knowledge of the Southern California Coastal Zone and Offshore Areas*. 3 vols. Southern California Ocean Studies Consortium, California State University Colleges, for Bureau of Land Management, U.S. Department of the Interior, Long Beach.

Dailey, M. D., D. J. Reish, and J. W. Anderson (eds.). 1993. *Ecology of the Southern California Bight*. University of California Press, Berkeley. 926 pp.

Dawson, E. Y. 1949. *Contributions Toward a Marine Flora of the Southern California Islands* I–III. Occasional Papers 8. University of Southern California, Allan Hancock Foundation, Los Angeles, Calif. 57 pp.

Dawson, E. Y., and M. S. Foster. 1982. *Seashore Plants of California*. California Natural History Guides, no. 47. University of California Press, Berkeley. 226 pp.

Ebeling, A. W., R. J. Largon, and W. S. Alevizon. 1980. Habitat groups and island-mainland distribution of kelp-bred fishes off Santa Barbara, California. In D. N. Power (ed.), *The California Islands: Proceedings of a Multidisciplinary Symposium*, pp. 403–31. Santa Barbara Museum of Natural History, Santa Barbara, Calif.

Engle, J. M. 1993. Distributional patterns of rocky subtidal fishes around the California islands. In F. G. Hochberg (ed.), *Third California Islands Symposium: Recent Advances in Research on the California Islands*, pp. 475–84. Santa Barbara Museum of Natural History, Santa Barbara, Calif.

Fagan, B. M., and G. Pomeroy. 1979. *Cruising Guide to the Channel Islands*. Capra Press, Santa Barbara, Calif. 206 pp.

Fitch, J. E., and R. J. Lavenberg. 1971. *Marine Food and Game Fishes of California*. California Natural History Guides, no. 28. University of California Press, Berkeley. 179 pp.

———. 1975. *Tidepool and Nearshore Fishes of California*. California Natural History Guides, no. 38. University of California Press, Berkeley. 156 pp.

Hedgpeth, J. W. 1962. *Introduction to Seashore Life of the San Francisco Bay Region and the Coast of Northern California*. California Natural History Guides, no. 9. University of California Press, Berkeley. 136 pp.

Hinton, S. 1987. *Seashore Life of Southern California*. California Natural History Guides, no. 26. University of California Press, Berkeley. 217 pp.

Howorth, P. C. 1976. The seals of San Miguel Island. *Oceans* 9(5):38–43.

Hunt, G. L., Jr., R. L. Pitman, and H. L. Jones. 1980. Distribution and abundance of seabirds breeding on the California Channel Islands. In D. M. Power (ed.), *The California*

Islands: Proceedings of a Multidisciplinary Symposium, pp. 443–60. Santa Barbara Museum of Natural History, Santa Barbara, Calif.

LeBoeuf, B. J., and M. L. Bonnell. 1980. Pinnipeds of the California Islands: Abundance and distribution. In D. M. Power (ed.), *The California Islands: Proceedings of a Multidisciplinary Symposium,* pp. 475–96. Santa Barbara Museum of Natural History, Santa Barbara, Calif.

Littler, M. M. 1980. Overview of the rocky intertidal systems of Southern California. In D. M. Power (ed.), *The California Islands: Proceedings of a Multidisciplinary Symposium,* pp. 265–306. Santa Barbara Museum of Natural History, Santa Barbara, Calif.

Lynch, J. F., and N. K. Johnson. 1974. Turnover and equilibria in insular avifaunas, with special reference to the California Channel Islands. *Condor* 76:370–84.

Murray, S. N., M. M. Littler, and I. A. Abbott. 1980. Biogeography of the California marine algae with emphasis on the Southern California Islands. In D. M. Power (ed.), *The California Channel Islands: Proceedings of a Multidisciplinary Symposium,* pp. 325–39. Santa Barbara Museum of Natural History, Santa Barbara, Calif.

Neushul, M., W. D. Clarke, and D. W. Brown. 1967. Subtidal plant and animal communities of the Southern California Islands. In R. N. Philbrick (ed.), *Proceedings of the Symposium on the Biology of the California Islands,* pp. 37–56. Santa Barbara Botanic Garden, Santa Barbara, Calif.

North, W. J. 1976. *Underwater California.* California Natural History Guides, no. 39. University of California Press, Berkeley. 276 pp.

Orr, R. T., and R. C. Helm. 1989. *Marine Mammals of California.* California Natural History Guides, no. 29. University of California Press, Berkeley. 93 pp.

Owen, R. W. 1980. Eddies of the California Current System: Physical and ecological characteristics. In D. M. Power (ed.), *The California Islands: Proceedings of a Multidisciplinary Symposium,* pp. 237–64. Santa Barbara Museum of Natural History, Santa Barbara, Calif.

Roetel, P. M. 1953. *Common Ocean Fishes of the California Coast.* Fish Bulletin 91. California Department of Fish and Game, Sacramento. 184 pp.

Seapy, R. R., and M. M. Littler. 1980. Biogeography of rocky intertidal macroinvertebrates of the Southern California islands. In D. M. Power (ed.), *The California Islands: Proceedings of a Multidisciplinary Symposium,* pp. 307–24. Santa Barbara Museum of Natural History, Santa Barbara, Calif.

———. 1993a. Rocky intertidal community structure on Santa Barbara Island and the effects of wave surge on vertical zonation. In F. G. Hochberg (ed.), *Third California Islands Symposium: Recent Advances in Research on the California Islands,* pp. 273–92. Santa Barbara Museum of Natural History, Santa Barbara, Calif.

———. 1993b. Rocky intertidal macroinvertebrates of the Southern California Bight: An overview and checklist. In F. G. Hochberg (ed.), *Third California Islands Symposium: Recent Advances in Research on the California Islands,* pp. 293–322. Santa Barbara Museum of Natural History, Santa Barbara, Calif.

Shane, S. H. 1994. Occurrence and habitat use of marine mammals at Santa Catalina Island, California, from 1983–91. *Bulletin of the Southern California Academy of Sciences* 93(1): 13–29.

Smith, R. I., and J. T. Carlton. 1975. *Light's Manual: Intertidal Invertebrates of the Central California Coast.* University of California Press, Berkeley. 716 pp.

Stewart, B. S., and P. K. Yochem. 1994. Ecology of Harbor Seals in the Southern California Bight. In W. L. Halvorson and G. J. Maender (eds.), *The Fourth California Islands Symposium: Update on the Status of Resources,* pp. 123–34. Santa Barbara Museum of Natural History, Santa Barbara, Calif.

Stewart, B. S., P. K. Yochem, R. O. DeLong, and G. A. Antonelis. 1993. Trends in abundance and status of pinnipeds on the Southern California Channel Islands. In F. G. Hochberg (ed.), *Third California Islands Symposium: Recent Advances in Research on the California Islands,* pp. 501–18. Santa Barbara Museum of Natural History, Santa Barbara, Calif.

Straughan, D., and D. Hadley. 1980. Ecology of Southern California island sandy beaches. In D. M. Power (ed.), *The California Islands: Proceedings of a Multidisciplinary Symposium,* pp. 369–94. Santa Barbara Museum of Natural History, Santa Barbara, Calif.

Northern Channel Islands

Breunig, E. E.(ed.). 1996. *Draft Conservation Strategy for Candidate and Proposed Species on the Northern Channel Islands: Community Assessment and Ecological Standards.* Channel Islands National Park, National Biological Service, and U.S. Fish and Wildlife Service, Ventura, Calif. 133 pp.

Chaney, R. W., and H. L. Mason. 1930. A Pleistocene flora from Santa Cruz Island, California. *Carnegie Institute of Washington Publications* 415:1–24.

Clark, R. C., and W. L. Halvorson. 1987. The recovery of the Santa Barbara Island Liveforever. *Fremontia* 15(1):3–6.

Daily, M. 1989. *Northern Channel Islands Anthology.* Occasional Paper Number 2. Santa Cruz Island Foundation, Santa Barbara, Calif. 177 pp.

Dash, B. A., and S. R. Gliessman. 1994. Nonnative species eradication and native species enhancement: Fennel on Santa Cruz Island. In W. L. Halvorson and G. J. Maender (eds.), *The Fourth California Islands Symposium: Update on the Status of Resources,* pp. 505–12. Santa Barbara Museum of Natural History, Santa Barbara, Calif.

Dunkle, M. B. 1942. Flora of the Channel Islands National Monument. *Bulletin of the Southern California Academy of Sciences* 41:125–37.

Halvorson, W. L., R. A. Clark, and C. R. Soiseth. 1992. *Rare Plants of Anacapa, Santa Barbara, and San Miguel in Channel Islands National Park.* Technical Report NPS/WRUC/NRTR-92/47. University of California, Davis. 134 pp.

Junak, S., T. Ayers, R. Scott, D. Wilken, and D. Young. 1995. *A Flora of Santa Cruz Island.* Santa Barbara Botanic Garden and California Native Plant Society, Santa Barbara. 397 pp.

Junak, S. A., M. C. Hochberg, R. N. Philbrick, and S. L. Timbrook. 1980. Plant communities of Anacapa Island, California. *Proceedings of the 2nd Conference on Scientific Research in the National Parks* 4:222–31.

Junak, S. A., R. Philbrick, and C. Drost. 1993. *A Revised Flora of Santa Barbara Island.* Santa Barbara Botanic Garden, Santa Barbara, Calif. 112 pp.

Klinger, R. C., P. T. Schuyler, and J. D. Sterner. 1994. Vegetation response to the removal of feral sheep from Santa Cruz Island. In W. L. Halvorson and G. J. Maender (eds.), *The Fourth California Islands Symposium: Update on the Status of Resources,* pp. 341–50. Santa Barbara Museum of Natural History, Santa Barbara, Calif.

Madden, C. T. 1981. Origin(s) of mammoths from Northern Channel Islands, California. *Quaternary Research* 15:101–4.

Miller, A. H. 1951. Comparison of the avifaunas of Santa Cruz and Santa Rosa Islands, California. *Condor* 53:117–23.

National Park Service, Channel Islands National Park. 1996. *Draft Resources Management Plan and Environmental Impact Statement for Improvement of Water Quality and Conservation of Rare Species and Their Habitats on Santa Rosa Island.* 130 pp.

Peart, D., D. T. Patten, and S. A. Lohr. 1994. Feral pig disturbance and woody species seedling regeneration and abundance beneath Coast Live Oaks (*Quercus agrifolia*) on Santa Cruz Island, California. In W. L. Halvorson and G. J. Maender (eds.), *The Fourth California Islands Symposium: Update on the Status of Resources*, pp. 313–22. Santa Barbara Museum of Natural History, Santa Barbara, Calif.

Philbrick, R. N. 1972. The plants of Santa Barbara Island, California. *Madroño* 21(5):329–93.

Roberts, L. J. 1983. *Anacapa Island*. McNally & Loftin, Santa Barbara, Calif. 97 pp.

———. 1993. Revising the history of San Miguel Island, California. In F. G. Hochberg (ed.), *Third California Islands Symposium: Recent Advances in Research on the California Islands*, pp. 607–16. Santa Barbara Museum of Natural History, Santa Barbara, Calif.

Schuyler, P. 1993. Control of feral sheep (*Ovis aries*) on Santa Cruz Island, California. In F. G. Hochberg (ed.), *Third California Islands Symposium: Recent Advances in Research on the California Islands*, pp. 443–52. Santa Barbara Museum of Natural History, Santa Barbara, Calif.

Stock, C. 1935. Exiled elephants of the Channel Islands, California. *Science Monthly* 41(3):205–14.

———. 1943. Foxes and elephants of the Channel Islands: New discoveries on the Channel Islands. *Los Angeles County Museum Quarterly* 3:6–9.

Stock, C., and F. L. Furlong. 1928. The Pleistocene elephants of Santa Rosa Island, California. *Science* 68:140–41.

Van Gelder, R. G. 1965. Channel Island skunk. *Natural History* 74(7):30–35.

Wehtje, W. 1994. Response of a Bishop Pine (*Pinus muricata*) population to removal of feral sheep on Santa Cruz Island, California. In W. L. Halvorson and G. J. Maender (eds.), *The Fourth California Islands Symposium: Update on the Status of Resources*, 331–40. Santa Barbara Museum of Natural History, Santa Barbara, Calif.

Yeaton, R. I. 1974. An ecological analysis of chaparral and pine forest bird communities on Santa Cruz Island and mainland, California. *Ecology* 55:959–97.

Southern Channel Islands

Beauchamp, R. M. 1987. San Clemente Island: Remodeling the museum. In T. S. Elias (ed.), *Conservation and Management of Rare and Endangered Plants*, pp. 575–78. California Native Plant Society, Sacramento.

Bowler, P. A., W. A. Weber, and R. E. Riefner, Jr. 1996. A checklist of the lichens of San Clemente Island, California. *Bulletin of the California Lichen Society* 3(2):1–8.

Coblentz, B. E. 1980. Effects of feral goats on the Santa Catalina ecosystem. In D. M. Power (ed.), *The California Islands: Proceedings of a Multidisciplinary Symposium*, pp. 167–70. Santa Barbara Museum of Natural History, Santa Barbara, Calif.

Doran, A. 1963. *The Ranch That Was Robbins: Santa Catalina Island*. Arthur H. Clark, Glendale, Calif. 211 pp.

Ferguson, H. L. 1979. The goats of San Clemente Island. *Fremontia* 7(4):3–8.

Foreman, R. E. 1967. *Observations on the Flora and Ecology of San Nicolas Island*. Publication TR-67-8. U.S. Naval Radiological Defense Laboratory, San Francisco. 79 pp.

Keegan, D. R., B. E. Coblentz, and C. S. Winchell. 1994. Ecology of feral goats eradicated on San Clemente Island, California. In W. L. Halvorson and G. J. Maender (eds.), *The Fourth California Islands Symposium: Update on the Status of Resources*, pp. 323–30. Santa Barbara Museum of Natural History, Santa Barbara, Calif.

Laughrin, L. L., M. Carroll, A. Bromfield, and J. Carroll. 1994. Trends in vegetation changes with removal of feral animal grazing pressures on Santa Catalina Island. In W. L. Halvorson and G. J. Maender (eds.), *The Fourth California Islands Symposium: Update on the Status of Resources,* pp. 523–30. Santa Barbara Museum of Natural History, Santa Barbara, Calif.

Lipps, J. H. 1967. Age and environment of a marine terrace fauna, San Clemente Island, California. *Veliger* 9:388–98.

Mautz, W. J. 1993. Ecology and energetics of the Island Night Lizard, *Xantusia riversiana,* on San Clemente Island, California. In F. G. Hochberg (ed.), *Third California Islands Symposium: Recent Advances in Research on the California Islands,* pp. 417–28. Santa Barbara Museum of Natural History, Santa Barbara, Calif.

Meighan, C. W. 1957. A prehistoric miner's camp on Catalina Island. *Masterkey* 31(6): 176–84.

———. 1959. The Little Harbor site, Catalina Island: An example of ecological interpretation in archeology. *American Antiquity* 24(4):383–405.

Millepaugh, C. F., and L. W. Nuttall. 1923. *Flora of Santa Catalina Island.* Botanical Series 5, Publication 212. Field Museum of Natural History, Chicago. 413 pp.

Moran, R. 1995. The subspecies of *Dudleya virens* (Crassulaceae). *Haseltonia* 3:1–9.

Oberbauer, T. A. 1989. Exploring San Clemente Island. *Environment Southwest* 524:4–7.

———. 1990. Twenty-six miles across the sea. *Environment Southwest* 527:14–19.

———. 1994. San Clemente Island Revisited. *Fremontia* 22(2):11–13.

Perlmutter, G. B. 1993. Preliminary studies on the distribution of native mice on Santa Catalina Island, California. In F. G. Hochberg (ed.), *Third California Islands Symposium: Recent Advances in Research on the California Islands,* pp. 429–32. Santa Barbara Museum of Natural History, Santa Barbara, Calif.

Powell, J. A., and D. L. Wagner. 1993. The microlepidoptera fauna of Santa Cruz Island is less depauperate than that of butterflies and larger moths. In F. G. Hochberg (ed.), *Third California Islands Symposium: Recent Advances in Research on the California Islands,* pp. 189–98. Santa Barbara Museum of Natural History, Santa Barbara, Calif.

Raven, P. H. 1963. A flora of San Clemente Island, California. *Aliso* 5(3):289–347.

———. 1967. Notes on the flora of San Clemente Island, California. *Aliso* 6(1):11.

Thorne, R. F. 1967. A flora of Santa Catalina Island, California. *Aliso* 6(3):1–77.

———. 1969. A supplement to the floras of Santa Catalina and San Clemente Islands, Los Angeles County, California. *Aliso* 7(1):73–83.

Townsend, W. C. 1968. Birds observed on San Nicolas Island, California. *Condor* 70:266.

Año Nuevo

LeBoeuf, B. J., and S. Kaza. 1981. *The Natural History of Año Nuevo.* Boxwood Press, Pacific Grove, Calif. 425 pp.

Farallon Islands

Ainley, J. D., and R. J. Boekelheide (eds.). 1990. *Seabirds of the Farallon Islands: Ecology, Structure, and Dynamics of an Upwelling System Community.* Stanford University Press, Stanford, Calif. 488 pp.

Ainley, J. D., and T. J. Lewis. 1974. The history of Farallon Island marine bird populations, 1843–1972. *Condor* 76:432–46.

Coulter, M. 1971. A flora of the Farallon Islands, California. *Madroño* 21(3):131–37.

Edgar, B. 1997. On the Farallones. *Pacific Discovery* 50(2):8–17.

LeBoeuf, B. J., D. G. Ainley, and T. J. Lewis. 1974. Elephant seals on the Farallones: Population structure of an incipient breeding colony. *Journal of Mammalogy* 55(2):370–85.

Vasey, M. C. 1990. The evolution of *Lasthenia maritima* (Asteraceae): An endemic of seabird-breeding grounds. M.A. Thesis, San Francisco State University. 156 pp.

San Francisco Bay

Anderson, P. K. 1960. Ecology and evolution in island populations of salamanders in the San Francisco Bay Region. *Ecological Monographs* 30(4):359–85.

Clauss, F. J. 1982. *Angel Island: Jewel of San Francisco Bay.* Angel Island Association, Tiburon, Calif. 87 pp.

East Bay Regional Park District. 1985. *Brooks Island Regional Shoreline Final Land Use–Development Plan/Environmental Impact Report.* 82 pp.

Greene, P. L. 1993. Marin Islands: Two for the Birds. *Pacific Discovery* 46(2):26–29.

Gustaitis, R. (ed.). 1995. *San Francisco Bay Shoreline Guide.* A California State Coastal Conservancy Book. University of California Press, Berkeley. 193 pp.

Hart, J., R. A. Beatty, and M. Boland. 1996. *Gardens of Alcatraz.* Golden Gate National Parks Association, San Francisco. 95 pp.

Howell, J. T. 1970. *Marin Flora: Manual of the Flowering Plants and Ferns of Marin County, California.* University of California Press, Berkeley. 366 pp.

Howell, J. T., P. H. Raven, and P. Rubtzoff. 1958. The flora of San Francisco. *Wasman Journal of Biology* 16(1). 157 pp.

Knight, W. 1980. The story of Brown's Island. *The Four Seasons* (East Bay Regional Park District) 6(1):3–10.

Lidicker, W. Z., Jr. 1966. Ecological observations on a feral house mouse population declining to extinction. *Ecological Monographs* 36(1):27–50.

———. 1973. Regulation of numbers in an island population of the California Vole: A problem in community dynamics. *Ecological Monographs* 43(3):271–302.

Lidicker, W. Z., Jr., and P. K. Anderson. 1962. Colonization of an island by *Microtus californicus,* analyzed on the basis of runway transects. *Journal of Animal Ecology* 31: 503–17.

Martini, J. 1991. *Fortress Alcatraz: Guardian of the Golden Gate.* Pacific Monographs, Kailua, Hi. 160 pp.

Ornduff, R., and M. C. Vasey. 1995. The vegetation and flora of the Marin Islands, California. *Madroño* 42(3):358–65.

Ripley, J. D. 1969. A floristic and ecological study of Angel Island State Park, Marin County, California. M.A. Thesis, San Francisco State College. 104 pp.

Shuford, W. D., and I. C. Timossi. 1989. *Plant Communities of Marin County.* Special Publication 10. California Native Plant Society, Sacramento. 32 pp.

INDEX

Page numbers for entries occurring in figures are followed by an f; those for entries occurring in tables, by a t.

Munz, Phillip, 158
Munzothamnus, Blair's, 9t, 29, 319t, 327
Muricea
   californica, 106
   fructicosa, 106
Murrelet, Xantus', 140, 145, 188, 271t, 272, 312t, 356
Murre, Common, 140, 144, 145, 188, 271t, 272, 371, 372, 373f
Muskrat, 398t, 405, 438
Mus musculus, 29, 178t, 194, 261, 329, 369, 399t, 404, 434, 438
Mussels, 75, 77, 88–90, 104–5
   Bay, 89–90, 430
   California, 66, 89–90, 105
Mustard family, 9t, 155t, 240, 280t, 294t, 319t
Mustards, 43, 242, 243, 390
   Black, 43, 434
   Field, 43
Mustelidae, 122
Mutiny on the Bounty (film), 157, 269
Myiarchus cinerascens, 301t
Myliobatis californica, 120f, 121
Myotis, *see* Bats
Myotis
   californicus, 178t, 191, 258, 270t, 285t, 300t, 312t, 333, 355t, 356
   evotis, 178t, 191, 258, 300t
   thysanodes, 333
Mytilus
   californianus, 66, 89–90, 105
   edulis, 89–90, 430

Nassella (=*Stipa*), 241, 431
   cernua, 241
   lepida, 241, 427
   pulchra, 241, 321
National Lighthouse Service, 306
National Marine Fisheries Service, 131
National Parks and Conservation Association, 39
National Park Service, 36, 39, 40, 46, 278, 306, 350, 379, 421
National Register of Historic Places, 439
National Science Foundation, 368
National Wildlife Refuge, 36, 368, 394, 400
Native Americans, 61, 62–63, 217
   of Alcatraz Island, 420, 421
   of Año Nuevo Island, 358–59

of Brooks Island, 429–30
diseases of, 33, 65, 150
impact on ecology, 31–33
kelps in diet of, 104
of Marin Islands, 425
meat in diet of, 189
medicinal plants of, 162, 163, 168, 310, 420
mussels in diet of, 90
of Northern Channel Islands, 199
plant food in diet of, 173, 309, 322, 385
plants introduced by, 44
of San Clemente Island, 64, 317, 333
of San Francisco Bay Islands, 378–79
of San Nicolas Island, 64, 334–35
of Santa Barbara Island, 354
of Santa Catalina Island, 64, 149–50, 151
of Santa Cruz Island, 292
of Santa Rosa Island, 277
tribes of, 63–66
of Yerba Buena Island, 418
Natural History Museum, Santa Barbara, 65
Natural History of Año Nuevo, The (LeBoeuf and Kaza), 362
Natural History of California, A (Schoenherr), 3, 70
Nature Conservancy, 36, 39, 46, 199, 288, 293
Navy, United States, 3, 36, 37–38, 40, 46, 194, 292–93, 314, 317–18, 325–26, 328–29, 333, 338–39, 344, 350, 379, 418, 419
Neanthes brandti, 90–91
Neduba
   morsei santacruzae, 299
   propsti, 23, 177
Needlegrass, 431
   Foothill, 241, 427
   Nodding, 241
   Purple, 241, 321
Neotoma, 178t, 191
Nepticuloidea, 20t
Nereocystis luetkeana, 78, 104
New York Slough, 435
Niche partitioning, 135
Niche shifts, 31
Nichols, W. I., 267
Nicoleños, 64, 334
Nidever, George, 336–37, 338, 339

Vizcaíno, Sebastián, 33, 62, 150, 276, 334, 348, 358

Volcanic rocks, 47, 55, 264, 289, 334, 380, 382, 409

Volcanism, 54–55

Vole, California, 329–30, 398t, 404, 434

Wallace, Gary, 154, 202, 318

Wallflower, Island, 240, 241f, 268, 310–11

Wandering Tatler, 403f

Wapiti, see Elk, Roosevelt

Warbler family, 252

Warblers, 252–54

  Orange-crowned, 31, 183t, 186, 253–54, 270, 271t, 284, 286t, 301t, 302, 312t, 313, 332t, 343t, 355t

Warning coloration, 100

Washingtonia

  filifera, 268–69, 339, 436, 438

  robusta, 156–57

Wasps, digger, 245f, 247, 299

Wasting disease, 95

Water birds, see Sea birds

Water Birds of California (Cogswell), 3

Water Cress, 414

Waterleaf family, 10t, 155t, 269t, 280t, 319t

Water pollution, 141

Waters, William G., 267

Water temperature, 70, 75, 142, 377

Waves, 72–74

Wave shock, 83t, 84–85

Weasel family, 122

Weather, see Climate; Temperature

Webster Point, 346

Weevils, 270

West Anacapa Island, 304

  sea birds of, 141

  terrestrial animals of, 244

  terrestrial vegetation of, 224, 228, 230, 307, 308, 309, 310, 311

West Brother Island, 382, 401, 439

West End Island, 366, 375

West Marin Island, 7t, 401, 425, 427–28

Whales, 136–39

  baleen (rorquals), 136, 137

  Blue, 137–38

  California Gray, 138–39, 313, *pl. 2A*

  Fin, 137

  Humpback, 138, *pl. 2B*

Killer, 136, 137

Minke, 137

Sperm, 136

toothed, 136

What I Saw In California (Bryant), 380

Whistler, McNeill, 305–6

White, Bill, 149

White-tailed Kite, 438

White-throated Swift, 183t, 271t, 286t, 301t, 312t, 332t

Wilken, Dieter, 202, 293

Willet, 402–3f

Willows

  Arroyo, 392, 433, 438

  Black, 392, 438

  Red, 174, 433

Wilson, Darryl Babe, 420

Wilson, E. O., 26, 28

Wilson Cove, 78, 317

Windle, Ernest, 149

Winfield B. Scott (steamer), 306

Winter Island, 435

Wintun tribe, 63

Wolf-eel, 117

Wolf-fish family, 117

Woodland Skipper, Santa Cruz, 20t, 299

Woodland Star, San Clemente Island, 11t, 320t, 327

Woodpecker, Acorn, 183t, 260, 301t

Woodrats, 178t, 191

Wooley site, 60

Worms

  blood, 80–81

  Capitella, 81

  Clam, 90–91

  flat, see Flatworms

  Lug, 80

  polychaete, 81

  Red, 80–81

  Sand-castle, 95–96

Wrasse, Rock, 108–9f, 111

Wrasse family, 110–11

Wrens

  Bewick's, 31, 182, 183t, 184–85f, 255, 284, 286t, 301t, 302, 312t, 313, 333, 343t, 344

  Marsh, 438–39

  Rock, 183t, 184–85f, 186, 255, 271t, 286t, 302t, 312t, 332t, 343t, 344, 355t, 371

Wren-tit, 31, 186

Wrigley, William, 151, 192

Wrigley Institute of Marine Science, 46, 195
Wrigley Memorial Botanical Garden, 158

Xantusia
    riversiana, 24–25, 29, 58, 179, 330–31f,
        342, 343t, 354, 355t, *pl. 1C*
    vigilis, 25, 178t, 179

Yarrow, 340
    Golden, 215
Yarrow Milfoil, 390, 410, 427
Yerba Buena (plant), 417, 419–20
Yerba Buena Island, 2, 416–20, *pl. 15A*
    comparison with other islands, 7t
    early history of, 61
    geology of, 382, 419
    history of, 378, 379, 380, 417–19
    terrestrial animals of, 397, 398t

terrestrial vegetation of, 382, 388,
    419–20
Young, David, 202, 293
Yponomeutoidea, 20t
Ypsolopha lyonothamnae, 13, 20t

Zalophus californianus, 66, 129–32,
    133–34, 135, 178t, 194, 270t, 273, 313,
    343, 345, 355t, 356, 364, 375, 406, *pl. 2C*
Zealous Bates Tower, 421
Zenaida aurita, 183t, 286t, 301t, 312t, 332t,
    344
Zigadenus fremontii, 390, 410, 411f
Zinc, 154
Zonotrichia leucophrys, 343t, 344f, 371
Zosteraceae, 92
Zostera marina, 92–93, 394
Zosteropoda clementei, 20t

Compositor:	Princeton Editorial Associates, Inc.
Text:	Minion
Display:	Franklin Gothic Book and Semibold
Printer:	Malloy Lithographing, Inc.
Color insert:	Pinnacle Press, Inc.
Binder:	Lake Book Manufacturing, Inc.